This is the first compendious study of the influence of Plato on the English literary tradition, showing how English writers used Platonic ideas and images within their own imaginative work. Source texts include Plato's Dialogues, and the writings of Neoplatonists and the early Christians who were largely responsible for assimilating Platonic ideas into a Christian culture; and there are essays on more than thirty English authors from the Middle Ages to the twentieth century, including Shakespeare, Milton, Blake, Wordsworth, T.S. Eliot, W.H. Auden and Iris Murdoch. The book is divided chronologically, showing how every age has reconstructed Platonism to suit its own understanding of the world, and there is a bibliographical guide to further reading. Established experts and new writers over a range of disciplines have worked together to produce the first comprehensive overview of Platonism in English literature.

PLATONISM AND THE ENGLISH IMAGINATION

Detail showing Plato from Raphael's *School of Athens*, engraved by G. Volpato (1778), reproduced from a print at the Fitzwilliam Museum, Cambridge. The original picture is in the Vatican Museum.

PLATONISM AND THE ENGLISH IMAGINATION

EDITED BY

ANNA BALDWIN and SARAH HUTTON

CAMBRIDGE
UNIVERSITY PRESS

CAMBRIDGE UNIVERSITY PRESS
Cambridge, New York, Melbourne, Madrid, Cape Town, Singapore, São Paulo

Cambridge University Press
The Edinburgh Building, Cambridge CB2 2RU, UK

Published in the United States of America by Cambridge University Press, New York

www.cambridge.org
Information on this title: www.cambridge.org/9780521403085

First published 1994
Reprinted 1995, 1996
This digitally printed first paperback version 2005

A catalogue record for this publication is available from the British Library

Library of Congress Cataloguing in Publication data
Platonism and the English imagination/edited by Anna Baldwin and
Sarah Hutton.
p. cm.
Includes bibliographical references and index.
ISBN 0 521 40308 1
1. English literature – History and criticism. 2. English
literature – Greek influences. 3. Philosophy, Ancient, in
literature. 4. Platonists – Great Britain. 5. Plato – Influence.
6. Neoplatonism. I. Baldwin, Anna P. II. Hutton, Sarah, 1948–
PR127.P57 1993
820.9′384–dc20 93-9341 CIP

ISBN-13 978-0-521-40308-5 hardback
ISBN-10 0-521-40308-1 hardback

ISBN-13 978-0-521-02168-5 paperback
ISBN-10 0-521-02168-5 paperback

Contents

Notes on contributors *page* x
Preface xiii

I ANTIQUITY 1

1 Plato and the Neoplatonists 3
Anne Sheppard

II THE EARLY CHRISTIAN PERIOD AND THE MIDDLE AGES 19

2 Introduction 21
Anna Baldwin

3 The Christian Platonism of St Augustine 27
Janet Coleman

4 Boethius and King Alfred 38
Janet Bately

5 Chaucer's use of Neoplatonic traditions 45
Yasunari Takada

6 Platonism in the Middle English Mystics 52
Andrew Louth

III THE RENAISSANCE AND THE SEVENTEENTH CENTURY 65

7 Introduction 67
Sarah Hutton

8 The transformation of Platonic love in the Italian Renaissance 76
Jill Kraye

9 Uses of Plato by Erasmus and More 86
Dominic Baker-Smith

10 Italian Neoplatonism and the poetry of Sidney, Shakespeare, Chapman and Donne 100
John Roe

11 Shakespeare on beauty, truth and transcendence 117
Stephen Medcalf

12 Platonism in Spenser's *Mutability Cantos* 126
Thomas Bulger

13 Reason, Recollection and the Cambridge Platonists 139
Dominic Scott

14 Platonic ascents and descents in Milton 151
Anna Baldwin

15 Platonism in some Metaphysical poets 163
Sarah Hutton

IV THE EIGHTEENTH CENTURY 179

16 Introduction 181
Pat Rogers

17 Blake and Platonism 186
Edward Larrissy

V THE NINETEENTH CENTURY 199

18 Introduction 201
Richard Jenkyns

19 Recollection and Recovery: Coleridge's Platonism 207
Keith Cunliffe

20 Wordsworth's *Ode on the Intimations of Immortality* 217
A.W. Price

21 Shelley, Plato and the political imagination 229
Jennifer Wallace

22 Arnold, Plato, Socrates 242
M.W. Rowe

23 Flux, rest and number: Pater's Plato 257
Anne Varty

VI THE TWENTIETH CENTURY 269

24 Introduction 271
Angela Elliott

25 Yeats and Platonism 279
Brian Arkins

26 Virginia Woolf and Plato: the Platonic background of *Jacob's Room* 290
Brenda Lyons

27 Plato and Eliot's earlier verse 298
Dennis Brown

28 The *Cantos* of Ezra Pound: 'to build light' 308
A.D. Moody

29 Platonism in Auden 319
Daphne Turner

30 Platonism in Iris Murdoch 330
Peter Conradi

Bibliography 343
Index 351

Notes on contributors

Editors

ANNA BALDWIN is an associate member of the English Faculty at the University of Cambridge. Her publications include *The Theme of Government in Piers Plowman* (1981).

SARAH HUTTON is Senior Lecturer in the School of Humanities and Education at the University of Hertfordshire. Her publications include *New Perspectives on Renaissance Thought*, edited with J. Henry (1990) and *The Conway Letters* (1992).

Contributors

ANNE SHEPPARD is a Lecturer in the Department of Classics at Royal Holloway College, the University of London.

JANET COLEMAN is a Reader in Ancient and Medieval Political Thought in the Department of Government at the London School of Economics.

JANET BATELY is a Professor in the Department of English at King's College, University of London.

ANDREW LOUTH is a Lecturer in the Department of Historical and Cultural Studies at Goldsmiths' College, University of London.

YASUNARI TAKADA is an Associate Professor in the Graduate School of Comparative Literature and Culture at the University of Tokyo.

JILL KRAYE is a Lecturer at The Warburg Institute, the University of London.

DOMINIC BAKER-SMITH is a Professor in the School of English at the University of Amsterdam.

JOHN ROE is a Lecturer in the Department of English and Related Literature at the University of York.

STEPHEN MEDCALF is a Professor in the School of European Studies at the University of Sussex.

THOMAS BULGER is Dean of the Arts Division of Siena College, New York.

DOMINIC SCOTT is a Lecturer in the Philosophy Faculty at the University of Cambridge.

PAT ROGERS is a Professor in the Department of Liberal Arts and Sciences at the University of South Florida.

EDWARD LARRISSY is a Lecturer in the Department of English at the University of Warwick.

RICHARD JENKYNS is a Fellow in Classics at Lady Margaret Hall at the University of Oxford.

KEITH CUNLIFFE is Museum Research Assistant at Moyse's Hall, Bury St Edmunds.

A.W. PRICE is a Lecturer in the Department of Philosophy at the University of York.

JENNIFER WALLACE is a Research Fellow at Clare College, Cambridge.

ANNE VARTY is a Lecturer in the English Department of Royal Holloway College, the University of London.

M.W. ROWE is a Visiting Research Fellow in the Department of Philosophy at the University of York.

ANGELA ELLIOTT is an Associate Professor of English in the Division of Liberal Arts, Centenary College, Hackettstown, New Jersey.

BRENDA LYONS is a Tutor at the University and at the Stanford Centre, Oxford.

BRIAN ARKINS is a Professor in the Department of Classics at University College, Galway.

DENNIS BROWN is a Professor in the School of Humanities and Education at the University of Hertfordshire.

A.D. MOODY is a Professor in the Department of English and Related Literature at the University of York.

DAPHNE TURNER is a Lecturer in the Department of Humanities at Kingston University.

PETER CONRADI is a Professor in the Department of Humanities at Kingston University.

Preface

This is a study of the way that Platonism and Neoplatonism run like a changing thread through the web of English literature. Not all of the authors here represented are English, and some did not even write in that language. But they have all contributed to a tradition which can be defined and which still continues. Our main aid to that definition has been to confine ourselves to writers who knew at least part of the corpus of Platonic texts at first hand. As can be seen from the bibliography, these texts include not only Plato's Dialogues but also the writings of the Neoplatonists, especially Plotinus, through whom Plato was read for so long. Our choice of writers has necessarily had to be selective but our chronological range from antiquity to the present offers, for the first time, a comprehensive overview of the influence of Platonism on English literature.

That very comprehensiveness is, of course, a source of danger, and our account must of necessity be both partial and personal. But this is also true of the readings of Plato and his followers by the writers who are discussed here. Plato himself was a rich and diverse writer, and every age has rediscovered Plato in a different way, and reinterpreted Platonism to suit its different understandings of the world. This is not the story of a nexus of mummified ideas carried forward by authors with a nostalgia for antiquity, but of particular people who read within a related group of philosophical texts and responded to them individually in very different contexts from the pagan culture in which Plato and Plotinus lived. The process of transmission was inevitably one of transformation: strands of Platonic and Neoplatonic thought were often used to question or redefine the beliefs of many of the authors discussed here. In some cases writers applied Platonic principles to the political circumstances of their own times. Others assimilated tenets of ancient philosophy to their Christian outlook. So this is often a story of non-conformity and debate, and often of the liberation of the imagination to explore meaning outside the confines of dogma.

It is always the imaginative use of Plato which we discuss: this is a collection of literary studies not a history of philosophy. We have, however, tried to give it some historical shape. Accordingly, we have divided it chronologically into periods so as to give a broad sense of how the perception of Platonism changes. There are both surprising correspondences between authors of very different dates, and diversity within each period. An account of each period is given at the beginning of each section, to set the chosen authors into a context, and to indicate some of the gaps which our telling of the story must leave. These introductions could all be read in sequence as a very general account of continuities and discontinuities of the Platonic tradition.

Each study has been specially commissioned to give an individual critical perspective on the writer or writers with which it is concerned. We begin with a summary of some of the principal strands of thought of the Platonic corpus (Anne Sheppard) and we include accounts of how they were to some extent incorporated into the Christian faith by Augustine and his predecessors (Janet Coleman), and how these and other Platonic authorities were used in Old and Middle English prose and poetry (Janet Bately, Andrew Louth and Yasunari Takada). We continue into the Renaissance by way of the Italian revival of Platonic studies (Sarah Hutton), exploring the role of Platonism in humanism (Dominic Baker-Smith and Thomas Bulger) and the philosophy of love (Jill Kraye), as well as the adaptions of Platonism in the love poetry of the Elizabethan era (John Roe and Stephen Medcalf). Religious issues dominate again in the seventeenth century in the eclectic Christian Platonism of the Cambridge Platonists (Dominic Scott) and the poetry of Milton (Anna Baldwin) and the metaphysical poets (Sarah Hutton). The eighteenth century marks a waning of interest in Platonism in general (Pat Rogers) although Blake continued to engage with it (Edward Larrissy). The renewal of interest in Plato in the nineteenth century (Richard Jenkyns) was at once more secular and more scholarly. And we find among the Romantic Poets and their Victorian successors a detailed focus on Recollection (Keith Cunliffe, A.W. Price), on society (Jennifer Wallace, M.W. Rowe) and on art (Anne Varty). The use of Plato to appraise society is even more characteristic of the twentieth century (Angela Elliott, Daphne Turner, Peter Conradi). Some writers reject or parody Platonic idealisation (Brenda Lyons), although others continue to exploit the transcendent symbolism of both Plato and the Neoplatonists (Brian Arkins, A.D. Moody). Plato is now generally treated very much as a philosopher whose dialectical method is itself a focus of interest (Dennis Brown), and who must be analysed by scholars rather than reinterpreted to buttress faith.

The bibliography provided at the end is not intended to be exhaustive but rather to enable readers to take their study of Platonism further and in directions not covered by this collection. This volume is thus presented as a point of departure rather than a definitive statement of the subject. For this reason it is entirely appropriate to conclude as we do with a study of someone whose philosophy and fiction testifies to the continuing vitality of the Platonic tradition in the twentieth century, Iris Murdoch.

ANNA BALDWIN
SARAH HUTTON

PART I

Antiquity

CHAPTER I

Plato and the Neoplatonists

Anne Sheppard

This chapter will be concerned both with Plato's own thought and with the Greek philosophers known as Neoplatonists who flourished from the third to the sixth century AD. Their understanding of Plato had a profound effect on later writers and thinkers and a proper appreciation of Plato's influence requires some knowledge of Neoplatonic thought. It is worth remembering however that Plotinus (AD204/5–270), the first Neoplatonist, lived nearly 600 years after Plato himself. The Neoplatonists treated Plato's thought as a unity and sought to interpret his works as a coherent whole. This sometimes led them to blur contradictions between different dialogues; in particular, they did not envisage any chronological development in Plato's views. Since the nineteenth century, Platonic scholarship has taken such development for granted. Plato is now usually seen as progressing from early dialogues such as the *Laches*, the *Ion* and the *Charmides* through the grand theory-building of the *Phaedo*, the *Symposium* and the *Republic* to a final phase of questioning and self-criticism represented by dialogues such as the *Parmenides*, the *Sophist*, the *Theaetetus* and the *Philebus*.

In most of Plato's dialogues his teacher, Socrates, is the main speaker. The early dialogues show Socrates searching for definitions of moral terms such as courage and temperance. He does this not by propounding definitions of his own but by testing definitions put forward by his interlocutors. These are regularly found wanting and the interlocutors' pretensions to knowledge are exposed as false and empty. Socrates' activity in these dialogues fits the picture given in Plato's *Apology of Socrates*. This purports to be Socrates' defence against the charges of impiety and corrupting the young, on which he was tried and put to death by his fellow-Athenians in 399BC. Although the *Apology* was probably written soon after 399 we do not know how close it is to anything Socrates actually said. However, in both the *Apology* and the early dialogues Plato seems to be attempting to recreate the style and atmosphere of Socratic conversation. By the time he wrote the middle dialogues, including the *Republic*, Plato had moved on from Socrates' sceptical questioning to develop philosophical theories of his own. Socrates still appears as a character and still asks questions but now Plato attributes to him doctrines such as the theory of Forms or Ideas which were never held by the historical Socrates. Whereas Socrates' teaching was informal, Plato himself founded a philosophical school, the Academy, and after his death in 347BC his successors, Speusippus and Xenocrates, developed his metaphysical theories further. Plato's most famous pupil, Aristotle, left the Academy and developed his own important and influential philosophical system.

Philosophy did not stand still between Aristotle and Plotinus. In the third and second centuries BC new schools of philosophy arose, the 'Hellenistic' schools of Stoicism, Epicureanism and Scepticism. We can see from Cicero's philosophical works that by the first century BC Plato, Aristotle and the Hellenistic schools all had their adherents. Already at this period philosophers of different schools were borrowing ideas from one another. In the subsequent centuries Stoicism and Platonism became the dominant philosophies. Not much survives from the works written by Platonist philosophers of the period but many of the ideas of these 'Middle Platonists' can be found in such philosophically educated writers as Philo of Alexandria (*c*.25BC–AD*c*.50) and Plutarch of Chaeronea (AD*c*.45–*c*.125).

In the first three centuries AD there were also a number of religious developments important for the subsequent history of Platonism. Christianity, pagan mystery-religions and Oriental cults all became increasingly popular in the Greco-Roman world. These religions picked up and used the philosophical ideas of the period and so we find Platonism in the Early Christian Fathers, particularly in Clement of Alexandria (AD*c*.150–216) and in Origen (AD185–254) and in the writings of Neopythagoreans, notably Numenius of Apamea (fl. AD*c*.150). Platonism is also reflected in two rather mysterious sets of religio-philosophical writings: the *Hermetica*, a heterogeneous collection produced in Egypt, mostly between the first and third centuries AD and ascribed to the mythical figure of Hermes Trismegistus; and the *Chaldaean Oracles*, composed in the second century AD and taken up by Neoplatonists after Plotinus. All the thinkers mentioned so far influenced subsequent ages and many of them will be mentioned again later in this book. The *Hermetica* in particular aroused great interest in the Renaissance. However, the influence of Aristotle and Aristotelian thought lies outside the scope of this volume, except in so far as certain Aristotelian ideas were absorbed into Neoplatonic thought. (The Neoplatonists tried to harmonise Plato and Aristotle as much as possible and offered largely Aristotelian accounts of both the structure of the human soul and the nature of the physical world.)

The work of Plotinus marks a new departure in philosophy because he developed a complex metaphysical system dependent on the One as its ultimate principle. Plotinus' One is envisaged as the transcendent source of all beings and is a more lofty supreme principle than any of those postulated by previous philosophers. Plotinus, however, saw himself as an interpreter of Plato[1] and his successors likewise regarded themselves just as Platonists. (The term 'Neoplatonism' is a modern invention.) Plotinus' philosophical writings were edited and arranged in six *Enneads* by his pupil Porphyry (AD232–*c*.305) after his death. Neoplatonic metaphysics was further developed by Iamblichus (AD*c*.250–*c*.325) who may in his turn have been a pupil of Porphyry. Iamblichean Neoplatonism was enthusiastically adopted by the Emperor Julian ('Julian the Apostate', AD331–363) and was taught in the Platonist philosophical schools at Athens and Alexandria in the fourth, fifth and sixth centuries AD. Proclus (AD410 or 412–485), who taught in Athens, was the most important and influential of these later Neoplatonists. He wrote extensive commentaries on a number of Platonic dialogues, including the *Timaeus* and the *Parmenides*. While his commentaries report and synthesise the views of many earlier commentators, his *Elements of Theology* offers a systematic presentation of later Neoplatonist metaphysics.[2]

Neoplatonist ideas continued to exert considerable influence on Christian thought. In the West, Augustine (AD354–430) and Boethius (AD480–524) both took over many Neoplatonist conceptions (see below Coleman, pp. 27–37 and Bately, pp. 38–40). In the East, the author known as Dionysius (Denys) the Areopagite in the late fifth or early sixth century composed works whose theology mirrors the metaphysical system of Proclus (see Louth, pp. 52–64 below).

[1] See especially *Enneads* v, 1.8.
[2] See Proclus, *The Elements of Theology*, ed. E.R. Dodds, 2nd edn (Oxford, 1963).

PHILOSOPHICAL THEMES IN PLATO AND THE NEOPLATONISTS

Since antiquity Plato himself has been admired not only as a philosopher but also as a writer. His skilful command of many different styles of writing helps to explain the extent and diversity of his influence. Some readers are most attracted by the colloquial, conversational tone of the early dialogues; others prefer the spare, abstract philosophising of the *Theaetetus* or the *Sophist*; still others respond most strongly to the lyrical, poetic style of Plato's myths. In philosophy too, successive generations of interpreters have concentrated on particular features of his work, ignoring or excluding others. The Neoplatonists stressed and developed certain aspects of Plato's metaphysics and of the resulting view of man. For them the important part of man is his soul and any discussion of the soul's abilities and aspirations must be seen in the context of the universe as a whole. An account of their philosophy must therefore begin with their metaphysics.

In a number of his dialogues and particularly in the *Republic*, Plato presents a contrast between two worlds, the world of absolute qualities ('Forms' or 'Ideas') on the one hand and on the other the everyday world of particular things accessible to sense-perception. So the Form of Beauty, for example, may be contrasted with particular beautiful things. The Forms are the only true objects of knowledge and only they are truly real. Although the particulars lack the perfection of the Form they are nevertheless regarded as 'imitating' the Form; they are like it even though they fall short of it. In the *Republic*, Forms are introduced in order to justify the claim that moral and political questions can be answered with absolute truth and certainty. Plato describes an ideal state, run by philosophers who, because they know the Form of the Good, rule with perfect wisdom. The members of the state are divided into three classes: the philosopher-rulers; the auxiliaries who, as professional soldiers, defend the state in war; and the workers, farmers and craftsmen. Plato draws an analogy between the state and the individual and finds three corresponding parts in the soul: reason, spirit and appetite. The philosopher whose soul is ruled by reason is the ideal ruler because only he has the genuine political expertise which comes from knowledge of the Forms.

The Neoplatonists took little interest in Plato's political theory but they developed the contrast between Forms and particulars into an elaborate metaphysical system in which each level of the universe reflects and imitates the one above. These levels were called hypostases and in the metaphysics of Plotinus there are three hypostases: the One, Mind or Intelligence (*nous*) and Soul. The transcendent One, inaccessible not only to sense-perception but also to the intellectual operations of the mind, is the source of all other things. This is how Plotinus describes the way in which the One gives rise to the rest of the universe:

> So if there is a second after the One it must have come to be without the One moving at all, without any inclination or act of will or any sort of activity on its part. How did it come to be then, and what are we to think of as surrounding the One in its repose? It must be a radiation from it while it remains unchanged, like the bright light of the sun which, so to speak, runs round it, springing from it continually while it remains unchanged. All things which exist, as long as they remain in being, necessarily produce from their own substances, in dependence on their present power, a surrounding reality directed to what is outside them, a kind of image of the archetypes from which it was produced: fire produces the heat which comes from it; snow does not only keep its cold inside itself. Perfumed things show this particularly clearly. As long as they exist, something is diffused from themselves around them, and what is near them enjoys their existence. And all things when they come to perfection produce; the One is always perfect and therefore produces everlastingly; and its product is less than itself. (*Enneads* v.1.6.27–40)[3]

Plotinus here uses the analogies of sunlight, fire and snow to make it clear that the One causes all things without itself suffering any diminution and that, unlike the God of Judaeo-Christian thought, it is not a deliberate creator.

Plotinus' view of the relationship between the One and the rest of the universe has significant implications for the Neoplatonist understanding of Plato's *Timaeus*. The *Timaeus*, somewhat neglected by modern philosophical interpreters of Plato, was much read in antiquity and was the only Platonic dialogue which continued to be available in Western Europe throughout the Middle Ages. In it Plato describes the making of the world by the demiurge. Taking the Forms as his model, the demiurge produces the visible world which is described as a cosmic organism, animated by a world-soul. Since antiquity, interpreters of Plato's account have disagreed on two fundamental issues: first, is the activity of the demiurge to be taken

[3] Cf. also *Enneads* v, 3.12.39–45; v, 4.1.23–42.

literally, implying that the world had a beginning, and secondly, does Plato imply that the material world is inherently evil? Two ancient interpreters, Plutarch of Chaeronea (AD*c*.45–*c*.125) and Atticus (AD*c*.150–200) understood Plato as holding that the world was created by the demiurge. It was not, however, created out of nothing but out of a previously existing disorder. In *Laws* x.896 sq. Plato had suggested that as well as a beneficent world soul there was a contrary soul which was responsible for evil. Plutarch combined this with the disorderly movement mentioned at *Timaeus* 30a and so made Plato a dualist in metaphysics who held not just that matter is evil but that the universe contains two opposing principles, one of good and one of evil. It is clear from the *Phaedo*, the *Republic* and other dialogues that Plato is a dualist in psychology, i.e. he thinks of the soul and the body as two separate entities of different kinds. It is debatable whether he is also a dualist in metaphysics. The Neoplatonists were dualists in psychology but not in metaphysics. They rejected any suggestion that the world had a beginning. Instead, they understood the *Timaeus*' creation-story metaphorically and argued against the existence of a principle of evil.[4] The Neoplatonic One did not bring the universe into being at any given time; rather, it is the cause of all things in the sense that it continuously sustains and underpins everything.

For Plotinus the Platonic Forms belong to the level of Mind, while Soul encompasses both the world-soul described in the *Timaeus* and individual human souls. Bodies and material things come below these hypostases and lack true reality. Matter is not so much evil as sterile. In passages such a *Enneads* 1.8.3.13–17 Plotinus describes evil entirely in terms of negation:

> one might be able to arrive at some conception of evil as a kind of unmeasuredness in relation to measure, and unboundedness in relation to limit, and formlessness in relation to formative principle, and perpetual neediness in relation to what is self-sufficient; always undefined, nowhere stable, subject to every sort of influence, insatiate, complete poverty.

This metaphysical picture was developed further by Iamblichus and his successors. They offered more detailed accounts of the three hypostases and their relation to one another as well as introducing

[4] Cf. the mention of the 'variable cause' at *Timaeus* 48a and see further R. Sorabji, *Time, Creation and the Continuum* (London, 1983), pp. 268ff.

some intermediate levels. In particular, we find in Proclus the notion that between the One and Mind there are divine 'henads' which mediate the transition from the One to the rest of reality. Proclus identified these henads with the traditional Greek gods, holding that each god, while primarily a henad, was also manifested at each of the lower levels. So, for example, as well as the henad which was Zeus there was an intelligible Zeus on the level of Mind and another Zeus on the level of Soul.

In the *Phaedo* Plato attempts to explain how we acquire knowledge of the Forms. He appeals to the Theory of Recollection (*anamnēsis*), arguing that the reason we can recognise particular sticks and stones as equal is that our soul has seen the Form of Equality in a disembodied existence before we were born. He had already used this theory in the earlier *Meno* to account for our *a priori* knowledge of mathematical truths and, by implication, of moral values, although the theory of Forms is not clearly present in that dialogue. In both dialogues, recollection is connected with the immortality of the soul and in the *Phaedo* it is made explicit that the soul's true home is the world of unchanging Forms; life in the body is only a temporary episode in the soul's timeless existence. In a third dialogue, the *Phaedrus*, Plato uses a myth to combine these ideas with the *Republic*'s tripartite division of the soul. He compares the soul to a winged chariot whose driver struggles to control two disparate horses, one good and one bad. Before it enters the body the soul inhabits the realm of the gods where reason, the charioteer, beholds the Forms. The unruly horse of appetite drags the soul down, pulling it away from pure intellectual contemplation. Some souls thus become 'burdened with a load of forgetfulness and wrongdoing' (*Phaedrus* 248c); they lose their wings and fall into bodies. There remains a possibility, at least for philosophical souls, of recollecting their former life and growing their wings again.

The Theory of Recollection implies that we are born with innate ideas and do not derive all our knowledge from sensory experience. Later chapters in this volume will show how both the Cambridge Platonists and the Romantics used Plato to develop anti-empiricist views of knowledge. (See Scott, pp. 139–50, Cunliffe, pp. 207–16, and Price, pp. 217–28). The Neoplatonists of late antiquity made little use of the Theory of Recollection but they did take up Plato's view of the relationship between the immortal soul and the perishable body and the *Phaedrus* myth provided them with a fruitful source of images and ideas for describing the fall of the soul and its return to the intelligible world; for Proclus, the myth actually revealed the structure of part of that world.[5]

More important for the Neoplatonists than the Theory of Recollection was Plato's account in the *Symposium* of the soul's ability in this life to ascend from the perception of particulars to a knowledge of the Forms. In the *Symposium* it is love (*erōs*) which provides the driving force behind the soul's progress from interest in beautiful bodies to concern for beauty of character and beauty of mind and so at last to a vision of true and unchanging Beauty, the Form itself. Plato describes that vision in a striking passage which combines lyrical enthusiasm with the language which he regularly uses to characterize Forms:

> Whoever has been initiated so far in the mysteries of Love and has viewed all these aspects of the beautiful in due succession, is at last drawing near the final revelation. And now, Socrates, there bursts upon him that wondrous vision which is the very soul of the beauty he has toiled so long for. It is an everlasting loveliness which neither comes nor goes, which neither flowers nor fades, for such beauty is the same on every hand, the same then as now, here as there, this way as that way, the same to every worshipper as it is to every other.
>
> Nor will his vision of the beautiful take the form of a face, or of hands, or of anything that is of the flesh. It will be neither words, nor knowledge, nor a something that exists in something else, such as a living creature, or the earth, or the heavens, or anything that is – but subsisting of itself and by itself in an eternal oneness, while every lovely thing partakes of it in such sort that, however much the parts may wax and wane, it will be neither more nor less, but still the same inviolable whole. (*Symposium* 210e–211b)

The ascent described in the *Symposium* may be related to the *Phaedrus*' mention of the soul's ability to grow its wings again and return to its former life among the gods. The *Phaedrus* myth occurs precisely in an account of love, which is described as madness, but a madness which can bring the greatest benefits. Plato's treatment of love became in the Renaissance one of the most influential aspects of his thought. In late antique Neoplatonism, however, the *Symposium* and the *Phaedrus* were read not so much for their view of love as for their picture of the soul's

[5] See Plotinus, *Enneads* IV, 8.1 and 4; V, 8.10; Hermias, *In Platonis Phaedrum Scholia*, ed. P. Couvreur (Paris, 1901); Proclus, *Platonic Theology* IV, 4–26 and pp. ix–xlv of the introduction by H.D. Saffrey and L.G. Westerink to their Budé edition of *Platonic Theology* IV (Paris, 1981).

ascent from the material world to a higher realm. A similar account is suggested by the Cave analogy in *Republic* VII. Here Socrates describes bound prisoners in an underground cave. Behind them is a fire and behind that a parapet along which are carried a series of images and statues. The prisoners, who are 'like to us' (*Republic* 515a) see only the shadows of the statues cast by the fire. If one of them were released he could not only turn round and see the fire and the statues but could also make his way out of the cave and gradually progress to the sight of objects in the world above ground and finally to looking at the Sun which, according to an earlier analogy in *Republic* VI, represents the supreme Form, the Form of the Good.

Republic VII, like the *Symposium* and the *Phaedrus*, suggests that the individual soul can ascend from a preoccupation with the shadows and images of the perceptible world to a grasp of true reality, found in the world of Forms. What for Plato is perhaps only a theory, expressed through myth and analogy, becomes in Neoplatonism an essential doctrine. For the Neoplatonists, the belief that the soul can ascend to higher levels of reality and thus return to its own ultimate origins is fundamental. In Neoplatonic terms, however, an ascent to the world of Forms is an ascent only as far as Mind. The Neoplatonists did believe that it was possible to go further and reach the level of the One. Since the transcendent One is strictly unknowable, any contact with it must be by means of mystical experience. Plotinus, indeed, describes himself as having often had such an experience; he achieved it four times during the six years Porphyry spent with him while Porphyry himself attained it only once. But Plotinus was a philosophical mystic and in the *Enneads* mystical experience is always regarded as something which comes only after the rigorous intellectual effort required to reach the level of Mind.[6]

Although later Neoplatonists continued to talk in a Plotinian way about mystical experience, they also practised the rites of theurgy, a type of religious magic associated with the *Chaldaean Oracles*. The belief that these could assist the soul in its ascent opened the way to a less severely intellectual approach to mysticism.[7] At the same time

[6] See Plotinus, *Enneads* IV, 8.1.1ff.; Porphyry, *Life of Plotinus* XXIII, 7ff.; E.R. Dodds, *Pagan and Christian in an Age of Anxiety* (Cambridge, 1965), pp. 83–91.

[7] It is unclear just how far the later Neoplatonists modified Plotinus' attitude here. Two recent discussions are G. Shaw, 'Theurgy: Rituals of Unification in the Neoplatonism of Iamblichus', *Traditio*, 41 (1985), 1–28, and A. Sheppard, 'Proclus' Attitude to Theurgy', *Classical Quarterly*, ns 32 (1982), 212–24.

their view of the universe and of the individual soul's place in it remained essentially the same as that of Plotinus.

I have already said that Plotinus saw himself as an interpreter of Plato and many of his treatises begin by discussing a problem raised by a Platonic text. The same is true of his successors. From the time of Porphyry onwards, commentaries were the main vehicle for the exposition of Neoplatonist ideas. The Neoplatonists commented on Aristotle as well as Plato, reflecting the close study of both great philosophers in the philosophical schools of the period. To the modern reader, the Neoplatonists appear to be reading their own metaphysics into passages of Plato that do not warrant it and to be misled by an excessive desire to explain away contradictions not only within Plato but between Plato and Aristotle. We must, however, remember that right up until the nineteenth century the Neoplatonists were seen as offering an understanding of Platonism, not a distinct philosophy. Many later writers read Plato through 'Neoplatonic spectacles', using the surviving works of Plotinus, Porphyry and Proclus as aids in the interpretation of Plato.

THE CONCEPT OF IMAGINATION

This book is mainly concerned with the use of Platonist and Neoplatonist ideas in literature. A number of the authors to be discussed found in Platonism a spur to literary creativity and poetic imagination. Yet Plato himself, for all his ability as a writer, is notoriously dismissive about the value of literature. To unravel this paradox we need to consider further both Plato's own view of literature and Neoplatonist attitudes to it. We shall find that here above all it was the Neoplatonist reading of Plato that turned him into a source of inspiration for later ages.

When Plato discusses literature he is concerned not with individual creativity or artistic imagination but with the truthfulness of poetic representations. He holds consistently that poets, however fine their work, lack the knowledge which is the hallmark of the philosopher. In the *Republic* he is concerned to decide what poetry, if any, is suitable for use in educating the future rulers of his ideal state. In *Republic* II and III he attacks much of Homer and tragedy as morally unedifying: it does not tell the truth about the gods and presents heroes as unsuitably prone to violent emotion. He also criticises dramatic representation *per se*, on two counts: he regards the acting of an evil character as potentially corrupting and, perhaps more importantly, he thinks that the versatility required of the actor will produce an unstable personality. In *Republic* x Plato presses his attack on poetry further, basing it now on the metaphysics of Forms and particulars expounded in Books v–vii. He uses a discussion of painting to make his points and compares the artist to someone who holds up a mirror and so produces reflections of everything in the visible world. While particulars imitate Forms, the products of the artist imitate particulars. They are only imitations of imitations. The same applies to poetry which is described as mere appearance, 'three removes from reality' (*Republic* 599a).

The *Republic* thus offers both moral and metaphysical reasons for not taking poetry seriously. Elsewhere however Plato's tone is different. In the *Ion* Socrates appears to praise poetic inspiration:

> For the poets tell us, don't they, that the melodies they bring us are gathered from rills that run with honey, out of glens and gardens of the Muses, and they bring them as the bees do honey, flying like the bees? And what they say is true, for a poet is a light and winged thing, and holy, and never able to compose until he has become inspired, and is beside himself, and reason is no longer in him. (534a–b)

That passage may be ironical since Socrates goes on to argue that rhapsodes (professional reciters of Homer) are inspired too and to use this point in demonstrating that the vain and pompous rhapsode, Ion, derives his ability to discourse fluently about Homer from inspiration rather than knowledge. Less equivocal is a passage in the *Phaedrus* 245a. Before he discusses the beneficial madness of love, Socrates considers three other good types of madness. One of these is the madness of the inspired poet and Socrates asserts that 'if any man come to the gates of poetry without the madness of the Muses, persuaded that skill alone will make him a good poet, then shall he and his works of sanity with him be brought to naught by the poetry of madness'. Poetic inspiration is clearly an irrational force here but it seems to be one of the very few such forces which Plato is prepared to welcome.

The *Phaedrus* puts the madness of the poet and the madness of the lover in the same category and it is tempting to turn to the *Symposium*'s account of an ascent to perfect Beauty, stimulated by love, as further evidence for a more welcoming attitude to aesthetic value. Care is needed here. Plato does not mention any art-form in that passage of the *Symposium* and the Greek word '*kalos*', often translated 'beautiful', is a very general term of commendation, as general as the English word 'fine'. It can be used to indicate moral goodness or noble birth just as well as aesthetic attractiveness. However, the possibilities which the *Symposium* offered to aesthetic theory were exploited by the Neoplatonists.

Modern interpreters of Plato's attitude to poetry have given greatest prominence to the *Republic*'s arguments against it. The Neoplatonists attempted to counter these arguments and drew on the *Symposium* and the *Phaedrus* in order to do so. Plotinus in *Enneads* I.6 uses *kalos* in a more clearly aesthetic sense than Plato in the *Symposium*, for he starts the treatise with the statement that 'Beauty (*kalon*) is mostly in sight but it is to be found too in things we hear, in combinations of words and also in music'.[8] Nevertheless, as he describes the ascent from these perceptible beauties to higher ones his concern, like Plato's, is with moral and metaphysical 'beauty' and he does not mention works of art. Art is mentioned in v.8.1 where Plotinus argues that an artist in creating his work imitates the Form directly. This contradicts Plato's argument in *Republic* x that the artist imitates only particulars and so produces only imitations of imitations. Plotinus mentions the statue of Zeus by the great Greek sculptor, Pheidias, as an example of a sculpture whose model is in the intelligible, not the sensible, world.[9]

Plato is always firm that the artist does not have knowledge. How then could a Platonist artist imitate the objects of the intelligible world? We might expect the Neoplatonists here to appeal to some capacity such as the imagination. This they do not do. Plotinus talks of the artist 'having the Form in his mind . . . because he had some share of art' but that is all he offers by way of explanation of the artist's grasp of the Forms. Proclus does give us an explanation, at least as regards poets, but the explanation is couched in terms not of imagination but of inspiration. Before we consider Proclus' account of poetic inspiration, it may be helpful to relate the Neoplatonist view of imagination to other ancient views of that faculty so as to see why it is that the Neoplatonists lack the concept of creative imagination.

[8] Plotinus does here draw on Plato but on *Hippias Major* 297e–298a rather than the *Symposium*.

[9] Plotinus draws on and develops a tradition here. See E. Panofsky, *Idea. A Concept in Art Theory*, trans. J.J.S. Peake (New York, 1968), ch. 2.

The Greek word, *phantasia*, which is regularly translated 'imagination', means originally 'appearance'. It is therefore applied as much to what we imagine as to the faculty of imagination, and ancient discussions of *phantasia* tend to contrast the imaginary with the true, the merely apparent with the real. Plato himself says very little about imagination but in *Sophist* 264b he defines *phantasia* as 'a blend of perception and judgement [*doxa*]'. In the same dialogue the related adjective, *phantastikos*, is used of the lower of two kinds of imitation. At *Sophist* 235ff. Plato contrasts 'eikastic' and 'phantastic' imitation or image-making. Both are of low value but 'eikastic' imitation is not quite as bad as 'phantastic'. While 'eikastic' imitation does at least produce accurate likenesses, 'phantastic' makes deceptive ones which appear at first to resemble the originals but on closer inspection turn out not to. For Plato, *phantasia* and the 'phantastic' belong firmly to the realm of appearance and illusion.

The notion of creativity is introduced in a completely different Platonic context, the account of the formation of the world in the *Timaeus*. Here the demiurge is presented as a divine craftsman who shapes and fashions the perceptible world. For Plato the activity of the demiurge is quite different from that of the human artist; nevertheless, the *Timaeus* provided a powerful impetus to later conceptions of man himself as creative: if the divine creator of the world is a cosmic artist then conversely the human artist could also be seen as a creator.[10]

Phantasia plays a more significant part in Aristotle's psychology than in Plato's. For Aristotle, *phantasia* is neither perception nor judgement but a distinct capacity of the soul, the capacity with which we respond to appearances, whether these come from sense-perception, from memory or from dreams.[11] In the Hellenistic period, the Stoics also gave *phantasia* an important role but they used the term rather of what appears to us, the presentation or impression which we receive when we perceive something with the senses.[12] The first writer to call the faculty of producing visual images *phantasia* is the sophist Philostratus, writing in the early third century AD. In his *Life of Apollonius of Tyana* Philostratus contrasts *phantasia* with imitation

[10] See further G. Watson, *Phantasia in Classical Thought* (Galway, 1988), pp. 80–93.
[11] See especially *De anima* III.3.
[12] See Watson, *Phantasia*, pp. 44–58; M.W. Bundy, *The Theory of Imagination in Classical and Medieval Thought* (Urbana, 1927), pp. 87–96.

(*mimēsis*). In VI.19 Apollonius is engaged in conversation with an Egyptian, Thespesion. When Apollonius ridicules the animal images of gods found in Egypt, Thespesion asks sarcastically whether such Greek sculptors as Pheidias and Praxiteles went up to heaven and copied the forms of the gods there. Apollonius replies that the Greek sculptures were made not by *mimēsis* but by *phantasia*, for *phantasia* can fashion even things which it has not seen. This does sound rather like the modern concept of imagination, although we should note that in Philostratus *phantasia* enables sculptors to conceive of independently existing gods, not to create something new.

Philostratus' concept seems to have emerged from the eclectic blending of philosophical ideas which characterised the culture of his time.[13] The Neoplatonists however stuck to an essentially Aristotelian account of *phantasia*. They divided the soul into a rational and an irrational part and most of them placed *phantasia* at the junction of the two, above sense-perception and below reason. They did not use the term to describe the imagination of the artist. We have seen that when Plato regards poetry with approval he speaks in terms of poetic inspiration; similarly, Proclus turns to the concept of inspiration to account for the poet's ability to reflect a transcendent world. In his *Commentary on the Republic* Proclus defends Homer against Plato's attack. Much of his defence takes the form of allegorical interpretation of the specific passages of Homer criticised by Plato. He also, however, takes up *Republic* x and argues that Plato there is attacking only imitative poetry, poetry which represents things in the world of sense-perception. Proclus claims that there are also two other types of poetry, the poetry of knowledge and inspired poetry. The poetry of knowledge states truths either about the physical world or about ethics. Inspired poetry, the highest kind, is the poetry described by Plato in *Phaedrus* 245a and, according to Proclus, in the *Ion*, which he takes at face-value. Homeric descriptions of the gods fighting or making love are to be understood allegorically as veiled presentations of higher realities. Such allegories can only be composed by the inspired poet whose soul is united with the gods in a madness more valuable than sanity.[14] Proclus' description of inspired poetry implies that the inspired poet even goes beyond the intelligible world to

[13] Watson, *Phantasia*, pp. 59–95; D.A. Russell, *Criticism in Antiquity* (London, 1981), pp. 108–10.

[14] *sōphrosynēs kreittōn*, Proclus, *Commentary on the Republic*, ed. W. Kroll, 2 vols (Leipzig, 1899), I, 178.24–5. Cf. Plato, *Phaedrus* 244d.

achieve a kind of mystical union with the supreme gods who are the divine henads. He thus uses the Neoplatonic belief in mystical experience as a way of claiming lofty and noble powers for the poet.[15]

Proclus is evidently distorting Plato in claiming that much of Homer is invulnerable to the *Republic*'s criticisms, yet he remains true to the spirit of Plato in appealing to inspiration rather than creative imagination to explain the poet's powers. It is not just that he has Platonic authority for praising inspiration and that, for a Platonist, imagination, *phantasia*, concerns only fleeting appearance, at best a distant reflection of reality. For Proclus, as for Plato, the highest praise goes to those who reveal the truth and that truth exists independently of its interpreters. We do not admire the poets for any ability to create new worlds but rather for an inspired capacity to reveal what is always there for those whose souls can rise to apprehend it.

The Neoplatonist inspired poet does not however report metaphysical truth directly; if he did, he would be a philosopher. He conceals the truth behind a veil of allegory. Proclus' examples of inspired Homeric poetry are of passages which he has already interpreted allegorically, such as the union of Zeus and Hera on Mount Ida in *Iliad* XIV. He contrasts the symbolic representation used in such passages with imitative representation (*mimēsis*):

> How could the poetry which interprets the divine through symbols be called imitative? For symbols are not likenesses [*mimēmata*] of the things of which they are symbols. Opposites could not be likenesses of opposites, the base of the fine and the unnatural of the natural; symbolic understanding [*theōria*] reveals the nature of things even through their complete opposites.[16]

This innovative theory rescues Homer at the cost of turning him into a Neoplatonist, harnessing the inspiration of the poet to the car of Platonist philosophy.

The Neoplatonists were philosophers, not poets, but they emphasised just the aspects of Plato which have made his philosophy attractive to the literary imagination: the belief in a world of higher realities,

[15] Proclus' theory of inspired poetry may be found in his *Commentary on the Republic*, I, 177–205. Parts of this text are translated in Russell, *Criticism in Antiquity*, pp. 199–201 and in A. Preminger, O.B. Hardison, Jr and K. Kerrane (eds), *Classical and Medieval Literary Criticism* (New York, 1974), pp. 313–23. For a complete translation, in French, see A.J. Festugière, *Proclus. Commentaire sur la république*, 3 vols, (Paris, 1970), I, pp. 197–201.

[16] Proclus, *Commentary on the Republic*, I, p. 198.13–19. The translation is my own.

beyond the fallible realm of sense-perception; the belief that the soul belongs in that higher world and can find its way back there; and finally the idea that the forces of love and of poetic inspiration can assist the soul in its return to its true home.

PART II

The Early Christian Period and the Middle Ages

CHAPTER 2

Introduction

Anna Baldwin

The story of the influence of Plato and the Neoplatonists on English literature cannot be told without some explanation of how these pagan ideas were Christianised. The original Greek texts were scarcely translated into Latin at all, and so were in a way lost until their rediscovery and complete translation in the Renaissance. But they were assimilated by key authors who had indeed read some Greek originals, and they were both transformed into something compatible with Christianity, and themselves became a major influence upon Christianity. It is this story which I will now briefly outline, to provide a context for the four chapters which follow.[1]

The process of transformation was made all the easier by the fact that Middle Platonism was itself one of the intellectual influences upon the New Testament. This influence is generally traced to the work of Philo, a Jewish philosopher who lived in Alexandria from about 20BC to AD50, and who made a systematic attempt to Hellenise Jewish theology, using (among others) Platonic and Stoic ideas. His account transformed the anthropomorphic Deity of much of the Old Testament into an immaterial Being, above space and time, whose manifestation in this world is through the *logos* (Word), described (to quote Chadwick), as '"the second God", the pattern and mediator of the creation, the archetype of human reason'.[2] Acting very much as the Demiurge in Plato's *Timaeus*, the *logos* makes the material world in imitation of the Divine incorporeal world, but out of an inferior material. Man is a composite being, and should attempt to release his spirit from the slavery of matter so that it can ascend and be flooded

[1] I have been greatly assisted in this by Peter Dronke and Andrew Louth.

[2] H. Chadwick, 'Philo', pp. 137–57 in *The Cambridge History of Later Greek and Early Medieval Philosophy*, ed. A.H. Armstrong (Cambridge, 1967), p. 143. See also C. Bigg, *The Christian Platonists of Alexandria* (Oxford, 1913), pp. 41–5.

with the Divine Light.[3] This is not the place to try to sort out the influences on or from Philo in any detail, but it is at least clear that there is an affinity between such ideas and parts of the New Testament. Most strikingly, Christ is understood very much as Philo understood the *logos* in the Prologue to St John's Gospel and in St Paul's Epistle to the Colossians 1.15–23. Philo's opposition between the body and the spirit reminds one of St Paul's opposition between the Old and New Adam (e.g. I Corinthians 15); and New Testament writers frequently urge the Christian to turn away from the material world towards the truth in Christ.[4]

During the next five centuries both Platonism and Christianity developed independently but with an increasing awareness of each other. Alexandria continued to be a centre for such discussion, where both Clement (*c.*150–213) and Origen (185–254) developed ideas about the nature of God which go back to Philo and ultimately, to Plato. Clement in particular accepted the Platonic emphasis on Reason, which he believed to be the image of the *logos* in the human mind, and urged the Christian to ascend beyond passion towards an 'apathetic love' which desires only that others should possess what it possesses so abundantly. Origen, using another aspect of the Platonic tradition, defined the Son and the Holy Ghost as 'hypostases', and believed it was the Holy Ghost who created in man the capacity to receive Christ and so to love as Christ loves.[5] These Trinitarian and other Christian ideas had a parallel development to some pagan Platonists of the time, including the great third-century Neoplatonists Plotinus and the (violently anti-Christian) Porphyry (see Sheppard, pp. 5–12 above). Their follower Proclus (*c.*410–485) developed a system of hierarchies, and a theology of negation and affirmation (reminiscent of both Philo and Plotinus), which inspired the mystical writings of Dionysius the Areopagite in the sixth century. Largely through the work of John Scotus Eriugena (d.870) this became an important part of the Western mystical tradition (see Louth,

[3] See *Philo*, ed. and trans. F.H. Colson and G.H. Whitaker, 10 vols. (Loeb Classics, London, 1929), *De Opificio Mundi*, I, 15–22, 69–71, 134–5; *Quis Rerum Divinarum Heres*, IV, 182–7, 205. Chadwick, 'Philo' cites many similar passages. See also D.J. Riunia, *Philo of Alexandria and the Timaeus of Plato* (Leiden, 1986).

[4] Bigg, *Christian Platonists*, pp. 31–50; Chadwick, *Philo*, p. 143; C.K. Barrett, *The Gospel according to St John: An Introduction with Commentary and Notes on the Greek Text*, 2nd edn (London, 1978), pp. 34–6, 73, 152–5.

[5] A. Louth, 'Apathetic Love in Clement of Alexandria', *Studia Patristica*, 18 (1989), 413–19; see also Chadwick, 'Clement of Alexandria' and 'Origen', pp. 168–92 in *Cambridge History of Greek and Medieval Philosophy*; Bigg, *The Christian Platonists*, pp. 72–90, 151–215.

pp. 52–64 below). But the inheritance of Plotinus was imported more immediately into the West by St Augustine (354–430), who was profoundly influenced by the numinous theology of Plotinus and Porphyry. Although it was he who finally made the break between Christianity and heathen Neoplatonism (see Coleman, pp. 27–37, below), it was not until he had already incorporated some of the most important Neoplatonic ideas into Western Christian theology, with a precision and perception which allowed them to develop without losing their character.[6]

Proclus had also developed the Neoplatonic notion of a progression out from God and a final return to Him, in terms of the Divine power of *eros* (love). This flows down through the cosmos, binding all into a unity and enabling what it touches to return to its source.[7] It may have been from him that Boethius, a Christian living in Rome *c.*480–529, derived his extraordinarily influential account of the chain of love with which God binds the Universe. However, since Boethius was also able to read Plato and Aristotle in Greek, his notion of *eros* is undoubtedly influenced by both of them directly. Sadly, his plans to Latinise Plato's (and Aristotle's) works, most of which were shortly afterwards virtually lost until the Renaissance, were frustrated by his imprisonment and death. But his imprisonment also gave him the time and the impulse to write his *Consolation of Philosophy*, which gave popular poetic embodiment to some of Plato's most important ideas. These include not only the ascent through *eros* to God, but also an epitome of the cosmology of the *Timaeus* and its account of the relation of time to eternity, an explanation of how the mind may recover its original knowledge of a higher world, and much encouragement to use this knowledge of the Good in order to pursue it entirely. Boethius was well known in England in his original Latin before as well as after King Alfred (849–901) translated him (see Bately, pp. 38–44, below) and is of course an influence on Chaucer (*c.*1340–*c.*1400), as well as on most other writers of the medieval period (see Takada, pp. 45–52, below).[8]

Chaucer was also interested in science and society, and used another, more secular part of the Neoplatonic tradition to analyse nature and man's place in the universe. This was the Latin tradition

[6] See J. Marenbon, *Early Medieval Philosophy 480–1150: An Introduction* (London, 1983), pp. 18–19; C.S. Lewis, *The Discarded Image* (Cambridge, 1964), pp. 70–4.

[7] J.M. Rist, *Eros and Psyche* (Toronto, 1964), pp. 213–20 (quote pp. 216).

[8] See Lewis, *The Discarded Image*, pp. 75–91; Marenbon, *Early Medieval Philosophy*, pp. 27–42; S. Gersh, *Middle Platonism and the Neoplatonic Tradition*, 2 vols. (London, 1986), II, pp. 647–718; H. Chadwick, *Boethius: the Consolations of Logic, Music, Theology and Philosophy* (Oxford, 1981).

inspired by the *Timaeus*, which had been partially translated (until 53b) by Calcidius in the fourth century. Calcidius added a commentary, heavily dependent on Porphyry, though also including some quotations from Plato's other works. The continuing availability of this text when all the other Dialogues were lost, ensured that Plato himself would be known throughout the Middle Ages as a great cosmologist, the wise pagan who had anticipated the doctrine of the Trinity. The *Timaeus*, and the writings of Plotinus and Porphyry, also influenced the *Commentary on the Dream of Scipio* by Macrobius (end of the fourth century), which includes an account of Neoplatonic Hypostases of The One, Mens (mind or *nous*), and Soul, as well as much about the Universe and man. Martianus Capella, writing in the fifth century, is even more encyclopaedic, collecting Neoplatonic as well as much other material about such enormous subjects as Nature, Art and Love.[9]

A renewed interest in these three authors is a feature of the 'twelfth-century Renaissance' centred on Chartres in Northern France. William of Conches wrote commentaries on the *Timaeus*, Macrobius, and Martianus Capella (this last transmitted indirectly, by way of a Florentine manuscript), and used them as well as Genesis in his great study of the created world, the *Philosophia mundi*. Bernardus Silvestris' *Cosmographia*, draws on these and a wide range of related texts, and Alain of Lille used them more metaphorically in his *De planctu Naturae*. An account of this Neoplatonic revival lies outside the scope of this book, but Takada illustrates how Chaucer's descriptions of love and nature owes much to this kind of learning.[10]

Also outside the scope of this book is any discussion of how Aristotle's works came to be rediscovered and translated in the twelfth century, and, in the thirteenth, to displace the interest in Platonism, at least for scholars. (In about 1160 the Sicilian scholar Henricus Aristippus also translated Plato's *Meno* and *Phaedo*, but they were not widely disseminated.)[11] However, literary figures continued to read Western Platonic texts such as Macrobius and Boethius, and

[9] On Calcidius, Macrobius and Martianus Capella, see Lewis, *The Discarded Image*, pp. 49–60; C.S. Lewis, *The Allegory of Love* (Oxford, 1936), pp. 78–82; Marenbon, *Early Medieval Philosophy*, pp. 10–12; Gersh, *Middle Platonism*, II, 421–646. T. Gregory, 'The Platonic Inheritance', pp. 54–80, in *A History of Twelfth-Century Western philosophy*, ed. P. Dronke (Cambridge, 1988).

[10] On the twelfth-century Renaissance, see Marenbon, *Early Medieval Philosophy*, pp. 111–27; D. Elford, 'William of Conches', pp. 308–27, in P. Dronke, *Twelfth-Century Philosophy*. P. Dronke discusses the Florentine Manuscript in *P. Dronke, Fabula: Explorations into the Uses of Myth in Medieval Platonism* (Leiden, 1974), ch. 3 and Appendix B.

[11] See L.D. Reynolds and N.G. Wilson, *Scribes and Scholars* (1968, Oxford 1065), p. 106; P. Dronke, *Twelfth-Century Philosophy*, p. 14.

the Eastern Platonism of Dionysius and Eriugena exercised a strong influence on at least one fourteenth-century English mystic, who wrote *The Cloud of Unknowing*. This also shows a deep knowledge of Augustine, as do the writings of his fellow mystics Walter Hilton and Julian of Norwich, and indeed most religious writers of the later Middle Ages. This is why Augustine has been included in a book about English literature, for it was largely because of him that a Platonic interpretation of Christianity continued to develop even after the impact of the new scholasticism inspired by Aristotle's analytic methods.

But outside this group of mystics it is hard to find writers who develop Platonic ideas in the English language until one arrives at Chaucer and his followers. William Langland, it is true, writes that Envy advised the friars to

> preche men of Plato, and preve it by Seneca,
> That alle thynges under heuene oughte to be in comune.
> B.xx.275–6[12]

But he may have been using pagan authorities' praise of common ownership (found in the Prologue to the *Timaeus* and Seneca's *Epistles* IX.3), rather than Luke's (Acts 2.44, 4.32) because he wanted to discredit the idea. A more positive affinity with Plato may be detected in the Middle English poem *Pearl*. Here an upper and a lower world are definitely depicted, and correspondences between them shown in terms of image and archetype. The whiteness of the Pearl-maiden is an image of the brightness of the Lamb, her innocence of His perfection, her adornment of His power to adorn and illumine the world. Although this kind of Platonism could be derived from Augustine or Boethius, might it have been the circling imagery of the *Timaeus* itself (36b) which inspired the author to compare the human soul to a spherical pearl, made in the image of a heaven which is 'endeles rounde and blythe of mode' (l.738)?[13]

What is most original about these authors' use of the tradition of Latin learning, including its Platonic elements, is their readiness to express it in English. It is with Chaucer that this elevation of the native tongue becomes thoroughly established, for he clearly aims to

[12] W. Langland, *The Vision of Piers Plowman*, ed. A.V.C. Schmidt (London, 1978), pp. 260, 357 for Seneca reference; the Plato reference was suggested to me by Peter Dronke.

[13] *Pearl etc.* eds A.C. Cawley and J.A. Anderson (London, 1962, 1976), p. 30. The Neoplatonism in the poem is discussed by Eugene Vance in '*Pearl*: Love and the Poetics of Participation', in *Poetics: Theory and Practice in Medieval English Literature*, eds. P. Boitani and A. Torti (Suffolk, 1991).

educate his vernacular readers. He knew Macrobius' work well, playing in several works with the notion of the soul's ascent, and he is also intrigued by the idea (which goes back to the *Timaeus* though he may have read it in Alain of Lille) that the creative power of Nature or the poet is an image of God, and shares some characteristics with Him. Above all his translation of Boethius, and his extensive use of his work in the *Knight's Tale* and *Troilus and Criseyde*,[14] may be seen as paving the way for the English Renaissance, in which the ascent of love is provoked as much by a particular woman as by a recognition of the Good.

[14] See e.g. *Knight's Tale* I, 2987–2990, *Parliament of Fowles*, 379–82 in which God or Nature appears to act as a craftsman, and compare *Timaeus* 30c, Boethius, *Consolations* IV, pr.6. He could have found the idea that language should be appropriate to its subject, which he ascribes to Plato (C.T. 742, IX, 208) in *Timaeus* 29b, or in Boethius, *Consolations* III, pr.2, or in *Romance of the Rose* 7099ff. (these three references from Robinson).

CHAPTER 3

The Christian Platonism of St Augustine

Janet Coleman

The writings of St Augustine (AD354–430) exercised a massive influence not only on the Western literary imagination but also on the development of medieval scholastic philosophy and theology, and the emergence of the Western mystical tradition. His doctrines also became central to the Renaissance and the Reformation. As the product of the Roman education system of the fourth century, he was one of a generation that absorbed in a highly eclectic fashion the themes that had been on the philosophical and theological agenda of pagan and Christian thinkers for more than four centuries and which stretched back to pre-Christian Stoicism and Hellenistic Judaism. During this period a kind of Platonism continued to be developed roughly contemporaneously with the rise and development of Christianity. Indeed, the early history of Christianity and the evolution of Christian asceticism can be described as the story of a selective incorporation of a range of Platonic insights into a Christian doctrine that explained the relationship between man and the created world and man and God.[1] But we must be aware of the eclectic nature of both Christianity and Platonism in this period. Just as what scholars now call Neoplatonism was not a fixed quantity, neither was Christianity from its inception to *c.*AD600. Indeed, the term 'Christian Platonism' for the first 1000 years AD covers so wide a variety of differences that it is difficult to define it accurately as a single thing.[2] By focusing on Augustine's Platonism, which was only one kind of Platonically influenced Christian

[1] Werner Jaeger, *Early Christianity and Greek Paideia* (Oxford, 1961).

[2] A.H. Armstrong, *St Augustine and Christian Platonism* (Villanova, 1967), reprinted with corrections in *Augustine, A Collection of Critical Essays*, ed. R.A. Markus (New York, 1972), pp. 3–37, p. 3.

thought,[3] we intend to highlight what, arguably, became the most influential rendering of the Platonic tradition for the Christian Latin West.

Augustine, the son of a Christian mother and a pagan father of humble means, came from a rural hill town in the Latin-speaking province of Roman North Africa (now Algeria). He was educated locally to pursue a career which eventually led him to become a professor of Latin rhetoric in Italy. He learned Greek to a level sufficient to translate quite technical philosophical texts although he never mastered Homer and Greek literature. Nor does he seem to have made a direct study of any Greek text of Plato although such were available.[4] We do not know if Augustine read Cicero's Latin translation of Plato's *Timaeus* on which Calcidius had written an elaborate commentary in the fourth century. In his own writings, Augustine never reveals which texts of the 'Platonists' he read or heard discussed, but it is clear that the form of Platonic philosophy that eventually captured him once he arrived in Italy to pursue his career, was the 'modern' Neoplatonism of the late third century of Plotinus and Porphyry. So enduring was their influence on him that when he finally lay dying at Hippo during the Vandal siege of his city, his last recorded words were a quotation from Plotinus.[5]

Augustine experienced a series of four conversions throughout his turbulent life: first to the philosophy of life expressed by Cicero, then to the dualist religious sect Manicheism, thirdly to pagan Platonism and finally to Christianity (386). In his *Confessions*, Augustine retells, stage by stage, the intellectual and spiritual journey he had undertaken throughout his life. He explains here how at first he thought the shift from Neoplatonism to Christianity to be easy, but gradually he reinterpreted the move as a painful break with old ways, a taking of sides and a cavernous divide. At first, however, he wrote works to demonstrate his optimistic commitment to the kind of Christian Platonism for which St Paul was only a short step further.

[3] We need only mention the variety of types of twelfth-century Platonism that derived not only from Augustine but from Boethius, Pseudo-Dionysius, Islamic Neoplatonism – principally from Proclus's *Liber de Causis*. See M.D. Chenu, *La théologie du douzième siècle* (Paris, 1957), chapter 5. Also R.A. Markus, *The End of Ancient Christianity* (Cambridge, 1990), p. xii.

[4] Henry Chadwick, *Augustine* (Oxford, 1986), pp. 7f. Augustine benefited from the Latin translations of Greek Neoplatonists made by Marius Victorinus. See Pierre Hadot, *Marius Victorinus, recherches sur sa vie et ses oeuvres* (Paris, 1971).

[5] Chadwick, *Augustine*, p. 25.

In these early works we see Augustine's debt to Cicero's Platonism,[6] to that precursor and source of Christian Platonic thinking, the Hellenistic Jew Philo of Alexandria,[7] to the Greek Fathers Clement of Alexandria, Origen, the Cappadocians (Basil of Caesarea, Gregory Nazianzen and Gregory of Nyssa) and to Plotinus and Porphyry.[8]

Writing with the hindsight of a convert to Christianity more than thirteen years after the event, Augustine tells us:

> Therefore You brought in my way by means of a certain man – an incredibly conceited man – some books of the Platonists translated from Greek into Latin. In them I found, though not in the very words yet the thing itself and proved by all sorts of reasons. [But not all of Christ was there]. (*Confessions*, VII. 9)[9]

In Book VIII.2 he writes: 'in the Platonists, God and His Word are everywhere implied'. He tells us that these Platonist books came from Athens and they spoke of Old Testament history and how the Jews

> changed the glory of Thy incorruption into idols and divers images . . . in fact into that Egyptian food for which Esau had lost his birthright . . . For it pleased You, O Lord, to take away the reproach of the inferiority from Jacob so that the elder brother [the Jews] served the younger [the Christians]: and You have called the Gentiles into Your inheritance. From the Gentiles indeed I had come to You; and I fixed my mind upon the gold which You willed that Your people should bring with them from Egypt: for it was Yours wherever it was. And You had said to the Athenians by Your Apostle [Paul] that in You we live and move and are, as certain of their own writers had said.

Augustine tells us that when he came to Italy and encountered Bishop Ambrose of Milan, a Greek reader who absorbed much from Philo,

[6] On Cicero's 'platonism', see Janet Coleman, *Ancient and Medieval Memories, Studies in the Reconstruction of the Past* (Cambridge, 1992), especially chapter 3, pp. 39–62. See Cicero's *De oratore*, I.12 on men gifted with divine eloquence; *Tusculan Disputations*, I, pp. xix–xxv on Plato's authority and on the self identified not with the body but with incorporeal soul.

[7] On Philo, see Henry Chadwick 'Philo', in *The Cambridge History of Later Greek and Early Medieval Philosophy*, ed. A.H. Armstrong (Cambridge, 1970), pp. 137–57, and H.A. Wolfson, *Philo*, 2 vols (Cambridge, Mass., 1947). See also *Philo, in ten volumes and two supplementary volumes*, ed. and trans. F.H. Colson, G.H. Whitaker and R. Marcus (London, 1929–62).

[8] See Jaeger, *Early Christianity and Greek Paideia*, pp. 43–4, and in general H. Chadwick, 'Clement of Alexandria' and 'Origen', in *Cambridge History*, ed. Armstrong, pp. 168–92 and 182–92 for editions of texts. In general, see Robin Lane Fox, *Pagans and Christians in the Mediterranean World from the Second Century AD to the Conversion of Constantine* (London, 1986). Also, Judith Herrin, *The Formation of Christendom* (Oxford, 1987).

[9] Translation of Augustine's *Confessions* used here: F.J. Sheed (London, 1944). Translations of other works of Augustine are my own.

Origen and Plotinus and then transformed their Platonism to produce a markedly ascetic image of the Church,[10] he did not think his own ideas on man and the universe that he had absorbed from Cicero and the 'Platonists' required any change. Some of the themes Augustine treats from the Christian Neoplatonist agenda of these early years can be outlined here.[11]

The world can be seen with human eyes and comprehended by the human mind as a measured and ordered hierarchy of beings. All being is good and God is the cause of good, never of evil. God, as the incorporeal, transcendent source of being, the transcendent One who is in Himself ineffable and unthinkable, 'known better in not being known' (*De ordine* II. 16.44), nonetheless communicates by descent through all levels of spirit and body, from His unity down to the multiplicity of matter and non-being, like light unto darkness. The human soul is created and therefore, is not part of God. Although fallen it retains some trace of the divine image and form through its rationality and freedom. It is in exile although immortal and it follows the hierarchical order to ascend vertically in reverse to its goal, its true home and origin. The material world is not evil although it is contrasted with the intelligible world. The sensible world is an image of the intelligible world which is its exemplar (*Contra academicos* III. 17.37: III. 18.40). The sensible, as an image, is therefore like the true (*verisimilem*). Therefore, he says that 'whatever is done in this world through the so-called civil virtues (which virtues are only like-the true virtues, while the true virtues are unknown to all but the few who are wise) cannot be called anything more than like-the true'.[12] For this reason, the body's rightful place in the hierarchical cosmos is as an instrument: its purpose is to enable intellect's work in the rational order as it is expressed at the lower levels of being. But the body can also be an obstacle to man's ascent and fulfilment. Evil, as a corruption of good, is a displacement from right order. Just as order

[10] Peter Brown, *The Body and Society, Men, Women and Sexual Renunciation in Early Christianity* (London, 1989), especially part III: 'Ambrose to Augustine', pp. 339–427.

[11] Edward Cranz, 'The Development of Augustine's Ideas on Society before the Donatist Controversy', *Harvard Theological Review*, 47 (1954), 255–316 and for a list of early works and their dates. This is reprinted in Markus (ed.), *Augustine*, pp. 336–403. Also see R.A. Markus, *Conversion and Disenchantment in Augustine's Spiritual Career* (Villanova, 1989). See A.H. Armstrong, 'Augustine and Christian Platonism' in *Augustine*, ed. Markus, pp. 3–37.

[12] *Contra academicos* III. 17. 37. See also *De libero arbitrio*, II, 15–33 and *De musica* VI. I. I, 3. Standard editions of Augustine's works are *Corpus christianorum series latina*, *Corpus scriptores ecclesiasticorum latinorum*, and, when texts are not available in these, *Patrologia latina*, edited by J.P. Migne.

brings about created being so its contrary, disruption of order, brings about non-being. And what undergoes corruption tends towards non-being.[13] Hence, sensual delight is distrusted and must be used rightly, for it is the rational mind, free from sensual slavery through reason's ordered control, that leads man to God (*De libero arbitrio* I.6.15). The ideal life is one of contemplation and a certain asceticism through which one withdraws from the distraction of material multiplicity. It is assisted by solitude and liberal studies that train the mind away from the order of sense, leading the spiritual mind to its goal within this life. Described here, then, is a certain *paideia* of the soul, an education of mind away from the changeable and corruptible things of the world to its true and natural focus, the incorporeal truths and God. Liberal studies are the means by which the soul is educated.[14]

In this life man is estranged from God, there is a gulf to be overcome and this can be achieved by a kind of human self-determination through moral discipline encouraged through the liberal studies of the classical Greek *paideia*, an instruction of mind concerning its true objects.[15] Augustine believed that nothing in the material world (*significata*) that is external to mind can, *in the last resort*, be regarded as the *source* of its knowledge. Neither the sense data of experience nor the signs that point to such sense data in language and gesture can give knowledge without the Interior Teacher who is the source of all truth and knowledge. This is Christ, dwelling in the mind. But the soul must begin at the beginning. Man's reason can move 'as it were by sure steps from things corporeal to things incorporeal' (*De musica* VI.1.1,3). There are stages in cognition that lead to salvation. There is a ladder of perfection consisting of the seven-fold work of the spirit which leads to God, beginning with fear and ascending through piety, fortitude, knowledge, counsel, understanding to wisdom, the supreme grade of perfection. Wisdom is of the intelligible order, 'for God's kingdom is the whole world which sense does not know' (*Soliloquia* I.3), and 'His law, fixed and unshaken in Him is, as it were, transcribed into wise souls' (*De ordine* II.8.25). This theory of mind's education from things corporeal to things incorporeal would be the most influential paradigm for all western theories of knowledge

[13] *De ordine* I. 7. 18; *De libero arbitrio* I. 16. 34, 35.
[14] These views influenced the *Secretum* of Petrarch in the fourteenth century. See Coleman, *Ancient and Medieval Memories*, pp. 551–4.
[15] *De sermone Domini in monte*, I. 2. 9; I. 4. 11, *De quantitate animae* 76.

during the middle ages until the reintroduction of Aristotle's writings, translated into Latin, during the twelfth and thirteenth centuries.

Just as there is a seven-stage ascent of the soul (*De quantitate animae* 76; *Sermo* CCLIX.2–3), so too the history of the universe is divided into six ages with a seventh when the saints and just men of God will enjoy the sabbath on earth.[16] This view would influence all historiography throughout the medieval period and beyond, the soul's own history paralleling the history of the universe. The passions can be integrated by subjection to reason's control and mind or reason is itself subject to what is above it in the hierarchy, God.[17] Ultimately, carnal desire must and can be tamed rather than eliminated and the consequent achievement of peace through a right subjection to God's order is the achievement of perfect wisdom in this life. Hence, man's quest is the quest of his soul for wisdom and it is achieved by one of two ways: either by reason guided by a Platonist understanding of the liberal arts, or by authority, which is Christ and his Ecclesia, which is a school of instruction. Indeed, the divine authority of Christ *is* the highest reason, for Christ is the wisdom of God (*De ordine* II.26–7). The teaching of the Church is 'Platonism for the multitude',[18] addressing unphilosophical minds in pictorial and figurative ways in order to guide their conduct with reason.

Man's identity is his contemplative mind and his sense experiences are merely images of a higher, intelligible world that can be contemplated by mind when it is divorced from the senses (*De trinitate* XIV.4–14; 24–5). The wise man's life is a progressive liberation from the world of sense, where the soul is called back to the intelligible world. 'This is the peace which is given on earth to men of good will, this is the life of the man who has achieved perfect wisdom'.[19] In the world of sense, the soul is blinded by darkness of error and made forgetful by bodily stains, images that would dominate the writings of St Bernard in the twelfth century and Petrarch in the fourteenth. Man must choose freely whether or not to accept right order and he has in himself and in his power all that is necessary for the right choices. To choose the proper order of soul is the necessary prerequisite to proper order in society. It *is* possible to attain justice, comprehensible in human terms, through the ordered arrangements

[16] *De Genesi contra Manichaeos* I. 23. 35, *De vera religione, passim*.
[17] *De Sermone Domini in monte* I. 2. 9; *De vera religione* 23, 44; *De musica* VI. 5. 13; 15. 50.
[18] Chadwick, *Augustine*, p. 25.
[19] *De sermone Domini in monte* I. 2. 9; *Contra academicos* III. 19. 42.

of social living. Justice is the order by which the soul serves God and dominates none but bestial and corporeal natures, images that would influence political theory and practice of medieval church and *regnum* ('state') for centuries. (*De musica* VI.15.50)

Augustine's early optimism consisted in the belief that the goal of human striving was attainable by human effort through rationality and he describes the apostles as having achieved it in this life.[20] The classical debate, to which Cicero had contributed, over the merits of the three kinds of life, active, contemplative or mixed, was decided in favour of an *otium liberale* (a withdrawal from public affairs to pursue liberal studies) (*De ordine* II.5.14). The life of action is linked with multiplicity and that of contemplation is linked with unity. The active life can only be considered the initiating step on the road to the soul's return for the soul begins life as a pilgrim, far from its home and seeks to steer itself to the harbour of philosophy,[21] images that would stir the imaginations of Renaissance thinkers. Hence, the main theme of Augustine's early works as a Christian Platonist is the soul's quest for wisdom and as a Christian he is certain that he will not depart from the authority of Christ. As a Neoplatonist he is equally certain that reason will find in Platonism what is in agreement with Christianity (*Contra academicos* III.20.43). Christianity is the one true philosophy, focusing as it does on the soul and the other, intelligible world. Augustine moves with ease from the philosophical distinction between the sensible and the intelligible to the Biblical distinction between flesh and spirit. Plato, St Paul and Cicero seem to be talking to one another. He has no difficulty in reconciling Plato with the Bible, identifying the stages of God's providence in history with the stages of the Platonist soul's ascent.[22] Jewish history is, therefore, read as an image of the Christian people and the consequence is an outline of history in terms of universal progress. History is God's gradual education of the human race (*De vera religione*).

Because Augustine began his career as an orator and became a professor of rhetoric it is probably not surprising that he has a theory of cognition that depends extensively on language. Indeed, much of the grammatical, logical and rhetorical tradition of antiquity was concerned with the ways in which language related on the one hand

20 *De sermone Domini in monte* I. 4. 12; I. 9, *De doctrina christiana* I. 27–8, *De libero arbitrio* II. 25. See Markus, *Conversion and Disenchantment*, p. 16.

21 *De libero arbitrio* II. 38. 53; *De beata vita* I. 1–2.

22 *De Genesi contra Manichaeos* I. 23. 35f., *De vera religione*, *passim*.

to non-linguistic reality (appearances and experiences) and on the other, to the way in which human minds think and speak about appearances and experiences. Augustine's writings introduced later ages to these ancient concerns and his teaching on language would be fundamental to medieval monastic and scholastic attitudes to texts and their interpretation.[23] Hence, his teaching on language would be central to later attitudes to the literary imagination.

In his *Soliloquies* Augustine speaks of an internal dialogue or conversation with the self in which the objects of knowledge are the participants, brought to consciousness through speech. Here the problem of knowledge is the problem of language as a system of signs. Augustine's discussion would greatly influence medieval monastic schools' treatment of divine and human language as signs especially through his further elaboration in his two early works the *De magistro* and the *De doctrina christiana*.[24] Here he explains there is a cognitive reality behind words and if we know what the words signify we are recalling an implicitly known truth which Augustine calls recollection. This is a modified Platonism because the truth is not innate in man's mind, for Augustine, but must be learned. The commemorative function of speech is most important for the Christian because Augustine believes that through prayer and the reading of the words of Scripture man's memory is stimulated. Through prayer a man is reminded of the reality of God whom he addresses. The knowledge of God is stored away in man's memory and the believer is aided by his memory of this anterior knowledge when he reads and studies the Bible. Christ the word acts as a prior, interior teacher and someone who has no anterior knowledge and memory of God within his mind cannot understand any meaning in the sacred page. But as St Paul had said, anyone who seeks God in the good things that are seen can find him. Men who have no anterior knowledge of God are without excuse (Rom.1.19–20). Augustine says that the vast majority of men require large quantities of human speech to orient them towards God and stimulate their memories of the interior teacher. But a small minority do not need to rely on the sensory stimulation provided by the sight and sound of words because they have access to the intelligible, acquiring faith through that inward divine speech achieved through contemplation. Signs signify divine realities, teaching us nothing, but pointing beyond and causing us to think of

[23] See Coleman, *Ancient and Medieval Memories*, chapters 1–7, pp. 3–111.
[24] See Markus, 'Augustine on Signs', in *Augustine*, ed. Markus, pp. 61–88.

what is beyond the impression the word, as sign, makes on the senses. This attitude was fundamental to future monastic *lectio divina* (reading of scripture).

Augustine would modify and refine his theory of cognition over the years but he would always retain his concern to establish a dominant role for the power of thought in order that it may break through the surface of appearance and habit, disclosing beyond it the objective, eternal, immovable structure of the nature of things, of man and of history, knowable to the contemplative mind alone. As a consequence he will maintain a Platonist hierarchy in the objects of thought that runs from a knowledge of temporal things to a knowledge of eternal objects and it is in the intellectual realm, divorced from all sense experience, that moral and philosophical truths reside, an intelligible world of ideas consonant with those of the divine mind. Such moral and philosophical truths divorced from sense experience were, for him, the manifestations of God's interior presence in the mind of man where Christ the word dwells in the human soul as the word of God, illuminated as the intelligible *verbum mentis* (word of the mind). Human speech, be it written or spoken, could bring forth that immutable truth, a confidence that was not shared by Plato but one which would inspire literary artists of the future to regard their works as capable of revealing prophetic truth.

If we were to stop here with the discussion of those early writings that demonstrate the overwhelming Neoplatonism of Augustine's early Christian years, we would have presented an Augustine that was more familiar to the Renaissance than to the Reformation. But Augustine's thinking did not stand still. Later ages would not read Augustine's works as having evolved and changed throughout his turbulent life and for this reason Augustine, like Socrates, would become all things to all men attracted to some kind of Platonically influenced Christianity. In fact, during the 390s when Augustine re-read St Paul, he gradually found it difficult to see how a pagan rhetor or a Neoplatonist could pass so easily into the ranks of the Christians.[25] His later works therefore argue for a dramatic renunciation of his past confidence in man's rational and moral capacities to achieve perfection.[26] The ordered cosmos, which he continued to believe in, was now not open to rational comprehension. It was, like

[25] Markus, *End of Ancient Christianity*, pp. 29, 48–51.

[26] *Confessions* VII. 21. See Markus, *End of Ancient Christianity*, pp. 50–6, and Gerald Bonner, *Augustine of Hippo, Life and Controversies* (London, 1963).

God's judgements, inscrutable. Likewise, he surrendered his early confidence in a possible ordering of men's lives, individually or socially.[27] There would be no enlightened ruler to control society with reason. Human experience and the Christian philosopher's striving towards felicity now seemed impossible of achievement except through God's grace. Man simply must believe. He cannot know. Sin took on a new power in men's lives to the extent that it seemed to Augustine that man was powerless to free himself without God's grace. Sin was no longer to be conceived as a disruption of the right order of the cosmos nor was it an ignorant surrender of reason to sensuality. The earlier *paedeia* describing a self-willed and self-performed perfectionism was rejected. Now good will can only be brought about in us by God's action. No longer was there a simple opposition between flesh and spirit, soul and body. Rather, the soul was to be seen as the battlefield of turbulence and the flesh, now neutral, became corrupted by the sins of the soul, by its various lusts – for the body and for domination of other men. There was to be no victory of mind over body in himself, nor a distinction between the rational philosophical Christian 'saved by liberal studies' and the average Christian, saved by the authoritative teaching of the Church providing 'Plato for the multitude'. Now God alone, not education, was seen to lead to truth (*Confessions* VII.20).

In the end there was only one division: between those destined to be saved and those who are reprobate, the city of God and the earthly city. The reason for this division was hidden in the inscrutable depths of God's will but what distinguished them in this life was the object of their love, be it self or God. If the ordinary Christian was now no further away from grace than the erudite or the ascetic, then imperfection is the inescapable condition for all alike here. Mankind after Adam is a mass of sin. Perfection – that distant goal after life and history – can only be due to God's will. God chooses His elect on the basis of His foreknowledge of His determination of their wills. Reading Neoplatonists with new eyes, Augustine finally insisted that the gulf between God and man could not be bridged through self knowledge but could be meditated by grace alone.

Augustine would continue to speak of our ignorance of God's essence as, nonetheless an informed ignorance, using Porphyrian language when he speaks of the believer contemplating God as an

[27] Markus, *Conversion and Disenchantment*, pp. 18–23, 36–40. See also Markus, *Saeculum, History and Society in the Theology of St Augustine* (Cambridge, 1970), pp. 87–92.

experience beyond intellection, such things being best known by not being known. He would still speak of salvation as, in a way, a deification by degree through participation in God. He would remain a Christian Neoplatonist to the end.[28] But after AD c.400 he would increasingly seek to draw upon Neoplatonist insights only to serve Christian doctrine as it had developed in the Latin West of the fourth and fifth centuries, rather than conforming Christian doctrine to Neoplatonist expectations. It was the writings of the older Augustine that would influence the Reformation's model of man.

[28] R. Russell, 'Neoplatonism in the *De civitate dei*', in *Neoplatonism and Early Christian Thought*, ed. H.J. Blumenthal and R.A. Markus (London, 1981), pp. 160–70.

CHAPTER 4

Boethius and King Alfred

Janet Bately

BOETHIUS

Any generalisation about the knowledge of Greek texts in medieval England is fraught with danger. However, it would appear that during the first half of that period acquaintance with the works of Plato was at second or even third hand, through the writings of authors such as Macrobius, Martianus Capella, Augustine, Boethius and (via Calcidius' translation of the *Timaeus*) John Scotus Eriugena, and through Latin and Old English texts drawing on one or other of these writings. The most important contribution in the vernacular was provided by the late ninth century reworking of Boethius' *De consolatione Philosophiae*[1] by Alfred, King of Wessex,[2] though Platonic or Neoplatonic ideas are also found in Alfred's *Soliloquies* (by way of Augustine)[3] and in a couple of Old English homilies (by way of Alfred's *Boethius*).[4] The earliest secure evidence for knowledge of the *Consolatio* in England is provided by Alfred's *Boethius*, although, thanks apparently to the Englishman Alcuin, it was being read on the continent from the Carolingian Renaissance onward. The works of Macrobius and Martianus Capella had also become known in England by the end of the ninth century, while commentaries on Capella and Boethius were in circulation there by the beginning of the tenth.

In the later medieval period, Calcidius' *Timaeus* was joined by the

[1] *Boethius*, ed. H.F. Stewart, E.K. Rand (1918), revised and trans. by S.J. Tester (London, 1973, reprinted 1978). Referred to hereafter as *Consolatio*.

[2] *King Alfred's Old English Version of Boethius De Consolatione Philosophiae*, ed. Walter John Sedgefield (Oxford, 1899). Referred to hereafter as *Boethius*.

[3] *King Alfred's Version of St Augustine's Soliloquies*, ed. Thomas A. Carnicelli (Harvard, 1969), especially p. 91.1–4.

[4] See M.R. Godden, 'Anglo-Saxons on the Mind', *Learning and Literature in Anglo-Saxon England*, ed. Michael Lapidge and Helmut Gneuss (Cambridge, 1985), pp. 296–8. Boethian ideas have also been detected (sometimes controversially) in a range of Old English poems.

twelfth-century Latin translations of the *Meno* and the *Phaedo* by Henricus Aristippus (d.1162). However, the importance of patristic and other major authors writing in Latin as transmitters of Platonic thought remained undiminished, with the *Consolatio* playing a key role. As in the earlier period, this text exerted its influence both directly (in the original or in translation) and through commentaries. Of these, the most influential seems to have been the Latin commentary of Nicholas Trevet, a work which incorporates material from both Alfred's *Boethius* and William of Conches' *Commentator*. Trevet's commentary was an important source for Chaucer's *Boece* (a prose translation of the *Consolatio*, which draws also on Jean de Meun's *Li Livres de Confort*) and for John Walton's Boethius (1410, a verse rendering which in its turn uses material from Chaucer).[5]

The importance of Boethius as the mediator of Greek philosophical learning to the Christian Western world cannot be overestimated. His writings reveal a profound intellectual debt to both Plato and the Neoplatonists. Indeed, the essential shape of the *Consolatio* has been described as 'a Neoplatonic thesis that the imperfections of this world are allowed to facilitate the return of the soul to its origin in God'.[6] The Platonic doctrines of Recollection and the Ascent of the Soul are combined and interpreted in terms of Plotinus' ascent of the soul to its original home. The questions 'If there is a God, whence comes evil? But whence comes good, if there is not?' are taken from Proclus (*Parmenides* 1056; *Consolatio*, I.pr.iv.105–6) along with a belief in foreknowledge by God, to whom everything is known, outside time, in the simultaneity of eternity (*Consolatio*, V.pr.vi.). God is seen to be working through Fate. However, while there are no overt references to Christian doctrines, such as the remission of sins, redemption, or eternal life, there is nothing of Plato that cannot also be found in Augustine.[7]

There are many reasons why Alfred should have chosen to make available to his people an English version of the *Consolatio*, a philosophical work of great power, originality and authority, coloured by its author's personal tragedy. Nearly 700 years later another English monarch – Queen Elizabeth I – was to undertake the same

[5] See *Boethius. His Life, Thought and Influence*, ed. Margaret Gibson (Oxford, 1981) and *The Medieval Boethius. Studies in the Vernacular Translations of De Consolatione Philosophiae*, ed. A.J. Minnis (Cambridge, 1987).

[6] H. Chadwick, 'Introduction', *Boethius*, ed. Gibson, p. 11.

[7] See further *Boethius*, ed. Gibson, Part 1, also Henry Chadwick, *Boethius. The Consolations of Music, Logic, Theology, and Philosophy* (Oxford, 1981, reprinted 1990).

task. Yet Alfred's is no close translation in the modern sense of the word. Rather, it is a reinterpretation, made in the light of his experience and obligations as a medieval Christian king, reflecting his own personal quest for an answer to the problems of a world in which evil and sin often seemed to have the upper hand. Even in the central discussions of Fate, Fortune, Freewill and Providence major differences emerge between the attitudes of the two men. Alfred certainly follows Boethius in his acceptance of Fate as the agent by which God's providence works out its will in the temporal world. However, he parts from Boethius in his emphasis on a personal God who is very clearly the Christian God. So, for instance, where Boethius takes from the Neoplatonists the image of concentric circles to represent Providence and Fate (*Consolatio*, IV.pr.vi.65–82), Alfred, introducing the Augustinian theme of the soul yearning for God, but reaching Him only through *contemptus mundi* (contempt for the world), uses instead the image of a cartwheel. Its axle represents God and the nave, spokes and fellies represent men, who are graded as the best, the middle sort and the least worthy, according to the extent to which they set their love near to God and despise earthly things (*Boethius*, 129.19–130.27). And as his ultimate answer to the problems of the secret workings of fate and fortune Alfred produces the doctrine of merit.

ALFRED'S BOETHIUS

It is not possible to do justice here to all the modifications and changes made by Alfred in his rendering of the *Consolatio*[8] and the variety of ways in which he handles those materials which Boethius himself had inherited from the Platonists. Exploration of three linked themes must suffice by way of illustration: the Platonic doctrines of the Pre-existence of the Soul, Recollection and the Ascent of the Soul. These, as we have seen, are doctrines which Boethius, following the Neoplatonists, explicitly associated together in the *Consolatio*, and Alfred reacts to them in a variety of ways. On one occasion where Boethius' Philosophia describes all human kind as from one origin, one father, who 'locked into limbs spirits brought down from their high abode' (*Consolatio*, III.m.vi.5), her English counterpart, Wisdom (*alias* Reason) summarises instead Christian teachings on the creation

[8] Book length studies include K. Otten, *König Alfreds Boethius* (Tübingen, 1964), and F. Anne Payne, *King Alfred and Boethius* (Madison and London, 1968).

of man (*Boethius*, 69.17–23).[9] On another occasion, Alfred preserves Boethius' references to recollection along with his Neoplatonist emphasis on self-knowledge, the turning-in upon itself of the soul:

> Whoever wishes to search deeply with inward mind after right and does not wish to be hindered by any man or any thing, let him begin to seek within himself what he previously sought outside . . . For no heaviness of the body nor any vice can completely take away the righteousness from his mind, so that he does not have something of it in his mind, though the sluggishness of the body and the vices often trouble the mind with forgetfulness and lead it astray with the mist of error, so that it cannot shine as brightly as it would, and nevertheless a grain of the seed of truth is ever dwelling in the soul while the soul and the body are united. (*Boethius*, 94.27–95.14)

For, he continues,

> it is a very true saying that the philosopher Plato spoke: 'Whoever', he said, 'is unmindful of righteousness, let him turn to his memory; then he will find the righteousness there, concealed by the weight of the body and by the tribulations and preoccupations of his mind'. (*Boethius*, 95.19–23)[10]

However, Alfred's rendering of this and the passage immediately following (*Consolatio*, III pr.xii. 1–4; *Boethius*, 95.24–31) contains no detail that requires interpretation in the light of Plato's Doctrine of Pre-existence, the emphasis being on forgetfulness by man of his essential righteousness.

In his version of *Consolatio*, IV.m.1, in contrast, Alfred preserves Boethius' reference to the soul's recollection of a former home. This meter begins with a description of the mind putting on Philosophia's wings and being borne aloft – itself an important Platonic image and one which is not only retained here by Alfred but may well have influenced him in the beautiful and original simile of the eagle that he puts into the mouth of Wisdom in Book II: 'But when I travel up with my servants, then we scorn this stormy world, just like the eagle, when he soars up in stormy weather above the clouds so that the storms cannot harm him' (*Boethius*, 18.11–14). On that occasion, Wisdom expresses a willingness to take *Mod* ('Mind', alias Boethius) up with

[9] Cf. Alfred's transformation of Book III.m.ix, 'O qui perpetua' (which draws heavily on Plato, *Timaeus*, and Proclus), into what is essentially a celebration of God and His creation, with the Platonic World Soul reinterpreted as the human soul.

[10] cf. *Consolatio*, III.m.xi 1–16, which concludes:

> If Plato's muse rings true,
> What each man learns, forgetful he recalls.

him – provided he return to earth again, for the sake of good men.[11] In *Consolatio*, IV.m.1, the soul, once it has ascended to 'the outside of the swift upper air' speaks only of remaining:

> If the road bring you back, returning to this place,
> Which you now seek, forgetful,
> 'This,' you will say, 'I remember, is my native land,
> Here I was born, here I shall halt my step'.
> (*Consolatio*, IV. m.i. 23–6)

In Alfred's version of this meter, Wisdom comments similarly:

> But if you ever come on that path and to that place that you have yet forgotten, then you will wish to say, 'This is my true homeland; I had formerly come from here and from here I was born; I now intend to stand fast here; I do not wish ever to depart from here'. (*Boethius* 105.20–4)

And in yet another striking passage the idea of a return home is actually inserted by Alfred, bringing together the themes of recollection and the ascent of the soul in an expansion of Philosophia's exhortation, 'Let us be raised up, if we can, to the height of that highest intelligence' (*Consolatio*, V. pr.5. 50). Having rendered this with some fidelity 'Let us now raise our minds as high as we can towards the high roof of the highest intelligence', he puts into Wisdom's mouth the further comment 'so that you may most speedily and easily come to your own home from where you previously came' (*Boethius*, 146.26–9).

The ideas of ascent and a journey home are also combined by Alfred in his version of *Consolatio*, III. pr.2.54, where Boethius uses his celebrated simile of the drunken man: 'man's mind, though the memory of it is clouded, yet does seek again its proper good, but like a drunken man cannot find by what path it may return home'). Alfred's extended version introduces the image of a steep slope:

> Now then although their minds and their natures are dimmed, and they have sunk down on the descent to evil and are inclined thither, nevertheless they desire the highest good, as far as they know how and are able to. Just as a drunken man knows that he should go to his house and to his rest and yet cannot find the way thither, so it is with the mind when it is made heavy by

[11] In a rewriting of a reference by Fortuna to her wheel (*Consolatio*, II.pr.2, 28–33). Just as Boethius has no place for Plato's gods in his system, so Alfred does not accept the personifications Fortuna and Natura.

the cares of this world; it is sometimes intoxicated and led astray by them, to the extent that it cannot very directly find the way to good (or God?) (*Boethius* 55.15–22)

We may compare Chaucer's exploitation of Boethius' drunken-man image in a very different context in the *Knight's Tale* (*c.*1382), where Arcite, having succeeded in obtaining his liberty, realises that he has in the process deprived himself of what was in fact even more important to him – sight of Emily.

> We witen nat what thing we preyen heere:
> We faren as he that dronke is as a mous.
> A dronke man woot wel he hath an hous,
> But he noot which the righte wey is thider,
> And to a dronke man the wey is slider.
> And certes, in this world so faren we;
> We seken faste after felicitee.[12]
>
> (ll.1260–6)

Perhaps the most interesting example of use of the Platonic doctrine of the Ascent of the Soul in Alfred's *Boethius* is, however, in the rendering of Book III. m.xii, a meter where the turning back of Orpheus as he leaves the Underworld is used – under the influence of the allegory of the Cave in Plato's *Republic* – to portray the failure of a soul in its ascent towards the light. According to Boethius' version the fable is intended for those who seek to lead their mind into the upper day:

> For he who overcome should turn back his gaze
> Towards the Tartarean cave,
> Whatever excellence he takes with him
> He loses when he looks on those below.

Alfred's Wisdom both provides a different moral[13] and shows greater compassion to the backslider:

these false tales teach every man who wishes to flee from the darkness of hell and come to the light of the true goodness (or God) that he should not look round at his old sins, so that he again commits them as fully as he once did. For whoever with entire will turns his mind to the sins that he previously abandoned and then fully commits them, and they then fully please him, and he does not think ever to forsake them, then he will lose all his former good, unless he atones for it again. (*Boethius*, 103.14–21)

[12] *The Riverside Chaucer*, 3rd edn, ed. L. Benson (Oxford, 1988).

[13] For the interpretations in contemporary commentaries, see Joseph S. Wittig, 'King Alfred's Boethius and its Latin Sources, a Reconsideration', 11 (1983), *Anglo-Saxon England*, 157–98.

Eternal punishment is the reward for evil, which Wisdom describes as the misuse of the freedom God has given to men (*Boethius*, 113.21–2).[14] But Alfred's God is a merciful God who allows for repentance (*Boethius*, 143.22–9) and there are plenty of escape clauses here for the less than hardened sinner. Platonic thought, as transmitted by Boethius, has been adapted and transformed by a medieval king, seeking for himself and his people a deeper understanding of man's place in the scheme of things.

[14] Alfred follows Boethius (Book III.pr.12, 80–2) in the Platonic view that evil is nothing 'because if evil were anything, then God would be able to do it' (*Boethius*, 100.3–4). However, his reasons for agreeing that evil men are happier when punished (*Consolatio*, IV.pr.4, 42–4, *Boethius*, 118.21–2) are that those who are unpunished for their wickedness in this world will face the worst retribution after this world (*Boethius*, 119.13–18). And whereas Philosophia claims that the wicked are punished because evil is its own punishment (IV.pr.3, 37–8), Wisdom on the one hand sees eternal punishment as the reward for evil (113.21–2), which, he claims, is the result of the misuse of the freedom God has given to men, but on the other hand maintains that God determined that if men sinned in that freedom, they might amend it afterwards with repentance in that freedom (143.22–9). There is nothing comparable to this in *Consolatio*, V.pr.4.

CHAPTER 5

Chaucer's use of Neoplatonic traditions

Yasunari Takada

There are notable references in Chaucer to the Neoplatonic *auctores* such as Martianus Capella, Boethius, Macrobius and Alain of Lille. They stand us in good stead in showing Chaucer working not in insular seclusion but in an active dialogue with the great continental tradition of Neoplatonism. The image of Chaucer as a cosmopolitan poet is indeed familiar enough, particularly to the reader of *Troilus and Criseyde*, where is suggested in a Dantesque manner the author's ambition to affiliate himself with the great European tradition of 'poesye', i.e. 'Virgile, Ovide, Omer, Lucan, and Stace' (v, 1792).[1] The transcultural negotiation here is in a sense simple and straightforward and even austere. But in the case of the dialogue with Neoplatonic *auctores* rather than those of 'poesye', things are as often as not characterised by obliqueness, a sense of humour and even irony. Perhaps this can be best seen if we focus our attention on some of the ideas and motifs which have a close association with Neoplatonism: love, the ascent to heaven, and Nature.

LOVE

To talk of these ideas and motifs in the intellectual milieu of the later Middle Ages means an inevitable reference, one way or another, to the so-called 'twelfth-century renaissance'. Among representative figures of the movement are Alain of Lille, William of Conches and Bernard Silvester, who derive their characteristically Neoplatonic ideas largely from the Latinised *Timaeus*, Boethius, Macrobius and Martianus Capella. It is characteristic of the movement to emphasise the teleological aspect of the created universe, where man as

[1] All quotations from Chaucer are from *The Riverside Chaucer*, general editor, L.D. Benson (Boston, 1987).

microcosm is in essentials ordained to act as part of and in harmony with the macrocosm. The cosmic (i.e. harmonious) correspondence, which is often invoked and variously envisaged in a poetic vision, can perhaps find its most basic and symbolic representation in the Boethian love, 'the holy bond of things'. Love is the overriding principle of harmony in both the macro- and microcosm. As might be expected, such a vision inevitably goes to form an important part of Chaucer's imagination; his Neoplatonism is derived from these twelfth-century authors as well as their sources.

To take for example Troilus' love: At the consummation of the love which he has long wished for, Troilus gives thanks to various gods and goddesses, including among others Hymen.

> Than seyde he thus: 'O Love, O Charite!
> Thi moder ek, Citheria the swete,
> After thiself next heried be she –
> Venus mene I, the wel-willy planete! –
> And next that, Imeneus, I the grete,
> For nevere man was to yow goddes holde
> As I, which ye han brought fro cares colde.
>
> 'Benigne Love, thow holy bond of thynges,
> Whoso wol grace and list the nought honouren,
> Lo, his desir wol fle withouten wynges?'
> (III, 1254–63)

Together with Hymen, the deities invoked are Love (or Cupid in the capacity of *caritas*), Venus (conceived as planetary deity as well), and once again Love (this time in the status of the Boethian 'holy bond of thynges'). The last-named Love, which is to be given an extended treatment some 500 lines later in the 'Canticus Troili' (1744–71), is a Chaucerian translation of the Metrum VIII of the *De consolatione*, and is here dovetailed into St Bernard's prayer to the Blessed Virgin (*Paradiso*, XXXIII.13–8). Faced with the apparent varieties of these amorous deities, the modern reader may well wonder how they can be accommodated in some kind of hermeneutic unity; the analytic mind is hard put to find a connecting link between charity and marital love.

To solve this hermeneutic conundrum, it seems helpful to take a brief look at the commentary tradition which was formed around the works of the *auctores*, especially in this particular instance, Martianus Capella's fifth-century *De nuptiis Philologiae et Mercurii* and its tradition of commentaries. Before coming down to the hand of Chaucer,[2] the *De nuptiis* had been furnished with commentaries by such figures as Johannes Scotus Eriugena and Remigius of Auxerre, and since the tenth century had been enlisted as one of the *auctores* in a normative curriculum.[3] The work opens notably with the hymn to Hymen, the god of marriage, and this Hymen is a personification of the Neoplatonic force of 'mutual attraction' by which are brought into fruitful harmony and coherence the varying elements that compose the universe.[4] The commentary tradition had interpreted this god as the Boethian cosmic harmonizer and bond of things. We find this in the so-called 'Florentine Manuscript'.[5] According to this manuscript, a series of notes on the *De nuptiis*, Hymenaeus can be interpreted in three ways: narrative, scientific and philosophical. At the last-named 'philosophical' level the commentary reads as follows:

> Take Hymenaeus as the natural power of propagation, that is to say the lovers which they (who love) cherish mutually in glory: and these lovers are regarded as reciprocal where Philosophia says:
>
> This order of things is bound
> by the love ruling earth and sea
> and dominating heaven.
> If this love relaxes its reins,
> all things that now love each other
> would at once wage war.
>
> This is the Holy Spirit, who infuses an ardent charity in all things. He is called god of weddings, that is, he composes the holy conjunction of elements.[6]

Identified first of all with 'the natural power of propogation', Hymen is then related, through the celebrated quotation from Boethius (*De consolatione Philosophiae*, II. m.8, 13–18), to the *spiritus sanctus*, 'who infuses an ardent charity [*caritas*] in all things'. The author of the 'Florentine Manuscript' is unknown, but it has been pointed out that

[2] For Chaucer's humorous reference to Martianus Capella's Hymen, see *The Merchant's Tale*, ll.1729–37.

[3] Johannes Scotus Eriugena, *Annotationes in Marcianum*, ed. C.E. Lutz (Cambridge, Mass., 1939); Remigius of Auxerre, *Commentum in Martianum Capellam*, 2 vols, ed. C.E. Lutz (Leiden, 1962); compare E. R. Curtius, *European Literature and the Latin Middle Ages*, trans. W.R. Trask (New York, 1953), p. 49.

[4] W.H. Stahl, R. Johnson and E.L. Burge, *Martianus Capella and the Seven Liberal Arts*, 2 vols, II, (New York, 1977), p. 3n.

[5] The 'Florentine Manuscript' (Florence, Bibl. Naz. Conv. Soppr. I. 1.28) is printed in selection in Peter Dronke (ed.), *Fabula: Explorations into the Uses of Myth in Medieval Platonism* (Leiden, 1974), pp. 114–18. See Appendix B for the strange fate of this fourteenth-century MS.

[6] Dronke, *Fabula*, p. 103.

the parallels which are found in William of Conches' *Philosophia mundi*, particularly in the exposition of Hymen, show at least the author was 'in significant respects under the influence of William Conches',[7] one of the representative intellects of the Chartrian Neoplatonic Renaissance.

Here in the case of the 'Florentine Manuscript' such disparate divinities as *caritas*, the Holy Spirit and the Boethian *amor* are effectively mobilised to a fuller understanding of Martianus Capella's Hymen. And if this mobilisation is made possible only by recourse to the spirit of Chartrian Neoplatonism, the same to a large extent holds true in the case of *Troilus and Criseyde*. It does not matter whether Chaucer had a chance to look at the commentary in the form of either the 'Florentine Manuscript' or *Philosophia Mundi*. The important thing is that Chaucer makes use of the characteristic Neoplatonic discourse of love in describing Troilus' ecstasy and joy, whose 'summer's lease', we may note, lasts only for a short period marked off by 'the double sorrow'.

THE ASCENT TO HEAVEN

What the above argument implies is that Chaucer is not completely positive about the Neoplatonic view of the world. There is a sense in which we see some irony in his use of Neoplatonic topos. The passage to consummation which Troilus undergoes in Book III is described by the analogy with the Neoplatonic 'cosmic flight' or *ascensus* and is actually compared by both Pandarus and the narrator to an ascent to heaven, be it earthly or celestial. 'Make the redy right anon,/ For thow shalt into hevene blisse wende', says Pandarus at the outset (ll.703–4) and, at the fulfillment of the journey, the narrator describes the hero's mental landscape as 'this hevene blisse' (l.1322). In this 'ascent' there is obviously felt Chaucerian irony and parody, which is detectable almost throughout, beginning with the point of departure, from the 'stewe' (l.601) – meaning 'brothel' as well as 'small room' – through Purgatorial parallel, and ending with the celebrated allusion to St Bernard's prayer to the Blessed Virgin,[8] which, as we have seen, is merged into the general Neoplatonic discourse of cosmic love.

[7] *Ibid.*, p. 179.

[8] Cf. Winthrop Wetherbee, *Chaucer and the Poets: An Essay on Troilus and Criseyde* (New York, 1984), pp. 145–78.

Apparently, the ascent of Troilus' mind has attained its heavenly destination, and yet 'this hevene' (l.1251) reached after an arduous itinerary locates itself nowhere but in Criseyde's body (ll.1247–50), arguably one of the most unreliable entities on earth. In the authentic topos of the *ascensus mentis ad deum* or *itinerarium mentis in deum* (the ascent of the mind to God) the mind finds itself at one with God in its ultimate vision, like the one we see at the end of the *Divine Comedy* or the Metrum I of Book IV of the *De consolatione*. By contrast, the vision of unity Troilus experienced when alive had nothing ultimate and transcendental whatsoever about it.

If Neoplatonic love is conceived of as the cyclical unfolding of an original overflowing (*emanatio*), which produces 'a vivifying rapture (*raptio*) whereby the earthly beings are drawn back to heaven (*remeatio*)',[9] 'the ascent' can be seen as consisting of the *raptio* (the mind mindful of its true home) and the subsequent *remeatio*. It is true that Troilus' spirit, ('goost') has finally gone to heaven at the end of the story of *Troilus and Criseyde*, but the ascent is not specifically characterised as *remeatio*, nor is his spirit by any means thought of as being taken in *raptio*. The employment of the topos rather finds its proper utility and power only in describing Troilus' this-worldly, vivifying but ephemeral *raptio*.

For all his frequent deployment of Neoplatonic topoi and discourse, Chaucer shows little predilection for the Neoplatonic transcendental vision, whose ultimate end is to be at one with the One. Rather, we find the orientation of his vision – particularly in *The House of Fame* and *The Parliament of Fowls* – directed in the final analysis to the opposite. Thus in Book II of *The House of Fame*, the cosmic flight of Chaucer the dreamer-poet is attempted after the manner reminiscent of Dante's *Paradiso*. But what seems to all intents and purposes to be the ultimate destination – which proves with some irony and bathos to be the foundationless House of Fame (Book III) – is further relegated to, and eventually replaced by the House of Rumour. At this properly unfinished end of the work we are left with a group of people, who inevitably remind us of the world of the *Canterbury Tales*. As it turns out, a fairly mundane horizon opens itself at the close of what has originally begun as a celestial ascent.[10]

9 Edgar Wind, *Pagan Mysteries in the Renaissance* (1958; Harmondsworth, 1967), p. 37.

10 For further discussion on the use of the Neoplatonic traditions in *The House of Fame*, see my 'From *The House of Fame* to Politico-Cultural Histories', in *Chaucer to Shakespeare*, ed. R. Beadle and T. Takamiya (Woodbridge, 1992) pp. 45–59.

NATURE

In the Neoplatonic vision, the *fons et origo* is essentially to be sought in the One or *nous*, from which everything emanates and to which everything ultimately returns. But equally important is the visionary moment in which this cyclic pattern is transferred to the sublunary world and consequently the latter attains the imaginative level where it can be conceived as (to use the Spenserian dictum) 'eterne in mutabilitie' under the procreative care of Goddess Nature. Such a visionary moment is given its best expression by Chartrian Neoplatonism in its characteristic mythico-allegorical mode, which makes much of the 'special awareness of a continuity between creation and redemption'.[11] Here redemption means man's imaginative restoration of his proper place in the natural order of things ordained by God. It is not a matter of linear providential history as characterised by the Incarnation and Redemption. As is typically seen in Alain of Lille's *De planctu Naturae*, one of the exemplary works of Chartrian Neoplatonism, it is not Christ but appropriately Genius, the priest of Nature, who is to accomplish redemption by pronouncing the decree of excommunication on those who act against the propriety of natural order. This is justified, in its turn, by her capacity as *vicaria Dei*, 'the vicaire of the almyghty Lord' (to use Chaucer's own rendering in *The Parliament of Fowls*). Here, God, Nature, Venus, and Genius are 'of imagination all compact', but the imagination, in contradistinction to the irrational dream vision of midsummer, characteristically belongs to rational order and cosmos. What is at stake in this visionary redemption is the sense of correspondence and continuity, psychologically envisaged, between man/microcosm and God's grand design/macrocosm – the essential bond between them being that of Boethian love.

Although it is the case, as we have seen in *Troilus and Criseyde* that Chaucer does take advantage of this kind of Chartrian Neoplatonic discourse, he makes only a limited use of it and hardly shows an inclination to commit himself whole-heartedly to that grand vision. Rather there seems to be a sense in which it is too much to treat Nature as *vicaria Dei*. He would also wish to avoid a reductionist

[11] For a standard study on Nature in the Neoplatonic tradition, see George D. Economou, *The Goddess Natura in Medieval Literature* (Cambridge, Mass., 1972). For the best introduction to the Chartrian Neoplatonism, see Winthrop Wetherbee, *Platonism and Poetry in the Twelfth Century: the Literary Influence of the School of Chartres* (Princeton, 1972).

treatment of the varieties of things and events under the moon. Nowhere is Chaucer's critical attitude towards the Chartrian Neoplatonic vision shown so clearly as in *The Parliament of Fowls*, that is in what purports to be the final episode of *The Parliament*. In spite of the explicit allusion to *De planctu Naturae*, where Nature is indeed the *vicaria dei*, the section on Nature's parliament can be read most appropriately as a Chaucerian critique of Alain. In this respect Nature's casual statement to the 'formel' seems crucial.

> But as for counseyl for to chese a make,
> If I were Resoun, thanne wolde I
> Consseyle yow the royal tercel take.
> As seyde the tercelet ful skylfully
> (ll.631–4)

Nature confesses that she is not Reason. But this would hardly be conceivable in Alain's vision. What guarantees the cosmic correspondence, the vital link that connects creation and redemption, is none other than the Nature of Chartrian Neoplatonism, and to function in such a position and capacity Nature should be an unreplaceable representative of divine Logos, or Reason. Nature's statement here is just another indication of the characteristic role that the Neoplatonic traditions have to play in Chaucer. They are indispensable traditions from which Chaucer most fruitfully grows.

CHAPTER 6

Platonism in the Middle English Mystics

Andrew Louth

To discuss the influence of Platonism on the Middle English Mystics is to consider something rather different from the other examples of Platonic influence in English literature discussed in this volume. Elsewhere it is usually possible to point to some Platonic text, either by Plato himself or one of his epigoni. With the Middle English mystics this is occasionally possible: various writings by St Augustine and Dionysius (or Denys) the Areopagite would have been available to the English mystics. But to concentrate on the influence of specific texts would be to misconstrue in a fundamental way the nature of the Platonic influence on medieval English mysticism. For that influence was, first of all, the influence of a *tradition*: a tradition of theology, concerned especially with ways of praying, that over the centuries had been decisively impregnated by Platonic ideas and ways of thinking. The history of the influence of Platonism on Christian theology goes back at least to the second century of the Christian era, if not earlier, and became so pervasive that it is almost impossible to envisage Christian theology apart from its Platonic dress.[1]

THE CHRISTIAN PLATONIC TRADITION

The principal reason for this influence is simply that Platonism and Christianity had so much in common: that, combined with the great respect accorded to Platonism by many of their pagan contemporaries, meant that Christian theologians soon came to look to Platonism for arguments with which to defend Christianity. And there was indeed

[1] On the history of the influence of Platonism on Christian theology see especially E. von Ivánka, *Plato Christianus* (Einsiedeln, 1964).

much that they held in common: belief in one transcendent God who cared for his world, belief in an afterlife in which human beings would be rewarded for the good they had done and punished for their wickedness, and a conviction that human beings were free to choose between good and evil. But it was not exactly the Platonism of Plato that they embraced as a providential ally, it was what their contemporaries indeed called Platonism, but what modern scholars have come to call 'Middle Platonism', a mixture of mainly Platonic and Stoic doctrines that can be traced back to Antiochus of Ascalon, the founder of the so-called 'Fifth Academy' in Athens early in the first century BC. Such Platonism, as R. E. Witt has put it, 'was characterized by its predominantly religious and theocratic world-view . . . Second-century Platonism is theological and otherworldly.' It was the product of an age 'attracted not so much by Plato the ethical teacher or political reformer, as by Plato the hierophant, Plato who (according to an old legend) had been conceived of Apollo and born of the virgin Perictione'.[2] Not that Christian theologians swallowed Platonism uncritically. Certain Platonic doctrines were fairly uniformly rejected, notably the doctrine of the Pre-existence of Souls; gradually the Christian doctrine of *creatio ex nihilo* came to distinguish Christian theology from developments in Platonic philosophy, notably in Neoplatonism, that explained the origination of everything from the One by means of a (mathematically inspired) theory of emanation;[3] and even though Christians embraced the Platonic notion of the soul's immortality, they sought to wed this to the wholly un-Platonic idea of the resurrection of the body. This piecemeal adaptation of Platonism makes it, in fact, difficult to put one's finger on unambiguously Platonic elements in Christianity. Christian monotheism is clearly not *derived* from Platonism: but it is often expressed in a way that owes much to the later Platonic doctrine that everything derives from an indivisible unity. It will be useful none the less to focus our discussion of the influence of Platonism on the Christian mystical tradition on one Platonic doctrine, viz. that of the two worlds.

[2] R.E. Witt, *Albinus and the History of Middle Platonism* (London, 1937; reprinted Amsterdam, 1971), p. 123.

[3] See J. Trouillard, 'Procession Néoplatonicienne et création judéo-chrétienne', in *Néoplatonisme. Mélanges offerts à Jean Trouillard* (Fontenay aux Roses, 1981).

THE DOCTRINE OF THE TWO WORLDS

It is fundamental to Platonism, in virtually any guise, that this world, the world we perceive through the senses and about which we hold a variety of opinions, is not the real world. This world is a world of change, decay, and, for all of us, death: all of which bear the mark of unreality. The real world is changeless, incorruptible, a place of enduring life: it is, for Plato, the realm of the Forms. One fundamental way of contrasting these two worlds is to say that one is material, the other spiritual: there are two worlds – the world of the senses, the *kosmos aisthetos*, and the world of spiritual (or intelligible) reality, the *kosmos noetos*. We human beings belong to both worlds: clearly to this world (which is why we call it *this* world), but in virtue of our possessing (or strictly: being) a soul (strictly: an intellect, *nous*), we belong to the spiritual world. For Plato the whole point of philosophy is to secure our passage to the spiritual world: philosophy is 'practising death', *meletē thanatou* (*Phaedo* 81a), for death is the separation of the soul from the body. But the spiritual world, as the place of eternal, changeless, incorruptible life, is the object of our deepest longing: our love (*eros*) for truth, for beauty, is only fulfilled when we free ourselves from the shadows of this world and gain entrance to the spiritual world, as Plato explains most compellingly through Diotima's speech reported by Socrates in the *Symposium* (201e–212b). The soul's gaining the spiritual world is experienced as a homecoming (*nostos*). Plotinus' writings are full of eloquent expression of the soul's nostalgia: in a passage that evokes the Greeks' longing for home outside the walls of Troy and Odysseus' flight from the enchantment of Circe and Calypso, he says, 'our fatherland is whence we have come, and there is the Father' (*Enneads* 1.6.8.21). Christians lapped this up. They too believed in two worlds. They felt themselves to be aliens (*peregrini*) in this world: 'here we have no abiding city' (Hebrews 13.14). They saw the human lot as exile from Paradise: there the dying thief had been received by Christ (Luke 23.43), there the martyrs were united with Christ,[4] there, too, Christians hoped to be welcomed if they died faithful to Christ. Or they thought of heaven and earth: the two worlds conjoined when human voices mingled with angelic song in the celebration of the

[4] See for example, Saturus' vision as recounted by Perpetua: *Passio SS. Perpetuae et Felicitatis*, 11f., and the apse in the Church of San Vitale, Ravenna.

Eucharist.[5] Platonism provided them with terminology with which to articulate such belief. It was not wholly satisfactory: in particular, Platonic language and concepts tended to elide the notion of two *successive* ages of Christian belief (this one and the age to come). But in doing that it only accelerated a tendency already present in Christian thought to move from what modern theologians call a 'futurist' to a 'realized' eschatology.[6]

The doctrine of the two worlds was open to many interpretations. For the rest of this chapter I want to take three of these and show how they are used by the English mystics of the fourteenth century. The three ways of interpreting the doctrine of the two worlds are these: first, the two worlds conceived as an inner and an outer world; secondly, as the world of angels and the world of human beings; and thirdly, as the world perceived by the spiritual senses in contrast to the world of the physical senses. These three ways cannot be kept in separate compartments: some overlap will be unavoidable.

INNER AND OUTER WORLDS

Plato never contrasts the two worlds as inner and outer but Plotinus clearly identifies the spiritual world with the inner world: 'we are each of us the intelligible world' (*Enneads* III.4.3.22). It lies behind one of his favourite metaphors for the relationship between the One and all other reality: that of a circle with the One as the centre and the rest of reality as the circumference. To seek the One is to seek within. This chimes in with the emphasis in Christianity on inward religion, as opposed to outward display.[7] The idea that the higher world is the inner world becomes axiomatic for Augustine, for whom God is *interior intimo meo et superior summo meo* ('more inward than my inmost self and higher than the highest part of my being') (*Confessions* III.6.11). The beginning of the search for God is to return within: *in te ipsum redi* ('return into yourself') (*De vera religione* 39.72). In a sense, interiority is all: *ergo intus age totum . . . in te ora* ('therefore act entirely within . . . pray within yourself')[8]. Such sentiments echo deafeningly in subsequent Christian tradition, so that Walter Hilton is repeating a

[5] See the words introducing the *Sanctus* in virtually any liturgy.

[6] This was a long-draw-out process. Colin Morris, *The Papal Monarchy* (Oxford, 1989), pp. 378–80, sees it still taking place in the twelfth century.

[7] See for example, Matthew 5.6–7.

[8] Augustine, *Tractatus in Joannis Evangelium* 15.25. The translations of this and the preceding quotations are mine.

commonplace of the Christian tradition when he says, 'there is one useful and deserving task on which to labour, and . . . a plain highway to contemplation . . . and that is for a person to go into himself to know his own soul and its powers, its fairness and its foulness'.[9] These final words remind us how far this Platonic idea has travelled from its Platonic source: inwardness is no longer *in itself* an unambiguous ascent, for the fracturing of reality as a result of the Fall reaches inward, and the interior reality of human beings needs healing before it can disclose the ultimate reality of God.

As important as such injunction to inwardness is the exploration of man's inner world. Here Augustine's importance is unparalleled. Both in his *Confessions*, especially in the introspective Book x, and in his profoundest theological work, *De Trinitate*, he explores the inner reality of the human mind. His guiding beacon here is the Biblical doctrine that man is created in the image of God, a doctrine that had already become pivotal in the theology of the Fathers. The idea that man, or more precisely the human soul, is created in the image of God makes the human mind the fulcrum on which the doctrine of the two worlds turns: the human mind is no longer simply poised between two worlds, it is a world on its own reflecting in itself divinity. The word Augustine turns to for this inner world (perhaps hampered by the limitations of Latin which has no word as evocative as the Greek *nous*) is *memoria*: more than memory, it recalls the Platonic doctrine of *anamnesis*, although by a transposition in which nothing of the soul's pre-existence remains. In *De Trinitate* ix–x, Augustine presses the idea that an image of a Trinitarian God must be itself trinitarian and analyses man's inner reality into *memoria*, *intelligentia*, and *voluntas* (or *amor*). Gradually, this way of understanding the soul established itself in the West and can be clearly seen in the psychology of both Walter Hilton (*Scale*, i.43) and the *Cloud of Unknowing*.[10]

This notion of man's inwardness reflecting the divine takes a curious twist in the West in the thirteenth century. The twelfth century had seen an enormous growth in the influence of St Augustine but it also saw the introduction of a significant influence of the writings of Denys the Areopagite. Denys had already been translated into Latin in the ninth century: once incomprehensibly by

[9] Walter Hilton, *Scale of Perfection*, i.42, trans. J.P.H. Clark and Rosemary Dorward (Mahwah, NY, 1991), p. 112.

[10] *The Cloud of Unknowing*, 63–7, ed. Phyllis Hodgson (218), (London, 1944), pp. 115–21. Early English Text Society.

Hilduin, Abbot of St-Denis, and once by the Irish scholar, John Scotus Eriugena, who may have hindered the influence of his translation of Denys by his own reputation for obscurity (and doubtful orthodoxy).[11] But it seems that it was John the Saracen's revision of Eriugena's translation, undertaken in the second half of the twelfth century at the behest of his friend John of Salisbury, that finally introduced Denys to the West. As Augustine had absorbed into Christian theology some of the Neoplatonism of Plotinus (and his disciple and editor, Porphyry), so Denys had absorbed Neoplatonism, but the rather different Neoplatonism that we associate with Proclus, the Platonic *diadochus* at the Athenian Academy, who died in 485. There are many differences between Proclus and Plotinus, but for our immediate purposes what we need to note is Proclus' systematic development of apophatic and kataphatic theology (theology of negation and theology of affirmation), with his privileging of the former over the latter (in fact, Plotinus is scarcely less apophatic than Proclus, but approached from Porphyry this side of him is much less evident). Denys embraced this warmly and found a Biblical symbol of apophatic theology in Moses' ascent into a cloud of impenetrable darkness on Mount Sinai in order to receive the Law from God (a traditional theme that goes back to Philo and that Denys had taken over from St Gregory of Nyssa).[12] Denys simply meant that in its ascent to God the closer the mind came to God the less it could make out: it was as if it entered an impenetrable cloud. The mind is reduced to a wondering silence, and held there by its love for God as He is in Himself, rather than by a love for anything it can get from God, for in the darkness it is aware of nothing. Such apophatic theology forms a refrain throughout Denys' writings, and attains concentrated expression in his short treatise, the *Mystical Theology*.

The author of the *Cloud* had translated John the Saracen's Latin version of the *Mystical Theology* into English and knew it well. He introduces the notion of the cloud of unknowing in an authentically Dionysian way: 'Lift up thin herte vnto God with a meek steryng of loue; and mene him-self, & none of his goodes. & therto loke thee lothe to thenk on ought bot on hym-self, so that nought worche in thi witte ne in thi wille bot only him-self' (*Cloud*, 3, p.16). But this Dionysian strand is introduced into a fundamentally Augustinian

[11] For a very brief survey of Denys's influence in the West, see my *Denys the Areopagite* (London, 1989), pp. 120–7.

[12] *Ibid.*, p. 87 for Denys on apophatic theology.

tradition. Augustinian psychology, analysing the human soul into memory, understanding and will, was open to an opposition between understanding (or intellect: *intelligentia*) and will (an opposition quite foreign to Augustine himself) that had already been exploited by St Bernard. Bernard is fond of setting up an opposition between truth and love (*veritas-caritas*), knowledge and feeling (*cognitio-affectus*), to the detriment of the former. It is love and feeling that touches man most deeply, it is at that level that man comes close to God. We learn of God with the heart: '*corde, . . . cordis affectu, id est voluntas*'.[13] The author of the *Cloud* is wholly of Bernard's mind: 'By love may he be getyn & holden; bot bi thought neither' (6,p.26). And he draws in Denys' apophatic theology to express this: 'for when I sey derknes, I mene a lackyng of knowyng' (4, p.23). Apophatic theology means, for the author of the *Cloud*, shutting down the 'principal worching might, the whiche is clepid a knowable might' and relying wholly on 'another principal worching might, the whiche is clepid a louyng might', for, as he says, 'of the whiche two mights, to the first, the whiche is a knowyng might, God, that is the maker of hem, is euermore incomprehensible; & to the secound, the which is the louyng myght, in ilch one diuersly he is all comprehensible at the fulle . . .' (4, p.19). Denys certainly did not mean that God was accessible to one human faculty but not to another: rather, for him, God is utterly unknowable. The author of the *Cloud* is in fact inconsistent here: already in chapter 3 he had said that 'this derknes and this cloude is, how-so-euer thou dost, bitwix thee and thi God, & letteth thee that thou maist not see him cleerly by light of vnderstanding in thi reson, ne felt him in swetnes of loue in thin affeccion' (3, p.17). These problems are probably traceable to different emphases in his sources. As Dom Justin McCann noted long ago,[14] the author of the *Cloud* introduced into his translation of the *Mystical Theology* the idea that God is known 'with affeccyon abouen minde'[15] from Thomas Gallus (d.1246): in other words the idea that the deepest faculty in man is the *principalis affectio* which alone is capable of God. But for the most part in the *Cloud* its author seems to stick closer to Augustine in seeing understanding and will as parallel, even though he entertains a doctrine that really requires an *apex*

[13] St Bernard, *Sermo in Cantica Canticorum*, 42.4.7 in *Sancti Bernardi Opera*, II, J. Leclerq OSB, C.H. Talbot and H.M. Rochais OSB (Rome, 1958), p. 37.

[14] In his edition of *The Cloud of Unknowing* (London, 1924), p. 252.

[15] *Deonise Hid Divinite*, 11.25f., ed. Phyllis Hodgson (EETS 231), (London, 1955), p. 2.

affectus, as Bonaventure called it:[16] the highest (or deepest) part of the soul that transcends the intellect and is the seat of love.

WORLD OF ANGELS AND WORLD OF MEN

Another way in which the doctrine of the two worlds is articulated is by seeing these two worlds as the world of angels and the world of human beings. It is an old idea, recalling both the Homeric distinction between gods and mortals, and the Biblical distinction between the heavenly court where God is surrounded by his angels and the earth. In Plato himself it is difficult to see his two worlds as foreshadowing the distinction between angels and men: the realm of the Forms is a realm of *objects* of intellection rather than purely intellectual beings. But in two places Plato introduces ideas that prepare the way for the realm of the Forms to becomes a realm of pure intellects. One place occurs in *Sophist* 249b–d where the Eleatic Stranger forces the concession that there must be change in the realm of the Forms if intelligence is to be found there. The other place is in *Symposium* 202e–203a where Plato introduces the notion of the daemon (*daimon*): a daemon is a being intermediary between the changeless perfection of the gods and the changeable imperfection of humans - Eros, the god of love, is such a daemon. Later Platonism developed both these ideas to produce a much richer upper world than Plato ever envisaged. For Plotinus the daemons are beings between gods and men, though he seldom mentions them: like everything else they ultimately derive from the One by emanation and seek to return there, but they are closer to the One than we and can assist us in our endeavours to return. In later Neoplatonism, however, especially that stemming from Iamblichus, daemons and other intermediary beings assume considerable importance: in his *On the Mysteries of Egypt*, Iamblichus has four ranks of beings mediating between gods and human souls – archangels, angels, daemons and heroes.[17] Iamblichus' mention of the Biblical angels and archangels reminds us that the traffic between the Platonic tradition and Christianity was not all one-way.

Christian theologians, following the example of their Jewish predecessors, found it easy to assimilate the Platonic doctrine of

[16] *Itinerarium mentis in Deum*, 7.4, in *Works of St Bonaventure*, ed. P. Boehner (St Bonaventure, NY, 1956), II, p. 98.

[17] *De mysteriis*, II.4(78), ed. E. des Places SJ (Paris, 1966), pp. 84–5.

daemons and the Biblical doctrine of angels: as Philo candidly put it, 'it is the custom of Moses [i.e. Scripture] to give the name of angels to those whom other philosophers call daemons'.[18] Most important for the medieval doctrine of angels was the contribution of Denys the Areopagite. He classified the angelic beings into three ranks of three: Seraphim, Cherubim, Thrones; Dominions, Powers, Authorities; Principalities, Archangels, Angels (in descending order).[19] This eventually became the accepted order of angelic beings in the Middle Ages (from about the end of the twelfth century: St Bernard, for example, still follows the order suggested by Gregory the Great).[20] What are these angels for? The short answer is that they are ministering beings who mediate between God and men: see the *oratio* for the feast of St Michael the Archangel (29 September). But it is a question that echoes in the fourteenth century.[21] It is not clear, however, that Julian of Norwich, or any of the English mystics, knew much about such Dionysian speculation. Richard Rolle knows that the angelic beings are ordered in three ranks of three: but he gives an ordering that is closer to Gregory the Great's (and Bernard's) than to the Areopagite's.[22] There was elaborate speculation about the angels on the continent in the thirteenth century. Such speculation projected the angelic hierarchies *inwards*, using them as a way of furthering the exploration of interiority we have already noticed: as Bonaventure put it, *efficitur spiritus noster hierarchicus* ('our spirit is made hierarchic').[23]

[18] *De gigantibus*, 6, in *Philo*, ed. F.H. Colson and G.H. Whitaker, 12 vols. (London, 1929–62), II, p. 448.

[19] For angels in general and Denys in particular, see Louth, *Denys*, pp. 33–51, and, more generally, J. Daniélou, *Les anges et leur mission* (Chevetogne, 1951).

[20] Dante introduced the disagreement between Gregory and Denys into his *Paradiso*:

> E Dionisio con tanto disio
> a contemplar questi ordini si unise,
> che li nomò e distinse com'io.
> Ma Gregorio da lui poi si divise;
> onde, sì tosto come li occhi aperse
> in questo ciel, di sè medesmo rise. (XXVIII.130–5).

[21] For example, Julian of Norwich, *A Revelation of Love*, 80, ed. Marion Glasscoe (Exeter, 1976), p. 97. E. Colledge and J. Walsh SJ attribute to Julian some knowledge of Dionysian angelology: see their *A Book of Showings to the Anchoress Julian of Norwich* (Toronto, 1978), p. 189.

[22] Rolle, *Ego Dormio*, 11.18–28, in *English Writings of Richard Rolle*, ed. Hope Emily Allen (Oxford, 1931), pp. 61–2.

[23] Bonaventure, *Itinerarium*, 4.4 (Boehner edition, pp. 74–6). On the important role of Thomas Gallus in such speculation, see J. Walsh SJ, 'Thomas Gallus et l'effort contemplatif', in *Revue d'Histoire de la Spiritualité*, 51 (1975), 17–42, and my 'The Influence of Denys the Areopagite on Eastern and Western Spirituality in the Fourteenth Century', *Sobornost*, 4 (1982), 185–200, especially pp. 191–3.

But I can find no trace of this in the English mystics. What we do find is development of an older and much more general idea that in contemplation the soul realises its kinship with the angels 'for both souls and angels are created spiritual beings': so Rolle closes his enumeration of the angelic ranks with this: 'this I say to kyndel thi hert for to covayte the felichip of aungels'.[24] Their fellowship is to be cultivated because of their closeness to God. In Walter Hilton we find the idea that in contemplation the purified soul can come to know the song of the angels:

Qwen a saule is purified be lufe of god, illumyned be wysdome, stabild be the myghte of god, than is he eyghe of the saule opynde to behalde gastly thyngys, as vertuse & aungels & haly saulys, & heuenly thyngys. Than is the saule habyl be cause of clenness to fele the towchynge, the spekynge of gude aungels. This towchynge and spekynge is gastly, and nought bodyly: ffor qwen the saule is lyfth & rauisched out of the sensualyte, & out of the mynde of any erthely thyngis, than in grete feruoure of lufe and lyghth of god, if oure lorde vouchesafe, the saule may here & fele heuenly sown, made be the presence of aungels in louynge of god. Nought that this songe of aungels es the souerayne Ioye of the saule . . . For the souereyn & the essencial Ioye es in the lufe of god be hym-selfe & for hym-selfe, and the secundarie es in commuynge & behaldynge of aungels & gastly creaturis.[25]

SPIRITUAL AND PHYSICAL SENSES

Hearing the angels' song leads us on to the third way in which the doctrine of the two worlds can be treated: as a contrast between the world of physical and the world of spiritual senses. This is a development of the *Christian* mystical – or Christian Platonic – tradition, though it is not without parallels in Platonism and Neoplatonism: for instance, in the way in which Plotinus tries to describe union with the One by calling it 'pressing toward touch' (*Enneads* VI.9.11.24) or, more significantly, in the distinction introduced by Pausanias in his speech in *Symposium* 180d between popular love and heavenly love – *eros pandemos* and *eros ouranios*. This distinction between popular and heavenly love is pressed into service by Origen in the prologue to his Commentary on the Song of Songs.[26] It parallels the distinction Origen develops at length in this part of the prologue between the

[24] *Ego Dormio*, 11.28f. (p. 62).
[25] From *Of Angels' Song*, in *Yorkshire Writers: Richard Rolle of Hampole*, ed. Christine Horstman (London, 1895), I, p. 178. Compare *Scale* II.46.
[26] Origen, *Commentary on the Song of Songs*, ed. and trans. R.P. Lawson (London, 1957), Prologue 2.

inner man and the outer man: the outer man, turned out towards the external world – not so much the physical world, as the world valued in terms of the external, a world of reputation and ambition, a world of possessions and consumption – and the inner man, turned inwards towards the spiritual world (understood as the inner world, as above). As the outer man experiences the outer world with his physical senses, so the inner man experiences the spiritual world with his spiritual senses. In this way, Origen is able to interpret the highly sensuous world of the Song of Songs in terms of the love between Christ and the Church,[27] the love of the soul for God, responding to His love for her. It can, I think, be regarded as an authentic development of the Platonic tradition in that the ascent of the soul described in the *Symposium*, or in *Phaedrus*, is realised in Christian terms in interpretation of the Song of Songs. The doctrine of the spiritual senses is used to express the way in which the soul wakes up to the world of inner spiritual reality and begins to experience that world by learning to use its new-found senses. As the soul grows to maturity in this newly revealed world, it develops a sensitivity to spiritual reality: so Origen says, 'that soul only is perfect who has her sense of smell so pure and purged that she can catch the fragrance of the spikenard and myrrh and cypress that proceed from the Word of God, and can inhale the grace of the divine odour'.[28]

The doctrine of the spiritual senses is developed in all sorts of ways in Origen's wake.[29] Its development is particularly bound up with the tradition of interpreting the Song of Songs of the mystical life:[30] in the East, the doctrine was developed in the fourth century by St Gregory of Nyssa, in the West, Bernard in his wonderful series of sermons on the Song of Songs developed the doctrine with a rare sensuousness. Among the English mystics the spiritual senses are most prominent in Richard Rolle who, alone among them, continues the tradition of commentary on the Song of Songs.[31] In his *Incendium amoris*, he maps

[27] Compare Ephesians 5.25–33.

[28] Origen, *Commentary*, II.11 (Lawson edition, p. 168).

[29] There are two important articles by K. Rahner SJ on the origins and medieval developments of the doctrine of the spiritual senses: in *Revue d'Ascétique et de Mystique*, 13 (1932), 113–45, and 14 (1933), 263–99. For English translations (with references somewhat abridged) see, Rahner, *Theological Investigations* (1979), XVI, pp. 81–134.

[30] On which see, recently, E. Ann Matter, *The Voice of My Beloved. The Song of Songs in Western Medieval Christianity* (Philadelphia, 1990). Also Ann W. Astell, *The Song of Songs in the Middle Ages* (Ithaca and London, 1990).

[31] See *Ego Dormio*, ed. Allen, pp. 60–72; *Oleum effusum nomen tuum*, in *Yorkshire writers*, ed. Horstman, I, pp. 186–91, and the beginnings of a Latin commentary in O. Madon, 'Le Commentaire de Richard Rolle sur le Cantique des Cantiques', in *Mélanges de science réligieuse*, 7 (1950), 311–25.

out the spiritual life in three phases – *calor, dulcor, canor*: all states of feeling. His lyrics are full of deeply felt emotion that flows over into definite experiences. In contrast there is a certain cautiousness about the spiritual senses in Hilton and even more in the author of the *Cloud*, though such caution can also be found in Rolle, in *The Form of Living* for example. Rosamund Allen is certainly right to stress that in his expressive sensuousness Rolle is drawing on the traditional doctrine of the spiritual senses:[32] but his spiritual feelings are real feelings, not a mere metaphor.[33] Walter Hilton, in *Of Angels' Song*, recognises both a genuine experience of hearing the song of the angels, and also a delusion that nothing but 'a fantasie caused of trubblyng of the brayne'.[34] A similar caution is found in the *Scale of Perfection* (I.46), while the author of the *Cloud* dwells at length on the dangers of confusing the physical and the spiritual (45-62 *passim*), and is even reluctant to use the language of interiority, preferring his own paradox: 'noghwhere bodely is euerywhere goostly' (68. p. 121).[35] At the root of all this there perhaps lies an unresolved problem for Christian Platonism: what is the true estimate of the body? Are spiritual and bodily senses simply to be opposed? Or are the spiritual senses a transfiguration of the bodily? Is Paradise a *purely spiritual* place (and therefore not a place at all), or is Paradise a place where there is complete harmony between the spiritual and the bodily? It is curious to note that chapters 63–7 of *The Cloud* seem to point in a different direction from the chapters that precede and follow: here the fracture between the physical and the spiritual is clearly ascribed to the Fall, rather than (*more platonico*) regarded as being intrinsic.

CONCLUSION

That the English mystics are to be regarded as heirs of the tradition of Christian Platonism has, it is hoped, been sufficiently demonstrated. The nature of this debt is also worth underlining. It is a severely *practical* interest: even when the English mystics betray awareness of speculative developments concerning the true centre of the human personality or the way in which the hierarchies of the angels may be

[32] In her introduction to *Richard Rolle: the English Writings* (London, 1989), p. 27.

[33] As Evelyn Underhill rightly notes in her introduction to *The Fire of Love . . . and the Mending of Life*, translated into Modern English from Richard Misyn's Middle English version by Frances M.M. Comper (London, 1914), p. xv.

[34] *Yorkshire Writers*, ed. Horstman, I, p. 180.

[35] It is possible that Hilton and the *Cloud* had Rolle in mind in their criticisms. See Dom David Knowles, *The English Mystical Tradition* (London, 1961), pp. 96, 107–9.

interiorized, they are only interested in practical conclusions that may be drawn. The author of the *Cloud* finds the imagery of darkness and unknowing something that helps him to understand a fundamental aridity in contemplative prayer that must simply be endured, rather than treated as a worrying symptom of something that needs to be put right (depression, or half-heartedness, or sinful habits) (*Cloud*,75). This lack of speculative interest has been noticed elsewhere in the English mystics. So Riehle says of their treatment of the term *grounde*:

> Just how far the traditional metaphor of the abyss is changed in English mysticism is apparent from the meaning of the commonly used metaphor *grounde*. At first sight it would seem to correspond to the Middle High German *grunt*, a synonym of *abgrunt* (abyss). But when the English authors speak of the divine *grounde* they leave aside the element of infinite unfathomable depth and tend rather to concentrate on another meaning which the word has, namely the meaning 'solid ground' in the sense of the Latin *fundamentum*.[36]

That the English mystics were essentially practical is a truth that their designation as 'mystics' perhaps obscures. The writings of the English mystics are concerned with prayer as a practical matter. For them the Platonic tradition was part of the fabric of a traditional wisdom about God and the soul that they drew on for the insight it gave into the practical business of living a life devoted to prayer.

[36] W. Riehle, *The Middle English Mystics* (London, 1981), p. 85.

PART III

The Renaissance and the seventeenth century

CHAPTER 7

Introduction to the Renaissance and seventeenth century

Sarah Hutton

The image of Plato which dominates the Renaissance is that of *Moses Atticus*, the Attic Moses, or Greek sage whose wisdom echoed the teachings of the Bible.[1] A striking visual representation of this is the portrait of Plato in Raphael's mural, now known as the School of Athens, located in the heart of Western Christendom, the Vatican itself. (An engraving based on this picture serves as the frontispiece for this volume.) The spirit of Raphael's portrait of Plato is very much the spirit of Plato invoked almost a century and a half later by Milton in 'Il Penseroso' where Plato is the seer of the soul, holding the secrets of 'the immortal mind that hath forsook / Her mansion in this fleshly nook' (ll. 88–9). Raphael's unwitting anticipation of Milton is a reminder that no account of Plato in Renaissance England can ignore the key importance of the Italian Renaissance in the recovery of the Platonic corpus and the transmission of Platonic thought. Raphael's grouping of Plato with other philosophers is a reminder that throughout the Renaissance and seventeenth century Plato was always seen in relation to other thinkers. Although considered *primus inter pares* by his admirers, he was linked with a constellation of what they believed to be like minds, Orpheus, Hermes Trismegistus and Plotinus among them. Nor did Platonism ever dominate the philosophical scene or succeed in dislodging Aristotelianism as the core of the university curriculum.[2] None the less, in the Renaissance the philosophy of Plato was read and valued more than at any time since the closure of the Athenian Academy by the emperor Justinian in AD 529.

[1] See D.P. Walker, *The Ancient Theology* (London, 1972).

[2] Some of Plato's dialogues did, however, figure on the curricula of Greek courses in European universities and grammar schools of the Renaissance, see P.O. Kristeller, *Renaissance Thought* (New York, 1961), pp. 60–1.

In the Middle Ages, Plato had been known through at most a handful of dialogues (See Baldwin, pp. 21–6 above), but in the fifteenth century Plato's entire extant *oeuvre* became known in Western Europe. An important herald of the new interest in Plato and Neoplatonism was Cardinal Nicholas of Cusa (1401–1464).[3] But it is to the humanists of the Renaissance that we owe the recovery and Latin translation of the Platonic corpus.[4] Here the lead was given by Petrarch (1304–1374)[5] whose high valuation of Platonic philosophy (on the authority of Cicero and Augustine) combined with his manuscript-collecting activities lent impetus to the recovery of the Platonic corpus, furthered by such figures as Luigi Marsigli, Francesco Filelfo (1398–1481) and Leonardo Bruni (1369–1444). Petrarch's knowledge of Plato was limited: even though he possessed a Greek codex of Plato,[6] his attempts to learn Greek came to nothing. It was only later with the promotion of Greek studies by such figures as the Florentines Coluccio Salutati (1331–1406) and Niccolo Niccoli that Plato's writings were read in Greek in Italy for the first time since antiquity. In the rebirth of Greek studies, as well as the new interest in Neoplatonism, a key role was played by Byzantine scholars who travelled to Italy, notably Manuel Chrysoloras (1350–1414) who taught Greek in Florence from 1397, George Gemistus Pletho (*c.* 1360–1452), a formative influence on the shaping of Renaissance Platonism[7] and Cardinal Bessarion (*c.* 1403–1472) who settled in Rome where he defended Plato from the attacks on him by George of Trebizond (1395–1484).[8] Contact with the Greek east was also a source for the supply of Plato MSS which were brought to Italy either by visiting Byzantines like Chrysoloras or by Italians like Filelfo who visited Constantinople. It was not until 1513, however, that the works of Plato were printed in the original Greek, by Aldus Manutius (see Baker-Smith, p. 87 below).[9]

The earliest attempts to translate Plato into Latin, the *lingua franca* of Renaissance Europe, concentrated on individual dialogues (for

[3] Charles Lohr, 'Metaphysics', in *The Cambridge History of Renaissance Philosophy*, ed. C.B. Schmitt (Cambridge, 1988) (hereafter CHRP), pp. 548–66.

[4] J. Hankins, *Plato in the Italian Renanssance*, 2 vols. (Leiden, 1990), pts I and II; B.P. Copenhaver and C.B. Schmitt, *Renaissance Philosophy* (Oxford, 1992), pp. 126–43.

[5] Kristeller, *Renaissance Thought*, pp. 57–8; P.O. Kristeller, *Eight Philosophers of the Italian Renaissance* (Stanford, 1964), pp. 9–10; N. Robb, *Neoplatonism of the Italian Renaissance* (London, 1935), pp. 17–56.

[6] Kristeller, *Eight Philosophers*, pp. 9–10. Petrarch owned sixteen Plato MSS: see Robb, *Neoplatonism*, p. 22.

[7] Hankins, *Plato*, I, p. 197.

[8] *Ibid.*, pp. 429–44.

[9] L.D. Reynolds and N.G. Wilson, *Scribes and Scholars*, p. 138.

example George of Trebizond's translation of the *Parmenides*, made at the behest of Nicholas of Cusa, and Leonardo Bruni's translations of the *Phaedo* and the *Republic*). It was the achievement of Marsilio Ficino (1433–1499) to translate all thirty-six dialogues of the Thrasyllan canon – a translation which was still current three and a half centuries later. Ficino's translation appeared in (1484).[10] Ficino also translated the *Enneads* of Plotinus (1492) and the Hermetic writings, *Pimander* and *Asclepius* (translated in the early 1460's, printed in 1471).[11] These writings, which contain a mixture of Neoplatonic, Gnostic and Jewish elements, were attributed to Hermes Trismegistus, believed then to have been an ancient sage living in pre-Christian times whose writings display intimations of Christian doctrine. Subsequently (1614) Isaac Casaubon demonstrated the spurious antiquity of these writings.[12]

Ficino was more than just editor and translator. He was also a commentator and philosopher who, in his prefaces and his *Platonic Theology* (*Theologia platonica*, written between 1469 and 1474),[13] bequeathed to the Renaissance an interpretative model which harmonised Plato and Neoplatonism with Western Christianity and endowed them with philosophical respectability in his own time.[14] Ficino's reading of Plato was very much a Neoplatonic reading: he regarded Plotinus and other Neoplatonists as authoritative propounders of Plato's philosophy. For this reason, the *fortuna* of Plato in the Renaissance cannot be separated from that of Neoplatonism. Furthermore, for Ficino the Hermetic writings were important confirmation of his reading of Plato as the divine Plato, *divinus ille Plato*. In Plato he found doctrines compatible with Christianity: that the world was created, not eternal; that the soul was immortal; even a version of the Trinity. Much of this wisdom was hidden beneath a veil of allegory. With the further authority of the early Christian Fathers, especially Augustine, Ficino cultivated the image of Plato as the sage whose philosophy accorded most closely with Christian doctrine.

[10] On Ficino as a translator, see Hankins, *Plato*, I, pp. 236–64.

[11] Frances Yates, *Giordano Bruno and the Hermetic Tradition* (London, 1964).

[12] A. Grafton, 'Protestant versus Prophet: Isaac Casaubon on Hermes Trismetgistus' and 'The Strange Death of Hermes and the Sybils' in Grafton, *Defenders of the Text* (Cambridge, Mass., 1991).

[13] This is not available in English, but there is a French translation: *Théologie platonicienne de l'immortalité des ames*, ed. and trans. R. Marcel, 3 vols. (Paris, 1964–70).

[14] M.J.B. Allen, *The Platonism of Marsilio Ficino* (Berkeley, 1989); and *Marsilio Ficino and the Phaedran Charioteer* (Berkeley, 1981); Copenhaver and Schmitt, *Renaissance Philosophy*, pp. 143–62; Kristeller, *Eight Philosophers*, pp. 37–53; Charles Lohr, *CHRP*, pp. 568–84.

This image entailed the view, adopted, from Byzantines like Pletho, that Plato was the heir to a line of philosophers going back to earliest times. In this scheme of things, Plato was the conveyor of ancient wisdom deriving ultimately from Adam and shared by others in a line of ancient sages which also included Zoroaster, Orpheus and Hermes Trismegistus. Thus in the Renaissance, the Neoplatonic interpretation of Plato rendered his philosophy at once more systematic as a coherent whole, and more eclectic, incorporating strands of thought not properly belonging to Plato. Renaissance Platonism was thus, paradoxically, at once a unified framework of thought and a flexible collection of doctrines.[15]

Ficino was not the only Renaissance translator and editor of Plato.[16] The 1578 edition by the Protestant Jean de Serres (Joannes Serranus) made in collaboration with Henri Estienne (Henricus Stephanus) has bequeathed to us the system of pagination still in use today. While it did not supersede Ficino's translation, Serranus' Latin translation of Plato which accompanied the Greek text was probably as well-known in England as Ficino's. The only English translation of Plato to be printed in the sixteenth century was the pseudo-Platonic dialogue *Axiochus* (London, 1592) translated from the French of Philippe du Plessis Mornay.[17] The earliest direct contact between Italian Platonism and England was Humphrey Duke of Gloucester, patron successively of two translators of the *Republic*, Leonardo Bruni and of Pier Candido Decembrio (1392-1477). An example of direct contact between Ficino and England is Sir Thomas More's friend, John Colet (*c.*1467–1519), who corresponded with Ficino and whose lectures on Romans 6–11 show clearly the influence of Ficino's theological thought.[18] Humanist visitors to England, like Desiderius Erasmus (*c.*1466/9–1536) and Juan Luis Vives (1492–1540), helped to disseminate Platonism in English humanist circles. None the less, in England, as on the continent, Platonic philosophy did not become institutionalised within traditional

[15] Kristeller, *Renaissance Thought*, pp. 48–69; Lohr, 'Metaphysics' in *CHRP*, pp. 537–638.

[16] For a list of the Renaissance translators of Plato, as well as an account of some of the most important ones, see Hankins, *Plato*, I, *passim*, and II, pp. 804–7, 819–22.

[17] The translation purports to be by one 'Edw. Spenser' from Greek. The same dialogue is translated in Mornay's *Six Excellent Treatises of Life and Death* (London, 1607). The French version was published by the printer Josse Badius in 1530. See A. Tilley, *Studies in the French Renaissance* (1922; New York, 1968), p. 145. The only dialogue to be printed in Greek was the *Menexenus* (Cambridge, 1587).

[18] Sears Jayne, *John Colet and Marsilio Ficino* (Oxford, 1963).

seats of learning,[19] but it is the case that colleges founded on humanist lines were well supplied with texts of Plato: an example is Corpus Christi College, Oxford, founded by Bishop Fox in 1517.[20] And there is evidence of assimilation of Platonism even by Aristotelians, such as the Oxford don, John Case.[21] Another source for the diffusion of Platonism in Renaissance and seventeenth-century England were compendia such as du Plessis Mornay's *A Worke concerning the trewness of the Christian Religion*,[22] Grotius' *De Veritate* (1627) and Pierre de la Primaudaye's *French Academy* (translated by 'T. B.', London, 1618), which was a source for the platonising poetry of John Davies of Hereford (*c.*1565–1618).

The appeal of Plato to the earlier humanists was enhanced by the authority of Augustine (see Coleman, pp. 27–37 above) and reinforced by their negative assessment of scholastic philosophy. Plato's concern with moral philosophy and his discussion of the nature of true eloquence coincided with the central pre-occupations of the humanists. Later humanists, notably Erasmus (1466/9–1536) continued to draw on Platonism as a repository of spiritual and moral values (see Baker-Smith, pp. 86–99 below). Sir Thomas More (1478–1535), on the other hand is distinctive for his interest in the political Plato. Although the humanist construction of Plato as guardian of moral wisdom undoubtedly served to recommend Plato to him, his engagement with Plato in *Utopia* is with Plato's questioning method of enquiry rather than with Plato the expounder of spiritual truth.

In secular literature the single most influential aspect of Ficino's Neoplatonism was his development of the doctrine of Platonic love in his commentary on Plato's *Symposium* (1469). Ficino's transformation of Plato's philosophy of love is the subject of Jill Kraye's paper (pp. 76–85 below) which also deals with the *trattati d'amore* which derived from it and which ensured Ficino's ideas a wide diffusion in the courts of Europe. In English circles the most influential of these treatises was Baldasar Castiglione's *Il cortegiano* (*The Courtier*). The Latin translation by the Englishman Bartholomew Clerke, *De curiali*

[19] On the continent, it flourished in newly founded academies, described by Kristeller as 'half learned society half literary club'. To my knowledge there were no such academies in England.

[20] The library of Corpus Christi College contained the translations of Plato by Ficino, Serranus, and the Aldine edition. See J.R. Liddell, 'The Library of Corpus Christi College, Oxford', *The Library*, 4th series, 13 (1938), 385–416.

[21] C.B. Schmitt, *John Case* (Kingston and Montreal, 1982).

[22] Mornay's *De la verité de la Religion Chrestienne* was first published in 1581. The translation by Sir Philip Sidney appeared in 1587.

sive aulico libri quatuor (1571), was more widely known in England than Thomas Hoby's English version, *The Courtyer* (1561), which is more famous today.[23] In addition to sources like Castiglione, Pietro Bembo and Pico della Mirandola, the Platonism of much English poetry was probably mediated indirectly to English writers from French sources such as Du Bellay and the Pléiade, every bit as much as Italian.[24] The doctrine of Platonic love was assimilated into secular love poetry, especially into the Petrarchan poetry so fashionable in the fifteenth and sixteenth centuries where it became an essential element of the language of courtly love. Spenser's *Amoretti* (1595) is a notable example of the idealising love poetry inspired by the Ficinian transformation of Plato's philosophy of love, while the Platonism of Drayton's sonnet sequence *Idea* is conveyed in its very title. Spenser's knowledge of Platonism extended well beyond the idea of Platonic love. As Tom Bulger shows (pp. 126–38, below), in his discussion of *The Faerie Queene*, he had a detailed acquaintance with a variety of Neoplatonic sources. In Sidney and Chapman (see John Roe, pp. 100-6, below) the idealising theory of love and beauty is given comic treatment. Their parody of Neoplatonism is light-hearted, by contrast with the dismissive ridicule of Platonic love by the libertine love poets of the seventeenth century. Neoplatonism continued to provide writers like Ben Jonson with a rich vein of idealism. In *The New Inn* (1629) he celebrates Platonic love, while Neoplatonism underscores the idealisation of monarchy in his masques for the Jacobean and Caroline courts.[25] Under Henrietta Maria's patronage, Platonic love was celebrated by writers like Davenant in the masques and drama of the court of Charles I's.[26]

THE SEVENTEENTH CENTURY

While the influence of Platonism is everywhere to be felt in the writing of the English Renaissance, the seventeenth century can justly be regarded as the golden age of English vernacular Platonic philosophy,

[23] J.W. Binns, *Intellectual Culture in Elizabethan England* (Leeds, 1990), pp. 258ff.

[24] Sears Jayne, 'Ficino and English Platonism', *Contemporary Literature*, 4 (1952), 214–38.

[25] See D. Gordon, *The Renaissance Imagination* (Berkeley, Los Angeles and London, 1980); D. Lindley (ed.), *The Court Masque* (Manchester, 1984); S. Orgel, *The Jonsonian Masque* (Princeton, 1965).

[26] S. Orgel and R. Strong, *Inigo Jones: the Theatre of the Stuart Court*, 2 vols (London, 1973), I, p. 55. See especially, chapter 4, 'Platonic Politics'. Also, K. Sharpe, *Criticism and Compliment: the Politics of Literature in the England of Charles I* (Cambridge, 1987), chapter 5, 'The Caroline Court Masque'.

on account of the appearance, mid-century, of the group of Cambridge-based philosopher theologians known now as the Cambridge Platonists (see Scott, pp. 139–50, below). The Cambridge Platonists were a relatively diverse group whose Platonism was a dominant element in an eclectic philosophical outlook which was also receptive to new philosophical currents, notably the philosophy of Descartes.[27] The leading members of this group, and the most prolific, were Henry More (1614–1687) and Ralph Cudworth (1617–1688). The one work of John Smith (1618–1652), his posthumously published *Select Discourses* (1660), surpasses them in its prose style, as does *Discourse of the Freedom of Will* (1675) by Peter Sterry (d.1672). Also associated with the group is Nathaniel Culverwell (d. *c.*1651), author of *An Elegant and Learned Discourse of the Light of Nature* (1652), and Benjamin Whichcote (1609–1683). The only aspiring poet among them was More, whose deep admiration of Spenser accounts for his adoption of Spenserian stanzas and allegorical mode in his first published adventures into Platonism. More's *Psychodia Platonica* (1642) treats a number of Platonic themes, notably the Immortality and Pre-existence of the Soul, in Spenserian stanzas.

With the Cambridge Platonists the Renaissance Neoplatonic synthesis is put to the service of religious peace in an age of religious strife. What distinguishes them as a group is their theological optimism, their latitudinarian spirit and their antipathy to the harsh predestinarian theology of Calvinism. Like Erasmus, they all (except Sterry) emphasise the freedom of the will. They all insist on importance of reason in religion, and accept a version of the Theory of Recollection. At the same time they adapted Renaissance Platonism to the demands of a period of intellectual turmoil – the scientific and philosophical revolution of the seventeenth century. Firstly, as in the case of the early humanists, Platonism offered an alternative to the increasingly irrelevant Aristotelianism still in place as the official philosophy of the universities. Secondly, by widening the traditional Platonic defence of the immortality of the soul to a defence of spirit in general, they sought to combat what they saw as atheistic tendencies in contemporary thought. Thus their antipathy to the deterministic philosophies of Hobbes and Spinoza matches their opposition to Calvinist predestination. More, with his concept of the 'spirit of

[27] For a fuller account of the Cambridge Platonists, together with a bibliography, see S. Hutton, 'Lord Herbert of Cherbury and the Cambridge Platonists', in *Routledge History of Philosophy*, vol. v, *British Philosophy and the Age of Enlightenment*, ed. Stuart Brown (forthcoming).

nature' and Cudworth in his concept of 'plastic nature' adapted the Platonic conception of the World Soul to explain the operations of the God in the natural world. In the case of Henry More's disciple, John Norris (1657–1712), Platonism came to be blended with the philosophy of Nicholas Malebranche (1638–1715), through which it could be said to have had something of a diffuse after-life in spite of the demise of Platonism in the eighteenth century.[28]

The roots of Cambridge Platonism can be traced back through the English Arminian theologian Thomas Jackson (1579–1640) who received his education at the humanist foundation, Corpus Christi College, Oxford.[29] Furthermore, Jackson can be identified as one channel through which Platonism was mediated to literary circles: he was linked to George Herbert through their close mutual friend Nicholas Ferrar, and through his patrons the Danvers and the Earl of Pembroke. He was also read by Thomas Traherne. Henry Vaughan was a student at Oxford in Jackson's time. The religious poetry of such writers as Milton, Vaughan, Traherne and Marvell is in many ways the poetic counterpart of the Cambridge Platonists philosophical theology (see Baldwin and Hutton, pp. 151–78, below).

In the seventeenth century, Plato and Plotinus were most frequently read in Latin, but also, by the more learned, in Greek. None the less, other vernacular sources should be noted, in particular John Everard's translation of the *Divine Pymander* of Hermes Trismegistus in 1650 – testimony to the fact that Isaac Casaubon's dating of the writings of Hermes as post-Christian took some time to take effect. The one Latin translation of Plato to be printed in England in the seventeenth century testifies to the longevity of Ficino's influence: as its title suggests, *Platonis de rebus divinis, dialogi selecti* (Cambridge, 1673) prints a small selection of dialogues (*Apology*, *Crito*, *Phaedo*, *Laws* x, *Alcibiades* II) that show Plato as an authority in divine matters. The only English translation of Plato to be printed in England in the same century also signals an interest in Plato as an authority on the soul, but there is a strong hint here of a more critical spirit. *Plato his Apology of Socrates and Phaedo or Dialogue concerning the Immortality of Mans Soul, and Manner of Socrates his Death* (London, 1675) is a confection of Serranus and Ficino, more usually following the former. It also

[28] On Norris's Malebranchism, see C.J. McCracken, *Malebranche and British Philosophy* (Oxford, 1983), and R. Acworth, *The Philosophy of John Norris of Bemerton (1657–1712)* (Hildesheim, 1979).

[29] On Jackson, see S. Hutton, 'Thomas Jackson, Oxford Platonist, and William Twisse, Aristotelian', *Journal of the History of Ideas*, 34 (1978), 635–52.

supplies background information ('Reflexions upon the Athenian Laws') and historical consideration of belief in the immortality of the soul ('The Antiquity of the Tradition of the opinion of the Soul's Immortality'), bringing this up to date by considering contributions of modern philosophers, namely Descartes and Boyle.

Finally, it is perhaps worth noting Plato's detractors in this period. Given the quasi-prophetic status accorded him by many of his admirers, the grounds of their attacks were mainly religious and moral. This kind of critique of Plato dates back to the fifteenth-century rediscovery of his writings, most famously in George of Trebizond's vitriolic attack on Platonism which prompted Cardinal Bessarion's equally famous apology for Plato.[30] In England, the seventeenth-century puritans William Twisse and John Owen may be cited for their objections to Plato as a pagan obfuscator. Even Plato's proponents often expressed reservations about the possible heterodox implications of his philosophy: Serranus, Jackson and Theophilus Gale[31] are examples. One of the most contentious subjects was Plato's Arian Trinity. Another was his doctrine of the pre-existence of souls, attacked by Nathaniel Culverwell but favoured by Henry More. In the wake of Cambridge Platonism, anti-platonism strikes a new note in Samuel Parker's *A Free and Impartial Censure of the Platonick Philosophy* (1666). The focus of Parker's attack is not Plato the moralist, whom he purports to admire, but what he sees as the flimsy and fantastical basis of Plato's theories grounded not on hard logic but on mere 'whimsies'. Parker's ridicule did nothing to diminish Plato's standing with More and Cudworth, but they strike at the very basis of the conception of Plato as 'Attic Moses', so heralding the end of an era of Plato interpretation that began in quattrocento Italy.

[30] See Hankins, *Plato*, I, pp. 236–63.

[31] See Theophilus Gale, *The Court of the Gentiles* (Oxford and London, 1669–78).

CHAPTER 8

The transformation of Platonic love in the Italian Renaissance

Jill Kraye

One of the most serious obstacles to the reception and adoption of Platonism by Italian scholars of the early fifteenth century was the theory of Platonic love. Yet by the middle of the sixteenth century this doctrine had become the most popular element of Platonic philosophy and was playing a significant role in the development of Italian literature. The transformation of Platonic love from an embarrassing liability into a valuable asset was a key episode in the history of Plato's reemergence during the Renaissance as a major influence on Western thought.

Through their knowledge of Greek, Italian humanists became familiar with a wider range of Platonic dialogues than had been known in the Middle Ages; but they did not always like what they read. Among the things they found particularly offensive was the homosexual and pederastic orientation of Platonic love. Leonardo Bruni, the most prominent early translator of Plato, felt obliged to bowdlerise his Latin versions of the *Phaedrus* (1424) and the *Symposium* (1435). In Bruni's translation, for instance, Alcibiades' attempted seduction of Socrates (*Symposium* 215a–22a) becomes a high-minded quest for philosophical enlightenment, with Alcibiades describing himself as 'inflamed with the desire for learning'. Fascinated though he was by the concept of divinely-inspired amatory fury, as expounded in the *Phaedrus*, Bruni was simply unable to accept Plato's explicit treatment of homosexuality.[1]

Bruni's contemporary in Florence, the Camaldulensian monk Ambrogio Traversari, had similar scruples. These led him to delete from his Latin version of Diogenes Laertius' *Lives of the Philosophers* (1433) the homosexual love poems attributed to Plato (III.29–32),

[1] James Hankins, *Plato in the Italian Renaissance*, 2 vols (Leiden, 1990), I, pp. 29–81; II, pp. 396–400. For his hatred of pederasty, see Leonardo Bruni, *Humanistisch-philosophische Schriften*, ed. H. Baron (Leipzig, 1928), pp. 40–1.

including the lascivious epigram about kissing Agathon. Virtually the only humanist to express appreciation of these poems was Antonio Panormita, author of a scabrous verse collection entitled *Hermaphroditus* (1425). The 'wanton' and 'effeminate' love poetry which Plato addressed to young men provided Panormita with classical precedent for his own pornographic efforts.[2] Rather than bolstering Panormita's case, however, this claim served to undermine further Plato's moral credibility. And worse was in store.

George of Trebizond published his *Comparatio Aristotelis et Platonis* (1458) as part of a one-man campaign to save Christendom from the irreligious and immoral doctrines of Platonism. He therefore went out of his way to portray Plato as a purveyor of sexual depravity and an unashamed pederast. Aristotle, whom George regarded as the bulwark of Western civilisation, may have been over fond of women, but at least he had not indulged in unnatural vice nor inflamed grown men with a desire for the youthful beauty of adolescent boys. In his lurid account of the *Symposium* – pointedly referred to as *De cupidine* ('On Desire') rather than by its customary title *De amore* ('On Love') – George deliberately distorted the speech of Aristophanes (189c–93d) so as to equate Platonic love with continuous sexual fulfilment, achieved when the two masculine halves of the original male creature were reunited.[3]

The aim of Cardinal Bessarion's *In calumniatorem Platonis* (1469) was to defend Plato against George's allegations, especially the damaging accusations of sexual misconduct. Bessarion did not deny that Platonic love was essentially homosexual in outlook, but he did insist that Socrates' attachment to young men such as Phaedrus was entirely honorable and chaste, and that it had nothing to do with lust. To reinforce this point, Bessarion stressed the similarity between Plato's concept of love and that praised in the Song of Solomon and the letters of St Paul. He also associated it with the cosmic love described by Dionysius the Areopagite in chapter 4 of *De divinis nominibus*, which had God as both its source and its goal. Contrary to what George had claimed, Plato's spokesman in the *Symposium* was not the raffish Aristophanes but the wise and noble Socrates. As for the amatory verses to Agathon and other boys, Bessarion maintained

[2] See his 1426 letter to Poggio Bracciolini in Antonio Panormita, *Hermaphroditus*, ed. D. Coppini (Rome, 1990), pp. 151–9; also Hankins, *Plato*, I, pp. 81, 131.

[3] George of Trebizond, *Comparationes phylosophorum Aristotelis et Platonis* (Venice, 1523), sigs N 6^v, O 3^v–5^v, T 5^r; see also John Monfasani, *George of Trebizond* (Leiden, 1976), pp. 156–8.

that Diogenes Laertius had wrongly attributed to Plato poems which were actually written by the voluptuary Aristippus of Cyrene.[4]

FICINO

Marsilio Ficino, equally anxious to discredit George of Trebizond's attack on Plato's character, had one of the characters in his *Symposium* commentary (1469) state, with obvious reference to George, that those who dared to slander Plato because 'he indulged too much in love' should be ashamed of themselves, 'for we can never indulge too much or even enough in passions which are decorous, virtuous and divine'.[5] Like Bessarion, Ficino too attempted to defend Socrates' reputation for moral probity. After noting that even in his trial Socrates had not been charged with immoral love affairs, Ficino asked: 'Do you think that if he had polluted himself with a stain so filthy, or rather, if he had not been completely above suspicion of this charge, he would have escaped the venomous tongues of such detractors?'[6] He also followed Bessarion's lead in reassigning to Aristippus the homosexual poems traditionally attributed to Plato.[7]

Ficino likewise took over Bessarion's tactic of associating Platonic discussions of love with those found in the Bible. He maintained, for instance, that the burning desire Socrates says he feels upon glimpsing Charmides' torso (155d) should be interpreted, like the Song of Solomon, allegorically.[8] Ficino, however, carried the Christianisation of Platonic love much further than Bessarion, even managing to impose a Thomist interpretation on the salacious speech of Aristophanes.[9] Another way in which Ficino made Platonic love more palatable was to emphasise its place within an elaborate system of Neoplatonic metaphysics. Relying heavily on Plotinus, *Enneads* I.6 ('On Beauty') and III.5 ('On Love'), Ficino turned Diotima's ladder

4 Cardinal Bessarion, *In calumniatorem Platonis* in L. Mohler, *Kardinal Bessarion als Theologe, Humanist und Staatsmann*, 3 vols. (Paderborn, 1927), II, pp. 442–93; also, Hankins, *Plato*, I, pp. 259–61.

5 Marsilio Ficino, *Commentary on Plato's Symposium on Love*, trans. S. Jayne (Dallas, 1985), p. 41; Latin text: *Commentaire sur le Banquet de Platon*, ed. R. Marcel (Paris, 1956), p. 143.

6 Ficino, *Commentary*, p. 155; *Commentaire*, p. 242.

7 Marsilio Ficino, *The Letters* (London, 1975–), III, p. 47; Latin text: *Opera omnia*, 2 vols. (Basel, 1576), I, p. 770.

8 Ficino, *Opera*, II, 1304; for a similar claim in his *Phaedrus* commentary, see M.J.B. Allen (ed. and trans.), *Marsilio Ficino and the Phaedran Charioteer* (Berkeley, 1981), pp. 78–9; Hankins, *Plato*, I, p. 313.

9 Ficino, *Commentary*, pp. 71–80; *Commentaire*, pp. 167–77.

(*Symposium* 210a–12a) into an ontological ascent from Soul, the hypostasis to which man belonged, through the Angelic Mind and ultimately to the One, the Neoplatonic equivalent of the Christian God.[10]

But Ficino's efforts to accommodate the theory to the values of a fifteenth-century audience did not include concealing or denying – it would hardly have been possible in a commentary on the *Symposium* – that the virtuous love practised by Socrates and promoted by Plato was homoerotic. Indeed, Ficino completely accepted the idea that Platonic love involved a chaste relationship between men, as can be seen from his dedication of the work to his friend Giovanni Cavalcanti. Giving Cavalcanti credit for having inspired the commentary, Ficino stated that although he had learned the definition and nature of love from Plato, 'the power and sway of this god was hidden from me for thirty-four years, until a certain divine hero, beckoning to me with heavenly eyes, demonstrated . . . how powerful love is'.[11] Further corroboration of the strictly masculine context of Ficino's conception of Platonic love comes from a contemporary biography of him, which states that 'he was enraptured by love just as Socrates was, and he used to discuss and debate the subject of love in the Socratic manner with young men'.[12]

Ficino differed from Plato in his outright condemnation of consummated homosexual love, which he described as 'against the order of nature'. But this did not stop him from endorsing Plato's belief that the soul's spiritual ascent to ultimate beauty was fuelled by love between men. The man who follows the lower sort of love, which seeks mere physical 'conception and generation' (*Symposium* 206e), desires, according to Ficino, a 'beautiful woman' to procreate 'handsome offspring'; but the man who pursues the higher and heavenly love, which pertains to the soul rather than the body, desires to teach 'men who are handsome', seeing in their external appearance a reflection of internal virtue.[13] On the heavenly journey, Ficino wrote to Cavalcanti, we should have God as our guide and a male friend as our companion.[14]

One of Ficino's followers, Girolamo Benivieni, was inspired by his

[10] Ficino, *Commentary*, pp. 136–45; *Commentaire*, pp. 230–9.

[11] P. O. Kristeller, *Supplementum Ficinianum*, 2 vols (Florence, 1937), I, p. 87.

[12] Giovanni Corsi's *Vita Marsili Ficini* in Ficino, *Letters*, III, p. 144; Latin text in R. Marcel, *Marcel Ficin* (Paris, 1958), p. 686.

[13] Ficino, *Commentary*, pp. 54, 131–2; *Commentaire*, pp. 155, 225.

[14] Ficino, *Letters*, I, pp. 96–7; *Opera*, I, pp. 633–4.

Symposium commentary to produce an elegant but obscure Italian *canzone*. The poem was itself commented upon, in 1486, by the young Giovanni Pico della Mirandola, who used this form to put forward his own interpretation of Platonic love, which differed in some respects from that of Ficino.[15] But Pico shared Ficino's conviction that while 'earthly love, that is, the love of corporeal beauty, is more properly directed towards women than towards men, the reverse is true of heavenly love', citing as his authority the speech of Pausanias (*Symposium* 180c–5c). In Pico's opinion, sexual love, which led to copulation, was less unseemly with the feminine sex than with the male. Heavenly love, on the other hand, was directed entirely towards the spiritual beauty of the soul or intellect, a beauty that was 'much more perfect in men than in women, as is true of any other attribute'. It was with this 'chaste kind of love', wrote Pico, that Socrates loved not only Alcibiades, but 'almost all of the cleverest and most attractive young men in Athens'.[16] Pico was by no means proof against female beauty – earlier in 1486 he had caused a scandal by attempting to abduct the wife of a government official from Arezzo – but, for him as for Ficino, what prompted the soul to start on its arduous spiritual ascent to God was the masculine beauty 'of Alcibiades, or Phaedrus, or some other attractive body'.[17]

Following in the footsteps of Bessarion and Ficino, Pico linked Platonic love to the Song of Solomon, adding, however, a new dimension by drawing on the Cabbalistic doctrine of the *mors osculi*, 'the death of the kiss'. This death, symbolised by a kiss, occurred 'when the soul, in an intellectual rapture, unites so completely with incorporeal things that it rises above the body and leaves it altogether'. Pico stated that the opening verse of the Song of Solomon: 'Kiss me with the kisses of thy mouth', alluded to this sort of kiss. Even more audaciously, he accepted the Platonic authorship of the poem about kissing Agathon, denied by Bessarion and Ficino, and asserted that it too referred to *mors osculi*.[18]

Through their interpretive skills, Bessarion, Ficino and Pico had removed from Platonic love the immoral connotations which had threatened to hinder the reception of Plato's philosophy by Renaissance

[15] See, e.g., Giovanni Pico della Mirandola, *Commentary on a Canzone of Benivieni*, trans. S. Jayne (New York, 1984), pp. 80–1, 97–8, 106, 149; Italian text: *De hominis dignitate . . . e scritti vari*, ed. E. Garin (Florence, 1942), pp. 465–6, 488–9, 499, 556.

[16] Pico, *Commentary*, p. 133; *De dignitate*, pp. 537–8.

[17] Pico, *Commentary*, p. 158; *De dignitate*, p. 567.

[18] Pico, *Commentary*, pp. 131, 150–1; *De dignitate*, pp. 535, 557–8.

thinkers. But while they expunged any taint of carnal homosexuality from Platonic love, they did not question its homoerotic nature, nor its relegation of heterosexual love to an inferior status on the grounds that love between the sexes resulted in physical procreation, whereas love between men led to spiritual perfection. This distinction is clearly enunciated in the writings of Lorenzo de' Medici, the unofficial ruler of Florence and the patron of both Ficino and Pico. In 1474 Lorenzo wrote a series of Platonic love letters to Ficino, demonstrating that he had thoroughly absorbed the lessons taught in his *Symposium* commentary.[19] Lorenzo was well aware that the spiritual love which he felt for Ficino was more exalted than the human love, directed towards women, which he celebrated in his poetry. In his *Comento* on his own poems, Lorenzo stated that they were not concerned with the love praised by Plato, which is 'the means for all things to find their perfection and to rest ultimately in supreme beauty, that is, in God'. His poetry dealt instead with a love, which, although not the supreme good, was nevertheless good in itself and natural, because it was necessary for the propagation of the species.[20] Yet despite his recognition of the difference between the two sorts of love, Lorenzo allowed himself to borrow certain Platonic themes from both Ficino and Pico, using them, alongside motifs taken from Ovid, Petrarch and the *Stil nuovo* poets, to elaborate the story of his love affair with his mistress.[21]

BEMBO

Lorenzo's appropriation of the language of Platonic love to describe some aspects of the romance between a man and a woman prepared the way for works such as Pietro Bembo's *Gli Asolani* (1505), in which both human and divine love were presented as unequivocally heterosexual. In this dialogue, set in the court of Asolo, a group of men and women gather together to converse on the subject of love. The inclusion of women is defended on the grounds that they 'as well as men have minds' and therefore have the right to seek knowledge of 'what one ought to flee from or pursue'; the love being discussed is clearly as relevant to them as the men in the group. Lavinello,

[19] Lorenzo de' Medici, *Lettere* (Florence, 1977–), I, pp. 496–508, 510–18; II, pp. 35–40.
[20] Lorenzo de' Medici, *Comento de' miei sonetti*, ed. T. Zanato (Florence, 1991), pp. 137, 140.
[21] Cf. Medici, *Comento*, pp. 189–90 with Ficino, *Commentary*, pp. 40–3, and *Comento*, p. 155 with Pico, *Commentary*, pp. 148–9.

attempting to strike a balance between the attack on love by Perottino and the overpraise of it by Gismondo, portrays an elevated, spiritual love, which obviously derives from the Platonic theory. But here, unlike previous treatments, women are envisaged as the object of Platonic love:

Who can fail to see that if I love some gallant, gentle lady, and love her rather for her wit, integrity, good breeding, grace, and other qualities than for her bodily attractions, and love those attractions not for themselves but as adornments of her mind – who can fail to see my love is good because the object of my love is likewise good?[22]

Most of the central ideas set out in Ficino's *Symposium* commentary are echoed by Bembo, but he transforms the latter's abstract, philosophical terminology into vivid, poetic metaphors. Ficino's doctrine that the beauty which provokes love can be perceived by the eyes and the ears alone of the five senses is expressed by Bembo through an image of love spreading and beating its wings: 'And on its flight two senses guide it: hearing, which leads it to the mind's attractions, and sight, which turns it to the body's'. While Ficino – and, for that matter, Plato (*Symposium* 201d) – provided only a perfunctory description of Diotima, Bembo carefully sets the scene for Lavinello's encounter with his guide to the mysteries of love: from a little grove on a charming mountaintop, surrounded by silvan quietude, emerges 'a solitary figure, a bearded white-haired man clothed in material like the bark of the young oaks surrounding him'. Although the message this hermit conveys is taken from Ficino, he speaks straightforwardly, avoiding any overtly philosophical language. Instead of erudite discourse on the Neoplatonic hypostases, the hermit explains to Lavinello that 'beyond this sensible, material world . . . there lies another world which is neither material nor evident to sense, but completely separate from this and pure . . . a world divine, intelligent and full of light'.[23] The aged hermit tells Lavinello that he now regards the sensual delights which he desired in his youth in the same light as a man, restored to health, might regard his fevered fancies. It is only when we grow older, he says, that 'our better part, namely the soul' is able to rule our worse part, the body, and that our reason is able to control our senses.[24] For Bessarion, Ficino and Pico, there was

[22] Pietro Bembo, *Gli Asolani*, trans. R. B. Gottfried (Bloomington, 1954), pp. 148, 156; Italian text: *Prose e rime*, ed. C. Dionisotti (Turin, 1960), pp. 458, 466.

[23] Bembo, *Asolani*, pp. 157, 169, 189; *Prose*, pp. 468, 479, 498; cf. Ficino, *Commentary*, pp. 40–1, 108.

[24] Bembo, *Gli Asolani*, pp. 181–2; *Prose*, pp. 490.

a complete separation between physical love, which had women as its object, and spiritual love, which was shared between men. By contrast, Bembo's version of Platonic love is unified and evolutionary, with male-female relationships gradually progressing, as one grows older, from a sexual to a spiritual plane.

CASTIGLIONE

Although *Gli Asolani* was widely read and influential, the new style of Platonic love formulated by Bembo reached its largest audience when his friend Baldesar Castiglione chose to cast him as one of the main characters in his hugely popular *Il libro del cortegiano* (1528). Castiglione sets out a vision of the perfect courtier and uses Bembo's speech, which is the culmination of the book, to describe what his attitude towards love should be. As in *Gli Asolani*, there is a progression from the sensual love of youth to the spiritual love of old age, both directed exclusively towards women. Moreover, Plato's pederastic ideal of an older and wiser man educating his young lover in virtue is given a novel heterosexual twist by Castiglione's Bembo, who states that the courtier should be at pains to keep his lady 'from going astray and by his wise precepts and admonishments always seek to make her modest, temperate and truly chaste'.[25] Much of the philosophical content of the speech is taken over from Ficino, but Castiglione gives these doctrines even more literary embellishment than Bembo had done. The Ficinian doctrine that beauty can be perceived only through sight and hearing becomes, in Castiglione, an admonition to the lover to 'enjoy with his eyes the radiance, the grace, the loving ardour, the smiles, the mannerisms and all the other agreeable adornments of the woman he loves' and to 'use his hearing to enjoy the sweetness of her voice, the modulation of her words and, if she is a musician, the music she plays'.[26] Castiglione carried on the trend, initiated by Bessarion, of giving Platonic love a strongly religious colouring. He has Bembo end his speech with a hymn, which is full of Biblical imagery, and in which love is identified with the 'searing power of contemplation' that ravished the souls of 'ancient Fathers', taking them from their bodies and uniting them with God. And from Pico, Castiglione takes the idea that the Song of Solomon

[25] Baldesar Castiglione, *The Book of the Courtier*, trans. G. Bull (Harmondsworth, 1986), p. 335; Italian text: *Il libro del cortegiano*, ed. V. Cian (Florence, 1947), p. 487.
[26] Castiglione, *Courtier*, p. 334; *Cortegiano*, p. 486.

refers to 'the death of the kiss'; but while he too alludes to the poem about kissing Agathon, unlike Pico he does not name the male dedicatee of these verses.[27]

Where Castiglione differs from all his predecessors is in the scepticism about Platonic love which he permits his characters to voice. Morello complains that he cannot understand the sort of love described by Bembo because in his view 'to possess the beauty he praises so much without the body is a fantasy'. Morello also does not believe that beauty is always as good as Bembo says, for he remembers 'having seen many beautiful women who were evil, cruel and spiteful . . . beauty makes them proud, and pride makes them cruel'. Bembo firmly denies that this is so and, dutifully toeing the Platonic line, affirms that 'one cannot have beauty without goodness' since 'outward beauty is a true sign of inner goodness'.[28] None the less, by introducing the down-to-earth objections of Morello, Castiglione raises doubts about the extreme idealism of the Platonic theory.

The combination of literary skill and psychological insight which Castiglione brought to the topic of Platonic love was the high point of the tradition. Now that Platonic love was safely in the heterosexual camp,[29] its themes were taken up in a stream of *trattati d'amore* (treatises on love). The inevitable price of such popularity was a drastic reduction in philosophical content and an increasing staleness, as once lively motifs became hackneyed through continual repetition.[30] A notable exception to this dreary picture is the *Dialoghi d'amore* of Leone Ebreo, written around 1501–2, but not published until 1535. Leone, a Portuguese-Jewish physician who emigrated to Italy after 1492, put forward his ideas on love in the form of a playful, but extremely erudite, conversation between the female Sofia (wisdom) and her male admirer, Filone (love). From the opening lines, Sofia's flirtatious teasing of the besotted Filone leaves the reader in no doubt as to the heterosexual nature of the love they speak about. Like other writers on Platonic love, Leone pointed out its compatibility with the tenets of religion: but, in his case, the religion was Judaism rather than Christianity. Again and again he noted that Plato's ideas derived from Moses and the Cabbalists: Aristophanes' myth of the

[27] Castiglione, *Courtier*, pp. 336–7, 342; *Cortegiano*, pp. 489–90, 498.

[28] Castiglione, *Courtier*, pp. 329–30; *Cortegiano*, pp. 479–80.

[29] See, however, Flaminio Nobili, *Il trattato dell'amore humano*, ed. P.D. Pasolini (Rome, 1895), fol. 16^{v}, who still regarded spiritual love as most appropriate between a man and a youth.

[30] *Trattati d'amore*, ed. G. Zonta (Bari, 1912); see also J.C. Nelson, *Renaissance Theory of Love* (New York, 1958), pp. 67–162.

androgyne, for instance, turned out to be nothing more than the Genesis account of the creation of Adam and Eve, amplified and polished 'after the manner of Greek oratory'.[31]

One of the last Italian Platonic love treatises was Giordano Bruno's *Eroici furori* (1585), written during his sojourn in England. In some respects this work – a series of sonnets written and commented on by Bruno – was quite conventional. There was the by now obligatory reference to the Song of Solomon, 'which under the guise of lovers and ordinary passions contains . . . divine and heroic frenzies, as the mystics and cabalistic doctors interpret it'. And in the dedication to Sir Philip Sidney, Bruno, like most authors of such treatises, attacked sensual love, calling it 'witless, stupid and odiferous foulness . . . worthy of pity and laughter'. But Bruno's polemic took an unexpected turn towards misogyny: 'and all this for those eyes, those cheeks, for that breast . . . that scourge, that disgust, that stink, that tomb, that latrine, that menstruum, that carrion, that quartan ague, that distortion of nature, which with...a shadow, a phantasm, a dream, a Circian enchantment put to the service of generation, deceives us as a species of beauty'.[32] This contempt for women was philosophically, not psychologically, motivated. Throughout the *Eroici furori*, Bruno deliberately subverts the metaphors of love poetry, bending them to his own metaphysical purposes. Thus, for him, female beauty is a symbol of the allure of the perceptible world; by downgrading it, he was indicating the immeasurable distance between sensible and intelligible beauty, between physical desire and heroic love – man's doomed but noble desire to understand the infinity of God. His aim was to recover the profound philosophical significance which Platonic love had had for Ficino and Pico, not to return to their homoerotic conception of it. That conception had been superseded by a notion of Platonic love which was better suited to the social, cultural and literary concerns of the Renaissance: a non-sexual, spiritually uplifting love between the sexes.

[31] Leone Ebreo, *The Philosophy of Love*, trans. F. Friedeberg-Seeley and J.H. Barnes (London, 1937), p. 345; Italian text: *Dialoghi d'amore*, ed. S. Caramella (Bari, 1929), p. 291.

[32] Giordano Bruno, *The Heroic Frenzies*, trans. P.E. Memmo (Chapel Hill, 1964), pp. 60, 62; Italian text: *Dialoghi italiani*, ed. G. Gentile and G. Aquilecchia (Florence, 1958), pp. 929, 932.

CHAPTER 9

Uses of Plato by Erasmus and More

Dominic Baker-Smith

Cultural influence is never a passive process. One striking feature of the Renaissance is the manner in which great figures of antiquity are brought into focus not so much for purposes of detached analysis, that would have to wait for the scientific classicism of a later age, but as potent presences or myths that could match contemporary expectations and perplexities. Of no figure is this more true than Plato, lauded by Petrarch, who hardly knew his writings, as a preferable alternative to the Aristotle of the scholars. Raphael's mural of the two philosophers in the Stanza della Segnatura effectively summarizes the myth: Aristotle extends his hand to the plane of terrestrial reality, the field of science, but the white-haired Plato points upwards to the transcendent order of spiritual truth (see frontispiece). Petrarch's intuitive preference reflected his concern with two issues: one was that of eloquence, of a linguistic medium that might touch subjective response and so convert thought into action; the other one, closely related, was a preoccupation with moral philosophy. One can detect in these issues the seeds of the humanist programme. The art of rhetoric is directed primarily at the will, the seat of moral responsibility; it moves it, arouses it and directs it towards desirable goals. The stock complaint in anti-scholastic polemic is that the *moderni*, the professional philosophers of the schools, have been trained in a dialectical system so formal and abstract that it has lost its purchase on actual life. Plato, the Plato of Renaissance myth, fits into this polemic because his philosophy is seen as eloquent and morally inspiring. Above all, it stresses the immortality of the soul, the ultimate ground of subjectivity.

The particular value of linking Erasmus and More is that they were closely associated at a critical juncture in the development of the Northern Renaissance, and yet in their individual encounters with Plato they embody quite distinct responses to his stimulus. Leaving aside the question of personal friendship, it is clear that between 1500 and 1520 they shared a common set of values and collaborated in a literary campaign which was highly critical of established attitudes and institutional forms. It is also clear that Plato was an important factor in this campaign. Moreover, their careers straddle the point at which the Greek text of Plato became generally available for the first time: the earliest printed Greek edition of Plato's works was issued by Aldus Manutius in Venice in 1513. Erasmus would have seen some of the manuscripts collected for this undertaking during his stay in Aldus' house in 1507. There is, then, the possibility of some manuscript encounter with the Greek, but we can be sure that both More and Erasmus based their initial impression of Plato on the growing number of Latin translations, such as those of Bruni, Decembrio and above all Ficino (see above, pp. 169–70) But it was Ficino's translation of the entire corpus, completed in 1469 and printed in 1484, which made possible any degree of intimacy with the range of Plato's works. Published in the exceptionally large run of 1,025 copies, it was sold out within six years and further printings followed, making it widely available.[1]

Among those works which Erasmus initiated during his stay in Paris (1495–1500) it is the *Antibarbari* which most clearly shows the impact of Ficino. Here Plato is praised as 'the most eloquent of philosophers', a significant pointer to Erasmus's general attitude: what he admires is the contagious quality of Plato's writing, and the moral acuity of Socrates.[2] Pagan wisdom is accepted as an endorsement of Christian truth, an approach which is justified by those church fathers, Augustine and Origen in particular, who see in Platonism the highest reach of natural wisdom. In a passage which may reflect later revision but which is representative of his general attitude Erasmus writes, 'For my part, I will allow myself to be called after any pagan so long as he was deeply learned or supremely eloquent; nor shall I go back on this declaration, if only the pagan teaches me more excellent things than a Christian'.[3] The point is not that the pagans are superior, or even equal, in their insight into truth but that an eloquent pagan does more to activate self-awareness in the moral subject than

[1] L.D. Reynolds and N.G. Wilson, *Scribes and Scholars* (Oxford, 1978), p. 138. See also the introduction to this section.

[2] *Collected Works of Erasmus* (Toronto, 1974, continuing) (hereafter *CWE*), XXIII, p. 39. For Ficino's influence see Maria Cytowska, 'Erasme de Rotterdame et Marsile Ficin son maître', *EOS*, 68 (1975), 165–79; P.O. Kristeller, 'Erasmus from an Italian Perspective', *Renaissance Quarterly*, 23 (1970), 1–14.

[3] *CWE*, XXIII, p. 58.

the impersonal technicalities of the professional theologians. Between 1499 and 1517 Erasmus visited England seven times, and he may have spent as much as six and a half years there, residing in London or Cambridge. This period marks the inception of his collaboration with Thomas More, and his encounter with a group of Englishmen committed to the advance of Greek learning. As he wrote enthusiastically to Robert Fisher, it scarcely seemed necessary to visit Italy, so stimulating were his encounters in England:

> When I listen to Colet it seems to me that I am listening to Plato himself. Who could fail to be astonished at the universal scope of Grocyn's accomplishments? Could anything be more clever or more profound than Linacre's mind? Did nature create anything kinder, sweeter or more harmonious than the mind of Thomas More?[4]

Apart from More, in any case a member of the younger generation, these new friends had all visited Italy and had significant intellectual ties with Florence – Colet actually corresponded with Ficino. But the identification of Colet, a theologian, with Plato indicates the distinctly religious character of their Platonism. It is not easy to pinpoint the exact nature of Colet's influence on Erasmus and More, but that he had an influence is beyond doubt.[5]

Something of it can be detected in the work that contains Erasmus' most characteristic use of Platonic themes, the *Enchiridion Militis Christiani* which he completed in the autumn of 1501 soon after his return from his first English visit. It reveals a loosely Platonic scheme of values, based on the primacy of the spiritual: a recurrent topic is the futility of basing judgement on the senses, since only spiritual values can lead to reality. Distinct from the recovery of Plato's own writings there was an indirect Platonism, linked to the influence of Dionysius the Areopagite, which disseminated key metaphors about the life of the spirit along the Rhineland in the fourteenth century, and surfaced in a number of writers, among whom Eckhart is the best known.[6] Erasmus would have met these metaphors before he read Plato, and when he did read him it appears that he did so in the spirit of this received tradition. One important feature of this 'northern' Platonism was a marked degree of hostility to the conventional forms of public

[4] *CWE*, I, pp. 235–6.

[5] On Colet's Platonism, see Leland Miles, *John Colet and the Platonic Tradition* (La Salle, Illinois, 1961) and Sears Jayne, *John Colet and Marsilio Ficino* (Oxford, 1963).

[6] R. Klibansky, 'Plato's *Parmenides* in the Middle Ages and the Renaissance', *Medieval and Renaissance Studies*, I (1943), 281–330.

religion: for Erasmus, the central Platonic tenet is the opposition of body, or flesh, and soul, of external and internal, of letter and spirit. In his writings a series of dichotomies marks out this opposition between a world experienced by the senses and the authentic values based on spiritual perception. The *Enchiridion* uses Plato's writings to give authority and precision to a scheme of values set up to counter a system of religious practice which had lost its soul. Much later, in 1515, when he was defending his *Praise of Folly* against Maarten van Dorp, it was entirely fitting that Erasmus should claim that the book dealt 'sub specie lusus' ('under the guise of play') with the same matters as the *Enchiridion.*[7] Here we can sense that there was for Erasmus, as for Thomas More, a continuity between the Platonic view of reality and satire: as the Platonist distinguishes material embodiment from animating principle, so the satirist distinguishes convention from motive, signifier from signified. It is in the gap between these two terms that Erasmus' satire operates, exposing the gulf that divides merely conventional actions from the original motives which should animate them – as with the Franciscan in the *Praise of Folly* who maintains the spirit of St Francis by avoiding all contact with money. He wears gloves when counting it.[8]

Thus, in the *Enchiridion*, Erasmus gives a surprisingly literal reading of Christ's judgement on the Pharisees (Matt.23.27): they are whitened sepulchres because they carry a dead soul around with them, an apt allusion to the *Cratylus* (400c). In common with most of his attacks on 'Judaising', Erasmus treats the pharisees as the representatives of a church which has lost inspiration and relies on ceremonies and an exaggerated theology of works.[9] The aim of the *Enchiridion* is, simply, to *reanimate* Christian observance, a strategy that has obvious Platonic overtones; this entails getting behind the signs to recapture the original inspiration, just as proper reading of the Scriptures involves getting behind the letter, the literal sense, to arrive at spiritual understanding. In a characteristic remark Erasmus compares the Biblical text to the Silenus figures mentioned in the *Symposium* (215b): little statues with a grotesque outer likeness which can be opened up to reveal images of the gods. The figurine with its contrast of ugliness and spiritual beauty is introduced by Alcibiades to represent the nature of Socrates, an ugly man with a beautiful soul (216d); just so, the Biblical text may seem arid until it is opened by the

[7] *CWE*, III, p. 115. [8] *CWE*, XXVII, p. 132. [9] *CWE*, LXVI, p. 29.

spiritual reader to reveal its divine power. The Silenus image appealed strongly to Erasmus and he returned to it later in the 1515 edition of the *Adages*. It is typical, too, of the way in which he drew on Plato, using the works to support a general scheme of values conveyed by metaphoric contrasts: inside and outside, spirit and flesh, light and dark.

Erasmus justifies his sympathy with Platonism in the *Enchiridion* by appealing to the favourable views of Augustine who rated the Platonists as the most perceptive of the pagans, 'not only because many of their ideas are perfectly consistent with our religion, but also because their figurative modes of expression . . . and frequent use of allegory are very close to the language of Sacred Scripture'.[10] Both the Platonists and Scripture demand interpretation, that is, they compel the reader to probe beneath the surface to a deeper sense. A Platonic locus that impressed Erasmus was the cave myth from the *Republic* (514a–517b): this allegory, like the Silenus-Socrates figure, involves a reversal of conventional values, and the 'wisdom' of the world turns out to be folly while the 'folly' of the wise, Socrates or Christ, turns out to be wisdom. Moral health requires divergence from common opinion, from the values of the *vulgus*, the mob guided by custom and convention: 'the crowd are those in Plato's cave, who, chained by their own passions, marvel at the empty images of things as if they were true reality'.[11]

It is not difficult to see, then, how the *Praise of Folly* could evolve from the moral concerns of the *Enchiridion*: the satirist makes us laugh at a world of empty images – rituals, vestments, regalia – which have lost their proper signification. There is even a similarity between the *Praise of Folly* and the process of ascent from the Cave; after an initial exposure of human fatuity (a soul shut in a body), Folly goes on to describe the ridiculous behaviour caused by social custom, the conventionalization of life into acts and gestures which have broken free of their original purpose and become ends in themselves. But, at the climax, Erasmus unexpectedly shifts the semantic load of *stultitia* from folly to the complex sense of St Paul's 'folly of the Cross'. What we encounter is a fusion of platonic/Pauline ideas about ecstasy or transcendent vision, and just as in the Cave myth Socrates anticipates that anyone who has ascended up to the light will seem blind and confused when they return to the shadows so Erasmus describes those

[10] *Ibid.*, referring to *The City of God*, VIII.5. On Augustine and Plato, see Coleman, pp. 27–37 above. [11] *CWE*, LXVI, p. 86.

visionaries who have glimpsed the world to come, 'They speak incoherently and unnaturally, utter sound without sense, and their faces suddenly change expression. One moment they are excited, the next they are depressed, they weep and laugh and sigh by turns; in fact they are quite beside themselves'.[12] If such ecstasy had been the experience of St Paul, it had also been that of Socrates.

The parallel between Platonists and Christians lies, then, for Erasmus, in their joint recognition of a higher reality, 'And as long as the mind makes proper use of the organs of the body it is called sane and healthy, but once it begins to break its bonds and tries to win freedom, as if it were planning an escape from prison, men call it insane'.[13] Both see the soul as stifled and weighed down by the fetters of the body, and both see philosophy as a preparation for death. In 1520, eleven years after composing the *Praise of Folly*, Erasmus explained this passage to Joris van Halewijn:

> The passage which troubles you in the *Moria* . . . will be clear to you if you remember the Platonic myth about the cave and the men born in it, who wondered at the shadows of things as though they were the reality. What we apprehend with our senses does not really exist, for it is not perpetual, nor does it always take the same form. Those things alone really exist which are apprehended by the contemplation of the mind.[14]

Erasmus' profound admiration for Socrates, the truly wise man who fell foul of conventional attitudes, is vividly expressed in the Silenus figure which he celebrates in one of the important 1515 additions to the *Adagia*, the 'Sileni Alcibiadis'. Here the Sileni also include Antisthenes, Diogenes, Epictetus, and even Christ, 'mirificus Silenus', who was born in obscurity to poor parents, called simple fishermen to be his disciples, and ended his life ignominiously on a cross; but 'in such poverty, what riches! in such weakness, what immeasurable strength! in such shame, what glory!'[15] In the elaboration of this paradox it is possible to recognise the consistency of Erasmus's perception of Platonism as a system of natural reason which is none the less a type or anticipation of Christian revelation. This fits his

[12] *CWE*, xxvii, p. 153. The key text for the foolishness of the cross is I Corinthians 1.18. Its importance for Erasmus is analysed in M.A. Screech, *Ecstasy and the Praise of Folly* (London, 1980), pp. 39–42 and *passim*.

[13] *CWE*, xxvii, p. 150.

[14] *CWE*, vii, pp. 316–17. For the psychology of Christian Platonism, see P.O. Kristeller, *The Philosophy of Marsilio Ficino* (New York, 1943), ch. xi.

[15] M.M. Phillips, *The 'Adages' of Erasmus* (Cambridge, 1964), p. 272; *Opera omnia Desiderii Erasmi* (Amsterdam, 1969) (hereafter, *ASD*), ii.5, 254.

generally positive view of pagan wisdom as a propaedeutic to the Gospels. In the adage 'Amicorum communia omnia' ('Between friends all is common') Plato is praised for his teaching on community of possessions, 'But it is extraordinary how Christians dislike this common ownership of Plato's, how in fact they cast stones at it, although nothing was ever said by a pagan philosopher which came closer to the mind of Christ'.[16] This virtual admission of Plato into the ranks of Christian sages is carried to its extreme in the colloquy 'The Godly Feast' of 1526, where it is obliquely hinted that some divine power may have prompted pagan wisdom. To make the point one of the speakers, Nephalius, alludes to the account of the death of Socrates in the *Phaedo*; reading such things, he asserts, 'I can hardly help exclaiming, 'Saint Socrates, pray for us''.[17]

This makes it clear that Erasmus does not engage with Plato as a philosopher, at least not in any rigorous sense, but rather as a rhetorician of spiritual experience, the instigator of a metaphorical system which coheres effectively with Pauline Christianity. In particular it is the figure of Socrates, the midwife of understanding in others, that holds a powerful attraction for him. Erasmus is often bracketed together with Thomas More as though they were identical in outlook, and certainly they had significant concerns in common. But their mental attitudes and their public commitments were distinct, and their different reactions to Plato demonstrate this. Erasmus, for one thing, must bear some of the responsibility for the image of More as a contemplative scholar dragged into public affairs. It is the case that More was deeply religious and carefully reserved part of his life for private meditation, but he was also an active and highly efficient public figure whose training in the common law was the prescribed Tudor preparation for an upwardly mobile career. Erasmus, in common with Ficino and his Florentine associates under the Medicis, showed little interest in the life of practical politics, even if he did engage in acerbic criticism of contemporary rulers. More's active spirit, by contrast, has something in common with the civic humanism that evolved in Florence prior to Medici domination; the active role he played in the affairs of the city of London, at least up to 1515, fits with his life-long resistance to absolutism. His early translation of the life of Giovanni Pico della Mirandola (1504) is suggestive in this regard: More so edits the original that a major

[16] *CWE*, XXXI, p. 30.

[17] Erasmus, *The Colloquies*, translated by C.R. Thompson (Chicago, 1965), p. 67, *ASD*, I.3, 254.

theme to emerge is the time-honoured debate over the contemplative and the active lives.[18] Platonists like Pico himself, or Cristoforo Landino in his *Disputationes Camaldulenses*, had touched on the matter and given priority to the contemplative life. But More leaves the question open. When he turns to Plato it is not in the spirit of Ficino, or even Erasmus, but rather as a student of politics turning to the originator of political science.

No doubt More cut his Platonic teeth on Ficino's Latin translation, though there is the possibility that he encountered the *Republic* in the version by Decembrio.[19] But some part in his discovery of Plato may have been played by the Hellenistic rhetorician and satirist Lucian of Samosata, a number of whose dialogues were translated by More and Erasmus as part of their joint Greek studies in 1504–06. Lucian's scepticism made him hostile to the Platonists and he enjoyed ridiculing Plato. One example relevant to More occurs in the *True History*, a satiric travel narrative which has its importance for *Utopia*: when the narrator reaches the Isles of the Blest and meets the great figures of Greek history Plato is absent. He is, it emerges, in his ideal city and is consequently invisible. It is a joke that points to the name of More's island – Utopia or no-place – and it alerts us to the nature of More's engagement with Plato, that is, a radical questioning of the ways in which the idealising imagination can engage with social institutions. To put it another way, what are the obligations of those who have climbed out of the cave to those left inside? It is also a distinct possibility that Lucian had the fortuitous effect of alerting More to what can best be described as Plato's intellectual playfulness. Thus one of the original features of More's platonism is that it shows little interest in Plato as the master of arcane, spiritual wisdom; rather, he is perceived as a creative, questing intelligence who challenges his readers to engage in a dialogue that extends beyond the text. As much is implied in the full title of More's most celebrated book, *De optimo reipublicae statu deque nova insula Utopia* (*Of the best state of a commonwealth and of the new island of Utopia*); this makes a declaration of genre, or genres, including a traveller's tale about a newly-found island, but also pointing to a tradition of debate *de republica* (on government) which looks back to Plato's *Republic* as its primal source.

[18] See D. Baker-Smith, *More's Utopia* (London, 1991), pp. 16–21.

[19] On More's access to Plato, see P.O. Kristeller, 'Thomas More as a Renaissance Humanist', *Moreana*, 17 (1980), 5–22; on Decembrio's translation, see R. Weiss, *Humanism in England during the Fifteenth Century* (Oxford, 1957), pp. 51–7.

An important link in the chain of transmission had been St Augustine's *City of God* which owes to Plato its distinction between the bogus community of the terrestial city and the city of God beyond the reach of time. It also, incidentally, contains fragments of Cicero's lost contribution to the debate, his *De Re Publica*, a point of some interest since More lectured on the *City of God* in 1501 at Grocyn's church of St Lawrence Jewry.

The Platonic credentials of *Utopia* are most aptly recognized by examining its name. If we slip back for a moment to that joke of the invisible Plato in Lucian's *True History*, it appears to allude to a key moment in the *Republic* at the end of Book IX when the political argument is brought to a close (592a–b), and a rather teasing close at that. To Socrates' declaration that the wise man will care for 'the established habit of his soul' Glaucon responds that he will not willingly participate in politics. Yes he will, affirms Socrates, 'in his own city . . . yet perhaps not in the city of his birth, except in some providential conjunction'. The fragile hope of such a conjunction has earlier been associated with the fusion of wisdom and political power in the philosopher-king, an improbable if not impossible figure (473d; 499b–c). Unless that ideal is realised the wise man apparently remains a political exile from the land of his birth, free only to participate in the life of 'his own city'. Glaucon sees the point: 'You mean the city whose establishment we have described, the city whose home is in the ideal, for I think that it can be found nowhere on earth'. This ideal city, literally one 'laid up in words' (*tē en logois keimenē*), is available as a pattern for contemplation; whether it comes into being or not, it alone will be the political homeland of the wise man.

No doubt the sceptical Lucian was only interested in the comic potential. But Thomas More accepted Plato's real point: that the intellectual reflection prompted by his sketch of a commonwealth goes some way towards bridging the gap between an ideal and our actual experience. The performance of political duty will, Plato hopes, be qualified by the intellectual (and affective) experience of reading the *Republic*. The aim is not exemplary but heuristic. This More seems to have perceived. The very name *Utopia* indicates as much: deriving from *ou-topos*, 'no-place', it was conceivably Erasmus' substitution while the book was in preparation for the press for More's original *Nusquama*, 'nowhere'. But just in case we miss the point, two items in the prefatory materials direct the humanistically trained reader in the right direction: these are the letter addressed to Jerome

Busleyden by Pieter Gillis, and the verses on Utopia supposedly by a certain Anemolius but actually by Gillis. It is clear in the prefatory materials that a complicated game is going on, and that Gillis is an accredited participant. This suggests that the idea of the book arose during More's stay in Antwerp as Gillis's guest in the summer of 1515, and there is a more than random chance that it was provoked by discussions of the Aldine Greek Plato. The verses make the point that Utopia rivals and even surpasses Plato since it manifests (*praestiti*) what he merely outlines *in words* (*literis/Deliniavit*). This distinction is further elaborated in the letter, where Gillis asserts that as he contemplates the island depicted by More, 'I am affected as if I were sometimes actually living in Utopia itself'.[20] This playfulness makes proper sense when it is grasped as an allusion to the ideal city which is the philosopher's true home.

This practice of bilocation – being in the world and yet out of it – can be taken either as a rejection of the political life or as an admonition to discerning involvement. One option results in a kind of political quietism as the philosopher avoids contact with a corrupting society, while the other demands a constant adaptation of the ideal to the exigencies of the actual. It is when Plato is about to introduce the idea of the philosopher-king that Socrates raises the critical question, 'Is it possible for anything to be realised in deed as it is spoken in word, or is it the nature of things that action should partake of exact truth less than speech . . . ?' (*Republic*, 473a). When we think of the city 'laid up in words', it is clear that the philosopher who is its true citizen is the only person who can mediate its conceptual possibilities to the actual world of deeds. Platonic politics need not involve the blind imitation of institutions proposed in the *Republic* but the adoption of a critical frame of mind, one that can mediate between the idealism of words and the resistant contingency of actions. This concern with the implementation of the ideal in the actual theatre of politics seems to be the most challenging aspect of Plato's thinking for More.[21] If the dream of the philosopher-king represents an ideal conjunction of political power and philosophical intelligence (*Republic* 473d–e), then within the terms of the Renaissance court the alliance of prince and counsellor might be presented in comparable terms, as indeed it is in

20 *The Complete Works of Sir Thomas More*, vol. 4, ed. F. Surtz and J.H. Hexter, (New Haven and London, 1965), pp. 19–23.

21 This is fully argued in the important article by Kevin Corrigan, 'The Function of the Ideal in Plato's *Republic* and St Thomas More's *Utopia*', *Moreana*, 27 (1990), 27–48.

Castiglione. The difficulty is, as Plato acknowledges in *Letter* VII, that wisdom and the life-style of princes cannot agree, the creative conjunction of speculation and action is inhibited by irrational forces; confronted by the hostility of Dionysius in Syracuse, 'I feared to see myself at last altogether nothing but words' (*Letters* 328c). Just such an anxiety motivates Raphael's angry rejection in *Utopia* of the proposal that he enter the service of some prince.

If Plato provides More with the starting point for his discussion 'de optime reipublicae statu' (about the best kind of state) he can also be recognised as the inspiration for many features in More's extraordinary island.[22] The central feature of Utopian life is its austere rationality; much as in *Republic*, the controlling consideration is spiritual worth – what will profit the soul. But in Utopia there are no distinctions of class and all citizens are expected to aim at the spiritual poise and self-control Plato proposes for his guardians. The absence of privacy, the standardised clothing and the rejection of all personal ownership, features listed by Socrates as necessary for the formation of an altruistic governing class (*Republic* 416b–17b), are basic to the Utopian polity. More's departure from Plato is to make a strictly rational life the goal of the entire community rather than of its governing elite alone, a point that has some importance for the role of women. Plato admits women to the elevated status of the guardians. This is arguably at the expense of their being women,[23] but in the classless society of Utopia both sexes preserve distinct areas of responsibility while sharing essential human concerns. Though political office seems to be a male preserve women oversee all matters relating to nurture. At the same time they may be admitted to the priesthood and, most important of all, they enjoy equal access to education and cultural life, the means of realising a common human potential. The monogamous ideal of Utopian marriage, likewise, underlines the complimentarity of the sexes, as Plato is modified in the light of a Christian anthropology.

The common basis of both republics is the primacy of soul, of rationality, over the pull of materialism or sensuality. This is most evident in the Utopian hierarchy of pleasures: any initial impression of indulgence is swiftly checked by the recognition that the islanders not only dismiss those pleasures based on custom or association but

[22] For a comprehensive survey of More's Platonic borrowings see Thomas I. White, 'Pride and the Public Good: Thomas More's Use of Plato in *Utopia*', *Journal of the History of Philosophy*, 20 (1982), 329–54.

[23] On this aspect see Julia Annas, *An Introduction to Plato's Republic* (Oxford, 1981), 181–5.

rigorously distinguish between satisfaction of the body and satisfaction of the soul, a lower pleasure cannot be allowed to interfere with the enjoyment of a higher one. A further, unexpected, consequence is the presence in this ideal society of slavery; but this is penal slavery, not hereditary, and can be read in almost metaphorical terms as the just consequence of irrational behaviour which forfeits the claim to human status. More's rational citizens, united in their pursuit of spiritual values, are a fictional embodiment of that ideal community sketched in the *Republic* (464d) and most emphatically expressed in the 'first-best society' of the *Laws* where all things combine in the common service and all citizens 'approve and condemn in perfect unison and derive pleasure and pain from the same sources' (739c–d). In the ideal society rationality underpins the solidarity which ownership would subvert.

Thus while More takes over a range of Platonic schemes and motifs to construct his alternative world, the most persistent echo of Plato in *Utopia* is the note of anxiety about the relation between intellectual ideals and the theatre of active politics. How keenly More felt the dilemma is revealed later in the *Responsio ad Lutherum* (1523) where Luther's church of the elect is derided as 'somehow imperceptible and mathematical – like Platonic Ideas – which is both in some place and in no place, is in the flesh and is out of the flesh'.[24] From his own Augustinian perspective, More sees Luther's doctrine as an attempt to anticipate the certainties of the City of God, to merge the ideal in the actual, when for him (as for Socrates) the human burden is to linger uncertainly between the two cities. And the reference to 'no-place', 'in nullo loco' has its utopian reverberations.

If we take this Platonic view of the political vocation as central to More's intentions in *Utopia*, the structure of the work becomes clearer. The central account of the island and its rational institutions, given to us in the form of a report by the traveller Raphael, is framed within an encounter that takes place in Antwerp after Mass, a parallel to the opening of the *Republic* in Piraeus after a religious festival. The conversation in an Antwerp garden fuses historical reality – a real city and real people, More and Gillis – with the fictional traveller Raphael, who has none the less been to the New World with the historical Amerigo Vespucci. When we add on to this the prefatory verses and letters prepared by More and Gillis, which touch on such matters as Raphael's present whereabouts and the precise location of

[24] More, *Complete Works*, vol. v, ed. J.M. Headley (New Haven and London, 1969), part 1, p. 167.

Utopia, we can see a deliberate device to alert the reader to the invisible frontier between fact and fiction, a narrative reflection of the equally obscure line between action and ideals. The tenuous thread by which the vision of a rational society is transported back to Europe and dispersed through the means of a reported conversation alerts the reader to the problematic ways in which ideals grate against established social customs.

The Platonic credentials of Raphael, our guide to Utopia, are beyond question. Plato is his favourite philosopher and his travels are compared to Plato's: new-found lands and the frontiers of thought are tacitly linked. Even his name, Hythlodaeus ('purveyor of nonsense'), may owe something to the dismissive term, *hythlos* (nonsense) that Thrasymachus, the voice of custom, directs at Socrates' idea of justice (*Republic* 336d). Finally, the disposal of his estate to relatives has something in it of Pico della Mirandola's otherwordly rigour; both the historical and the fictional Platonist refuse to compromise, to sacrifice independence or integrity to political engagement. More devised Book I as an example of existing societies based on custom in order to prepare us for the vision of the rational society of the Utopians, but its central episode is the clash between Raphael and Morus (More's own persona in the fiction) over this basic question of engagement. Against Raphael's 'academic' philosophy which refuses to compromise with the irrational, Morus advocates discretion and flexibility, an 'indirect approach' which may at least minimize evil even if it doesn't uproot it.[25] The issue returns on the final page of Book II: after the account of Utopia Morus is left still sceptical about the feasibility of emulating the ideal yet equally ill-at-ease about the aspects of things as they are. His dilemma becomes a model for our own reception of the book: as in the *Republic*, it is the interaction of 'there' and 'here' within the perceptive reader, the essential act of accommodation, that is the intended aim of the narrative. Otherwise why use fiction? The terms we encounter in the book are not those on which we are allowed to rest.

In certain respects, then, More and Erasmus develop their Platonic interests in contrasting modes. What stands out is the fertility of the tradition and its adaptability in bridging the gap between imagined worlds and mundane experience in a manner that offers, if not transformation, at least the elevation of immediate affairs. Hence its

[25] More, *Complete Works*, IV, pp. 99–101.

potential for destabilising entrenched custom. If the Neoplatonic rhetoric of the soul adopted by Erasmus seems to diverge from the institutional focus pursued by More, the fact remains that both find in Platonism a radical challenge to the complacencies of the day. While Erasmus in his depiction of inward life remains faithful to a tradition of interpretation which includes Origen as well as Ficino, More shows a powerful originality and penetration in his response to the epistemological challenge of the *Republic*. It is intriguing to reflect that this rare perception may owe something to the provocation of a Lucianic joke.

CHAPTER 10

Italian Neoplatonism and the poetry of Sidney, Shakespeare, Chapman, and Donne

John Roe

ITALIAN NEOPLATONISM

Much of the influence of Neoplatonism on Elizabethan erotic poetry can be traced directly to the impact made by Castiglione's *Il cortegiano* (see Hutton, pp. 72–3, above). The pertinent ideas of Ficino concerning the body's beauty and that of the soul, as well as Ficino's novel arrangement (following Plotinus *Enneads* 1.6) of the senses according to a hierarchy of values, find expression in Bembo's famous speech in Book IV of *Il cortegiano*. These are the ideas which principally shape those poems of Sidney, Shakespeare, Chapman, and Donne which provide the material for this chapter. I propose to examine in turn the Neoplatonic features of *Astrophil and Stella*, *Venus and Adonis*, *Ovids Banquet of Sence*, and *The Songs and Sonets* of John Donne, concluding with 'The Ecstasy'.

Immediately striking about the English encounter with Italian Neoplatonism is how the latter's influence on the poetry operates, the philosophical ideas being adapted, not to say redirected, to poetic ends. This makes the poets I am dealing with quite different in tone and intention from Spenser whose abstract thinking in his most overtly Neoplatonic work *The Fowre Hymnes* traces a more orthodox Platonic design (see Thomas Bulger's chapter in this volume.) For example, the figure represented as Astrophil in Sidney's sonnet sequence directs the Platonic theory of pure love to the ends of seduction, while Venus the spokeswoman of desire in Shakespeare's poem artfully modifies the order Ficino gives to the senses to vindicate those of them upon which Ficino (and Castiglione) would place least value (see below, pp. 108–10). This seems to draw a rejoinder from Chapman (whose title *Banquet of Sence* refers most obviously to Ficino), for while Chapman also gives the bodily senses a higher status than Ficino assigns to them the tone and tenor of his poem seems markedly in contrast to that of Shakespeare's.

To begin then by resuming the Italian arguments (for more of which see Kraye, pp. 76–85 above): Ficino, emphasising harmony as the principal determinant in the relationship between love and beauty, makes it clear that the intellect, which he considers to be a sense, and the eyes and ears have priority over the other organs:

Beauty, therefore, is three-fold: of souls, of bodies, and of sounds. That of souls is known through the intellect; that of bodies is perceived through the eyes; that of sounds is perceived only through the ears. Since, therefore, it is the intellect, seeing, and hearing by which alone we are able to enjoy beauty, and since love is the desire to enjoy beauty, love is always satisfied through the intellect, the eyes, or the ears. What need is there for smell? What need is there for taste, or touch?[1]

Castiglione takes up the argument concerning the senses in the celebrated fourth book of *The Courtier* in which Cardinal Bembo, speaking on behalf of Platonic love, elaborates the Ficinian distinctions in a tone and style more in keeping with courtly *sprezzatura* (nonchalance):

Let him lay aside therefore the blinde judgement of the sense, and enjoy with his eyes ye brightnesse, the comelinesse, the loving sparkels, laughters, gestures, and all the other pleasant furnitures of beautie: especially with hearing the sweetnesse of her voice, the tunablenesse of her wordes, the melody of her singing and playing on instruments (in case the woman beloved bee a musitian) and so shall he with most daintie foode feede the soule through the meanes of these two senses, which have little bodily substance in them.[2]

Castiglione appears to omit the Ficinian insistence on the intellect as a third sense on a par with those of sight and hearing (and superior to touch, taste, smell), concentrating rather on the visual and auditory as pure means of perceiving beauty. He also gives, in keeping with the work as a whole, a more courtly context to his depiction of the senses, which in Ficino have a methodical abstract status (Ficino's model of three higher and three inferior senses provides an abstract pattern which Castiglione does not adopt). But he observes the important Ficinian distinction of spiritual as opposed to corporeal love and beauty, and the role assigned to Bembo is that of a spokesman for the ethical end of love which is to eschew sense gratification and concentrate on self-perfection through virtue.

Before turning to the application of Italian Platonic ideas in

[1] Marsilio Ficino, *Commentary on Plato's Symposium on Love*, trans. and ed. Sears R. Jayne (Dallas, 1985), p. 41.

[2] Baldassare Castiglione, *The Book of the Courtier*, trans. Sir Thomas Hoby (1561) (London, 1928; reprinted with revisions, 1974), p. 313.

Elizabethan poetry, we should note one important addition made by Castiglione to the Ficinian scheme, and that concerns the activity of kissing which Castiglione favours as long as its purpose is chaste:

For since a kisse is a knitting together both of bodie and soule, it is to be feared, less the sensuall lover will be more enclined to the part of the bodie, than of the soule: but the reasonable lover woteth will, that although the mouth be a parcell of the bodie, yet it is an issue for the wordes, that be the interpreters of the soule, and for the inwarde breath, which is also called the soule. (*The Courtier*, p. 315)

The emphasis on 'inwardness' will shortly call to mind Sidney's sonnet sequence in which Astrophil pay special, Platonic tribute to the 'inward sun' (of virtue) which shines in Stella (see sonnet 71). Similarly, in language which will summon up Donne's 'The Ecstasy', Castiglione's Bembo continues:

And one alone [i.e. soul] so framed of them both ruleth (in a manner) two bodies. Whereupon, a kisse may be saide to be rather a coupling together of the soule, than of the body, because it hath such force in her, that it draweth her unto it, and (as it were) separateth her from the bodie. For this doe all chaste lovers covet a kisse, as a coupling of soules together. And therefore Plato the devine lover saith, that in kissing, his soule came as farre as his lippes to depart out of the bodie. (*The Courtier*, p. 315)[3]

Neoplatonism influences then the literary convention of courtliness – a concern which in varying ways had been the subject of the first three books of *The Courtier*. Ficinian Neoplatonism does not enter in a 'pure' way into literary works but with alternately modifying and modified effect, and it is to some of its modifications that we now turn.

[3] As the passage continues, Castiglione refers to the kiss in the Song of Solomon, which shows incidentally that his source at this point is not Ficino but Giovanni Pico della Mirandola. See the *Commentary on a Canzone of Benivieni*, trans. Sears R. Jayne (New York, Berne, Frankfurt-on-Main, 1984), p. 151. Pico is a slightly misleading authority as, contrary to his assertion, Plato says nothing about the kissing of Agathon in the *Symposium*. According to Edgar Wind, Pico is really alluding to Diogenes Laertius (or perhaps the *Anthologia graeca*) who ascribes an epigram on kissing to Plato. See Wind, *Pagan Mysteries in the Renaissance*, 2nd edn (London, 1967), p. 155. See Wind's chapter also for the influence of the Cabbalistic *mors osculi*, and Kraye, p. 000 above. For a particularly detailed discussion, see Nicholas James Perella's *The Kiss Sacred and Profane* (Berkeley, Los Angeles and London, 1969), pp. 158–88. Finally, Marlowe seems to be drawing on the Platonic as influenced by the *mors osculi* tradition in his description of Helen's kiss in *Dr Faustus*. See *The Works of Christopher Marlowe*, ed. C.F. Tucker Brooke (Oxford, 1910), p. 189.

SIDNEY

Sidney declares his position on Platonic morality in the *Defence of Poetry* where he attempts to answer Plato's objection that poetry is a false and deluding art. Sidney deals with this criticism, which is made chiefly in *The Republic*, by contending that Plato's own practice as a moralist, whose purpose must surely be to encourage active and not merely contemplative virtue in others, owes more to the art of poetry or feigning than it does to the drier, less inticing skill of dialectic:

> Where the philosophers, as they scorn to delight, so must they be little content to move – save wrangling whether *virtus* be the chief or the only good, whether the contemplative or the active life do excell – which Boethius and Plato well knew, and therefore made mistress Philosophy very often borrow the masking raiment of poesy.[4]

Sidney is not above employing a debater's tactics in reminding his audience of Plato's authorizing of 'abominable filthiness' (a charge of homosexual tendencies), or of the fact that *The Republic* advocates free love.[5] But while seeking to lessen the strength of Platonist opposition to poetry with such tactics, on the whole he seeks to enlist Plato as an authentic, if sometimes unacknowledged, ally of the poetic cause:

> And a man need go no further than to Plato himself to know his meaning: who, in his dialogue called *Ion*, giveth high and rightly divine commendation unto poetry. So as Plato, banishing the abuse, not the thing, not banishing it, but giving due honour unto it, shall be our patron, and not our adversary. (*Misc. Prose*, p. 108)

Such distinctions are put with precision in *The Defence*, where they enable Sidney to steer a painstaking course through the treacherous shoals of moral ambiguity. Are the arguments of poetry a force for virtue or evil? Exposing the contradictions in Plato's own statements, and playing the more positive side deftly against the lesser, Sidney manages to dismiss the threat he poses to poetry while retaining him as a supporter. Sidney uses a similar ploy in his sonnet sequence *Astrophil and Stella*, where his speaker Astrophil pleads that his love for Stella is pure; but on this occasion the morality of the argument is confused and uncertain rather than enlightening. The reason perhaps is that Astrophil takes the ideal of feminine beauty, which in *The Defence* Sidney employs as an image of an equally ideal heroic poetry,

[4] *Miscellaneous Prose of Sir Philip Sidney*, ed. Katherine Duncan-Jones and Jan van Dorsten (Oxford, 1973) (hereafter *Misc. Prose*), p. 93.

[5] *Ibid.*, p. 107.

and uses it directly of the woman herself. In speaking of heroic or virtuous ideals (as in the inspiring deeds of Achilles, Cyrus, Aeneas, etc.) Sidney cites Plato (and Cicero) to the effect that to recognise the good is to love it, illustrating the argument with the image of a beautiful woman:

if the saying of Plato and Tully be true, that who could see virtue would be wonderfully ravished with the love of her beauty – this man (i.e. the heroic poet) sets her out to make her more lovely in her holiday apparel.[6]

To love virtue in the image of female beauty and to love its *embodiment* as such are two quite separate things; in bringing them together Sidney (or perhaps Astrophil) eliminates distinctions alarmingly. Astrophil, who from an early point displays a mischievous talent for sowing confusion, says to Virtue:

I sweare, my heart such one shall shew to thee,
That shrines in flesh so true a Deitie,
That *Vertue*, thou thy selfe shalt be in love.[7]

In the same sequence, Astrophil applies a blend of Christianised Platonism only to overturn it defiantly:

True, that true Beautie Vertue is indeed,
Whereof this Beautie can be but a shade,
Which elements with mortall mixture breed:
True, that on earth we are but pilgrims made,
And should in soule up to our country move:
True, and yet true that I must *Stella* love.
(5, ll.9–14)

Astrophil and Stella admits of no single interpretation, critical opinion being sharply divided on the degree of sympathy we should accord its spokesman for passion, Astrophil. There is no doubt that the love he proposes is technically adulterous – or would be were Stella to accede to it – since she is a married lady. The earlier sonnets indicate that a comedy of seduction is in progress; but for Sidney the spiritual consequences of behaviour also matter a good deal. Hence one of

[6] *Ibid.*, p. 98. His editors note (p. 201) that here Sidney receives his Plato from Cicero in the *De Officiis*. Sidney's direct knowledge of Plato was well served by the edition of Henri Estienne sent to him in 1579 (*Misc. Prose*, pp. 63–4).

[7] *Astrophil and Stella*, sonnet 4, ll.12–14. All references are to *The Poems of Sir Philip Sidney*, ed. William A. Ringler, Jr (Oxford, 1962). P.J. Croft compares Sidney's Platonism with the more idealistic, self-denying kind which appears in his brother Robert's poetry. See his edition of *The Poems of Robert Sidney* (Oxford, 1984), pp. 54–62.

Astrophil's tactics in defending the rightness of his love for Stella is to protest seriously that her marriage itself is a shameful thing (see sonnet 78), and that his own feelings cannot be put down to mere lasciviousness:

> If that be sinne which in fixt hearts doth breed
> A loathing of all loose unchastitie,
> Then Love is sinne, and let me sinfull be.
> (14, ll.12–14)

As we have just seen, in the early sonnets Astrophil employs logic to establish that the body-soul dualism turns on too fine a distinction to be able to separate the one from the other: Stella so embodies virtue that to desire her person is to engage in spiritual worship. While a Platonic spokesman such as Castiglione willingly admits that a lover of sufficient maturity and self-awareness can be trusted to tell pure from improper feelings, he would undoubtedly baulk at Astrophil's cheerful identification of spiritual refinement with bodily pleasure. Astrophil himself eventually acknowledges the strain Platonic thinking imposes on the erotic by representing desire's distress at the thin nourishment provided by the mind:

> So while thy beautie drawes the heart to love,
> As fast thy Vertue bends that love to good:
> 'But ah,' Desire still cries, 'give me some food'.
> (71, ll.12–14)

Always adept at drawing on arguments that may redound to his advantage, Astrophil as the sequence goes on seems to apply the Platonic kind of kissing which Cardinal Bembo advocates (see p. 102, above and Kraye, pp. 83–4) to broader ends. The kiss famously celebrated in the eighth and ninth decades of the sonnet sequence fuses Italian Platonism with the older *basia* tradition deriving from Catullus, sensual enjoyment acquiring a spiritual basis:

> O kisse, which doest those ruddie gemmes impart,
> Or gemmes, or frutes of new-found *Paradise*,
> Breathing all blisse and sweetning to the heart,
> Teaching dumbe lips a nobler exercise.
> O kisse, which soules, even soules together ties
> By linkes of *Love*, and only Nature's art.
> (81, ll.1–5)

As Sidney's editor William Ringler points out, these lines distinctly echo the Castiglionian Bembo's description of kissing;[8] and as we

[8] *Ringler*, p. 402.

have seen already, a kiss may be imbued with a seriousness of purpose that far exceeds the ordinary motives of delight. Yet there is no doubt from the temper of his remarks in the kissing sequence that such delight is what Astrophil chiefly aims at. For that matter, it is not entirely clear whether at this point Astrophil wishes to celebrate a kiss bestowed or merely one anticipated. Sidney draws an exceptionally fine line between presenting Stella as a willing, conniving lover of the troubadour school or as a Petrarchan woman whose concern for chastity outweighs all other considerations; and it is this latter vision of her which ultimately prevails. To that degree, despite the freedom he allows Astrophil to parody Ficinian Neoplatonism in sonnet 71, Sidney appears to endorse the aim of Castiglione's Bembo's to restore the code of honour to its original *stilnovistica* status.

Shortly following this comes the famous rupture between the lovers, whereby a bewildered Astrophil finds himself confronting the fact of Stella's sudden and hasty withdrawal: having dallied briefly with the notion that sincerity of heart condones technical adultery, she has in the event thought better of accepting Astrophil's suit. To betray the marriage bed would certainly exceed the Bembian mandate which supposes a pair of lovers for whom physical union, within marriage or without, is a far lesser aim than a love in which the body understands its proper subordination to the authority of the soul. This is indeed what Astrophil is left with as the sequence enters its final phase; feelings of desolation are mitigated by his constant sense of Stella's worth. Even though deserted, he continues to nourish hopes that Stella will acknowledge him if he fulfils a Petrarchan vow of chastity similar to the restraint practised by her. Astrophil's continuing commitment to the living Stella, which the poet seems to endorse, if we are to judge by the elegiac mood of the concluding sonnets, would prevent Sidney from responding with any warmth to Giordano Bruno's later appeal to abjure the flesh and concentrate on love as a wholly symbolic abstraction (see Kraye, p. 85 above). But this is not quite all. The drama of the final phase deepens and is enhanced by the poetry's apparent drawing on one of Plato's most famous myths, that of the figures in the cave in *The Republic*. Darkness and light constitute a carefully maintained paradox throughout *Astrophil and Stella*: though her eyes are black an uncommon brightness shines from them. Deprived of this light by her absence, Astrophil finds himself in a 'darke place' where he has recourse to false or artificial lights in the form of lesser and, as he insists to her, merely companionable women. Though no explicit reference is made to Plato's Cave (*Republic*, VII), the poetic idea seems to derive closely from it. That Stella still feels affection for Astrophil seems proved by his concluding tercet which, like John Donne in some of his lyrics (see below, pp. 112–13), offers the Platonic ideal as a means of consolation:

> Deere, therefore be not jealous over me,
> If you heare that they seem my hart to move,
> Not them, ô no, but you in them I love.
> (91, ll.12–14)

Astrophil and Stella is above all a sonnet sequence affected by the tradition of Romantic love (similar to that operating in Malory's *Morte d'Arthur*), and so it depicts a conflict of loyalties: Stella's division of feeling over her love for Astrophil and her regard for her married status, and Astrophil's sense of being betrayed by Stella and yet needing to prove his worth both in her and the world's eyes. Neoplatonism has bearing on the sequence in various ways, as I have tried to show: sometimes it is parodied by a no-nonsense Astrophil who would rather eat his cake than have it (as in sonnet 71); but it also lends itself to a finer and more poised sense of the conflict between love and duty, which is itself further refined by additional notions of loyalty and restraint. It is unlikely that the delicate mixture of bitterness and resolution which defines Astrophil at the close (desolation mitigated by a strengthened awareness of Stella as an ideal) would have acquired the form it does without the intervention of Neoplatonic ideas. Yet the closing sequence of sonnets (roughly from 87 to the end) transfers attention from Ficinian ideas of self-refinement (grasped mainly through Castiglione) to the terrain of Plato himself in a dramatic and original adaption of the analogy of the watchers in the Cave (*Republic* VII). This in turn gives a new perspective on the conventionally romantic situation of the enchained lover, whose dark and wretched plight is occasionally alleviated by perceptions of true light, of which the lady – and not some transcendental ideal – is the proper source.

SHAKESPEARE

I turn now to the intervention of Neoplatonism in Shakespeare's erotic and amusing Ovidian masterpiece *Venus and Adonis* (1593) which may have provoked a rejoinder in George Chapman's pointed and paradoxically titled *Ovids Banquet of Sence* (1595). Venus, the goddess of love, attempts to woo the young Adonis who embodies male beauty. The youth meets her suit with a somewhat arch disdain, but he also expresses a shy innocence which attracts the goddess even as he attempts to repel her. A stalemate occurs which is only broken, and then unavailingly, when Adonis gets himself killed by the boar whom he has so rashly hunted. As in the Ovidian source, Adonis is then transformed into a flower which Venus cradles in her bosom and over which she pronounces a gentle farewell elegy.

Neoplatonism is intermittent rather than systematic in Shakespeare's poem for the tone is never quite circumscribed by the kind of seriousness which we associate with Bembo's speech in *The Courtier*.[9] But it is arguable, as with Sidney, that Shakespeare's peculiar blend of tragi-comic pathos required the Neoplatonic as a refining or contributory principle. As in the growth of sophistication in techniques of painting, in the poem those few degrees' extra shading in the employment of Neoplatonic definition make for a finer balance in the play of oppositions which determine the effect. This can be seen where Venus, like Astrophil before her, makes parodic use of the Neoplatonic scheme of the senses. Referring first to the enchanting quality of Adonis' voice, Venus says:

> 'Had I no eyes but ears, my ears would love
> That inward beauty and invisible;
> Or were I deaf, thy outward parts would move
> Each part in me that were but sensible:
> Though neither eyes nor ears, to hear nor see,
> Yet should I be in love by touching thee.
>
> 'Say that the sense of feeling were bereft me,
> And that I could not see, nor hear, nor touch,
> And nothing but the very smell were left me,
> Yet would my love to thee be still as much;
> For from the stillitory of thy face excelling
> Comes breath perfumed, that breedeth love by smelling'.[10]

Shakespeare, or Venus, artfully varies the Ficinian order of the senses by introducing the poignant idea of sensory deprivation, enhancing the value of whichever organ remains. The phrase 'inward beauty', quite possibly an echo of Sidney's 71st sonnet, expresses the

[9] For an argument favouring a fuller integration of Neoplatonism in the poem, see Lennet J. Daigle, '*Venus and Adonis*: Some Traditional Contexts', *Shakespeare Studies*, 13 (1980), 31–46; in contrast, I am concerned with what Shakespeare makes of Ficino.

[10] *Venus and Adonis*, ll.433–44, in *Shakespeare: the Poems*, ed. John Roe (Cambridge, 1992).

Neoplatonist insistence on the inwardness of virtue. Venus then makes clear her allusion to the *Symposium* and its Italian adaptation in the stanza which follows:

> 'But O what banquet wert thou to the taste,
> Being nurse and feeder of the other four.
> Would they not wish the feast might ever last . . ?'
> (ll.445–47)

As this stanza shows, Venus intends not merely to vary the Neoplatonic hierarchy but to invert it. Taste is now the culminating sense (whereas for Ficino it would either be the mind itself or the mind in some combination with sight and or hearing), and this allows Venus to repeat her earlier request for a kiss from Adonis wherein, as here, the insistence on one sense's being of more value than another is challenged in the name of equivalence:

> Look in mine eye-balls, there thy beauty lies:
> Then why not lips on lips, since eyes in eyes?
> (ll.119–20)

Within this same passage Venus seems to propose herself as the Venus Pandemos of Italian Platonism in order to encourage the procreative impulse of the young man:

> 'Things growing to themselves are growth's abuse.
> Seeds spring from seeds, and beauty breedeth beauty;
> Thou wast begot, to get it is thy duty.
>
> 'Upon the earth's increase why shouldst thou feed,
> Unless the earth with thy increase be fed?
> By law of nature thou art bound to breed,
> That thine may live when thou thyself art dead'.
> (ll.166–72)[11]

As well as drawing upon her secondary role as the goddess of earthly fertility, in which, as she is quick to point out, her function is underwritten by nature's laws, Venus reminds Adonis of his destiny with the Platonic scheme: the perfect embodiment of an ideal form of beauty, his self-perpetuation through the flesh ensures the appearance of that ideal to worldly eyes (the same point is urged repeatedly by Shakespeare to the young man in the first seventeen of his *Sonnets*). The irresolvable conflict between these two embodiments of beauty

[11] The Venus Pandemos of Plato's *Symposium* is not noted for her procreativity, which is rather a Medieval and Renaissance development. See Earl G. Schreiber, 'Venus in the Mythographic Tradition', *Journal of English and German Philology*, 74 (1975), 519–35; and Daigle, '*Venus and Adonis*'.

and love at the more mundane level of attraction and dislike means that the Platonic ideal manifests itself only fitfully and has no shaping role in the poem as a whole. This said, it must also be acknowledged that the concluding pathos of the work, following the death of Adonis, owes something to Venus' recasting of his memory according to one of the ideal figures of Platonic love, Orpheus:

> 'To see his face the lion walked along
> Behind some hedge because he would not fear him;
> To recreate himself when he hath sung,
> The tiger would be tame, and gently hear him;
>   If he had spoke, the wolf would leave his prey,
>   And never fright the silly lamb that day.'
> (ll. 1093–98)[12]

Shakespeare makes use of the Platonic in order to bring greater delicacy to the terms of opposition acted out by Venus and Adonis in their frustrated love match. Like Sidney previously, Shakespeare parodies the Neoplatonic ideal, gently and comically rearranging Ficino's careful hierarchical ordering of the senses; but also like Sidney, especially where he appears to draw upon the Platonic idea of the Cave, Shakespeare, in introducing the Neoplatonic, effects a deepening of pathos which might not have been possible had the poem avoided it altogether. As a carefully applied refining principle, the poem's Platonism prevents the tone from descending to the sort of crude farce in which an improbably wimpish boy seeks to escape the clutches of a sweaty mature woman. But while ensuring that decorum never falters in this respect, Shakespeare includes enough of a hedonistic current to maintain for the poem a conventional Ovidian poise. It is quite possibly the success of his venture which induced George Chapman, Shakespeare's more straightforwardly moralistic contemporary, to manage the 'banquet' in reverse, that is, enlist the Ovidian erotic on behalf of the Platonic.

CHAPMAN

The situation of Chapman's poem is one in which Ovid overhears his mistress Corinna playing the lute and singing while at her bath. She is bathing outdoors in a pleasant, secluded grove. For the Elizabethan reader the story has the Biblical overtones of Bathsheba observed

[12] For the Platonist Orpheus, see D.P. Walker, 'Orpheus the Theologian', *Journal of the Warburg and Courtauld Institutes*, 16 (1953), 100–20.

bathing by David or Susannah by the Elders, an indication perhaps that Chapman means to set the Ovidian theme of shameless scopophilia in a more serious key. Like the Shakespearean Venus before him, though more fully and extensively, Ovid enjoys the presence of Corinna through each of the senses: first he listens to her song, then savours the odour of her fragrance, after which he surreptitiously watches her. But to show he is no sly voyeur he openly declares his presence assuring her of his good intentions. Indeed he claims a kiss (i.e. taste) to show no harm has been done. Shortly afterwards Ovid makes his final request to Corinna which is to grant him the favour of touching her; she complies by unveiling her breast. Put thus baldly, the poem may sound like a mischievous seduction piece along the lines of Ovid's own *Art of Love*; but the narrative, like Corinna's robe, unfolds with a visionary solemnity which is the reverse of licentious in tone:

> Close to her navill she her Mantle wrests,
> Slacking it upwards, and the foulds unwound,
> Showing *Latonas* Twinns, her plenteous brests
> The Sunne and *Cynthia* in theyr tryumph-robes
> Of Lady-skin; more rich than both theyr Globes.

After more description he touches her breast, which,

> made her start like sparckles from a fire,
> Or like *Saturnia* from th'Ambrosian pride
> Of her morns slumber, frighted with admire
> When *Jove* layd young *Alcydes* to her brest.[13]

As with each depiction of sensual appreciation Chapman amplifies and dignifies the context in a progressively heroic manner, the reference to Jove's and Saturnia's powerful son being the culmination. In the process sensuality is transformed into an ideal description of itself whereby, as in this instance, a particular action of touching seems to resonate with universal significance, the image of the lover's contact with the breast merging instantly with that of the infant Hercules endowed with immense strength of hand.[14]

As the poem approaches what in a classical context would be the

[13] *Ovids Banquet of Sence*, ll.950–4 and 992–5, in *Elizabethan Narrative Verse*, ed. Nigel Alexander (London, 1967).

[14] Frank Kermode finds evidence of Chapman's subtle undermining of Ovid's eroticism in the lines on Corinna's breasts (*Shakespeare, Spenser, Donne* (London, 1971, p. 115). But '*Latonas* Twinns' are the sun god and moon goddess, i.e. '*heavenly globes*'. There is nothing here to suggest irony.

moment of *concubitus* or sexual culmination, Chapman's Ovid utters a complaint about the metaphysical condition of love whereby the soul must resort to an unsatisfactory fleshly medium for its expression:

> Alas why lent not heaven the soule a tongue?
> Nor language, nor peculiar dialect,
> To make her high conceits as highly sung,
> But that a fleshlie engine must unfold
> A spiritual notion.
>
> (ll. 1,001–5)

For all its contemplation of erotic delight the poem concludes, somewhat grudgingly, by giving the body a necessary but decidedly inferior place in love's scheme. And while, like Shakespeare, he inverts the sense order as prescribed by Ficino and Castiglione, unlike Shakespeare he ends by affirming the Ficinian primacy of the soul.

Although stylistically *Ovids Banquet of Sence* must be counted as one of the most awkward of the more distinguished Elizabethan long poems, fluency and gracefulness occurring only intermittently during its progress (while many of its statements are fussily resistant to precise interpretation), it succeeds in its aim of converting the Ovid of bawdy reputation into an eloquent spokesman for the erotic as a potential expressor of virtue; and to do this Chapman draws notably on Neoplatonism. To a significant degree he differs in intention from both Sidney and Shakespeare in that he never takes the philosophical ideas lightly; but if Chapman follows a more consistent and serious Neoplatonic design than either of them, both Sidney and Shakespeare make fuller use of such ideas when it comes to including that element of pathos without which the cleverest comedy may achieve no more than witless, brutal farce. In that respect the three poets unite in turning Neoplatonism to account in terms of what it may say about the dignity of instinct and the heroic aspect of flawed human experience.

DONNE

This brings us to the Neoplatonic example of John Donne who in his *Songs and Sonets* gives us a more versatile, more original encounter with Platonism than perhaps any other Elizabethan poet. Donne sometimes uses the Platonic argument for consolation, as most famously in his poem of leave-taking, 'A Valediction: forbidding mourning':

Dull súblunary lovers' love
(Whose soul is sense) cannot admit
Absence, because it doth remove
Those things which elemented it.

But we, by a love so much refin'd
That ourselves know not what it is,
Inter-assurèd of the mind,
Care less, eyes, lips, and hands to miss.
('A valediction', ll.13–24)[15]

These stanzas draw clearly on the Platonic idea that the body is only a vehicle for the soul and that it is dispensable for anybody who has the art to perceive the soul's essence truly. But we remember, none the less, that the speaker of these lines is offering solace to his lover (possibly his wife) at a moment of tender and painful parting. In a seriously witty fashion (characteristic of Metaphysical poetry's paradoxical style) he attempts to make light of the pain which for both of them is all too material. Similarly, in another poem which strikes an even more heartfelt note of grief, 'A Nocturnal upon St Lucy's day', Donne appears moved to invoke the Platonic condemnation of flesh-centredness as a means of overcoming both his despair at having lost her and his envy of those still in possession of their lovers:

You lovers, for whose sake the lesser sun
At this time to the Goat is run
To fetch new lust, and give it you,
Enjoy your summer all:
Since she enjoys her long night's festival,
Let me prepare towards her.
('A Nocturnal', ll.38–43)

The 'lesser sun' is evidently a symbolic equivalent of the earthly Venus of Neoplatonism, but in this poem such a sun's light is felt to be inferior to the spirituality emanating from the darkness of St Lucy's night, while the unmistakably scornful tone with which the speaker repudiates the lovers' fascination with 'lust' reinforces the moral implications of 'lesser'. Donne uses the Neoplatonic framework to speak personally and enforce oppositions which in the philosophy would be kept in harmonious relation. A more extreme example of the same thing occurs in 'The Undertaking *or* Platonic Love', which

[15] *The Songs and Sonets of John Donne*, ed. Theodore Redpath, 2nd edn (London, 1983).

repudiates the flesh, especially female flesh, in the following harsh images:

> But he who loveliness within
> Hath found, all outward loathes,
> For he who colour loves, and skin,
> Loves but her oldest clothes.
> ('The Undertaking', ll.13–16)

Here Platonism combines with the medieval tradition of misogynistic satire to produce a voice of stern rebuke which again differs in its tone markedly from the accomodating accents of Ficino and Castiglione; and such a manoeuvre is in keeping with poetry's modifications and often strategic adaptations of Platonism as outlined above.

But it is in 'The Ecstasy', a poem which carefully analyses the body–soul relationship in a manner which sustains the erotic mood convincingly, that Donne makes his greatest and undoubtedly most challenging statement about the impact of the Neoplatonic on love poetry.[16] The poem describes a situation in which the two lovers sit together on a 'pregnant bank' gazing into one another's eyes. They appear to do nothing except hold hands ('So as to intergraft our hands, as yet / Was all our means to make us one', ll.9–10). Each lover's soul seems to leave the body (the title of course refers to the Greek word '*ekstasis*', meaning a standing forth) and interact with the soul of the other:

> But as all several souls contain
> Mixture of things, they know not what,
> Love these mix'd souls doth mix again,
> And makes both one, each this and that.
> ('The Ecstasy', ll.33–36)

The issuing forth and commingling of the souls appears to owe something to Castiglione's description of such a process during a chaste kiss between a man and woman who know how to love each other with propriety (see above, p. 102). Donne markedly says nothing about a kiss in developing his point about the soul's intermingling. This may be the result of an uncustomary feeling of caution with regard to so delicate a subject, but the more likely reason is that he is holding back the sensual part of his argument to the final and most dramatic phase of the poem in which an urgent appeal is launched on the body's behalf:

[16] For good summaries of the various critical and scholarly approaches to the poem, see Redpath (*Songs and Sonets*), pp. 323–7 and Merritt, Y. Hughes, 'Some of Donne's "Ecstasies"', *PMLA*, 75 (1960), 509–18.

But oh alas, so long, so far
  Our bodies why do we forbear?
They are ours, though they are not we, we are
  The intelligences, they the sphere.
(ll.49–53)

As lovers who have met each other in bodily form, the poet and his mistress 'owe [their bodies] thanks because they thus / Did us, to us, at first convey' (ll.53–4). The pertinent question is *how* should such an obligation be discharged?[17] My reading of this is that the body can and must be enjoyed but without compromising the serious attitude which is maintained from the start. Such a reading is endorsed by the authoritative tone of the decisive stanza:

So must pure lovers' souls descend
  To affections, and to faculties,
Which sense may reach and apprehend,
  Else a great Prince in prison lies.
(ll.65–8)[18]

Is this prince the soul, the body, or some compound of the two? Italian Neoplatonism would conventionally identify it as the soul,[19] but the lovers' souls, far from being prisoners, actively assist the process of liberation; and they *descend* in order to do so, whereas the normal Platonic argument would describe a movement upwards out of the body's cage. If the lovers' souls are already free and eager to assist, then the 'great Prince' still seeking his liberty must be either the body, awaiting release into a superior evaluation, or some compound of body and soul which differs from the usual idea of the transcendance of the one (body) by the other (soul). And this compound must surely be love itself, which Donne in another Neoplatonic lyric describes as needing to take or occupy a body rather than merely existing.[20] If this is the case, the subtlety of the poetic argument makes it hard to decide what weighting, if any, is being given to either the body or the soul in their reciprocal relationship; furthermore the poet's enigmatic closing statement ('. . . he shall see / Small change when we are to bodies gone', ll.75–6) indicates his reluctance to spell matters out any more

[17] See Legouis, *Donne the Craftsman* (Paris, 1928), pp. 68–9; and Gardner, 'The Argument about "The Ecstasy"', in *Elizabethan Studies Presented to F. P. Wilson* (Oxford, 1959, p. 283).

[18] It is well put by, among others, Earl Miner, although he maintains, as I would not, that the purpose of bodily interaction is to procreate the rational soul. See *The Metaphysical Mode from Donne to Cowley* (Princeton, N.J., 1969), pp. 81–2.

[19] See, for example, Bembo's own treatise *Gli Asolani*: 'egli (the soul) in questa prigione delle membra rinchiuso', in Nesca Robb, *Neoplatonism of the Italian Renaissance* (London, 1935), p. 186.

[20] 'Love must not be, but take a body too' ('Air and Angels', l. 10; *Songs and Sonets*, p. 196).

clearly. But his very diplomacy would surely mean that he is arguing for a more than usually prominent role for the body and that his purpose is to dignify the erotic rather than to eclipse or abjure it. The poem's erotic statement neither parodies Neoplatonism, as in Shakespeare's example, nor does it end by submitting to its orthodoxy.

Unlike George Chapman who at the end of *Ovids Banquet of Sence* deplores the fact that the loving soul is compelled to express itself through a physical medium, Donne celebrates the erotic as a valued element of the process. Note the different force Donne's climactic 'alas' has from Chapman's in the key moment of each poem:

> But oh alas, so long so far
> Our bodies why do we forbear?
> ('The Ecstasy', ll.49–50),

and,

> Alas why lent not heaven the soule a tongue?
> Nor language, nor peculier dialect,
> To make her high conceits as highly sung,
> But that a fleshlie engine must unfold
> A spirituall notion.
> (*Ovids Banquet*, ll.1,001–5)

Because of his success in finding an authoritative role and position for the erotic in what is normally, in Neoplatonic philosophy, the exclusive preserve of the soul, Donne is, in 'The Ecstasy', the most original and adventurous of Elizabethan poetic thinkers to engage with the Platonic mode.

CHAPTER 11

Shakespeare on beauty, truth and transcendence

Stephen Medcalf

Venus, in Shakespeare's *Venus and Adonis*, is given subtle understanding of the Neoplatonic doctrine that Beauty is an absolute quality which is conferred from on high on other qualities like pleasingness of colour and proportion, from which it is distinct. But she combines this with a simple misunderstanding by identifying absolute Beauty with her beloved. When Adonis lived, she says,

> his breath and beauty set
> Gloss on the rose, smell to the violet.[1]

While without him

> The flowers are sweet, their colors fresh and trim,
> But true sweet beauty lived and died with him.
> (ll.1079–80)

In Sonnet 53, Shakespeare picks up Venus' statement and, speaking as himself the lover of the Beautiful, transforms it into a paradoxical, but much more serious play with Platonic logic. He addresses the beloved young man as the reality behind not only Adonis, the paradigm of male beauty, but Helen, the paradigm of female beauty; not only as a pattern for human beauty, but for that of the spring and autumn; not only as a pattern for 'beauty' but also for 'bounty'. The third of these pairs recalls the sentence in which Hoby, rendering Castiglione's *Courtier* and indirectly Plato's *Symposium*, speaks of the Beautiful as 'the beawtye unseperable from the high bountye'.[2] The young man is addressed not only as if he were the Beautiful itself, but as the Good, which is in fact what Plato implies by *to kalon*, although it

[1] *Venus and Adonis* lines 935–6. All quotations from Shakespeare's poems are from *The Poems*, ed. Kenneth Palmer (London, 1960).
[2] Baldassarre Castiglione, *The Book of the Courtier*, translated by Sir Thomas Hoby, with an introduction by W. Raleigh (London, 1917), p. 360.

is inadequately translated as 'the Beautiful'.[3] Furthermore, the relation between the young man and every instance of good is underlined by the conflation for which there seems to be no parallel, of all Plato's models for the relation between forms and particular things. First the vivid, vague and pregnant image of 'strange shadows', recalls Plato's account of the relation of forms to things in the Myth of the Cave in *Republic* VII. Secondly, Shakespeare evokes Plato's logically more precise but also more difficult concepts of imitation ('counterfeit' and painting) and of participation ('In all external grace you have some part') (*Parmenides* 131–2, *Republic* X). Finally, at the end of the poem, Shakespeare reveals the logical relation which underlines them all, i.e. likeness: 'But you like none, none you, for constant heart'. In this last line, correctly stating the principal way in which the Form of the Beautiful should *not* be like its particulars, that of being subject to transience, he also gives the real difficulty in identifying it with a person. This he was presently to explore.

The uncanny alliance of mystery and logic in this sonnet approaches Plato's higher flights so nearly as to suggest that Shakespeare had been improving his knowledge of him: a suggestion confirmed by *The Phoenix and the Turtle*, which he published in 1601. At whatever time he read Plato, it would have been not in Greek, of which the evidence is he knew little, but in Latin. For as the most recent writers on his learning, the Martindales, put it, 'his "small Latin" (as Jonson saw it) would have allowed him to read Latin books if they were not too difficult, without translation where necessary'.[4] And the Latin of the most widely available translations (Ficino and Serranus) is far from difficult. It is possible that it was Ben Jonson himself who introduced Shakespeare to Plato in Latin, for they collaborated in the volume *Loves Martyr* in which the *Phoenix and the Turtle* appeared. The two had some acquaintance since at least 1598, when Shakespeare acted in Jonson's *Every Man in his Humour*, and by Jonson's own witness their friendship was in the end close. Now Jonson's knowledge of Plato was good. He later owned Serranus' edition and translation in Latin of Plato's works, and may already have owned Ficino's.[5] One of the

[3] Shakespeare may have been following suggestions from Sidney, e.g. *Astrophil and Stella*, 91. See John Roe's chapter, pp. 100–161.

[4] C. and M. Martindale, *Shakespeare and the Uses of Antiquity* (London and New York, 1990), p. 11.

[5] Jonson's copy of Serranus' edition is in the Chetham Library, Manchester. His library was fluid, suffering at least one fire, and several disposals to pay his debts (Herford and Simpson, *Ben Jonson*, I (Oxford, 1925), pp. 250–71). The British Museum's copy (C.107 K.3) of the edition of Ficino's Plato printed in Lyons in 1590 has a pencilled note, 'Ben Jonson's copy with 219 Annotations in his hand 33 Trefoil marks in his hand', though it is not clear on what evidence.

earliest and one of the latest of his masques – *The Masque of Beauty* (1608) and *Loves Triumph through Callipolis* (1630) – are expositons of Plato on love, the latter a dazzling presentation of how Love drives false followers of his out of Plato's ideal city. In his play *The New Inne* (1629) a gentleman called Lovel describes love, following the *Symposium* closely, and at times Ficino's commentary on it.[6] Now, although in this play Jonson is anticipating a new fashion for spiritual, Platonic love based on Honoré d'Urfé's pastoral romance *Astrée*, which only took hold at court with William Davenant's masque *The Temple of Love* in 1635,[7] his thought and style look back thirty years. An anti-Platonic, Lord Beaufort, comments derisively on Lovel's speeches by conjuring up Chapman's *Ovids Banquet of Sence* (compare Roe, pp. 110–12 above):

> I relish not these *philosophical* feasts;
> Give me a banquet o'sense, like that of *Ovid.*
> (*The New Inne*, III.ii.125–6)

Lovel's Ficinian lines could not be bettered as an introduction to *The Phoenix and the Turtle.* Love is, he says

> a flame, and ardor of the mind.
> Dead, in the proper corps, quick in anothers;
> Trans-ferres the Louer into the Loued.
> The he, or she, that loues engraues, or stamps
> Th'*Idea* of what they loue, first in themselves:
> Or, like to glasses, so their minds take in
> The formes of their belou'd and them reflect.
> (III.ii.96–102)

Chapman, as well as Shakespeare and Jonson, took part in *Loves Martyr.* So did John Marston. But Jonson, who had some close association with Sir John Salusbury, to whom the whole book is dedicated, is perhaps the most likely person to have put it together.[8]

The Phoenix and the Turtle is an episode in a sequence begun by someone otherwise unknown called Robert Chester. Nature, fearing that the Phoenix of the present will have no successor, causes her

6 Herford and Simpson, *Ben Jonson* (Oxford, 1938), VI, *The New Inne*, III.ii. The commentary in X (Oxford, 1950), gives some of the sentences in Ficino, pp. 319–20, although oddly with a mistaken reference. It should be Commentary on the *Symposium* II.viii. See *Commentarium in Convivium Platonis*, ed. R. Marcel (Paris, 1956).

7 Kathleen M. Lynch, *The Social Mode of Restoration Comedy* (New York, 1926), chs 2 and 4.

8 Robert Chester's 'Loves Martyr', ed. A.B. Grosart, 1878. Most of the literature on *The Phoenix and the Turtle* is competently summarised in R.A. Underwood, *Shakespeare's The Phoenix and the Turtle; A Survey of Scholarship* (Salzburg, 1974). See also P. Dronke's 'The Phoenix and the Turtle', *Orbis Litterarum*, 23 (1968), 199–222, and editions of Shakespeare's *Poems* by W. Empson (1972), John Roe (Cambridge, 1992) and Maurice Evans (1989).

union with the Turtle dove. They join in the mutual flame of love and death which Shakespeare celebrates. The story continues after him with the poems by Marston, Chapman and Jonson celebrating the appearance of a new Phoenix. It is an allegory, relating to the lives of people of the time, probably to Sir John Salusbury's family. Its detail has not yet been clearly interpreted, but it gives us entry to the civilisation for which it was created, to a world of people acting out elaborate, vivid and extreme moral parts, whose characteristic form of art is the masque. It makes it easier to understand how known and recognisable people could be seen in a dream or vision as the forms of Beauty and Truth. In this allegory, Shakespeare being given or choosing for himself the moment of suspense between the death of the former Phoenix and the epiphany of the new one, was enabled to treat once again the theme of the unique person with whose death beauty and truth have passed from the earth. He made of it a kind of divine nursery rhyme, like *Who Killed Cock Robin?*, some early version of which may have been in his mind, and discovered in it the enchanted purity which belongs to the songs of Ariel, songs that express the non-human life of an elemental spirit, an emanation of Renaissance Neoplatonism. The first five verses of *The Phoenix and the Turtle* summon up a child's equivalent of such a world, with emblematic birds in place of spirits. The anthem which follows, sung by one or all the birds, is more genuinely Neoplatonic, resembling both Ficino and *The New Inne*. It proclaims positively for four verses the mutual indwelling, in the flame that is at once love and death, of the two lovers, in whom the distinction between two and one is lost because either lives with the life and sees with the sight of the other. In the next four, Property and Reason together stress the converse truth that what looks like one is still two. Property is appalled 'That the self was not the same', Reason puns on true, 'actual', and 'faithful':

> How true a twain
> Seemeth this concordant one!

Reason admits to being unable to comprehend love –

> Love hath reason, Reason none,
> If what parts can so remain.

As a consequence of this admission, Reason makes a lament, in which Shakespeare once again picks up the paradoxical identification of the beloved with Beauty. He reverts or progresses from the paradox of Sonnet 53, in which the beloved is the Beautiful while still living, personal and particular, and makes the identification, as in *Venus and Adonis*, only in death. With the death of the Phoenix and the Dove, he says, 'Truth may seem but cannot be' (l.62) – a gnomic statement of the place of Truth in the world of appearance which concentrates a great deal of Plato. He paralles this with something that recalls what is said in *Phaedrus* 250d, that in this world Beauty alone of the forms shines 'most clearly through the clearest of our senses':

Beauty brag, but 'tis not she;
Truth and beauty buried be.
(ll.63–4)

This last line of a very Platonic verse is signalled as a Platonic allegory by its logical incompatibility on the literal level with what follows:

To this urn let those repair
That are either true or fair
(ll.65–6)

People with some share of truth and beauty, then, do exist in this imperfect world of experience. They owe their duty to the mythical place in this world where ideal Truth and Beauty, who are in heaven, are closest. There let them, 'For these dead birds sigh a prayer' (l.67). This prayer is also perhaps a lamentation for the absence of perfect Truth and Beauty, and request for their continued presence in those who pray.

The image of a contradiction of this world as representing its transcendence turns out, when one looks back, to run through the poem. It opens with an image that has perplexed interpreters, of 'the bird of loudest lay / On the sole Arabian tree', which cannot be anything but the Phoenix: no other bird has the right to be on that tree. If so, the Phoenix is calling the other birds to its own funeral. The priest it calls is the swan, who sings only when it dies. Only, and immediately, when Reason recognises that it is confounded by love, does it make its lament. It is in the moment that the creatures of this world are confounded that they sing and love: it is nature's, reason's, identity's business to transcend itself. The poem is about ecstasy, and its style is ecstatic, which does not prevent its being, as it says, tragic. The childlike purity of its language is made up of scholastic subtleties, and the nursery-rhyme simplicity of its thought is governed by paradoxes which descend from Aquinas on the Trinity, Plotinus, and Plato.[9]

[9] J.V. Cunningham, 'Idea as Structure: *The Phoenix and the Turtle*', *Collected Essays* (Harmondsworth, Chicago, 1976), 169–209.

Plato is not only the Plato of the myths. He put his philosophy forward not as a code of doctrine, but dramatically as a set of explorations, in dialogues that look like plays. Shakespeare was therefore behaving in a thoroughly Platonic way when, within a year or so of publishing *The Phoenix and the Turtle*, he tried his hand at a play in which people try to argue philosophically – *Troilus and Cressida*. That Shakespeare meant *Troilus and Cressida* to be a philosophical play is clear from the sheer quantity of philosophical statement and debate which happens in it: the Greek debate about their lack of success, which includes Ulysses' speech on degree, the Trojan debate about the continuance of the war which becomes a discussion of value, and Ulysses' argument with Achilles about the need to demonstrate one's qualities publicly. Shakespeare seems to have read Greek philosophers for these debates.[10] Kenneth Palmer has persuasively argued that the twelve lines of Hector's last speech in favour of returning Helen, which begin with an appeal to Aristotle, are so packed with arguments and ideas from Books I –V of the *Nicomachean Ethics* as to suggest Shakespeare's direct aquaintance with those books, though not with the rest of the *Ethics*.[11] The same habit of reading – hasty, brilliant, impatient, intuitive – is suggested by the impression that the dialogue of Plato's which is powerfully present in *Troilus and Cressida* is the one in which is put first in Cornarius', and Serranus' editions and in the 1602 printing of Ficino's: the *Euthyphro*.[12]

The centre of the philosophical debate in the play is Shakespeare's taking as an agonising problem the acknowledgement of a single actual person as the standard and guarantee of value, which previously he had treated as a positive insight. The problem comes to a head in Troilus' speech on seeing Cressida in the arms of Diomede, which is a kind of mirror inverse of *The Phoenix and the Turtle*. In both *The Phoenix* and *Troilus* reason is confounded by division. In both love, beauty and truth slip from our grasp. In both unity loses its rule, because in the poem two people are one though remaining two, in the play one person is, and is not, herself:

[10] Ulysses and Achilles' discussion of a book saying that a man only knows his own qualities by reflection, III.iii.94–122, may be a reference to Plato's *Alcibiades* I, where the argument first occurs: but it became a commonplace.

[11] *Troilus and Cressida*, ed. K. Palmer (London and New York, 1982), Appendix III, pp. 311–20.

[12] I.A. Richards, *Speculative Instruments* (London, 1955), pp. 198–213, '*Troilus and Cressida* and Plato'.

This, she? – No, this is Diomed's Cressida.
If beauty have a soul, this is not she;
If souls guide vows, if vows be sanctimonies,
If sanctimony be the gods' delight.
If there be rule in unity itself,
This is not she.

(Vii 136–141)

The argument goes in two directions, like an arch with its keystone at the idea of vows. The first side of the arch forms a satisfactory argument in itself. Troilus knows that it is Cressida whom he has seen: but Cressida is beautiful, and beauty expresses the soul. Souls express themselves in vows. Therefore, if Cressida breaks vows, her soul cannot be her soul: the argument could go straight to the summing up, 'If there be rule in unity itself / This is not she'. But on the other side of the arch, Troilus develops a different argument, by which Cressida cannot have been seen breaking vows, not by reason of unity of personality, but because vows in themselves have sanctimony. 'Sanctimony' is a word which Shakespeare only uses three times, all three probably within a year or two of each other – here in *Troilus and Cressida* (probably late 1602); in *All's Well that Ends Well* (*c.*1602–4) where Helena's pilgrimage is said to be a 'holy undertaking [which] with most austere sanctimony she accomplished' (IV.iii.52–3); and in *Othello*, where Iago describes the guarantee of Othello's and Desdemona's marriage as 'sanctimony and a frail vow' (I.iii.349). In each case it implies fulfilling a commitment which has religious sanctions. Troilus extends the idea: 'If sanctimony be the gods' delight . . .' He may be arguing for the preciousness of sanctimony, in that even the gods regard it as precious, or for its bindingness, in that the gods themselves validate it. The line and its ambiguity call to mind a question of Socrates in the *Euthyphro*: 'Is what is holy holy because the gods approve it, or do they approve it because it is holy?' (10a). It is an attractive possibility that 'sanctimony' entered Shakespeare's vocabulary briefly because he was trying to find a word to express the element of absoluteness in the holy, in Ficino's translation *sanctum*, and that he associated it with 'vows' because Ficino presently translates Socrates' definition of *sanctum*, 'a science of sacrifice and prayer' '*scientiam quandam vovendi atque sacrificandi*', (14c).

There is implicit in Shakespeare's line the argument of the whole *Euthyphro*, concentrated in this question. In the form, whether the good is good by the determination of God, or God is good because He loves the good, it became later in the century crucial to the Cambridge Platonists' revolt against Calvinism,[13] and it would clearly be of no less interest in the same way in 1602. In a more abstract form, whether the value of any particular thing is intrinsic, or at least partly determined by the decision of gods or men, it is what Troilus and Hector argue about earlier in the play. Hector paraphrases Socrates' argument for the objectivity of value, namely that a thing is loved because of what it is, it is not what it is because it is loved:

> But value dwells not in particular will:
> It holds his estimate and dignity
> As well wherein 'tis precious of itself
> As in the prizer. 'Tis mad idolatry
> To make the service greater than the god.
> (ii.54–8)

Here the striking use of the term 'service' of the god, another definition of *sanctum* (*Euthyphro* 12e), may owe its presence to Socrates' investigation of whether the gods gain anything from our service to them.

The person whose value Hector and Troilus are arguing about is of course the paradigm of beauty, Helen. Hector says that she is not worth the number of lives lost on her. Troilus wants to say *both* that she is worth all that and more, *and* that it does not matter whether she is or not, because value depends on the valuer, and the valuer's commitment to what is valued. Clearly what he says about her is mixed up with his own feelings about Cressida, so we are brought back to the belief that the beautiful and beloved is at the heart of value.[14]

What we find then, when Troilus speaks after seeing Cressida in Diomede's arms, is first a doctrine which has Platonic roots, that beauty like Cressida's guarantees truth to its lover. This has been put to an agonising confutation, first because Cressida, being herself divided, is the exact opposite of lovers like the Phoenix and the Turtle and second, because the commitment in love, with which Troilus tries to support the intuition that beauty means truth, is hard to continue

[13] See especially Ralph Cudworth's *A Sermon Preached before the House of Commons* (Cambridge, 1647), reprinted in C.A. Patrides, *The Cambridge Platonists* (London, 1969) and G.R. Cragg, *The Cambridge Platonists* (Oxford and New York, 1968), whose use of the the *Euthyphro* is on pp. 102 and 384 respectively.

[14] Ulysses' speech on degree may also draw on *Euthyphro* 14b, where Euthyphro argues that piety saves the family and the state, whereas impiety 'upsets all and ruins everything', while ironically his own conviction of knowing what piety is leads him to prosecute his father for murder, which Socrates probably thinks equivalent to parricide. See *Troilus and Cressida*, I.iii.109–15.

except when it is accepted by both lovers, by both a Phoenix and a Turtle. Furthermore, this doctrine is joined by a question that seems likely to come directly from Plato, whether value is intrinsic, or is imposed from outside. Shakespeare, who began in *Venus and Adonis* with doctrines derived from Plato and diffused in the poetic circles which he was then entering, has in *Troilus and Cressida* come to wrestle with the kind of problems from which Plato himself began.

CHAPTER 12

Platonism in Spenser's Mutabilitie Cantos

Thomas Bulger

Spenser's fascination with Platonism continually manifests itself in his poetry. The ideological and allegorical possibilities of Platonism continually act as a catalyst in Spenser's imagination. Within *The Faerie Queene*, there are numerous occasions where Spenser employs Platonic doctrines to suit his fictional needs; a salient example of this is in the Garden of Adonis episode (III.vi), where Spenser reflects and refracts Platonic notions of the soul and of generation.[1] Spenser draws on Platonic doctrines and assumptions in other poems as well. Most notably this occurs in the *Fowre Hymnes*, which trace the interrelationship and integration of Platonic concepts of earthly and ideal love with their Christian counterparts.[2]

Precisely where and from whom Spenser derived his Platonism is difficult to determine.[3] Much of his understanding of Platonism came from writers steeped in the Platonic tradition, such as Macrobius,

[1] The Platonic background for the Garden of Adonis episode is extensively discussed in a series of articles written by Josephine Waters Bennett and Brents Stirling. See Bennett, 'Spenser's Garden of Adonis', *PMLA*, 47 (1932), 46–80, and Stirling, 'Spenser's "Platonic" Garden', *JEGP*, 41 (1942), 482–6.

[2] The *Variorum* edition of Spenser's works attributes the 1592 English translation of *Axiochus* (then thought to be by Plato) to Spenser. Although there is not absolute certainty about this attribution, in the *The Spenser Encyclopedia*, ed. A.C. Hamilton (Toronto, 1990), Harold Weatherby states that the evidence 'weighs in favor' of Spenser's authorship of this translation, p. 77. All Spenser citations are taken from *The Works of Edmund Spenser: A Variorum Edition*, ed. Edwin Greenlaw, Charles Osgood, and Frederick Padelford, 9 vols. (Baltimore, 1932–47). *Mutabilitie* is conventionally labelled as the seventh book of *The Faerie Queene*, according to the publisher's headnote.

[3] In his seminal study, *Neoplatonism in the Poetry of Spenser* (Geneva, 1960), Robert Ellrodt demonstrated the difficulty of pinpointing exact sources for Spenser's Platonic references. Unfortunately, Ellrodt also minimises and dismisses the impact of Platonism on Spenser, a position that has since been challenged successfully. For the most comprehensive and most recent refutation of Ellrodt's thesis, see Elizabeth Bieman, *Plato Baptized: Towards the Interpretation of Spenser's Mimetic Fictions* (Toronto, 1988). Jon Quitslund provides a succinct summary of Spenser's Platonism in *The Spenser Encyclopedia*, pp. 546–8.

Boethius (whose *Consolation* was transmitted to Spenser via Chaucer's *Boece*), Bernard Silvestris, Alain de Lille (whom Spenser refers to by name in the *Mutabilitie Cantos*), and Dionysius the Areopagite (whose angelic hierarchies are mentioned in *Hymne of Heavenly Beautie*, ll.85–98). As the notes to the *Variorum* edition of Spenser's works confirm, Spenser was also familiar with the poetic and prose redactions of Platonism of such writers as Castiglione, Tasso, Leone Ebreo, and Giordano Bruno. Given the subject matter and phrasing of the *Fowre Hymnes*, it is virtually certain that Spenser read Ficino's commentary on Plato's *Symposium*, the well known *De Amore*; and it may well be that Spenser read Ficino's 1492 translation of the *Enneads*, thus making Spenser one of the first English authors to read Plotinus directly.

That Spenser is deeply versed in Platonism as an intellectual system as well as a psychology of love is revealed in what is generally agreed to be his poetic coda, the *Mutabilitie Cantos*[4], which engage the tenets and methods of Neoplatonic hermeneutics consistently, consciously, and profoundly. Where the *Fowre Hymnes* assimilate Platonic theories of love, *Mutabilitie* incorporates the fundamental principle of Platonism, its ontological gradations of the universe, as an architectonic strategy. The hypostasis of Soul is represented in the confrontation of Mutabilitie and Jove (the World Soul) in canto VI; the higher hypostasis of *nous* is personified in the numinous figure of Nature, who appears in canto seven; and the supreme hypostasis, the One above all and the source of all, coincides with the divine ineffability remarked on in canto VIII.[5] *Mutabilitie* examines how the cosmological and teleological structures of Neoplatonic thought bridge the gap between 'pagan' metaphysics and Christian doctrine; as such, the cantos stand as a positive counterpoint to Book VI of *The Faerie Queene*, which arrives at a pessimistic answer (the disappearance of Colin Clout's vision on Mount Acidale, the seeming triumph of the Blatant

[4] An argument that the *Mutabilitie Cantos* is an attempt at closure by Spenser to his unfinished *Faerie Queene* is made by William Blissett, who calls the cantos 'a detached retrospective commentary on the poem as a whole'. Blissett, 'Spenser's Mutabilitie', *Essays in English Literature from the Renaissance to the Victorian Age Presented to A.S.P. Woodhouse*, ed. Millar MacLure and F.W. Watt (Toronto, 1964), p. 26.

[5] In so organising his poem, Spenser invokes and inverts what Ficino's disciple Diacetto says is the appropriate format for a Neoplatonic hymnist: 'He sings, I say, first to the divine Henad of the sun, then he sings to the Mind, and lastly he sings to the soul; since One, Mind, Soul, are the three principles of all things'. Cited by D.P. Walker, *Spiritual and Demonic Magic From Ficino to Campanella* (London, 1958), p. 33.

Beast in the last canto) in addressing the question of the relationship of created and imperfect nature with a transcendent and ideal world. *Mutabilitie* is Spenser's final attempt to reconcile the ceaseless tension between being and becoming that permeates *The Faerie Queene*; the solutions he considers are both philosophical (the Platonic notion of emanating hypostases) and theological (the Christian prayer in the canto's concluding stanza).

The cantos open with Mutabilitie's challenge to the authority of Jove, the god who in the 'mythological grammar'[6] of Platonic commentators is regularly associated with the hypostasis of the World Soul: 'to cosmogonists Jupiter is the soul of the world.'[7] Spenser's Jove occupies a similar ontological role. Jove is 'wont to wield the world unto his vow, / And even the highest Powers of heaven to check; (VII.vi.22). Concomitantly, when arguing his case before Nature, Jove defines his function in terms identical to the Plotinian World Soul:

> But who is it (to me tell)
> That *Time* himselfe doth moue and still compell
> To keepe his course? Is not that namely wee.
> Which poure that vertue from our heauenly cell,
> That moves them all, and makes them changed be?
> (VII.vii.48)

Since the soul descends into the lower world through the agency of the planetary spheres, and since Jove 'in his principall Estate' (VII.vi.19) rules the other heavenly bodies, Spenser follows the Platonic convention of using Jove to symbolise the *anima mundi* (World Soul).

If Jove in the cantos operates as the rational governing principle of the World Soul, this raises immediately the question of Mutabilitie's relation to Jove. An answer suggested through Mutabilitie's genealogy:

> For, *Titan* (as ye all acknowledge must)
> Was *Saturnes* elder brother by birth-right;
> Both, sonnes of *Vranus*: but by unjust
> And guilefull meanes, through *Corybantes* slight,
> The younger thrust the elder from his right.
> (VII.vi.27)

In Platonic thought, the introduction of time into the universe is signified by the descent of the Titans from Saturn (Chronos). This

6 Michael J.B. Allen's term, in *The Platonism of Marcilio Ficino: A Study of His Phaedrus Commentary, Its Sources and Genesis* (Berkeley, 1984), p. 35.

7 Macrobius, *Commentary on the Dream of Scipio*, trans. William Stahl (New York, 1952), p. 158.

explains why Mutabilitie as 'Titanesse' (VII.vi.4) brings forth the pageant of the 'times and seasons of the yeare' (VII.vii.27) as proof of her sublunary powers. The Titans are also associated with the division of the One into many, as an adjective from Pico illustrates: 'we shall at one time be descending, tearing apart, like Osiris, the one into many by a titanic force; and we shall at another time be ascending and gathering into one the many, like the members of Osiris, by an Apollonian force'.[8] The conflict of Jove and Mutabilitie is therefore between two ontological equals, two aspects of the World Soul. Jove is the higher, connective, static, eternal dimension of the World Soul; Mutabilitie, its lower, disruptive, dynamic, temporal dimension. Their antagonism exemplifies the tension at the level of the World Soul between order and disorder, stability and change, reason and irrationality, ascent to the unity of the One versus descent into the multiplicity of the sensible cosmos.

Regarding this dispute in terms of the hypostasis of the World Soul explains the paradoxical quality of Mutabilitie's audacity. When the narrator describes her discursively as a discarnate, cosmic principle, she seems an unmitigated evil:

> For, she the face of earthly things so changed,
> That all which Nature had establisht first
> In good estate, and in meet order ranged,
> She did pervert, and all their statutes burst.
> (VII.vi.5)

But in actuality, she is also beautiful; even Jove finds her irresistibly attractive:

> But, when he looked on her louely face,
> In which, faire beames of beauty did appeare,
> That could the greatest wrath soone turne to grace
> (Such sway doth beauty euen in Heaven beare)
> He staide his hand.
> (VII.vi.31)

Hers is the multiple beauty of the corporeal universe which arises from the inevitable mixture of good and evil in the lower world. Plotinus notes this compound beauty in *Enneads* I.8.15:

[8] Giovanni Pico della Mirandola, 'On the Dignity of Man', in *On the Dignity of Man, On Being and the One, Heptaplus*, trans. Charles Wallis, Paul Miller, and Douglas Carmichael (Indianapolis, 1965), p. 10.

Because of the power and nature of good, evil is not only evil; since it must necessarily appear, it is bound in a sort of beautiful fetters, as some prisoners are in chains of gold, and hidden by them, so that though it exists it may not be seen by the gods, and men may be able not always to look at evil, but even when they do look at it, may be in company with images of beauty to remind them.

Mutabilitie's physical beauty proceeds from the One; and as degenerate as this process of dissemination may become, all creation retains vestiges of the ethereal and divine beauty of the One.

The peculiar digression to the Faunus episode in canto VI also becomes clear if viewed through 'Neoplatonic spectacles'.[9] This fable has always posed interpretative difficulties.[10] But the sudden transition from the cosmic saga of Mutabilitie to the comic tale of Faunus becomes more coherent if placed within the context of Spenser's Platonic preoccupations. The Faunus-Molanna tale both concretely manifests, and further extends, the principle of devolution espoused by Mutabilitie. The episode is an allegorisation of how far removed the hypostasis of matter is from the first and highest hypostasis, the One, the folly of a descent into the material world. Mutabilitie's rashness (she is called a 'foolish gerle' by Jove just before the Faunus episode) is paralleled by the thoughtlessness of Faunus:

There *Faunus* saw that pleased much his eye,
And made his hart to tickle in his brest,
That for great ioy of some-what he did spy,
He could him not containe in silent rest;
But breaking forth in laughter, loud profest
His foolish thought. A foolish *Faune* indeed,
That couldst not hold they selfe so hidden blest,
But wouldest needs thine owne conceit areed.
Babblers vnworthy been of so diuine a meed.
(VII.vi.46)

In not being silent at the sight of the perfection embodied by Diana,[11] Faunus proves himself incapable of distinguishing between the

[9] Anne Sheppard's phrase in the 'Introduction', p. 12.

[10] John Guillory's comment is representative of the critical confusion: 'We are also uncertain about the gravity of Faunus' crime, but we can give it a familiar tag: Faunus is guilty of "laughing in church". The nature of this impropriety is obscure, to say the least'. In *Poetic Authority: Spenser, Milton, and Literary History* (New York, 1983), p. 56.

[11] In the notes to his 1792 translation of the Orphic hymns, Thomas Taylor cites the *Platonic Theology* of Proclus to this effect: 'Diana (who is the same with the Moon) is so called, because she finishes or perfects the essential perfection of matter'. *The Hymnes of Orpheus* (Los Angeles, 1981), p. 126.

sensible and the ethereal. Fittingly, the wood-god is chastised by Diana's nymphs, traditional tutelary daemons of matter:

The Nymphs are divinities presiding over generations; accordingly, they are said to dwell in streams or woods, since generation is accomplished through wetness and descends to the wood, that is, to prime matter.[12]

As his punishment indicates, Faunus is not primal matter itself. Faunus is hounded in the manner of Actaeon (VII.vi.52), not only because both commit a sacrilege against Diana, but because Faunus (like Actaeon) epitomizes the rending of the One into the many. At the same time, however, Faunus avoids the fate of Actaeon, and escapes a more serious retribution:

> At length, when they had flouted him their fill,
> They gan to cast what penaunce him to giue.
> Some would haue gelt him, but that same would spill
> The Wood-gods breed, which must for ever liue.
> (VII.vi.50)

Faunus is not castrated, cannot be castrated, because he (like Adonis at III.vi) is the source of the seminal principles that give form to matter.[13] Thus Faunus lives on in the infinity of matter, which is the basis for the concept of quality-in-matter referred to by Plotinus in *Enneads* II.4 and elevated to a hypostasis by Ficino:

Quality, when it partakes of the limit, forms matter and possesses the one property appropriate to its nature. But when it degenerates into matter's infinity, it can always be relaxed in its degrees to infinity or intensified to infinity.[14]

The degeneration caused by the descent of quality into matter is reflected by the state of affairs in Ireland consequent to Diana's indignant flight:

> Thence-forth she left; and parting from the place,
> There-on an heauy haplesse curse did lay,
> To weet, that Wolves, where she was wont to space,
> Should harboured be, and all those Woods deface,
> And Thieues should rob and spoile that coast around.
> (VII.vi.55)

[12] Marsilio Ficino, *Commentum cum summis capitulorum*, in M.J.B. Allen, *Marsilio Ficino and the Phaedran Charioteer* (Berkeley, 1981), p. 134.

[13] In *Source and Meaning in Spenser's Allegory: A Study of 'The Faerie Queene'* (Oxford, 1971), John Hankins demonstrates the ties between Adonis and the Platonic notions concerning seminal principles, referring to a number of Ficino's texts for support. Hankins does not remark on the parallel of Faunus to Adonis (pp. 246–9).

[14] For Ficino's elaboration of the hypostases of Plotinus, see Michael J.B. Allen, 'Ficino's Theory of the Five Substances and the Neoplatonists' *Parmenides*', *Journal of Medieval and Renaissance Studies*, 12 (1982), 19–44.

The pervasive water imagery in this canto is a further indication that this episode represents a regression from the goodness of limit (the One) to the malignity of indeterminacy (the amorphous many). Water as an image of prime matter is a Platonic commonplace, prominently mentioned by Porphyry in *The Cave of the Nymphs* and invoked by Pico in the *Heptaplus*:

This world is symbolized by water, a flowing and unstable substance . . . Here there is an alternation of life and death; there, eternal life and unchanging activity; in the heavens, stability of life but change of activity and position. This world is composed of the corruptible substance of bodies.[15]

The plight of Molanna, who is punished for abetting Faunus, bears witness to the corrupt nature of matter in and for itself: 'When, back returning to Molann' againe, / They, by commaund'ment of Diana, there / Her whelmed with stones' (VII.vi.53).

Yet the procession from the absolute good of the One to the flowing inchoation of the many does not entail an absolute split between the highest and lowest levels of reality. Slender though it may be, there remains a sinuous thread connecting the greatest to the least. Molanna's physical deterioration paradoxically leads to a more substantial unity:

Yet Faunus (for her paine)
Of her beloved *Fanchin* did obtaine,
That her he would receiue vnto his bed.
So now her waues passe through a pleasant Plaine,
Till with the *Fanchin* she her selfe doe wed,
And (both combin'd) themselues in one faire riuer spred.
(VII.vi.53)

However imperfectly it may be realised, the longing for unity is found even in the lowest forms of matter. This impulse springs from a desire to return to the One, the third stage in the Platonic triad *emanatio-raptio-remeatio*.[16]

The outcome of the Faunus episode adumbrates both the resolution of the Mutabilitie-Jove dispute and the concluding stanza of the cantos, wherein the narrator petitions for his divine reconciliation.

[15] Pico, *Heptaplus*, p. 75.

[16] This process is described by Edgar Wind in *Pagan Mysteries in the Renaissance*, 2nd edn (New York, 1968), p. 37: 'the bounty bestowed by the gods upon lower beings was conceived by the Neoplatonists as a kind of overflowing (*emanatio*), which produced a vivifying rapture or conversion (called by Ficino *conversio*, *raptio*, or *vivificatio*) whereby the lower beings were drawn back to heaven and rejoined the gods (*remeatio*)'.

But at the close of canto VI, the dispute of Mutabilitie and Jove remains at an impasse. Therefore, Mutabilitie demands arbitration from 'the highest him, that is behight / Father of Gods and men by equall might; / To weet, the god of Nature' (VII.vi.35). Too often it is assumed that Mutabilitie in these lines is appealing directly to Nature, who does indeed appear shortly thereafter. In subsequent lines, however, Spenser is careful to preserve the distinction between the god of Nature and Nature itself. Though androgynous, Nature is consistently referred to in the feminine gender by both Mutabilitie and by the poet himself:

> Then forth issewed (great goddesse) great dame *Nature*,
> With goodly port and gracious Maiesty;
> Being far greater and more tall of stature
> Then any of the gods or Powers on hie:
> Yet certes by her face and physnomy,
> Whether she man or woman inly were,
> That could not any creature well descry.
>
> (VII.vii.5)

So it is not the Christian God the Father (analogous to the Platonic One above and beyond all being) who answers Mutabilitie's summons. Nor is this figure to be equated with medieval personifications of Nature. The narrator explicitly invites readers to compare his Nature with the Natura of Chaucer and Alain de Lille:

> So hard it is for any living wight,
> All her array and vestiments to tell,
> That old *Dan Geffrey* (in whose gentle spright
> The pure well head of Poesie did dwell)
> In his *Foules parley* durst not with it mel,
> But it transferd to Alane, who he thought
> Had in his *Plaint of kindes* describ'd it well:
> Which who will read set forth so as it ought,
> Go seek he out that *Alane* where he may be sought.
>
> (VII.vii.9)

Yet if therse putative sources are indeed sought out, a significant divergence between the medieval Natura and Spenser's creation is discovered. Whereas Nature is in most medieval literature either overtly Christian (the 'vicaire of the almyghty Lord' in the *Parliament of Fowls*) or a thinly disguised version of the Platonic *anima mundi*, Spenser's Nature is far more mysterious.[17]

The description of Nature that the poem unfolds is an intricate composite of Christian and classical concepts. Nature's ineffable radiance has both religious and philosophical import:

For that her face did like a Lion shew,
That eye of wight could not indure to view:
But others tell that is so beautious was,
And round about such beames of splendor threw,
That it the Sunne a thousand times did pass,
Ne could be seene, but like an image in a glass...

Her garment was so bright and wondrous sheene,
That my fraile wit cannot devize to what
It to compare, nor find like stuffe to that,
As those three sacred *Saints*, though else most wise,
Yet on mount *Thabor* quite their wits forgat,
When they glorious Lord in strange disguise
Transfigur'd sawe; his garments so did daze their eyes.
(VII.vii.6–7)

This comparison is suggestive rather than prescriptive. Nature's brilliance is at once akin to, yet distinct from, Christ's transfiguration. For Christian Platonists such as Ficino and Pico, the symbolic resonances of the sun as a metaphor for the emanation of divine illumination holds open the possibility of connecting Platonic concept to Christian doctrine. In Pico's words:

We can picture Christ by nothing more fitting than the sun. He placed his tabernacle in the sun, and he sprang from the tribe of Judah, whose emblem is the lion, the animal of the sun, and when Plato in the Republic calls the sun the visible son of God, why may we not understand it as the image of the invisible Son? If he is the true light illuminating all minds, does he not have his most exact likeness the sun, which is the light of the senses illuminating all bodies?[18]

The belief in a tripartite cosmos enabled Renaissance Neoplatonists to view the three primary Plotinian hypostases as vestiges of the Holy

[17] In *Renaissance Chaucer* (New Haven, 1975), p. 42, Alice Miskimin observes that Spenser's Nature here is 'far more ornate and complex than its predecessors'. Josephine Waters Bennett identifies Spenser's Nature with the World Soul in 'Spenser's Venus and the Goddess of Nature in the *Cantos of Mutabilitie*', *Studies in Philology*, 30 (1933), 163. This interpretation is refuted by Ellrodt in *Neoplatonism in Spenser*, p. 64. Guillory, in *Poetic Authority*, p. 61, also argues against those readings which equate Spenser's Nature with the Platonic *anima mundi*.

[18] Pico, *Heptaplus*, p. 163.

Trinity, wherein *nous* is the pagan equivalent to Christ as the eternal Logos.[19] As a threshold figure mediating between visible and invisible worlds, Spenser's Nature evokes resonances both of *nous* as 'the image of the One . . . as the sun's rays tell of the sun' (*Enneads* v.i.7) and of Christ's incarnation and transfiguration.

There are also distinct affinities between the functions of Nature and those of the Platonic *nous*.[20] Spenser's Nature and the Platonic *nous* simultaneously embody stasis and change. Ficino emphasises this coincidence of opposites as being central to the distinction of Soul from *nous*:

> The soul, being moved by itself, moves others, there must be something before the soul which moves others and is motionless. But the intelligence moves and is motionless; it is steadfast and always operates in the same ways . . . The intelligence moves, is not moved.[21]

As an unmoved mover, *nous* combines essence and existence, being and becoming, unity and plurality, presence and transcendence, time and eternity. Spenser accords these paradoxical attributes to Nature:

> Great *Nature*, euer young yet full of eld,
> Still moouing, yet unmoued from her sted;
> Vnseene of any, yet of all beheld.
> (VII.vii.13)

The clearest indication that Nature is operating as the Spenserian equivalent to the Platonic *nous* is in Nature's resolution of the debate between Mutabilitie and Jove. Nature's answer is articulated in terms of classical philosophy ('fate'), not Christian providence:

> I well consider all that ye haue sayd,
> And find that all things steadfastnes doe hate
> And changed be: yet being rightly wayd
> They are not changed from their first estate;
> But by their change their being doe dilate:
> And turning to themselues at length againe,

[19] A full discussion of vestiges of the Trinity is in Wind, *Pagan Mysteries*, p. 242. See also Milton Anastos, 'Pletho's Calendar and Liturgy', *Dumbarton Oaks Paper*, 4 (1948), 290.

[20] A number of medieval Neoplatonic commentators (in particular, members of the school of Chartres) linked Nature (emissary of the divine) with *nous* (the intelligible emanation of the One). In the *Cosmographia* of Bernard Silvestris, a work it is likely Spenser knew, Noys and Nature are presented as complementary entities. As Brian Stock remarks about the *Cosmographia*, 'Noys never appears on stage alone. She is virtually always accompanied by Natura'. Stock, *Myth and Science in the Twelfth Century: A Study of Bernard Silvester* (Princeton, 1972), p. 95. In *De planctu Naturae*, Nature 'coins the pure ideas of Noys'. Alain de Lille, *The Complaint of Nature*, trans. Douglas Moffat (New Haven, 1908), p. 11.

[21] M.J.B. Allen, *Marsilio Ficino: The Philebus Commentary* (Berkeley, 1979), p. 98.

> Doe worke their owne perfection so by fate:
> Then ouer them Change doeth not rule and raigne;
> But they raigne ouer change, and doe their states maintaine.
> (VII.vii.58)

Telescoping perfection and change in this way, Nature's sentence has sometimes been accused of intellectual inconsistency.[22] But these logical contradictions are excusable and indeed appropriate if Nature is regarded as the intuitive, apprehensive wisdom of *nous* that Plotinus distinguishes from discursive reason (*Enneads* V.I.II). As Rosalie Colie notes, this speech has a precise Neoplatonic import, recalling the fifth *Ennead*'s discussion of the dilation of forms from Form.[23] Nature's speech also is similar to the following passage from the sixth *Ennead*:

> The soul's movement will be about its source; to this it will hold, poised intent towards that unity to which all souls should move and the divine souls always move, divine in virtue of that movement; for to be a god is to be integral with the Supreme. (*Enneads* VI.9.8)

Seeking to return to the pure being of the One, each created being engages in the process of perfecting itself within the limits of its own peculiar nature. Nature's answer reconciles the simultaneous existence of being and becoming. In this presentation of Nature, the poem suggests a circular equation: Nature = Being; Being = *nous*; *nous* = Beauty; Beauty = Being; Being = Nature.

Canto VII closes with a celebration of the mysterious unity that reigns over the universe. Mutabilitie is chastened and subdued, 'put downe and whist' (VII.vii.59). In turn, Jove is 'confirmed in his imperiall see' (VII.vii.59), restoring the hierarchical order in the World Soul. Having reconciled the two warring oppositions in the World Soul, Nature disappears 'whither no man wist' (VII.vii.59). Nature's vanishing hints at the mystical ecstasies that Plotinus speaks of as resulting from a union with the Absolute One. Yet Nature's final words are a reminder that this transcendent harmony cannot be known, described, or realised with the limits of temporality: 'But time

[22] For instance, see Arnold Davidson, 'Dame Nature's Shifting Logic in Spenser's *Cantos of Mutabilitie*', *Neuphilologische Mitteilungen*, 83 (1982), 451–6.

[23] Rosalie Colie, *Paradoxica Epidemica: The Renaissance Tradition of Paradox* (Princeton, 1966), pp. 345–6.

shall come that all shall changed bee, / And from thenceforth, none no more change shall see' (VII.vii.59).

Until canto VIII, Mutabilitie demonstrates the compatibility of classical metaphysics and Christian theology in addressing ontological and epistemological matters. Platonism and Christianity are analogous in that they both articulate the soul's desire to return to a transcendent One. And for Spenser as well as the Florentine Platonists, Platonism is an important vehicle in arriving at an intellectual appreciation of the various dimensions of being. But all such intellectual constructs, all words, all images, are inadequate – whether by accident or design, the last canto is entitled, 'The VIII. Canto, unperfite'. Perfection in its absolute eschatological sense will always remain incommunicable and incomprehensible.

So it is that poem closes not with philosophic acceptance but with a Christian prayer; appropriately for a Christian humanist, Spenser completes his literary Platonic hymn with a liturgical Christian hymn.[24] The final stanza is not a request for a perfection of vision occuring in time but for a sight of divine perfection beyond time. Prior to canto 8, *Mutabilitie* has shown the value and validity in Platonism's ontological categories. The Christian elements Spenser introduces in his description of Nature are the first signs that *Mutabilitie* even as it incorporates the framework of Platonic thought (the three hypostases) also goes beyond this framework. But it is only at the very highest level of being that the hermeneutics of Platonism and Christianity stand apart. The crucial difference lies in the personal relationship between God and soul found in Christianity but absent from Neoplatonic conception of a transcendent, impersonal One. The intellectual solace provided by the concept of the Platonic Ones does not match the spiritual comfort of a caring and concerned creator. The poem ends unambiguously not with a hymn to the Neoplatonic One but to the God of Christianity: 'O that great Sabbaoth God, graunt me that Sabaoths sight' (VII.viii.2). The cosmic piety of the Platonic hymn is not finally a substitute for or identical to the monotheistic piety of the

[24] That *Mutabilitie* draws on the properties of the hymn is suggested not only by its content but also by its form. A tripartite structure informs classical hymns: a divine power is invoked, followed by a discussion of the god's impact on creation, ending with a prayer for salvation. The narrative unfolding of *Mutabilitie* displays a comparable pattern. This pattern of moving from Platonic to Christian hymn may be seen in Synesius, who completes his cycle of nine Platonic hymns with a tenth Christian hymn. Synesius, *The Essays and Hymns of Synesius of Cyrene*, translated by Augustine Fitzgerald, 2 vols (Oxford, 1930).

Christian hymnist. Thus, though *Mutabilitie* shows the many correspondences between Neoplatonic and Christian concepts of the soul's ascent to divine illumination, the poem also confirms the significant differences separating these two epistemologies that preclude any absolute synthesis.

CHAPTER 13

Reason, recollection and the Cambridge Platonists

Dominic Scott

The Cambridge Platonists had a distinctly ambivalent attitude towards one of Plato's most well-known doctrines, the Theory of Recollection (*anamnēsis*). (See Anne Sheppard, pp. 9–10). On the one hand they embraced a close relative of the theory, the doctrine of innate ideas, which was bound up with their laudably Platonic belief that learning is essentially a matter of drawing upon one's own resources rather than relying wholesale on extrinsic sources. On the other hand they rejected, for a variety of reasons, any literal version of recollection itself. This essay will explore what led them into something of a love–hate relationship with Platonic recollection.[1] I shall confine my discussion to those of them whose writings were most extensive on this subject, Whichcote, More and Cudworth. First, however, a note about the theory itself. It first appears in Plato's *Meno* (81a sq.), and Socrates attempts to demonstrate it by taking a slave boy and asking him questions about a geometrical figure drawn in the sand. At first the slave gives the wrong answers but after repeated questions solves the problem. At the end, Socrates insists that he never taught the boy anything, but only asked questions (85b–d). As the boy has never been taught geometry before in his life, Socrates concludes that he must have had the knowledge within him even before he entered his body: the retrieval of this knowledge is recollection. The theory reappears in the slightly later dialogue, the *Phaedo* (72e sq.) where it is bound up with the newly emerging theory of forms. Again, the soul is said to have knowledge before it enters the body, but now the objects of this knowledge are 'forms' – such as those of beauty, goodness, justice and equality – which are not accessible to sense-perception. Apart from these two passages, and a brief reference

[1] For a fuller treatment of this subject, see my 'Platonic Recollection and Cambridge Platonism', *Hermathena*, 149 (1990), 73–97.

in the *Phaedrus* (249b–c), the theory is not mentioned anywhere else in Plato. Whether or not this is because Plato ceased to believe in it is a notoriously difficult question. But whatever the answer, one thing is certain: the theory itself has become one of Plato's most famous doctrines.

WHICHCOTE

The leading figures of the Cambridge Platonist movement were Benjamin Whichcote, Henry More and Ralph Cudworth, and the theory of innate ideas played a central role in their thought. I shall start with Whichcote, concentrating on his theology, not because the views expressed are exclusive to him – they were also pervasive in More and Cudworth – but because it is in his works that they are set out with the greatest clarity. Whichcote believed that religious truth comes from two sources: one is the light of reason which is the light of God's creation, the other the light of scripture or revelation.[2] God teaches man first by instilling principles into his very nature and then by biblical revelation. The second source is necessary because man, after his fall, has apostatised from his natural principles and needs to be recalled. Whichcote describes the light of reason as being,

> connatural to Man, it is the light of God's creation, and it flows from the principles of which Man doth consist, in his very first Make: this is the soul's complexion. (*Sermons*, III, 20)[3]

Examples of these truths, or 'truths of the first inscription', are:

> good Affection and submission towards God, the instances of justice and righteousness towards men, and temperance to himself. (*Sermons*, III, 28)

For Whichcote these concreated principles flow from man's essentially deiform nature: man was made in God's image and his reason is a 'deiform seed'. In another analogy, Whichcote talks of reason as the 'Candle of the Lord', a light derived from God to direct us towards Him. (*Sermons*, III, 187; cf. Proverbs 20.27) These principles are thus natural to man, 'part of his very make' (*Sermons*, III, 52, 210, 346; IV, 58), and their naturalness is a vitally important theme for Whichcote. (*Sermons*, III, 53, 166) He stresses that nothing could be more

[2] Whichcote, *Moral and Religious Aphorisms* (1703; London, 1753), Aphorism 109.
[3] Whichcote, *Sermons*, 4 vols (1698: Aberdeen, 1753).

unnatural than disobedience to the principles of our reason or conscience. (*Sermons*, III, 142, 346) As he puts it elsewhere,

> It is not more natural for light things to move upward, and heavy things downward, than for mind and understanding to move toward God. (*Sermons*, III 347, 190)

> Nothing is deeper imprinted in Human nature, than righteousness, fairness, benevolence. (*Sermons*, IV, 43–4; cf. III, 187)

Whichcote sees reason as a seed sown by God or a 'seminal principle':

> when God made a rational creature, he made a creature more proportional to the effects of reason and so to religion than when he made any natural principle in the world: and if a man do not walk up to the principle of reason he is a monster. (*Sermons*, III, 211)

So far we have heard nothing of the term 'innate idea' and it may seem difficult to see why Whichcote's 'truths of first inscription' amount to any sort of doctrine on innate ideas. To make the connection it helps to borrow an analogy from Descartes. He talked of ideas being innate to the mind like diseases in certain families, such as gout. Whereas members of such families will only contract some other disease, if exposed to certain specific conditions they are predisposed to contract gout whatever their external conditions – even if they never touch a drop of port in their lives. Similarly, there are some ideas or beliefs which we form only if exposed to a very specific range of stimuli (e.g. that pineapples have yellow flesh). But there are others, such as the idea of God, that we are predisposed to form whatever our experience. These are the innate ideas. To be precise, it is not the ideas themselves that are innate but the predispositions to form them.[4] This Cartesian analogy helps to explain Whichcote's position. The truths of first inscription are those that all men by their very nature are predisposed to form wherever, whenever, and however they happen to live. The acceptance of these truths is natural and inevitable, and the truths that derive from reason, as opposed to those of the scriptures, command universal consent as much from heathens as from Christians (*Sermons*, IV, 109, 352–3, 436).

Although truths of first inscription are connatural to us, we fail to

[4] For Descartes' innatism, see *Meditation* III, in *The Philosophical Works of Descartes*, trans. E.S. Haldane and G.R.T. Ross, 2 vols (Cambridge, 1984), I, p. 160. Descartes draws the analogy with innate disease in *Notes against a Certain Programme*, *Philosophical Works*, I, p. 442.

live up to them (*Sermons*, III, 52), and so we need revelation to recall us to our true selves, i.e. our rational selves. (It is on this issue of redemption that Whichcote's Platonism is most explicit: in his account of man's fall and redemption he recalls the myth of the fallen charioteer in Plato's *Phaedrus* – II.172; II.160) Whichcote's espousal of concreated truths natural to man does not lead him to neglect the necessity for revealed truth because we need scriptural revelation, the second source of God's illumination (*Sermons*, I, 370–2; 380; IV, 78), to awaken and return us to the natural light (*Sermons*, III, 190). Nevertheless, in a number of passages he does give natural light priority over revelation: it has a 'deeper foundation' (III, 122), revelation being in certain respects dependent upon reason. Revelation is necessary only for the sake of bringing us back to the natural light, had we never apostatised from the natural principles there would be no need for it. Further, revelation must presuppose natural truth: revealed truth would mean nothing to us if we did not already have within us the light of reason, however dim it may be. We would not be able to understand what we were being recalled to:

> For had there not been a law written in the heart of man, a law without would have done very little. No man can prove anything to him that grants nothing: and he that knows nothing grants nothing. (*Sermons*, III, 122)

The dependence of revelation upon natural truth brings us to one of the most distinctive features of Whichcote's thought: again and again he tells us never to accept anything in religion not agreeable to reason. There must be an acceptance from within of the truths of revelation. If someone espouses scriptual truth without understanding it in the light of their own reason their religion will be hollow. It is only when revelation is referred back to reason that it can make any sense. It is not enough then for someone to be well educated and instructed in religion or to accept it because it is the religion of their culture. They must weigh up and examine that religion for themselves and only then can it be firmly rooted. Elsewhere he makes this point by distinguishing between someone who merely accepts dogma like a vessel and someone who assents to the truth because they have understood it. Here Whichcote is showing a strongly anti-Calvinist leaning. What emerges from a number of sermons is a radical disagreement between Whichcote's rational theology and the Calvinist view that man's faculties are so feeble as to preclude the use of reason almost completely from religion. To a Calvinist, it is not reason on which we should rely but the Bible. For Whichcote, man's reason is a derived light enabling him to see the truth of certain principles. Hence, man has his own contribution to make through his God-given reason. Whichcote was thus utterly opposed to what he perceived as the Biblical dogmatism of certain Calvinists (*Sermons*, IV, 142).[5]

As I said at the beginning of this section, although these views are so closely associated with Whichcote, he is not their only advocate. More and Cudworth both agree with him on the essential point that the mind of man is not a passive thing, a vessel that simply has truths poured into it, but is endowed with its own power of coming to accept moral and religious truth. In his *Sermon preached before the House of Commons* in 1647,[6] Cudworth insists that religion without the inner light is empty canting; and More's antipathy to the non-rational surfaced in his opposition to religious 'enthusiasm': the belief that one is directly inspired by God and so has no need to consult authority, scripture, or even reason: 'one man, one religion'. Like Whichcote, he saw enthusiasm as the enemy of rational consideration: it 'disposes a man to listen to the magisterial dictates of an over-bearing phansy, more than to the calm and cautious insinuations of free reason'.[7] For Biblical dogmatism substitute frenzied and fanciful conviction in one's own inspiration. But the result is the same: an unthinking and uncritical acceptance of principles which, even if they are true, can only be accepted at the most superficial level.

MORE AND CUDWORTH

Let me now turn to the philosophical aspect of innatism. More and Cudworth argued at length for the priority of spirit over matter,[8] especially for the priority of the human mind over its body and it was this that led them to espouse innate ideas. If spirit and mind are prior to matter, human thought is the product not of material bombardments on our senses but of the creative activity of the mind. The theory of innate ideas was thus central to their view of man and led them to engage in some fierce anti-empiricist polemic.

More does so at the beginning of his *Antidote Against Atheism* (1653) where he attacks the *tabula rasa* theory on the grounds that many of

[5] Compare Whichcote's third letter to Tuckney, *Aphorisms*, pp. 108–9.

[6] *The Cambridge Platonists*, edited by C.A. Patrides (London, 1969), p. 108.

[7] More, *A Collection of Several Philosophical Writings*, 2 vols (London, 1662), I, *Enthusiasmus triumphatus*, p. 1.

[8] *Cambridge Platonists*, ed. Patrides, pp. 25–31.

our ideas are not implanted by external objects but merely stimulated by them; the mind has an 'active sagacity' that, when prompted, will produce ideas from within itself. Perception does not produce the ideas as if they had never been there before in any form: it acts merely as a catalyst for bringing out those latent ideas into full consciousness. He then compares this to a musician who is asleep but is then awakened by a friend and asked to sing a song, given the opening words. 'Upon so slight an intimation' the musician is jogged into a full-blown recital.[9]

Cudworth championed the essentially active nature of the mind as a source of innate truth both in the *Treatise concerning Eternal and Immutable Morality* and the *True Intellectual System of the Universe*.[10] At one point in the *System*, as part of a sustained attack against atheism, he attempts to demolish the claim that the idea of God is an invention of astute politicians devised as a means of subduing their subjects (p. 693). After pointing out the difficulty this thesis has in explaining why the concept of God is so similar in all places, he asks how the politicians could impose the idea of God on the subjects if these subjects did not have it already. Ideas cannot simply be poured into people as if into vessels. The idea has to come from within. Here Cudworth is insisting that the human mind is not a passive thing that can be manipulated by politicians, any more than by sense-perception. It comes with its own active sagacity, and no ideas can be created except by that means, which derives ultimately from God.

There is a common strand that runs throughout the philosophical anti-empiricism of More and Cudworth and Whichcote's theological innatism. In both contexts the mind is seen to have its own connatural and active sagacity. Far from being the creature of external factors, it comes to those influences with its own natural resources. In theology the external factor is revelation acting as a reminder of our internal state. With no innate resources scripture could not mean anything to us and could produce no religion. In the philosophical fight against empiricism the position is analogous. If there were no internal sagacity all the bombardments of sense would be powerless to produce our ideas: however many similar objects we saw, we would

[9] More, *An Antidote against Atheism*, I.v, p. 17 in *A Collection*, I. As if to recall the *Meno*, More's first examples of innate ideas come from geometry, but ultimately, he wishes to show that the idea of God as necessarily existent is innate.

[10] Cudworth's *Treatise* was published posthumously (London, 1731). His *System* was published in London in 1678.

have no idea of similarity; if we had no innate idea of God, no one could lead us to form the idea. Neither the Bible nor politicians nor sense impressions will have any effect without an innate source.

RECOLLECTION AND PRE-EXISTENCE

Interestingly enough Whichcote, More and Cudworth all compare their theories of innate ideas to recollection. As Whichcote puts it, 'No sooner doth the Truth of God come to our soul's sight, but our soul knows her, as her first and old Acquaintance' (*Sermons*, III, 18). In More's analogy of the musician reminded of a tune, he talks of the soul's active sagacity being merely 're-minders' (*Antidote*, I.v.2). For Cudworth, the soul's apprehension of its ideas is like someone looking into a crowd of unknown faces and then suddenly recognising one of them as that of an old friend (*Treatise*, p. 128).[11] Here they all invoke recollection as a metaphor for the way in which, in some sense, knowledge is already in us. But metaphor was as far as they would go: recollection in its literal form is kept firmly out of bounds. An obvious reason for this might seem to be that it involves a doctrine, the pre-existence of the soul, which conflicts with the orthodox Christian view that the soul is created along with the body. We need, however, to tread carefully here. Pre-existence need not be considered inimical to the very essence of Christianity. Some Christians have believed in it, among them the church father Origen, according to whom God created all souls at the beginning of time, and all but one, by the exercise of their individual wills, proceeded to fall away from Him. Eventually, some fell so far away that they were punished with incarnation. The one soul that remained true became so close to God that it became divine, i.e. Christ (*De principiis*, II.9.6).

Now Cudworth had no sympathy at all with this position. For him, God's majesty must be realised in the perpetual creation of souls. The notion of a God who creates all souls at the beginning of time and then sits back as a spectator letting nature look after itself as if it were a godless world is at variance with His true nature (*System*, pp. 43–4). Thus for Cudworth the case against recollection was simple: it involved an unacceptable commitment to the pre-existence of the soul. But More, who also rejected recollection, must have had other reasons because he, like Origen before him, cheerfully espoused

[11] See the Preface to 'The Pre-existency of the Soul' in More's *Philosophical Poems* (Cambridge, 1647) and *The Immortality of the Soul* (London, 1659), II, pp. 12–13.

pre-existence. In his *Poems* (1647) he hazarded the view that pre-existence was a reasonable opinion; later (1659) he embraced the doctrine whole-heartedly, citing Origen among others. Yet, although More believed in pre-existence, he did not accept recollection along with it. In one of his attacks on Thomas Vaughan he argues against recollection explicity:[12] admitting that Plato was quite right in the *Meno* to point out that the slave boy's learning comes from within, he takes issue with Plato's inference from this to recollection on two counts: first, there is no perception or awareness of recollection; and second, the slave boy's achievement could equally well be explained by God's creating a soul, endowing it with knowledge of geometry and then incarnating it.

In the second criticism of recollection in the *Meno* More argues that the inwardness of learning does not have to imply pre-existent souls – another possibility is that God equipped the boy to learn. This of course is the line that Whichcote and Cudworth would take. Remember that the reason of man is the candle of the Lord; it is a God-given, hence derived light, enabling us to see the eternal truths. Recollection is thus unnecessary. The point had already been made by Augustine (*De trinitate* XII.15): making a parallel between sensible and intellectual vision he said that in order to see we do not need memory, only light; similarly for intellectual vision we do not need memory of the Platonic variety, only the divine light. So More accepts pre-existence but denies recollection: the soul in its previous state would originally have had explicit knowledge but, as its fall approached, failed to keep up its rational and intellectual activity. In its incarnate state the soul cannot remember anything of its previous state, not even the intellectual truths it once contemplated. This does not mean, however, that the soul does not have access to those truths by a route other than recollection. Both now and before its incarnation, the soul can know these truths by the divine light which accounts for its active sagacity. Recollection is unnecessary because the faculty by which the soul knew before is still intact.

More, like the other Cambridge Platonists, had substituted the theory of illumination for recollection and if we now set these two theories side by side we can see the true significance of the differences between them. In proposing recollection in the *Meno* and the *Phaedo*, Plato attempted to explain human learning by appealing to facts about the soul's past, but making no appeal to the presence of any

[12] More, *The Second Lash of Alazonomastix* (Cambridge, 1651). See reprint in *Immortality*, p. 209.

divine agent. Conversely, More explicitly excludes reference to the soul's previous history in explaining human learning and instead appeals to the continuing presence of the divine light. In as much as recollection makes no mention of a divine agent working in man, it is unacceptable to the Cambridge Platonists. For them, to overlook the presence of light is almost to deny the presence of God in man, and yet God's continued and continual illumination is at the core of their thought. Indeed, one of the most important aspects of the appeal to light as a metaphor is that it directs us to the notion of divine presence. Recollection as the sole source of our knowledge, on the other hand, would imply that God has left man to his own devices. This is something that all the Cambridge Platonists would have strongly denied. Whichcote, for instance, often talks of God dwelling in man, or man as the 'mansion' of God (*Sermons*, IV, 74; III, 212), and Cudworth's sermon to the House of Commons talks of the divine light as a living spirit.[13]

These grounds for the rejection of recollection are important for our comparison between Plato and the Platonists because they rest on an opposition between recollection and an inescapable tenet of Cambridge Platonism – divine illumination and divine presence. None of their other objections to recollection rest on a point so crucial to the Cambridge movement as this. Cudworth's argument against pre-existence, for instance, was disputed by More, his own colleague. But while they could tolerate friendly disagreement on this issue, it is difficult to see how they could have remained in the same movement if one had denied the perpetual presence of the divine light in man. Thus it is here that we find a fundamental disagreement between Plato and the Platonists, one which stems from the theological significance of their catch-phrase, 'candle of the Lord'[14].

INWARDNESS OF LEARNING

At this point it might be tempting to conclude that as far as recollection is concerned the differences between Plato and the Cambridge Platonists are considerably more significant than the similarities. But it would be a mistake to let Plato's theory drop out of the picture altogether because from another angle there is a parallel between the

[13] Cudworth, *Sermon*, in *Cambridge Platonists*, ed. Patrides, p. 108.

[14] This disagreement is specifically with the author of the *Meno* and the *Phaedo*. When we come to the *Republic* and its analogy between the form of the good and the sun, there is greater scope for agreement between Plato and the Cambridge Platonists.

two theories that touches both philosophies at their source. Consider the background to Plato's theory as it is set out in the *Meno*. Most of the exposition of recollection is concentrated into the examination of the slave-boy in which Socrates tries to show that what the boy learns comes from within: we know that he has never had the opportunity to learn these things before, and we witness that Socrates is not teaching him, i.e. not giving him the answers or instilling opinions into him. He is playing the part of the catalyst and getting the slave boy to make use of his own resources and to draw the knowledge out from within. In many respects the examination is a demonstration of what should have been happening between Meno and Socrates when they discussed the nature of virtue in the first part of the dialogue (70a–80d). Indeed, the dialogue between Socrates and slave-boy seems to mirror the earlier one between Socrates and Meno: questions are asked, answers confidently given, then a state of puzzlement ensues.

But Socrates is not simply enacting a re-run of his conversation with Meno when he examines the slave-boy: he is offering some advice to both. The slave-boy, he claims, is drawing knowledge from within and provided he continues to do this for himself will attain genuine understanding (85d). But what the slave-boy has just done is in sharp contrast to what we are told (implicitly) about Meno's previous intellectual history. Meno, it transpires, is a pupil of the sophist Gorgias, and in his brash self-confidence has claimed to have learnt the nature of virtue from his master. (*Meno* 71c, 73c, 76b, 98d)[15] Socrates uses the method of cross-examination to expose the shallowness of Meno's learning and, in doing so, also exposes the barrenness of the method by which he was taught. The method in question was that of memorising what the master has said; and it seems that Meno's teacher Gorgias was a keen advocate of it.[16] Now contrast this with Socrates' reluctance to take on the role of teacher rather than that of questioner. Aware of this difference between himself and Gorgias, he implies – less and less subtly as the dialogue progresses – that Meno has not attempted to understand what Gorgias said, but merely accepted uncritically the pronouncements of a famous name, and attempted to recite them upon demand.[17] What

[15] It should be noted that what Gorgias was professing to pass on to Meno was an answer to the question 'what is virtue?' *Meno* 95c shows that Gorgias did not claim to teach virtue itself.

[16] For evidence of Gorgias' teaching methods, see Aristotle, *Sophistici elenchi* 183b.

[17] On this see my 'Innatism and the Stoa', *Proceedings of the Cambridge Philological Society*, 3rd series 34 (1989), 131–2, especially note 20.

he failed to do was to draw knowledge from within; what Gorgias failed to do was to act as a catalyst to help his charge learn for himself. Instead he took on the role of the one who simply pours water into a vessel.

Although these ideas about education were originally Socratic in character they remained firmly entrenched in Plato's own thought, and not simply as a convenient stepping-stone to the theory of recollection. He is keen to insist upon the first theme quite independently of the second. A good example comes from the *Phaedrus* which features a paradoxical attack on the usefulness of the written word: writing can only remind us of what we already know (274c–277a). This passage is much later than the reference in that dialogue to the theory of recollection, and so quite independent of it. Now Plato's theory of recollection disappears from his works after the *Phaedrus*. The same cannot be said of the insistence on the inwardness of learning. In a later dialogue which makes no mention of recollection, the *Theaetetus*, Socrates invokes the analogy of midwifery to describe the role he will play in helping his interlocutor to draw answers from within himself as if they were babies(148e sq.). As in the *Meno*, Socrates disclaims any ability to teach his interlocutor; nevertheless, the most promising way of making progress will be for Socrates to help Theaetetus to draw ideas out from himself.

It should not be difficult to see the clear parallel between Plato and the Cambridge Platonists. For Whichcote, the true use of reason involves thinking for yourself and the use of reason is essential for an understanding of revealed truth. Without the one, anything learnt from the other is superficial. What Whichcote had to say about the deficiencies of a Calvinist education had also been said by Plato about Gorgias in his dealings with Meno. There is also a remarkable parallel between Plato's attitude in the *Phaedrus* to the written word and Whichcote's to revelation: ultimately, writing and revelation can only bring us back to what we already know. Cudworth, even if he does not accept recollection, completely endorses the 'maieutical' elements in it. When arguing against the atheistical notion that the idea of God was put into the minds of men by devious politicians, he draws upon the analogy of the midwife. Ideas are not put into men by mere words, and even if learning is not reminiscence, 'yet is all teaching but maieutical and obstretitious; and not as the filling of the soul as a vessel, meerly by pouring into it from without, but the kindling of it from within' (*System*, p. 693). In the *Treatise* the Platonic parallel is at its most explicit. In the course of another anti-empiricist argument, Cudworth claims that true knowledge is best attained when we retire into ourselves and attend to our inward notions. He continues:

And therefore it is many times observed that over-much reading and hearing of other men's disourses, though learned and elaborate, doth not only distract the mind, but also debilitates the intellectual powers, and makes the mind passive and sluggish, by calling it too much outwards. For which cause that wise philosopher Socrates altogether shunned that dogmatical and dictating way of teaching used by the Sophisters of that Age and chose rather an Aporetical and Obstreticious method; because knowledge was not to be poured into the soul like liquor but rather to be invited and gently drawn forth from it; nor the mind so much to be filled therewith from without, like a vessel, as to be kindled and awakened. (*Treatise*, p. 137)

Cudworth is really speaking for his colleagues as well here: it is in exactly the same spirit that More rebukes the enthusiast and Whichcote the Bible-canting Calvinist. They may have rejected the Theory of Recollection in its literal version, but they did espouse the ideas that gave rise to it and that were maintained even in dialogues from which it is absent; and, if it is true that for Plato himself the inwardness of learning is more basic than recollection itself, this point of agreement between Plato and the Cambridge Platonists is ultimately more significant than their differences.

CHAPTER 14

Platonic ascents and descents in Milton

Anna Baldwin

It is usual for critics to find evidence of Platonic influence on Milton mainly in his early poetry, notably in *Comus* (1634), where I too will start. Here Milton seems to use a 'dualist' view of nature, in which spirit, which is good, is contaminated by matter, which is bad. Although I will argue that he discards this view in *Paradise Lost* (written about 1658–63), I will show that he replaces it not by an orthodox Christian view of nature, but by another kind of Platonism, the 'emanationist' view associated with Plotinus, and that this vivifies his understanding of nature and of man. Though both uses of Platonism can be set in the context of the actual seventeenth-century debates about the relationship between the mind and the body, we should see Milton's use of them as largely metaphoric, ways of approaching the mysteries of nature and man, rather than offering philosophical explanations. For as Madsen reminds us: 'The only relevant question is what function do these ideas have in the poem itself'.[1]

COMUS

Plato's dualism is easy enough to find. The *Phaedo*, the *Republic*, and the *Timaeus* (all of which Milton knew), describe the soul as being imprisoned in a body driven by its own imperfect passions, and which must be rejected if the reason and intellect inherent in the soul are to survive. The body cannot help its imperfection, because it is made of matter, which is ultimately subject to an 'Errant Cause' outside God's

[1] W.G Madsen *et al.*, *Three Studies in the Renaissance* (New Haven, 1958), p. 233. Studies of Milton's Platonism include: M. Agar, *Milton and Plato* (Princeton, 1928) Ch. 2; R.B. Levinson, 'Milton and Plato', *Modern Language Notes*, 46 (1931), 85–91; D. Saurat, *Milton, Man and Thinker* (London, 1944), pp. 113ff.; I. Samuel, *Plato and Milton* (Cornell, 1947); E.C. Baldwin, 'Milton and Plato's *Timaeus*', *PMLA*, 35 (1920), 210–17; S. Fallon, *Milton among the Philosophers* (Columbia, 1991), pp. 79–89, setting the poet in context.

control.[2] Following the lead given by critics such as Jayne,[3] we can use these philosophical tenets to explain the symbolism of *Comus*. The Lady wanders 'In the blind mazes of this tangled wood'(l.180)[4] like the prisoners Plato describes in the *Republic*. The Attendant Spirit, on the other hand, has escaped 'this pinfold' (l.7), and is free to inhabit the aether which fills the space above the moon. The Lady can inhabit this purer realm in her mind, but not in her body, and though she may win the verbal battle with Comus, he has power to make her immobile. He therefore seems to represent the 'Errant Cause' which controls matter, though not the incorporeal upper world of ideas which the mind can inhabit through reason and virtue. The Lady's steadfastness in these qualities prevents Comus from turning her head into an animal's and so losing 'the express resemblance of the Gods' (l.69), that 'round shape of the universe' which the creative gods in the *Timaeus* had copied in forming the human head (44d). Her mind remains free, then, but her body is still imprisoned, and she needs the grace of Sabrina to release her from immobility (and indeed from the play-world itself).

Yet Sabrina herself seems to suggest a goodness in the material world, as 'Goddess of the silver lake' (l.864). And even Comus' animal-like attendants seem to have retained the ability to 'recognise the harmonies and revolutions of the world' which Socrates recommended as the fittest objects of study (*Timaeus* 90d). For Comus claims that:

> We that are of purer fire
> Imitate the starry quire,
> Who in their nightly watchful spheres,
> Lead in swift round the months and years.
> (ll.111–14)

The quickening rhythm of this enchanting passage certainly seems true imitation of that 'swift round' of the planets. If Comus does represent the dangerous demands and powers of matter, he is also a being who can recognise and be affected by truth (ll.261–3, 799–805), and can be led up to it by the higher influence of the Lady. If Comus has a good side, and a capacity to change, does this not contradict the

[2] See *Republic*, 507–21 (similes of sun, line and cave); *Phaedo passim.*; *Timaeus* 48a–e (the Errant Cause). Quotations from the *Timaeus* are taken from the translation by J. Warrington (London, 1963).

[3] S. Jayne, 'The Subject of Milton's Ludlow Masque', *PMLA*, 74 (1959), 533–43 and references given note 1 above.

[4] Quotations from Milton's poems are from *The Poems of Milton*, ed. J. Carey and A. Fowler (London, 1968), p. 5.

Attendant Spirit's unequivocal rejection of the earth in favour of some incorporeal marriage between Psyche and the Celestial Cupid (ll. 1002–1010)? The alternatives of earth and heaven which the masque form would separate, are in effect fused by Milton's own imagination, which valued the creativity of Comus' music as well as the rationality of the Lady's pentameters. He needed a more flexible philosophy than dualism to satisfy his ideals without sacrificing his tastes. And he needed one which was more compatible with Christianity, in which God can be incarnate, and the body resurrected in heaven.

PARADISE LOST

The alternative Milton chose in about 1656 for *De Doctrina Christiana* and for *Paradise Lost* was derived from Plotinus' identification of goodness not with spirit (wholly incorporeal), but with being (including both corporeal and incorporeal being). Only God truly exists, and so all things must emanate from and out of God, and will eventually return to Him again. This conception of *creatio ex deo* (creation out of God) implies that the material world is good in its nature, and not under the degradation of an 'Errant Cause'. Plotinus explains this at several places in the *Enneads*, often half-metaphorically:

> [Intellect] reports that he has seen a god in labour with a beautiful offspring, all of which he has brought to birth within him, and keeping the children of his painless birth-pangs within himself... one son alone of all, has appeared outside . . . But he says that it was not without purpose that he came forth from his father; for his other universe [the material world] must exist, which has come into being beautiful, since it is an image of beauty . . . [and] since it comes from that higher beauty. (*Enneads* v.8.12)[5]

This essentially monist philosophy comprehends evil as the deprivation of being or Form (so that matter would be evil only if it were formless: I.8.10). I will be turning to the question of evil at the end of this paper, but now I want to look at the Creation in *Paradise Lost* as a kind of emanationist account. For in order to describe an unfallen world, a world as God intended it to be, Milton needed a philosophy which would not lead inevitably to the Fall and the Atonement. It was precisely because Neoplatonism does not accommodate ideas of Original Sin and God's Atonement that Augustine, in his later

[5] *Plotinus*, ed. and trans. A.H. Armstrong, 7 vols (Loeb Classical Library) (Cambridge, Mass., 1966–88).

writings, had directed Christian theology away from it. (see Coleman, above pp. 27–37). In the *City of God*, he rejects the optimistic Platonic account of Creation for a doctrine of Creation out of nothing (*creatio ex nihilo*), which is both closer to Genesis and more illustrative of the power and freedom of God. In all nature only man appears to have the capacity for good, and he loses this almost entirely after the Fall, becoming even more dependent on God's grace.[6] In choosing an older and less orthodox Creation theory for his poem, Milton was evidently setting the scene for a possible alternative destiny for mankind, not dependent upon the Redemption, but upon the natural goodness of a world and a humanity which had come from God rather than from nothingness, and was all meant to return to Him. Only then would the Fall of Man come as a tragedy which could have been avoided.[7]

Milton need not have read Plotinus (though Ficino's Latin translation was widely available) to have found these ideas. They were Christianised early on by Byzantine thinkers like Gregory of Nyssa, Dionysius the Areopagite and Maximus, who had been assimilated into the Latin West largely through John Scotus Eriugena in the ninth century. His systematised account of Nature, the *Periphyseon*, opens with an 'emanationist' explanation of how all Creation flows out from God, and is destined to ascend back to Him. Adamson has demonstrated, albeit briefly, that Milton's account of nature sometimes follows Eriugena so closely as to suggest direct influence. Milton also appears to use Hermetic ideas about the creativity of matter, which he may well have got through Robert Fludd, whose *Mosaicall Philosophy* (1638 in Latin, 1659 in English) was another attempt to reconcile Genesis with pagan philosphy.[8]

At first Milton's description of Creation in *Paradise Lost* VII seems too anthropomorphic to be genuinely philosophical:

> And thou my Word, begotten Son, by Thee
> This I perform, speak thou, and be it done.

[6] See in particular Augustine *City of God*, XI.6; *Confessions*, VII (quarrel with Platonism), XI.5–6 (creation); rejected by Milton, *De Doctrina* I.7.

[7] Milton's Creation is particularly discussed in P.A. Fiore, *Milton and Augustine* (Pennsylvania, 1921), ch. 1; D. Saurat, *Milton*, pp. 113ff.; A.S.P. Woodhouse, 'Notes on Milton's Views on the Creation: The Initial Phases', *Philological Quarterly*, 28 (1949), 211–35; J.H. Adamson, Milton and the Creation', *JEGP*, 61 (1962), 756–78; J.M. Evans, *Milton and the Genesis Tradition* (Oxford, 1968); J.H. Adamson, 'The Creation' in *Bright Essence*, ed. W.B. Hunter *et al.* (Utah, 1973), pp. 81–102.

[8] Other studies of Milton's Neoplatonic sources include M.H. Nicolson, 'The Spirit World of Milton and More', *Studies in Philology*, 22 (1925), 433–52; Woodhouse, 'Milton's Views of the Creation' (citing Fludd and More). Milton may also have known Philo, *De Opificie Mundi*.

My overshadowing spirit and might with thee
I send along, ride forth, and bid the deep
Within appointed bounds be heaven and earth,
Boundless the deep, because I am who fill
Infinitude, nor vacuous the space.
Though I uncircumscribed myself retire,
And put not forth my goodness.

(VII, 163–71)

This is neither the creation out of pre-existent chaos found in the (*Timaeus* 52d–53d), nor the *creatio ex nihilo* found in St Augustine. But Milton is not being vague; he is in fact defining two kinds of emanation from God in order to support his *creatio ex deo* theory. First God creates matter (which shares His substance but has as yet no form), and then He begets His son (who shares his essence) and commands him to make matter participate in form. Kelley, in *The Great Argument*, distinguishes between Creation and Generation very carefully, and points out that the Son is made clearly secondary as a Cause:

Generation concerns the begetting of the Son; creation, the making of highest heaven and the material universe . . . Thus the Son [by whom all things were made] signified only a delegated power, a secondary efficient cause. Only the Father himself is the primary efficient cause, and only the Father, embracing all causes is the material cause of the Universe.[9]

By dignifying the substance of Creation, and reducing the status of Christ, Milton has prepared the way for his analysis of the freedom of not only man, but of all creation. Nothing could be further from the imperialist role sometimes assigned to Milton's God. All things come from Him and so all have value and, in some sense, the capacity to act for themselves.

Milton may have found this doctrine, which he worked out more explicitly in *De Doctrina*, I.7, in Eriugena's *Periphyseon*, Book I, where God is argued to be the embodiment of all the causes, including the material one, acting through Christ:

Do not be surprised that bodies are created from incorporeal causes . . . while the causes themselves are created by, and proceed from, one and the same Cause that is creative of all things. For from the Form of all things, namely, the only-begotten Word of the Father, every form is created. (I, 502A)[10]

[9] M. Kelley, *The Great Argument* (Gloucester, Mass., 1962), pp. 93–4.

[10] *The Periphyseon*, Books I and II, ed. and trans. I.P. Sheldon-Williams (*Scriptores Latini Hiberniae*, VII and IX, Dublin, 1968 and 1972). On Eriugena, see J. Marenbon, *Early Medieval Philosophy* (Routledge, 1983), pp. 58–70.

Having proceeded directly from God, chaotic matter is thrown out to its greatest distance from God, lacking even form. Its distance from God lends it freedom (as Danielson has argued),[11] and its origin from God means it has the capacity to use that freedom to return to God through generating forms (once it is assisted in this by Christ). The natural goodness of Chaos is clearly defined in the *De Doctrina*,

> It was a substance, and derivable from no other source than from the fountain of every substance, though at first confused and formless, being afterwards adorned and digested into order by the hand of God.[12]

So also does Eriugena introduce infant matter as 'the hulk of the earthly body . . . not yet decked out (*ornata*) with the divers genera and species of buds, fruits and animals' (II, 548C).

The first act which Christ performs to initiate the return of Chaos to God, is to give to part of this material his Divine attributes of form and creativity. He does this by sending his Spirit to warm and to incubate the waters:

> on the watery calm
> His brooding wings the spirit of God outspread,
> And vital virtue infused, and vital warmth
> Throughout the fluid mass, but downward purged
> The black tartareous cold infernal dregs
> Adverse to life . . .
>
> (VII, 234–9)

From this point on the elements themselves participate in creation, and this serves as a wonderful opening proof that God's creatures have the freedom to create and to ascend, as well as to destroy and to fall. It is as if Milton were anticipating the Darwinian vision of self-propelled evolution, and that Christ is like Charles Kingsley's character Mother Carey, who can make the creatures make themselves (*The Water Babies*, ch.7). To enrich the metaphor, Milton introduces some Hermetic ideas, which he could have read either directly in Ficino's Latin translation or Everard's English translation (see Hutton p.74 above) or found in Fludd. Using the Platonic conception of creation as a Living Creature, the *Hermetica* saw creative power in the Universe (or *Kosmos*) itself, in the sun, and in water:

11 D.R. Danielson, *Milton's Good God* (Cambridge, 1982), p. 48.

12 J. Milton, *Of Christian Doctrine*, Book I in *Prose Works*, ed. and trans. C.R. Sumner, 5 vols (London, 1953), IV, p. 179.

The Kosmos is to the things within it as a father to his children in that it is the author of their generation and nutrition, but it has received from God the supply of good . . . For God's Word, which is all-accomplishing and fecund and creative, went forth, and flinging himself upon the water, which was a thing of fecund nature, made the water pregnant.[13]

Fludd develops this principle and tries to reconcile it with the Bible. He affirms that although the sun contains the spirit of God which vivifies the world and carries the soul down into it, the material part of the universe in fact derives from the waters (which are one of the three primary elements, the others being light and darkness):

But the world is composed only of heaven and earth, and therefore it followeth that the whole world is made and existeth of the waters . . . and the compound-Creatures . . . namely Animal, vegetable or minerall, must in respect of their materiall part or existence proceed from waters.[14]

Milton uses both principles, the fecundity of water, and the supportive and generative power of the sun (each of which he could have accepted on a purely metaphorical level), to suggest that the Son only has to release this creative potential for the plants and animals to burst from the primary elements. Water was made first, and from it springs light (243–5) and earth:

> The earth was formed, but in the womb as yet
> Of waters, embryon immature involved . . .
> (VII, 276–7)

Having been fermented by the 'warm / Prolific humour' (ll.279–80) of the waters, the earth begins 'to conceive' (l.281) not only mountains and rivers, but plants to adorn them (l.314) and, in time, animals to enjoy them:

> The earth obeyed, and straight
> Opening her fertile womb teemed at birth
> Innumerous living creatures, perfect forms . . .
> (ll.453–5)

Christ makes the lights of heaven Himself, though retaining the fecund imagery ('And sowed with stars the heaven thick as a field', l.358), but their warmth and 'sweet influence' (l.375) further vivify

[13] *Hermetica*, ed. and trans. W. Scott (Oxford, 1924), I, pp. 189, 545, cited pp. 331–2 in W.B. Hunter, 'Milton and the Thrice-Great Hermes', *JEGP*, 45 (1946), 327–36; see also *Timaeus* 30–1, and Carey's note to *Paradise Lost*, VII.233.

[14] R. Fludd, *Mosaicall Philosophy: Grounded upon the Essentiall Truth or Eternal Sapience* (London, 1659), p. 48, quoted in A.G. Debus, *Robert Fludd and his Philosophical Key* (Science History Publications, New York, 1979), pp. 12–13, see also pp. 78–9 in that treatise, and W.H. Huffman, *Robert Fludd and the End of the Renaissance* (Routledge, 1988), pp. 105–10.

the lower elements. The waters generate fish (l.388) and the 'tepid caves, and fens and shores / Their brood as numerous hatch' (l.417–8) of reptiles and birds. Form seems to be born of matter, not imposed on it, and when God finally makes man 'a living soul' (l.528),[15] this is a phrase which has been used before of the fish (l.388). Man is special in being breathed on by God, which gives him an internal and an external resemblance to his maker, but he is not special in being composed of both material and immaterial parts, nor in being fruitful and able to participate in the creation of others (wife and children), nor in being free to develop his capacities.

It is important to realise that the birth of form from original matter is part of the return of matter to God. For Eriugena the original chaos should be described as 'mutable formlessness' which begins to ascend when it begins to participate in 'adornment and form and species' (I, 501B) passing from a kind of insubstantial matter only recognisable by the mind, into real and tangible matter. At the other end of its journey it will pass again into spirit, and this Eriugena describes in mystical language at the beginning of his treatise:

> the sound intellect must hold that after the end of this world every nature, whether corporeal or incorporeal, will seem to be only God, while preserving the integrity of its nature, so that even God, Who in Himself is incomprehensible, is after a certain mode comprehended in the creature, while the creature itself by an ineffable miracle is changed into God. (I, 451B)

It seems to be precisely this hope which Raphael offers to Adam in Book V, in a crucial passage describing an alternative ending to *Paradise Lost*:

> O Adam, one almighty is, from whom
> All things proceed, and up to him return,
> If not depraved from good, created all
> Such to perfection, one first matter all,
> Indued with various forms, various degrees
> Of substance, and in things that live, of life;
> But more refined, more spiritous, and pure,
> As nearer to him placed or nearer tending
> Each in their several active spheres assigned,
> Till body up to spirit work, in bounds
> Proportioned to each kind.
>
> (V, 469–479)

[15] Man as 'living soul' is discussed D. Saurat, *Milton*, p. 118; J.M. Hanford, *A Milton Handbook* (New York, 1926), p. 232.

There are also analogues to this passage in Plato's *Symposium*, in Plotinus, and in Ficino's conflation of the two, where the ascended soul is rewarded, as Raphael promised Adam, by heavenly food.[16] Centred as it is on an act of eating, *Paradise Lost* makes much of the metaphor of digestion, and Milton seems to use Eriugena again to describe how the normal process of digestion is from the material to the incorporeal:

> Man's nourishment, by gradual scale sublimed,
> To vital spirits aspire, to animal,
> To intellectual, give both life and sense,
> Fancy and understanding, whence the soul
> Reason receives, and reason is her being.
> (v, 483–7)

But whereas for Milton this is a natural process with a continuation – at least for unfallen man – into the supernatural world, for Eriugena it is only the elect who are so transformed. Quoting Gregory of Nazianzen he affirms

> the bodies of the saints shall be changed into reason, their reason into intellect, their intellect into God; and thus the whole of their nature shall be changed into Very God. (I, 451A)

Raphael offers the same transformation, but to all men – so long as Adam keeps God's one condition:

> Your bodies may at last turn all to spirit
> Improved by tract of time, and winged ascend . . .
> If ye be found obedient . . .
> (v, 497–501)

But of course man is not found obedient, and at the moment of Fall Milton must abandon this Platonic vision of the ascent of nature, for Augustine 'reality' of a ruined world, where man seems destined to choose evil ways until finally rescued by Christ.

It seems clear then that Milton used a Neoplatonic line of argument, taken from some such source as Eriugena's *Periphyseon* to establish the fundamental goodness and freedom of nature and man by showing them to be part of the free and good God. But what then can we say about evil and Satan? Milton is still Platonic, but in a much more orthodox way, for Augustine had taken over wholesale

[16] *Symposium* 209C–212C; Plotinus, *Enneads* III.8.1. 8; F. Jayne, 'Ficino's Commentary on the *Symposium*', *University of Missouri Studies*, 19 (1944), 120–80, pp. 161–2 (ch. VI); Eriugena discusses the Return at length in *Periphyseon* V.

from Plotinus the argument that evil is a deprivation of being, the absence of existence as well as the absence of good. Plotinus had argued this in *Enneads* I.8 (*On What are and Whence come Evils*) explaining the non-existence of evil dynamically as a falling away from Authentic Existence (God), towards formlessness, lifelessness, and darkness. The Tractate abounds in rhapsodic contradictions:

So if evil consists in privation, it will exist in the thing deprived of form and have no independent existence . . . But . . . if the privation in the soul is privation of good . . . soul then has no good in it, so then it has no life in it . . . So then soul will be soulless. (I.8.11)

Augustine works out the moral and historical implications of this in the *City of God* (particularly Books XI and XII), but the argument rests on the same premises. All nature is good, and therefore evil is a turning away from the good which is the true end of natures. He adds further that it is a turning towards itself, its own will, and so self-created:

The evil will therefore cause evil works, but nothing caused the evil will . . . For the will turning from the superior to the inferior [i.e. from the love of God to the love of self], becomes bad, not because the thing whereunto it turns is bad, but because the turning is bad and perverse. (XII.6)[17]

Milton not only develops the moral implications of these Neoplatonic premises, but also embodies them poetically. If evil is a contradiction of being, then Hell should be described in oxymoronic terms, perhaps suggested by Plotinus' definition of absolute evil as 'the place of Unlikeness' – a phrase taken from Plato and repeated by Augustine – where the soul sinks into the 'mud of darkness' (*Enneads* I.8.13).[18] If it is self-created, then Satan may be shown as the kind of opposite creator to God, making non-existent substances (allegorical personifications like Sin and Death) out of his own self-will. The two effects can be seen operating together in this description of the birth of Sin (rather implausibly described by herself):

All on a sudden miserable pain
Surprised thee, dim thine eyes, and dizzy swum
In darkness, while thy head flames thick and fast
Threw forth, till on the left side opening wide,
Likest to thee in shape and countenance bright,

[17] *The City of God in John Healey's Translation*, edited by R.V.G. Tasker (London, 1945; reprinted 1967), p. 349 (XII.6); see Fiore, *Milton and Augustine*, pp. 18ff.

[18] See Armstrong's note to *Enneads*, I.8.13 (pp. 308–9) referring to Plato's *Statesman*, 273d–e and Augustine's *Confessions*, VII.10.16. 'The mud of darkness' is also discussed by Moody in this volume, pp. 311–12 below.

Then shining heavenly fair, a goddess armed
Out of thy head I sprung.

(II, 752–8)

Satan's own thoughts of conspiracy create 'miserable pain', blindness, both 'darkness' and 'flames', and a rupture on the left side of his head which anticipates the end of the war in Heaven, when the

crystal wall of heaven . . . opening wide
Rolled inward, and a spacious gap disclosed
Into the wasteful deep.

(VI, 860–2)

The bad angels throw themselves into a 'place of Unlikeness' where that 'miserable' pain is embodied within the flaming darkness:

No light, but rather darkness visible . . .
Regions of sorrow, doleful shades . . .
O how unlike the place from whence they fell!

(I, 63, 65, 75)

Moreover this 'place of Unlikeness' is verbally self-destructive, its adjectives denying what has just been affirmed (how can darkness be visible?), and its nouns suggesting the fabulous, the unreal, the creatures of the corrupted mind:

A universe of death, which God by curse
Created evil, for evil only good,
Where all life dies, death lives, and nature breeds,
Perverse, all monstrous, all pernicious things . . .
Gorgons and Hydras, and Chimeras dire.

(II, 622–8)

It is not so much 'God by curse' (surely a mistaken phrase?) but Satan himself, who has created Hell, just as he has created Death by becoming perversely enamoured of Sin, his own image and creature. Milton is allegorising the development of evil as a series of self-reflective images, each looking back to itself rather than looking forward to the true ascent of being towards God.

The natures of the fallen angels, as Augustine (still following Plotinus) insisted, remain good, though they become corrupted by the evil will inhabiting them and so gradually lose existence:

Good therefore may exist alone, but so cannot evil; because the natures that an evil will has corrupted, though in so far as they be polluted they are evil, yet in so far as they are natures they are good. (*City of God* XII.3)

Their degeneration is shown in the poem as a reversal of the ascent of Nature from the corporeal to the incorporeal which is described by Raphael in Book v. The devils are shown becoming less divine, less rational, metamorphosed into animals, and even into the substance of Hell itself. At first their nature preserves its innate goodness, and consequently suffers from the presence of its contrareity in Hell, but gradually they become entirely at home in the location they had invented, so that they are finally what Satan had always affirmed they were – genuinely self-created. This progression is actually hoped for by Belial:

> Our torments also may in length of time
> Become our elements, these piercing fires
> As soft as now severe, our temper changed
> Into their temper; which must needs remove
> The sensible of pain.
>
> (II, 274–8)

Ultimately they will lose reason, freedom, even voice in a prophetic transformation into snakes (x, 539). And surely Milton wants us to notice the choice between Belial's waste of 'the length of time' (II, 274) which will lead only to loss, and Raphael's hope that man would use 'the tract of time' (v, 498) to ascend to God.

Sadly, Adam and Eve follow Satan's path, and learn to love reflections of themselves more than images of God, and to believe that by eating privileged food they will rise immediately to God's level, rather than the truth, which is that by slowly ascending through the levels of being they will one day share angels' food. They are forgiven partly because they repent, and partly because they were taught by another, but surely also because they had attempted only to anticipate their natural destiny, which was to attain the Platonic vision of a Return to the Author of their being.

CHAPTER 15

Platonism in some Metaphysical Poets: Marvell, Vaughan and Traherne

Sarah Hutton

There is a Platonic element in much Metaphysical poetry. Indeed, it is arguable that it is most metaphysical, in the philosophical sense, when it is most Platonic. In what follows I shall discuss this aspect of Metaphysical poetry in relation to three poets, Andrew Marvell (1621–1678), Henry Vaughan (1622–1695) and Thomas Traherne (1637–74). However, before doing so, it must be acknowledged that Platonism is often present in Metaphysical poetry only to be attacked: much Metaphysical love poetry contains a strong anti-Platonic streak. Not only is libertine repudiation of Platonic love a motif in Donne's *Songs and Sonets*, but the term 'Platonic' is used pejoratively, commonly as a synonym for 'chaste' if not 'frigid' (Cleveland, 'Antiplatonick'; Cartwright, 'No Platonique Love'). Such ridicule can be explained in part as a reaction to the vogue for Platonic love in Elizabethan love poetry and to the courtly cult of Platonic love promoted under Queen Henrietta Maria at Charles I's court (see above, p. 72).[1] One exception to the rule of ridicule of Platonism in love poetry is Edward Lord Herbert of Cherbury who, in his several poems entitled 'Platonic Love' and in 'Idea' preserves the construct of Platonic love without sacrificing the licentious intent of the poems.

By contrast with the secular poets of the seventeenth century, the religious poets of the period often found a natural affinity with Platonism. The emphasis here is not on Platonic love but on those aspects of Platonic and Neoplatonic thought which appeared to men of the Renaissance to make it compatible with, if not a foreshadowing of, Christianity. In particular they draw on Plato's teachings on the immortality of the soul. The syncretic Christian Platonism of the Renaissance finds its strongest literary expression in religious poetry.

[1] K. Sharpe, *Criticism and Compliment: the Politics of Literature in the England of Charles I* (Cambridge, 1984).

Just as in mid-century Cambridge men of moderate puritan temper and eirenic disposition turned to Neoplatonism as the philosophical handmaid (*ancilla*) of their liberal theology (see Scott, pp. 139–50 above), so also in the poetry of Marvell, Vaughan and Traherne, Neoplatonism is an important vehicle for expressing personal spirituality that transcends the doctrinal divisions of the day. While the writings of Plato and Plotinus offered a rich source of images to convey the personal spirituality of each, their Platonising accounts of the soul are all tinged with heterodoxy. I shall illustrate the connection between heterodoxy and Platonism in the reworking of the doctrine of Recollection by Marvell and Vaughan. I shall then go on to examine the rich web of Platonic allusion which underlies Traherne's extreme theological optimism.

MARVELL

Among those of his poems concerned with the soul, Marvell's 'The Garden' is his most enigmatic. The wit and word-play of the poem belie its serious metaphysical content. The one biblical reference (to Eden – stanza 8) comes second to the inverted Ovidian metamorphoses of stanza 4 and the evocation of *Rejouissance* naturalism in stanza 5. The withdrawal from the world into the vegetable paradise described here is also a withdrawal of the soul from body and of the highest faculty of the soul, the mind (or *nous*) into its own transcendent world of intelligible forms. The progress of the soul away from the many ('busy companies of men', l.4) to the one ('delicious solitude', l.16), the discarding of body ('casting the body's vest aside', l.52)[2] in preparation for the next stage of this spiritual journey, suggests Plotinus' account of the re-ascent of the soul through the various hypostases to be re-united with the One (*Enneads* III.8.1). This preparation for ascent is not explicitly described as a return to a former state, although, by reference to Plotinus, it can be read as a re-ascent. If read in this way it would suggest the pre-existence of the soul.

Plotinus' cycle of descent and return is also evoked in 'A Drop of Dew'. But here it is made clear that the anticipated journey of the soul is a return to a former state. The idea that the soul has come from God and will return to Him, is not, by itself, unorthodox. But the return is

[2] Quotations from Marvell are from *Andrew Marvell*, ed. Frank Kermode and Keith Walker (Oxford, 1990).

placed firmly within a framework of pre-existence of the soul by the striking double reference to the Theory of Recollection in the account of the soul, which,

> Remembering still its former height,
> Shuns the swart leaves and blossoms green,
> And recollecting its own light.
>
> (ll.22–4)

'Remembering' and 'recollecting' combine with other allusions to Platonism (the restlessness of the soul, the metaphor of light) to bring out not simply the Christianised Platonism of the poem, but the heterodox doctrine of the pre-existence of souls.

VAUGHAN

The Theory of Recollection and the cognate doctrine of the Pre-existence of the soul is also important for Vaughan's 'The Retreat'. This poem makes no direct reference to Platonic *anamnesis*: rather the whole poem is cast as an act of recollection – in this case of childhood innocence. It does make specific mention of the soul's pre-existence in the dominant theme of longing to return to the former state of the soul, represented by childhood ('angel infancy', l.2),

> O how I long to travel back
> And tread again that ancient track!
> That I might once more reach that plain,
> Where first I left my glorious train.
>
> (ll.21–4)[3]

These lines indicate that the 'angel-infancy' for which he longs is not actually childhood but an angelic former existence, the celestial city, 'shady city of palm trees', mentioned two lines further on (l.26). Furthermore, as Louis Martz has noted, the image of the drunkenness to describe the embodied soul, the soul in its 'second race' in next lines, alluded to *Phaedo* 79c–d.[4]

> But (ah!) my soul with too much stay
> Is drunk and staggers in the way.
>
> (ll.27–28)

[3] Quotations from Vaughan are from *George Herbert and Henry Vaughan*, ed. Louis Martz (Oxford, 1986).

[4] Louis Martz, *The Paradise Within* (New Haven and London, 1964), pp. 29–30. The analogy is made clearer in Jowett's translation to which Martz refers, since Jowett uses the simile 'like a drunkard'. Cf. Boethius, *Consolatio* III. pr. ii.

To Martz's observation it might be added that in both 'The Retreat' and *Phaedo* this image of the drunken soul immediately leads on to an account of immortal condition of the soul separated from the body. Plato describes how the soul, 'passes into the realm of the pure and everlasting and immortal and changeless . . . and strays no longer, but remains, in that realm of the absolute, constant and invariable, through contact with beings of a similar nature' (*Phaedo* 79d–e). For Vaughan, the soul's release from the body is death, but death is the return to its former condition:

And when this dust falls to the urn
In that state I came return.
(ll.31–2)

The Platonism of these poems cannot be described as the single key to their interpretation,[5] because it is blended with other elements in a patina of allusion to express an essentially Christian spirituality – albeit a spirituality that is generalised, personal and non-dogmatic, even heterodox in its implications. This fusion of Platonism with Christian piety is made possible by the fact that the Platonism on which the poets draw had already been Christianised. It is the eclectic Platonism promoted by Ficino (see Hutton, pp. 69–70 above) and propounded by the Cambridge Platonists (see Scott, pp. 139–50 above). Selective in the doctrines it emphasises, it takes for granted the synthesis of Platonism with Neoplatonism. Whether Marvell's or Vaughan's use of Platonic themes was the result of a broad assimilation from a general stock-in-trade of Platonic *topoi*, or whether it was the result of study, is impossible to say. The well-documented Hermeticism of his brother, Thomas, suggests Henry Vaughan may have direct contact with specific sources.[6] Besides, even if Aristotelianism held sway in the university curricula when Marvell and Vaughan were undergraduates, Platonism had its influential proponents in both universities, as the examples of Thomas Jackson and the Cambridge Platonists show. In some cases, interest in Platonism accompanied a revival of interest in Origen, the Christian father who argued in favour of the pre-existence of the soul (see Baldwin and Louth, pp. 23 and 61–2 above). Even if Origenist

[5] I am mindful here of Frank Kermode's caveats against distorting the Platonic dimension of Marvell by focusing on that at the expense of other elements in the make-up of the poetry. See 'The Argument of Marvell's "Garden" ', *Essays in Criticism*, 2 (1952), reprinted in M. Wilding (ed.), *Marvell, Modern Judgements* (London, 1969).

[6] A.E. White, *The Works of Thomas Vaughan* (London, 1919).

teachings never gained acceptance with the religious authorities, the interest of Henry More and George Rust certainly gave them wider currency. Marvell and Vaughan's poems of meditative withdrawal mirror their authors' political disengagement from the turmoil of civil war, and their coming-to-terms with the royalist defeat. Theirs is an unworldly, non-denominational spirituality. It is no accident that they gave expression to it by recourse to a doctrine of spiritual nostalgia for a 'happy former state', a doctrine which spelled the hope of return to former innocence.

TRAHERNE

A similar combination of elements is to be found in the poetry of another royalist sympathiser, Thomas Traherne. A dominant theme of his poetry is nostalgia for a former state of innocence and purity expressed through images of nature and childhood, recollection and pre-existence. The Platonism of Traherne, like that of Marvell and Vaughan, is not self-advertising, but transmuted by the Christian spirituality it serves to express, and the surface quality of the poems does not immediately suggest a deeply studied Platonism. But unlike the cases of Vaughan and Marvell, if we look at Traherne's prose writing we can see the extensive heritage of Renaissance Platonism that underlies his poems.

The rapturously rhapsodic character of Traherne's writing, his visionary account of the mundane and his repeated use of dominant images, particularly of light and sight, invite a mystical interpretation. Images of light and sight are certainly to be found in accounts of mystical experience, especially those influenced by Dionysius the Aereopagite. None the less, they are also features of the systematised Neoplatonic theology of Marsilio Ficino.[7] Traherne's poetry is not overtly Platonic in the sense that he names his mentors, or expounds the framework that underlies his concept of the soul. His account of recollection, for example, often seems to owe more to his own experience that to Neoplatonic metaphysics. This is particularly the case with his account of childhood experience which seems to anticipate Wordsworth's. In 'Shadows in the Water' he recounts how 'in unexperienc'd Infancy' he saw 'Another World' reflected in 'som

[7] See, for example, Ficino, *Theologia platonica*, VI.ii and iii; VII, xiii (*Théologie platonicienne de l'immortalité des ames*, ed. and trans. Raymond Marcel, 3 vols (Paris, 1964–70), I, pp. 229–37, 297–8, 321–2).

Puddle' next to where he happened to be playing. Viewing the reflections of people apparently living and moving in the water, he comments, ''Twas strange . . .'

And yet I could not hear them talk:
That throu a little watry Chink,
Which one dry Ox or Horse might drink,
We other Worlds should see
Yet not admitted be;
And other Confines there behold
Of Light and Darkness, Heat and Cold.[8]

The poem is one of many that celebrate visible creation as the outward manifestation of spiritual reality, as, for example, 'The Recovery', where he says of God's works,

In all his Works, in all his Ways,
We must his Glory see and Prais.
(ll. 21–2)

Or in 'The Improvement',

His *Wisdom* Shines in Spreading forth the Skie,
His *Power's* Great in Ordering the Sun,
His *Goodness* very Marvellous and High
Appears, in evry Work his Hand hath done.
(ll. 12–16)

Such statements are of course the staple fare of Christian prayer and praise, with obvious parallel in the Psalms. In Traherne's prose writings their Platonic undertones are made more explicit. In the *Centuries*, Traherne observes, 'Nothing can be but it exhibits a Deity' (*Centuries*, II. 24) or, more Platonically: 'The World is a Mirror of Infinite Beauty' (*ibid.*, I.31).

Although he celebrates the beauty and harmony of the natural world, things in themselves have no value: 'I *Things* as *Shades* esteem' ('The Review', ll.19) –

Things are but dead: they can't dispense
Or Joy or Grief.
('The Inference', ll.17–18)

Physical objects have value only in so far as they manifest the divine: 'You never Enjoy the World aright, till you see how a Sand

[8] 'Shadows in the Water', ll.27–32. Thomas Traherne, *Poems, Centuries and Three Thanksgivings*, ed. Anne Ridler (Oxford, 1966). Unless otherwise indicated all quotations from Traherne's poems and *Centuries* are from this edition.

Exhibiteth the Wisdom and Power of God' (*Centuries*, 1.27). It is the internal, spiritual world that Traherne regards as real:

Thought! Surely *Thoughts* are tru:
They pleas as much as *Things* can do:
Nay Things are dead,
And in themselvs are severed
From Souls; nor can they fill the Head
Without our Thoughts. Thoughts are the Reall things
From whence all Joy, from whence all Sorrow springs.
('Dreams', ll.50–6).

This vividly suggests a Platonic turning away from the material to the intelligible world.

Even in his most rapturous outbursts, Traherne's writing is remarkable for its consistent framework of ideas. Far from being wholly intuitional and subjective, it bespeaks a thorough knowledge of Renaissance Neoplatonism. His notebooks show just how studiously that knowledge was acquired. As Carol Marks has shown, Traherne was steeped in contemporary Platonism: his Commonplace Book is a collection of exerpts from Thomas Jackson, Theophilus Gale and Henry More, as well as Ficino.[9] His so-called 'Ficino Notebook' is a compilation from the *argumenta* accompanying Ficino's translations of Plato, Hermes Trismegistus and Plotinus.[10] He also made extensive use of John Everard's translation of Hermes, *Divine Pymander*.[11]

If we look at Traherne's notebooks we can see evidence of a close link between Traherne's extensive note-taking and his writing of poetry. The most recently discovered Traherne manuscript, the 'Commentaries of Heaven', now in the British Library,[12] is an alphabetically arranged collection of quotations, comments and poems, in which the subject matter of the poems is directly linked to

[9] Oxford, Bodleian Library MS, Eng. Poet. c.42. Carol Marks, 'Thomas Traherne's Commonplace Book', *Papers of the Bibliographical Society of America*, 58 (1964). See also Marks, 'Thomas Traherne and Cambridge Platonism', *PMLA*, 81 (1966), 521–34.

[10] London, British Library MS Burney 126, on which see Carol Marks Sicherman, 'Traherne's Ficino Notebook', *Papers of the Bibliographical Society of America*, 63 (1969), 73–81.

[11] Carol Marks, 'Thomas Traherne and Hermes Trismegistus', *Renaissance News*, 19 (1966), 118–31.

[12] 'Commentaries of Heaven. Wherein the Mysteries of Felicitie are opened, and All Things Discovered to be Objects of Happiness', London, British Library MS Additional 63054. I am grateful to the British Library Board for permission to quote from this manuscript. See Alan Pritchard, 'Traherne's "Commentaries of Heaven"', *University of Toronto Quarterly*, 53 (1983), 1–35; J.J. Smith, 'Thomas Traherne from his Unpublished Manuscripts', in A.M. Allchin *et al.*, *Profitable Wonders: Aspects of Thomas Traherne* (Oxford, 1989). *Commentaries of Heaven. The Poems*, ed. D.D.C. Chambers (Salzburg, 1989) prints the poems from the manuscript, but, unfortunately, without the prose into which they are embedded in the manuscript.

the content of the prose passages. Although there is no entry on Plato because only the entries for letter A and some of B survive, it is possible to extract a good deal of information on Plato from entries on other subjects, especially the entry on Aristotle, which includes 'A Comparison of Aristotle and Plato'. Much of this is exerpted from one of Traherne's favourite sources, Theophilus Gale's *Court of the Gentiles*. Of course, the notebooks by themselves are not necessarily a sure guide to Traherne's acceptance of their content,[13] especially since in *Christian Ethicks* he exhibits a measure of caution about the heathen philosophy. He notes that 'The Heathens who invented the name Ethicks, were very short in the Knowledge of Mans End' (*Christian Ethicks*, p. 14) and affirms that, 'The best actions of the prophaner Heathen fell under the notion of *Dead* Works' (*Christian Ethicks*, p.61). Even the writings attributed to Hermes Trismegistus, from which Traherne drew in both *Christian Ethicks* and *Centuries*, are not above criticism: Traherne conjectures, in the former, that on the matter of the immortality of the soul, Trismegistus 'did not understand the end (or at least not clearly) for which it was implanted'. (*Christian Ethicks*, p. 226). This kind of reserve about the value of pagan philosophy in general and of Platonism in particular, is to be found among other English Platonists, notably Jackson and Gale. It has its roots in the early Christian debates about the compatibility of Plato's teachings with those of the church (see Coleman and Baldwin, pp.21–37 above), a debate which was reopened in the fifteenth century with the humanist interest in Plato (see above, pp. 68 and 77).

These reservations about pagan philosophy notwithstanding, Traherne appears to hold Plato himself in high esteem. Although he does not name Plato among 'the more Knowing and Learned' heathens whom he commends for their 'Conscience of Sin' (*Christian Ethicks*, p. 126), neither does he name Plato in his strictures about heathen philosophy. Traherne's high valuation of Plato can be seen in his 'Commentaries of Heaven', in spite of their being no extant entry on Plato. Both the entry on Aristotle and the accompanying poem are remarkable for their acknowledgement of Aristotle as a natural philosopher, 'ye Greatest Philosopher in nature' (fol. 125^{v}). Traherne praises Aristotle as the founder of many branches of philosophy:

[13] Note-taking can, after all, indicate a negative intent. There is the added problem that a good number of the notes are made in the hand of an amanuensis, which means one must be cautious about inferring Traherne's acceptance of the passages recorded.

'father of Ethicks, Oeconomicks, Politicks, Rhetorick, Logick, Arithmetick, Astronomy, Astrologie, Geographie &c.', the 'Benefit' of which 'is unspeakable and endless'. Although Aristotle is therefore like the sun to all nations, 'diffused as a Blessing', Traherne notes his greatest failing as being his neglect of divinity. 'Learning is', Traherne insists

> A Sacred Heavenly Flame
> That shining for us upon Earth by Night
> Restores the World unto its Ancient Light
> The native characters of Bliss, that were
> Engraven in the Soul.
>
> (ll.6–10)[14]

Although useful, the compass of Aristotelian philosophy fails to include 'Divinitie':

> Transcendent Metaphysicks soar, abov
> The reach of Physicks, to Eternal Lov,
> Discovers GOD, and brings the Angels down
> Makes known the Soul, and what it shews doth crown.
> It walks among Invisibles.
>
> (ll.45–9)

This 'Poeticall Reflection' on Aristotle's philosophy which accompanies the prose entry does not mention Plato. Even so his preference for Plato is implicit in his reference to the doctrine of Innate Ideas when he describes the key to happiness as innate, 'engraven in the Soul'. His admiration of Plato is made explicit in the 'Comparison of Aristotle and Plato' which precedes the poem. This makes clear that 'comparing y^{m} in Metaphysicks & Divine Contemplations, 'tis evident y^{t} Aristotle was far inferior to Plato'. From his acquaintance with Jewish traditions (here Traherne is following Gale), Plato 'obtained great Notices of Divine Mysteries, especialy such as Related to ye Origene of ye Univers, ye Spiritual Nature & Perfection of GOD, ye Immortality of ye Soul &c.' (fol. 129^{v}) Indeed Traherne condemns Aristotle for having repudiated or adulterated 'ye more sublime & Divine of Plato's Traditions' (fol. 128^{v}). Furthermore, in an earlier entry, 'Amendment', Traherne singles out for praise Plato's teacher, Socrates, because he 'did upon design omit natural philosophie wch toucheth visible & material Beings; y^{t} he might make men acquainted

[14] 'Aristotle's Philosophie', in Thomas Traherne, *Commentaries*, ed. Chambers, p. 76.

wth Spiritual & Invisible Things'. (fol. 91[r]). Although it is composed almost entirely of extracts from others, Traherne's 'Commonplace Book' confirms the picture of Plato to be gleaned from 'Commentaries' of Heaven: Plato is metaphysician and moralist par excellence, with profound insight into the mysteries of divinity.[15]

Just as Ficino's Platonic theology entails an eclectic blend of selective elements of Platonic and Neoplatonic philosophy so Traherne displays the same ability to read his sources selectively. It is in this vein that he defends the *Pimander* of Hermes Trismegistus:

> This is the Philosophy of the ancient Heathen: wherein though there be some Errors, yet he was guided to it by a mighty sence of the interiour Excellency of the Soul of Man, and the boldness he assumes is not profane, but that it is countenanced here and there in the Holy Scriptures. (*Christian Ethicks*, p. 226)

Thus a Christian reading justifies recognising prefigurations of Christian truth in the *Pimander*. Such a reading in turn justifies the use of Hermes as a pagan witness of that truth, even though he may be guilty of 'some Errors'. Traherne's writings abound in selective readings of this kind. Occasionally he acknowledges the source of his borrowings but more often these can be recognised as adopted and adapted from a general stock in trade of Platonic and Neoplatonic doctrines and metaphors. Perhaps the important example is Plato's analogy between the soul and the faculty of sight. In *Republic* VI, he writes that when the eyes

> are directed upon objects illumined by the sun, they see clearly, and vision appears to reside in these same eyes . . . Apply this comparison to the soul also in this way. When it is firmly fixed on the domain where truth and reality shine resplendent it apprehends and knows them and appears to posses reason. (*Republic* 509d)

The same analogy occurs repeatedly in Traherne's poetry and prose writings. On one occasion he names Plato as the source, although he does not give a specific reference to *Republic* VI:

> *Plato* makes him [God] the very *Light* of the understanding, and affirms, that as three Things are necessary to *Vision*, the Eye rightly prepared, the object conveniently seated, and Light to convey the *Idea* to the Eye; so there are three things required to compleat and perfect Intelligence, an understanding Eye, an Intelligible Object, and a Light intelligible in which to conceive it. Which last is GOD. (*Christian Ethicks*, p.41)[16]

[15] Oxford, Bodleian Library MS Eng. Poet c. 42, fol. 77[v], and passim. See Marks, 'Thomas Traherne's Commonplace Book'.

[16] A longer version of the same passage is recorded in 'Select Meditations', III.16: see Traherne,

The analogy between the eye and the soul is, of course, developed by Plotinus (*Enneads* I. 6. 9; V. 3. 8–9; V. 6. 4) and used extensively by Hermes Trismegistus, through both of whom it became an important metaphor in Ficino.[17] Traherne was acquainted with the writings of these latter three, in whom the recurrence of the image undoubtedly reinforced this selective reading of Plato. The image recurs many times in Traherne's poetry (e.g. 'The Preparative', 'The Vision', 'Sight', 'An Infant-Ey'). In 'Commentaries of Heaven', he says of 'A Soul in Act' that in it 'Objects shine to many Eys / In a Diviner Light' ('Act', ll.46–7, *Commentaries*). Connected with this is the image of the soul as the mirror of the divine. 'In ye Glass of His [man's] Abilities He may see the Nature of GOD, as ye Sun in a Mirror' ('Abilitie', 'Commentaries', fol. 7^{r}). 'A Soul in Act' is 'Image and Mirror of Himself [God]' ('Act', III, l.53, *Commentaries*). In 'Apprehension, he describes that faculty as 'Thou Map and Mirror of Eternitie' (l. 40, *Commentaries*, p. 71).[18] In 'Application', where in accordance with Plato, God's mind is both the divine archtype, 'Prototype . . . Original and Pattern' of the poet's mind, the mirror image is reversed: the divine mind is also its mirror (ll.4–6, *Commentaries*, p. 70). Linked with these are metaphors of light:

> The Soul of Man was made an Endles Sphere
> Of Pure and Comprehensive Light . . .
> ('Affinity', ll.7–8)

This image of the soul as an all-containing, shining sphere recalls Plotinus *Enneads* V.8.9 ('Let there be, then, in the soul a shining imagination of a sphere, having everything within it either moving or standing still'). In 'All in All', the soul released from the body is made 'all Pure power / Being made all Life itself, an Endless Bower of Immaterial Light' (ll.26–7, *Commentaries*, p. 56). This image too echoes Plotinus' description of the soul from which the body has been stripped away which 'apprehends the eternal by its eternity . . . having become an intelligible universe full of light, illuminated by the truth from the Good' (*Enneads* IV.7.10; cf. *Phaedrus*, 250c). The sun 'is an Emblem of God' (*Christian Ethicks*, p. 140). In nature it is a

Christian Ethicks (1675), ed. C.L. Marks and G.R. Guffrey (Ithaca, 1968), note for p. 41, ll.25–6.

[17] See, for example, *Théologie platonicienne*, I. p. 68–9. Compare Plotinus, *Enneads*, IV.3.18.

[18] Compare, 'Thoughts I': 'As in a Mirror Clear, / Old Objects I / Far distant do even now descrie' (ll.15–17); 'Ye hidden nectars': 'Ye Images of Joy that in me Dwell' (I, ii, 5). 'The powers of ye Soul . . . in these as in a Mirror the face of GOD is seen' (Abilitie) – God/Soul are 'many mirrors reflecting sun ('Assimilation') – Thought is the mirror of God: 'The Soul thus Thinking is a Compleat Act In wch as in a Glass you may see ye Deitie'.

reminder of God: 'To see ye Sun is a prospect of Exaltation y^{t} makes Beholder Acquainted with GOD! It fills him with Ideas of His Life & Goodness' ('Accident', 'Commentaries', fol. 20^{v}). But the sun is also a metaphysical metaphor of the soul, 'Its Beams are Accidents of another Kind: even living Rays & Feeling Appearances wch tho they Shine not wth Material Lustre like Splendor to Ey; are More Noble & Invisible, Carrying ye Benefit of other, filling ye Spiritual World, seating its Glories, & ye Glories of ye Sun in ye Soul' ('Commentaries', fol. 20^{v}).

In the poem 'Sight' (*Poems*, p.122) the images of sight, light and reflection are brought together to contrast the external, outward world of sense, viewed with the 'Two Luminaries in my Flesh . . . Those Eys of Sense' and the inward landscape of invisibles made visible by the invisible eye of the mind.

> I own it was
> A Looking-Glass
> Of signal Worth; wherin
> More than mine Eys
> Could see or prize,
> Such Things as Virtues win,
> Life, Joy, Lov, Peace, appear'd: a Light
> Which to my Sight
> Did Objects represent
> So excellent;
> That I no more without the same can see
> Than Beasts that have no tru Felicity.
> (ll. 49–60)

The image-cluster of light, vision and reflection, echoing as it does biblical images (e.g. Psalms xxxvi, 9; John i, 4–7 & viii 12; 1 Corinthians xiii, 12) are appropriate for Christian meditations on the human soul and its relationship to God and His creation. Understood Neoplatonically they bring epistemological and ontological significance to a spiritual metaphor. In Plato, Plotinus and Ficino they are important for explaining both how the soul derives from God and how it may participate in the divine. In Neoplatonic perspective the epistemological connotations of the eye image are unmistakable, pointing to Traherne's central concern with the nature and function of the soul. This is made clear at the opening of 'An Infant Ey' in which light figures as the light of knowledge, and the innocent eye had god-like powers of insight:

A simple Light from all Contagion free,
A Beam that's purely Spiritual, an Ey
That's altogether Virgin, Things doth see
Ev'n like unto the Deity:
That is, it shineth in an hevenly Sence,
And round about (unmov'd) it's Light dispence.
(ll. 1–6)

What the inward eye sees is, of course, an immaterial world, and it is striking that no less than five poems from the Dobell Folio are on the subject of 'Thoughts'. Many others celebrate the power of thought.[19] In his poetry as in his *Meditations*, Traherne celebrates spiritual reality, the inward temple of the mind. This is another image which recurs in the *Centuries*, *Christian Ethicks*, 'Commentaries of Heaven' and the poems.[20] The temple of the mind is as much an intellectual as a spiritual reality for the mind in its contemplations is the crowning part of the soul: 'By Thoughts alone the Soul is made Divine' ('Thoughts III')[21] Reason is thus, as in Ficino, spiritualised. After all, it is the rational power of thought that gives the soul its unique insight into the world and its special relationship with God. 'To think well,' Traherne writes, 'is to serv God in the Interior Court: To hav a mind composd of Divine Thoughts' (*Centuries*, I. 10). Thoughts are the link between soul and God,

Thoughts are the Wings on which the Soul doth flie,
The Messengers which soar abov the Skie,
Elijah's firey Charet, that conveys
The Soul, even here, to those Eternal Joys.
('Thoughts IV', ll 1–4)

Thoughts are the Angels which we send abroad
To visit all the Parts of Gods Abode
('Thoughts III', ll. 1–2)

Like Augustine (*De Trinitate*) Traherne sees reason as evidence that man is made in the image of God. Traherne uses the Neoplatonic image of the soul as mirror to express this: 'The Soul thus Thinking is

[19] See, for example, 'Walking', 'Dreams', 'The Inference', 'The Review'.

[20] See 'Thoughts II', 'The Inference, II' and *Christian Ethicks*, p. 252, for the temples of David and Solomon. 'Thoughts IV', ll.80–8: 'His Omnipresence . . . It enters in, and doth a Temple find / Or make a Living one within the Mind'. 'Thoughts I' describes 'a Spiritual world within' (I, 44).

[21] Compare *Commentaries*, 'The Mind of Man for ever shall endure / And is a Region of diviner Light ('Accident' ll. 13–14, edn cit. p. 7) and *Poems*, 'For 'tis by Thoughts that even she [the soul] is Bright. / Thoughts are the Things wherwith even God is Crownd', 'Thoughts IV' (ll.14–15).

a Compleat Act In wch as in a Glass you may see ye Deitie'. The ideas in the mind come directly from God

> Thoughts are the highest Things,
> The very Offspring of the King of Kings.
> ('Thoughts III', ll.27–8)

As in the *Phaedo* (66a, 82c) and *Enneads* v it is by exercising his reason that man can become godlike:

> O give me Grace to see thy face, and be
> A constant Mirror of Eternitie.
> Let my pure soul, transformed to a Thought,
> Attend upon thy Throne.
> ('Thoughts IV', ll.95–9)[22]

In this way Traherne assimilates to the Christian concept of the relationship of God and the soul Plotinus' conception of the relationship of *nous* to *psyche*. And like the intellect in Plotinus (*Enneads* V.9. 9–10), and the soul in Plato (*Timaeus* 36d–e), the mind is, for Traherne, a world in itself, an interior world, a microcosm that epitomises the external macrocosm.

> A Delicate and Tender Thought
> The Quintessence is found of all he Wrought
> ('Thoughts II', ll.1–2)

Man is the 'Comprehensor' of his celestial environment (*Centuries*, I. 100).[23] To comprehend, in Traherne's usage means not only to understand, but to contain. 'God hath made your Spirit a Centre in Eternity comprehending all and filled all about you in an Endless maner with infinit Riches' (*Centuries*, II. 80). In 'Thoughts II' Traherne emphasises that God delights not in His creation as such, but in Man's enjoyment of His Works. For by seeing the works of creation and recognising them as a reflection of the divine, we are led to God. The visible world will decay, but it is preserved in the mental images it conjures up in the mind.

This leads us back to Traherne's celebration of childhood. Only a purified mind, unsullied by sinfulness can apprehend the world rightly, recognise the eternal and infinite behind the temporal and finite. Hence Traherne's emphasis on the innocent eye of the child, able to 'giv to Things their tru Esteem':

22 Cf. 'Commentaries', 'Appetite': 'The Rational Appetite like an Eagle soars up aloft to Celestial Things'. BL Additional MS, 63054, fol. 112^{v}.

23 'I being the Living TEMPLE and Comprehensor of them [Angels etc.]. *Centuries*, I.100.

How wise was I
In Infancy!
I then saw in the clearest Light.
('Right Apprehension', ll.5–7)

The human soul's unique observer status underlies Traherne's astonishingly anthropocentric (even egocentric) theology. Instead of bemoaning human frailty, Traherne rejoices in his humanity, 'That you are a Man should fill you with Joys, and make you overflow with praises' (*Centuries*, II. 24). This optimism about human nature sets Traherne apart from even the most liberal theologians of the seventeenth century. But it is not unique to him. In more modified form, it is a feature of the theology of his Platonising contemporaries, all of whom repudiated extreme Calvinist stress on original sin and human incapacity for salvation. Among them Jeremy Taylor perhaps comes closest to Traherne in his insistence on the innocence from sin of unbaptised infants. The principle difference in Traherne's optimism about human nature is the degree to which he takes it. His optimism is fed by the humanist character of his Platonic sources. Indeed, in his fullest celebration of man as the miracle of creation in the *Centuries*, II, he quotes extensively from Pico della Mirandola's *Oration on the Dignity of Man*.

The personal and mystical character of Traherne's poetry, combined with the fact that it remained unpublished for three centuries, have resulted in Traherne's being regarded as an isolated figure. His interest in Neoplatonism during the age of the new science appears to confirm this. However, recent work on his biography is beginning to show that he did not live a life apart.[24] As an exponent in verse (but also in prose) of the eclectic Platonism forged by Ficino and propounded by More, Cudworth and Smith, he must be set alongside the Cambridge Platonists. Like theirs, Traherne's is a spiritualised and Christianised Platonism, deeply imbued with Neoplatonism. Like them he takes for granted the religious character of Platonic philosophy and its compatibility with Christian doctrine. Although Traherne's Neoplatonism is in many ways a late flowering, 200 years behind Ficino's time, when it is properly placed in its seventeenth-century English context it is possible to recognise both how closely interconnected it was with currents of thought of its own day and the originality of Traherne's development of Platonism.

[24] Julia Smith, 'Thomas Traherne and the Restoration', *The Seventeenth Century*, 3 (1988), 203–22.

PART IV

The eighteenth century

CHAPTER 16

Introduction

Pat Rogers

In speaking of the 'three provincial centuries' marked by British neglect of Plato, W. B Yeats lumped together the period from 1600 to 1900. But the start is too early and the end too late, for Plato's sojourn in the shadows cannot plausibly be dated prior to the death of the Cambridge Platonists, nor construed as surviving undiminished through the Victorian age. Yeats really had in mind the high noon of empiricism, Newtonianism and Enlightenment. He meant, to be blunt, the eighteenth century.

Abundant evidence exists to show that Plato, direct or mediated, counted for less in this age than in previous or succeeding phases of British culture. Three levels of neglect can be discerned. In the first place, there is the comparatively low level of concern in the eighteenth century with matters Greek. One striking index of the general situation lies in the fact that the great historian of the ancient world, Edward Gibbon, learnt no Greek at Westminster or Oxford: he had to teach himself the language as a mature private student. In the major public schools which set out the national curriculum for educated males, hardly any attention was paid to Greek prose of any description; the philosophers and historians were still 'untrodden ground' at Westminster as late as the 1820s. Until a major shift of interest from Latin to Greek in the second quarter of the nineteenth century, which was initiated by Butler of Shrewsbury and Thomas Arnold of Rugby (who daringly introduced Plato into sixth-form studies), the bulk of school-work was devoted to Latin. (Before 1800 Greek was learnt from textbooks written in Latin, not English.) The Greek tragedians started to make headway in the curriculum of the leading schools around the middle of the century, though the scabrous Aristophanes seldom joined them, and lyric poetry remained a staple element in classical studies, largely one imagines for philological and pedagogic reasons. At the universities, things were not very different: Latin predominated, and the range of Greek prose texts studied was pitifully narrow. As M.L. Clarke states, 'The professorships of Greek had become mere sinecures, and their holders apart from an inaugural oration gave no lectures'. Recent attempts to salvage the reputation of the ancient universities from the hostile comments of observers like Gibbon have not succeeded in burnishing the reputation of these institutions as regards the teaching of Greek.[1]

The second level of neglect is illustrated by the paucity of editions, translations and commentaries. In 1701 there was a two-volume abridgment of Plato's *Works*, but this was translated from the French of André Dacier.[2] Occasionally, versions of individual dialogues appeared: Harry Spens translated the *Republic* (1763), and Lewis Theobald, the first hero of the *Dunciad*, attempted the *Phaedo* (1713). But the only concerted project of any importance was conducted by a largely forgotten Oxford scholar named Floyer Sydenham (1710–87), who undertook a comprehensive translation between 1759 and 1780: it is readable if not outstandingly felicitous. Of course, Plato was not alone in suffering such neglect. Aristotle, though more admired and influential, had no full translation until Thomas Taylor's in 1812: Henry Fielding remarked in the *Covent-Garden Journal*, no. 10 (1752) that his works, like those of Plato, were 'not completely made English, and consequently are less within the Reach of most of my Countrymen'.[3] This in an era which could boast the Greek scholarship of Bentley at the start and Porson at the end of the century, as well as significant lesser lights such as Joshua Barnes, Jeremiah Markland and Jonathan Toup. The fact remains that until Thomas Taylor (1758–1835) undertook his widely read versions of the dialogues in the 1790s, and augmented these with the Orphic Hymns, Plotinus, Proclus and Porphyry, little of Plato was available for the general reader.

How can we explain this circumstance? Plato did not have the good fortune, as did Homer, to be caught up in the cultural battles of the age, and so to stand at the heart of any current critical debate.

[1] Information in this paragraph is drawn chiefly from M.L. Clarke, *Classical Education in Britain 1500–1900* (Cambridge, 1959): quotations from pp. 50–2, 68, 76–80. See also Clarke's *Greek Studies in England 1700–1830* (Cambridge, 1945), pp. 112–20, for a good account of attitudes to Greek philosophy in the period. Clarke finds 'as we should expect, a general indifference to the Greeks' (p. 115). The most detailed review of scholarship in the period, unsupplanted by Pfeiffer, remains J.E. Sandys, *A History of Classical Scholarship*, 3 vols (Cambridge, 1903–08), II, 401–39, though the treatment is sketchy and occasionally inaccurate.

[2] *The Works of Plato abridg'd with an Account of His Life, Philosophy, Morals and Politics, together with a Translation of his Choicest Dialogues* (London, 1701).

[3] *The Covent-Garden Journal*, ed. B.A. Goldgar (Oxford, 1988), p. 75.

Equally, none of his translators had the clout or centrality of Pope. When issues related to Greek antiquity did surface in the popular consciousness, as with the great *querelle* of Ancients and Moderns, Plato was never directly implicated. The discoveries of the sites of the classical world, publicised by the new breed of archaeologists and promoted by the Dilettanti Society, did little to humanise the rarified ideas of Plato. It is doubtful whether the rise of Romantic Hellenism can be put back into the eighteenth century; Timothy Webb's interesting collection, by focusing on such matters as the debate about Homeric epic, conceals the severe limits to Greek influence in the first part of the eighteenth century.[4] We are still left with the fact that Plato was no great beneficiary of the trend. And here we touch on the third level of neglect. Plato's name was further besmirched, in the eyes of many, because of a curious guilt by association. Neoplatonism had come to seem a kind of secret-society activity, equivalent to Rosicrucianism or freemasonry: and these things were suspect until mysticism re-entered the European mind towards the end of the century. At a time when many people wished to show that not just Christianity but all serious thought was 'not mysterious', as John Toland's deistic slogan had it, the hermetic side of Neoplatonic doctrine (part of its appeal to later generations) limited both its own attraction and that of its ultimate progenitor.

To attribute these forms of resistance to the huge currency of John Locke may only be to shift the argument one stage back without further illumination of the issues. None the less, it must be significant that James 'Hermes' Harris, the most obstinate Platonist in the literary world of mid-eighteenth-century England, nurtured a 'seething dislike' of Locke.[5] Harris followed in a line of Salisbury metaphysicians including John Norris of Bemerton, Arthur Collier and Thomas Chubb, but the principal influence on him was his uncle, the third Earl of Shaftesbury. Like Shaftesbury, Harris favours the dialogue form in his characteristic works such as *Three Treatises* (1744); neither master nor pupil ever achieves the dramatic cut and thrust of Plato's own dialogues, substituting for their sharp interplay of question and answer, self-revelation and exposure, something more like a mere exchange of dialectical positions. It is true that some parts of Shaftesbury's *Characteristicks* (1714) do achieve a fervour and sense of

[4] See Timothy Webb, *English Romantic Hellenism 1700–1824* (Manchester, 1982).

[5] See Clive T. Probyn, *The Sociable Humanist: The Life and Work of James Harris 1709–1780* (Oxford, 1991), for a good and sympathetic account of Harris as Platonist: quotation from p. 243.

ecstasy otherwise almost wholly absent in Augustan writing: his 'philosophical rhapsody' entitled *The Moralists* relates the quest for the good to the search for happiness in impassioned prose. But there are few such moments in eighteenth-century literature. Mark Akenside in his *Pleasures of the Imagination* (first version 1744) makes free use of abstractions like *truth*, *beauty*, *knowledge* and *wisdom*, but the import of these terms is Christianised to the point where any Platonic sense has drained away.[6] Even Thomas Gray, who had spent more time reading Plato than most people of the age, shows little impress in his poetry. By this time the 'sublime', a secularised way of approaching the transcendental, was in full sway.

It is clearly possible to argue that Swift was in part responding to the *Republic* when he wrote *Gulliver's Travels*, even though it is Socrates rather than Plato who figures as one of the 'sextumvirate' of mighty dead to which 'all Ages of the World cannot add a Seventh'. (*Gulliver's Travels*, III, chap. 7).[7] Sir Thomas More is another, and he is more clearly Swift's model, but there are aspects of the Island of the Houyhnhms which may derive directly from Plato – for example the horses are committed to truth and have no word for lying. However, to show a truly rational society attainable only by placid and passionless horses is ultimately to question its relevance for humans. Swift's heroes tend to grow two ears of corn where only one grew before, and thus to do more service to their country than the whole race of philosophers put together (see *Gulliver's Travels*, II,7).

So we are left with the fact that literature before the time of Blake (discussed by Edward Larrissy in the following chapter) scarcely makes a nod at Platonism. This only changes in the era of Thomas Taylor, with the designs of John Flaxman and of the vogue for neoclassic art: and these involve the break-up of the high Augustan dispensation. Taylor and Flaxman were contemporaries of Blake, and in Blake old enthusiasm joins hands with new Romanticism. Old enthusiasm reveals itself to be politically as radical as ever. Men and women start to take Plato's political ideas seriously, something that

6 Akenside does refer to Sophocles in his notes to the poem, but it is perhaps indicative that he cites Xenophon's *Memorabilia* rather than Plato. See *The Works of the English Poets*, ed. Alexander Chalmers, 21 vols (London, 1810), XIV, 76. One occasionally finds the vestiges of a Platonic vocabulary in other poets of the age, e.g. William Mason in *The English Garden* (1772) speaks of giving 'local form to each Idea'; but the words have forgotten their lost originals.

7 See M.M. Kelsall, '*Iterum* Houyhnhm: Swift's Sextumvirate and the Horses', *Essays in Criticism*, 19 (1969), 34–45. Also T.O. Wedel, 'On the Philosophical Background of Gulliver's Travels', in *Swift, Gulliver's Travels, a Casebook*, ed. R. Gravil (London, 1974).

had never really happened in the easy-going Whig consensus of earlier years. An age of revolution made it possible, if not indeed necessary, to reconsider absolutes. The eighteenth century, broadly speaking, had revered not pure intellectual categories but the working divisions thrown up in ordinary life, just as it had preferred to use language muddied by everyday contact with the world rather than the philosophically exact terms of the Academy. With a few notable exceptions, Augustan thinkers had seen the cosmos not as a mysterious reflection of a higher reality, but as an intelligible system of forces governed by physical laws. They had distrusted philosopher kings advocated by visionaries like Bolingbroke, and settled for practical statesmen like Robert Walpole. Like Samuel Johnson and Joshua Reynolds, they had viewed art as a *technē* with its own disciplines and identifiable rules, to be practised with conscious purpose and rarely attended with sudden illumination or spontaneous bursts of self-validating enthusiasm. The Enlightenment had canonised the worldly, and made the pursuit of happiness a civic right instead of a metaphysical quest. We can place the breakdown of this way of viewing the world as occurring around 1775, or 1789, or 1798, or when we will; but until a radical shift in pervasive values took place, there could be little room for a Platonic dialect in the language of the arts.

CHAPTER 17

Blake and Platonism

Edward Larrissy

'There Exist in that Eternal World,' says Blake, 'the Permanent Realities of Every Thing which we see reflected in this Vegetable Glass of Nature' (E555/K605).[1] These words from his Notebook, which were penned in 1809 or 1810, agree with much that he wrote at least after about 1803. And it might be argued that they continue, with a different emphasis, certain themes from his earlier work respecting vision and imagination. Blake is among those poets who seem more obviously indebted to Platonism. The problem has always been to gauge the character and extent of that indebtedness. Some things, however, are clear: Blake must have read Plato in the translations of Thomas Taylor, who was familiar with members of his circle.[2] He must also have read Taylor's commentaries and his translations of the Neoplatonists. From these he derives a Neoplatonic vocabulary – 'Generation', 'Non-Entity', 'Hyle', 'Forms Eternal', 'Intellect', and (with some twisting) 'Emanation' – which he uses not infrequently in his later work. These facts have led some scholars, notably George Mills Harper and Kathleen Raine, to see Blake as capable of being described, with only a degree of qualification, as a Neoplatonist.[3] Their works demonstrate the incontestable fact of his detailed familiarity with the tradition. It might therefore seem wiser

[1] *The Complete Poetry and Prose of William Blake*, ed. David V. Erdman with commentary by Harold Bloom; newly revised (New York, 1988) (referred to hereafter as E, with page number). *The Complete Writings of William Blake*, ed. Geoffrey Keynes (Oxford, 1972) (referred to hereafter as K, with page number).

[2] Kathleen Raine, 'Thomas Taylor in England', introduction to *Thomas Taylor the Platonist: Selected Writings*, ed. Kathleen Raine and George Mills Harper (London, 1969), pp. 13–15.

[3] George Mills Harper, *The Neoplatonism of William Blake* (Chapel Hill and Oxford, 1961); Kathleen Raine, *Blake and Tradition* (The A.W. Mellon Lectures in the Fine Arts, 1962), 2 vols. (Princeton and London, 1969). The influence of Neoplatonism on Blake was first suggested by S. Foster Damon in *William Blake: His philosophy and Symbols* (Boston and New York, 1924). It is also an assumption of Milton O. Percival, *William Blake's Circle of Destiny* (New York, 1938).

to take 'Blake and Neoplatonism' as our subject. However, Blake makes a number of comments on Plato, and a couple on Socrates, which make it clear that he thought he could form a judgement about the originators of Platonism to some extent independently of whatever he may have thought about their successors. But only to some extent, surely; for it seems reasonable to assume that these comments are nevertheless relevant to an understanding of the part played by Neoplatonic terms in his work. The word 'Platonism', then, covers all the phenomena. And now a brief initial reminder of the complexities of this subject: most, though not all, of Blake's references to Plato himself are hostile.

In the past the importance of Platonism to Blake's work has been widely, and sometimes summarily, denied. One can understand why Kathleen Raine once claimed, of Blake, Coleridge and Yeats, 'the 'darling studies' of the poets are just those their academic commentators would like to disregard'.[4] And still many readers and some critics of Blake are inclined to dismiss such studies in advance. They are emboldened by his hostile references to Plato, and by the perceived bluntness and political immediacy of some of his best-known works. Why bring in all that unwieldy arcane lore? Such readers regard Blake's Neoplatonic terms and are inclined to dismiss them as forming a small strand of creative borrowings in the work of a notably creative borrower. The general form of a rebuttal of such objections must include a glance at some of those other borrowings. Raine's work, but not only Raine's, has made it clear that Blake is indebted also to philosophical alchemy, and that he shows some knowledge of Gnostic doctrine. Blake himself thought he owed much to the alchemical tradition, avowing the importance of Paracelsus and Boehme ('Behmen') in some remarks in *The Marriage of Heaven and Hell*, and in a letter to Flaxman of 12 September 1800 (E707/K799). He seems to have inherited from the antinomian Protestant tradition a tendency to syncretism in these matters and his prophetic political radicalism. An interest in Paracelsus and Boehme was very common among the sects of the English Revolution period.[5] And one may instance the confluence of such currents in a striking individual of that time: John Everard (1579–1650), translator of the Hermetic *Pimander* (see Sarah

[4] Kathleen Raine in *Thomas Taylor*, p. 4.

[5] Christopher Hill, *The World Turned Upside-Down* (Harmondsworth, 1976), Chapter 14, *passim*, Keith Thomas, *Religion and the Decline of Magic: Studies in Popular Beliefs in Sixteenth and Seventeenth Century England* (London, 1971), pp. 270–1.

Hutton p. 74 above) who believed in God's immanence, and in the idea that heaven and hell were in the human heart.[6] Although there are differences of emphasis, most scholars have come to accept the idea that Blake's political radicalism and his 'occult' interests are facets of a single tradition. It is because this tradition produced only one great artist that Blake used to seem so absolutely *sui generis*. An interesting question follows: how does this inheritance interact in his work with contemporary Romantic ideas and forms?[7] But that is another tale.

THEL AND LYCA

The first place chronologically where one encounters an indisputably Platonic echo in Blake's work is at the end of *The Book of Thel* (1789 [1789–91]; E3–6/K127–30). At the beginning of the poem the maiden Thel has wandered in 'the vales of Har'. Unlike her sisters, who are happy to lead 'their sunny flocks' around, she is preoccupied with the melancholy of transience and mortality, and 'in paleness' seeks 'the secret air', lamenting. She proceeds to ask the Lily, the Cloud, the Worm and the Clod of Clay why they do not also lament their transience. All but the Worm reply, and the burden of their responses is that they enjoy existence while it lasts and at its end are re-born to fuller life. It is not entirely clear that Blake is referring to a life after death, and there are a number of hints that he is making use of the language of the after-life to symbolise the redemption of time by entry into an 'eternal' state of mind in this life. Perhaps the bluntest hint of this occurs when Thel complains that she will have lived 'without a use' and will be 'at death the food of worms' (plate 3, ll.22–3). The Cloud replies:

> Then if thou art the food of worms. O virgin of the skies,
> How great thy use. how great thy blessing; every thing that lives,
> Lives not alone, nor for itself.
> (plate 3, ll.25–7)

The 'matron Clay', as if to settle the question whether mortality is to be feared, invites Thel into her house, telling her to 'fear nothing'. There follow, on plate 6, the concluding lines, which are (like 'Thel's Motto') a late addition to the poem. The style of script is one which

6 See Michael Ferber, *The Social Vision of William Blake* (Princeton, 1985), p. 93.
7 See Edward Larrissy, *William Blake* (Oxford, 1985), pp. 20–1, 29–37.

Blake began to adopt in 1791, while that of the rest of the poem is congruent with the date of 1789 on the title page. No doubt these lines replace an earlier ending. They are in Blake's Ossianic-Biblical sublime mode. The Platonic reference is to be found in their opening: 'The eternal gates terrific porter lifted the northern bar: / Thel entered in & saw the secrets of the land unknown'. Here is surely a reference to Porphyry's *De antro nympharum*, of which Blake would have been aware from Taylor's *History of the Restoration of the Platonic Theology* (1789).[8] Porphyry takes as his text the description of the Cave of the Nymphs on Ithaca from *Odyssey* XIII, and Blake himself later in his life makes this passage the subject of a great tempera painting, the Arlington Court Picture of 1821. In *The Odyssey* the nymphs weave purple webs inside the cave, which is full of perpetually flowing waters and has two gates: a northern one for mortals to descend through, and a southern for ascending immortals. Porphyry interprets the cave as this material world in its aspect of inertness, and the waters as its aspect of flux and generation. The nymphs are souls descended into this world. The northern gate is the one through which such souls descend, and the southern that through which not gods, but immortal souls, return to be the companions of gods.

So Blake at first asks us to see Thel as encountering death in some aspect, and then suggests either that she is a soul descending into the material world according to a Platonic conception, or that there is some analogy in her actions with such a descent. There is no contradiction for the Platonist in the first alternative: 'Our birth is but a sleep and a forgetting'. But it seems unlikely that Blake is using the motif from Porphyry in an orthodox fashion. For one thing, the place from which Thel descends, and to which she swiftly returns, is described as 'the vales of Har' (plates 2, l.1; 6, l.22). We know from Blake's 'Tiriel' (*c.* 1789) that Har is associated with what John Beer calls 'innocent Reason' and 'faded vision'.[9] Secondly, the period in which Blake was writing the end of Thel is somewhere around the time when he was composing those famous lines from *The Marriage of Heaven and Hell*, plate 4, about how 'Energy is the only life and is from the Body' (E34/K149), for plate 3 was composed in 1790. There is room for interpretation of this remark, especially in view of the neighbouring one 'that calld Body is a portion of Soul discernd by the five Senses'. But reading both remarks against Blake's indisputable

[8] *Thomas Taylor*, p. 296. [9] John Beer, *Blake's Visionary Universe* (Manchester, 1969), p. 70.

and well-known celebration of desire in this period, one must feel that he is attempting to expound a non-dualist conception of soul and body, or soul-body.

The Platonic allusion, then, is being employed figuratively. It seems to Thel as if she has fallen into a world of fearful limitations, of which death is only the last and direst expression. Coming to 'her own grave plot', she hears the following voice, which it is reasonable to assume is that of her own fear:

> Why cannot the Ear be closed to its own destruction?
> Or the glistning Eye to the poison of a smile!
> Why are Eyelids stord with arrows ready drawn,
> Where a thousand fighting men in ambush lie?
> Or an Eye of gifts & graces, show'ring fruits & coined gold!
> Why a Tongue impress'd with honey from every wind?
> Why an Ear, a whirlpool fierce to draw creations in?
> Why a Nostril wide inhaling terror trembling & affright.
> Why a tender curb upon the youthful burning boy!
> Why a little curtain of flesh on the bed of our desire?
> (E6/K130)

There are several related points which need to be made about this. First, there are good grounds for believing that Blake is thinking here of the influence of empiricism, the dominant school of philosophy at the time, which held that all knowledge is ultimately derived from simple sense experience: Blake calls it the 'Philosophy of Five Senses' in *The Song of Los* (plate 4, l.16). We have just seen that in *The Marriage* he remarks that 'that calld Body is a portion of Soul discernd by the five Senses': these, he continues in the same place, are 'the chief inlets of Soul in this age'. 'Inlets' is a word familiar from the empiricist tradition, as is the notion of the five senses being, so to speak, separate windows on the world. Blake does not, of course, hold with empiricism. Those who are subject to its conceptions place bounds on their imaginations. Yet within these bounds they are still expressing imagination, in however stunted a form. It is a fair inference that Thel's vision is to some extent vitiated by a narrow view of experience, for Blake makes clear that it is bounded by the five senses. But we may also assume that there is a degree of truth in what she sees.

What, then, does she see? She sees both limitation and sublimity: we are in the realm of 'The Tyger' and also of 'The Sick Rose', from *Songs of Experience*, a world in which wrath and deceit co-exist with sublime beauty ('a whirlpool fierce to draw creations in'). Here sexuality, though acknowledged (unlike in the state of Innocence) is seen to be subject to irksome constraints. In sum, she sees the state of Experience. The subject of her vision is analogous with the eye that perceives it. For just as the five senses are vehicles which both obstruct and permit vision, so the world they here reveal is both expressive and destructive of beauty. On the whole, though, the emphasis is negative, and it is not surprising to find that Thel flees back 'with a shriek' to 'the vales of Har'. She can see mainly the terror of the state of Experience, and sees its sublimity only as terrible. She would not perceive any wisdom in Blake's contemporary 'Proverbs of Hell', from *The Marriage*, in which he asserts that 'The tygers of wrath are wiser than the horses of instruction' (plate 9), and also that 'The roaring of lions, the howling of wolves, the raging of the stormy sea, and the destructive sword, are portions of eternity too great for the eye of man' (plate 9). These would certainly be too great for Thel's 'eye'. Blake would have us open our own eyes to the infinite in such a way that we could reach some accommodation with the terrifying 'Energy' revealed in the state of Experience. Blake had just completed *Songs of Innocence* (1789) and was writing *Songs of Experience* (finished 1793). There is little reason to disagree with the widely, though not universally, accepted theory that Thel is over-timorously fleeing from Experience back into a faded Innocence whose limitations she has also discovered.

The true path is more akin to that taken by Lyca, the heroine of 'The Little Girl Lost' and 'The Little Girl Found', a linked pair of poems which Blake composed for *Songs of Innocence* and then moved to *Experience* (E20–22/K112–15). As a girl lost in the world of generation Lyca has one obvious point of similarity with Thel, and it is just possible that Blake may here have been thinking of what Kathleen Raine calls 'The Myth of the Kore', from *κόρη*, the Greek for 'maiden'.[10] The myth is that of Persephone, who was often called Kore. The Neoplatonic interpretation of the later Olympiodorus sees Persephone's descent into the underworld as a symbol of the soul's descent into generation.[11] Yet read in the light of the facts already outlined about Blake and his development, these poems can easily be seen as recommending some accommodation of the energies of Experience, including wrath and sexuality: leopards and tigers play around Lyca as she sleeps in the wild; the lion licks her bosom, while the lioness undresses her, and she is then carried, naked and asleep, to a cave. When the grieving parents approach, seeking their child, they

[10] Kathleen Raine, *Blake and Tradition*, I, pp. 126–65. On 'The Little Girl Lost' and 'The Little Girl Found', see pp. 130–49. [11] *Ibid.*, p. 133.

encounter a lion who turns into 'A spirit arm'd in gold' and leads them to their daughter:

> To this day they dwell
> In a lonely dell
> Nor fear the wolvish howl,
> Nor the lions growl.

It may be, as Kathleen Raine says, that the 'palace deep' in which this spirit lives is the underworld, and that he is Pluto: figuratively the patron of the caves of generation, then.[12] Yet the use to which Blake puts these allusions, if such they be, suggests that the underworld is not such a bad place when properly understood. Miss Raine recognises this fact, and refers it to Blake's indebtedness to the alchemical principle that 'that which is beneath is like that which is above': God is at work, then, even in the 'lowest effects' of the world of generation.[13] As we have seen, there is reason to believe that philosophical alchemy is very important to Blake. But at least at this relatively early stage of his career there are, as we have also seen, grounds for believing that he interpreted the famous Hermetic principle in a radical anti-dualist manner.

But to return to Thel: she has a point about this world, and here is where the allusion to Porphyry begins to make sense. For ours is indeed a world where limitation can occur, and can all too readily encourage fear and failure of vision. Escape into Blake's 'infinite' is in this period to be attained by cleansing 'the doors of perception' (*Marriage*, plate 14), not by entering a world of spirits. But granted these qualifications one can see how entry into Experience can be figured as descent into a realm of imperfection, mutability and limitation, when it is encountered without courage and vision. For this reason the way forward is to trust the positive aspects of Innocence while integrating them with the energies of Experience. In this sense, at least, Blake's conception of the importance of childhood is comparable to that of Wordsworth, who believed, as A. W. Price points out, that 'infant sensibility' should be 'augmented and sustained' (see p. 223, below).

URIZEN AND THE DEMIURGE

Blake, as is well known, creates his own mythology, with his own invented names and terminology. One of the most important and

[12] *Ibid.*, p. 145. [13] *Ibid.*, p. 146.

striking figures in this system acts as a culprit for the limitations encountered in the state of Experience. Blake calls him 'Urizen', the white-haired tyrant deity. He will be familiar to many from the great frontispiece to *Europe* (1794) which is sometimes known as 'The Ancient of Days', where he is seen holding a pair of dividers. His name owes something to the Greek infinitive *ὁρίζειν* ('to set bounds, limits'). From *The Book of Urizen* (1794; E70–83/K222–37) it might seem that he creates the fallen world of limitation. He is associated with Reason (his name also puns on 'Your Reason'); he divides and measures the universe (plate 3); and he and his world go through seven ages of growth (plate 10, l.35–plate 13, l.19) which, though they undoubtedly refer to the Biblical seven days of creation, may also reflect knowledge of the seven numbers which express the proportions in which the Artificer divides the World Soul in the *Timaeus* (35b–c). This series, as is well known, could be expressed on a pair of dividers. For all these reasons Urizen is often compared to the Demiurge or Artificer in *Timaeus* 28c sq. But only on a superficial reading can Urizen be seen as a creator. In fact he is spurned by the other Eternals because of his lack of energy (plates 2, 3), and has to be separated from them in an action which may represent Blake's adaptation of the doctrine of *Tsimtsum* in the Lurianic Cabbala: that is, separation of the deity from his creation.[14] It is not Urizen but another of Blake's mythological creations, Los, who really does the creating. Los is 'The Eternal Prophet' (plate 10: 15), the spirit of poetry or imagination. He is the true equivalent of the Demiurge, and it is he who has the task of giving, even to Urizen and his world, such form as they possess. Even the seven-fold changes referred to above are given form by Los. Such is Blake's way of asserting that Reason can build nothing, and that even those concepts and world-views that it fancies it has produced are simply the codification or measurement of ideas which really derive from imagination.

More than to Platonism, Blake is indebted to Gnosticism for his concept of Urizen.[15] An important difference between Gnosticism and Platonism is the Gnostic conception of the Demiurge as evil, as the creator of a world of evil. The appearance of a limited universe, bound by the five senses, is the work of an evil creator, and this,

[14] For a discussion of *Tsimtsum*, see Gershom G. Scholem, *Major Trends in Jewish Mysticism*, 2nd rev. edn (New York, 1946), p. 260. Blake could have encountered this idea in Robert Fludd's *Mosaicall Philosophy*, trans. from Latin (London, 1659), p. 44: here Elohim effects 'Separation'.

[15] Cf. Stuart Curran, 'Blake and the Gnostic Hyle', *Essential Articles for the Study of William Blake, 1970–1984*, ed. Nelson Hilton (Hamden, Conn., 1986), pp. 23–4.

combined with the fact that Blake makes Urizen look very much like the Old Testament God, gives immediate plausibility to the identification of Urizen as a Gnostic demiurge. Hans Jonas describes the Gnostic doctrine thus:

The world is the work of lowly powers which though they may mediately be descended from Him do not know the true God and obstruct the knowledge of Him in the cosmos over which they rule.[16]

Sometimes, in the case most relevant to Blake,

this role is reserved for their leader, who then has the name of *demiurge* (the world-artificer in Plato's *Timaeus*) and is often painted with the distorted features of the Old Testament God.[17]

It was the diarist Henry Crabb Robinson who first detected the Gnosticism in Blake's thought during discussions with him.[18] And Blake could easily have come across descriptions of Gnostic doctrine in the works of Joseph Priestley, who was a member of his early circle, or in J.L. Mosheim's *Ecclesiastical History*.[19] Yet Platonism has, I think, something specific to add to our understanding of Urizen. Thomas Taylor, in his commentary on the *Timaeus*, notes that 'by the *demiurgus* and *father* of the world we must understand Jupiter'.[20] Blake's opinion of 'the Jupiter of the Greeks' can be gauged from his letter to William Hayley of 23 October 1804:

I have entirely reduced that spectrous Fiend to his station, whose annoyance has been the ruin of my labours for the last passed twenty years of my life. He is the enemy of conjugal love and is the Jupiter of the Greeks, an iron-hearted tyrant, the ruiner of ancient Greece. (E756/K851–2)

This means that Blake feels he has been under the emotional sway of abstraction. It should not be assumed, as some commentators do, that he had given intellectual assent to such a Jupiter for twenty years, nor that he had emerged from a Neoplatonic 'Grecian period'.[21] For in 1795, in the middle of that time, he explicitly notes in *The Song of Los* that 'To Trismegistus, Palamabron gave an abstract Law: / To

[16] Hans Jonas, *The Gnostic Religion: The Message of the Alien God and the beginnings of Christianity* (Boston, 1958), p. 42.

[17] *Ibid.*, pp. 43–4.

[18] *Blake, Coleridge, Wordsworth, Lamb, Etc: Being Selections from the Remains of Henry Crabbe Robinson*, ed. Edith J. Morley (Manchester, 1922), p. 23.

[19] Joseph Priestley, *An History of Early Opinions Concerning Jesus Christ*, 4 vols (Birmingham, 1786), I, 166–7; J.L. Mosheim, *An Ecclesiastical History, Ancient and Modern*, trans. Archibald Maclaine, 2 vols (London, 1765), I, 113–16.

[20] Thomas Taylor, *The Cratylus, Parmenides And Timaeus Of Plato. With Notes On the Cratylus, And An Explanatory Introduction to Each Dialogue* (London, 1793), p. 402.

[21] Harper, *Neoplatonism*, p. 35.

Pythagoras Socrates & Plato' (E67/K246). Palamabron is in fact transmitting this law from Urizen. We may infer that Urizen is 'the Jupiter of the Greeks, an iron-hearted tyrant', and that Platonism is at least implicated in the ruin of Greece because of 'abstract Law'.

Art and imagination are Blake's chief subjects. The ruin of Greece was its artistic ruin. It is therefore important to realise that one may associate this Platonic abstraction with Blake's later thoughts about 'Grecian' Form. Thus, in *On Virgil* (*c.* 1820) he notes: 'Mathematic Form is Eternal in the Reasoning Memory. Living Form is Eternal Existence. / Grecian is Mathematic Form / Gothic is Living Form' (E270/K778); and in [The Laocoön] (*c.* 1820) he asserts that 'The Gods of Greece & Egypt were Mathematical Diagrams See Plato's Works' (E274/K776). It must be realised, however, that the distinction between Grecian and Gothic Form, *so defined*, is a feature only of Blake's later work. His first known reference to Greek art is more equivocal. Writing to Dr Trusler, on 16 August 1799, Blake avows that 'the purpose for which alone I live' is 'to renew the lost Art of the Greeks' (E701/K792). What does he mean by 'lost'? It is quite likely that he imagines that the best Greek art is no longer extant, possibly because it has been ruined by worship of 'Jupiter'. One can see how this might be from Blake's *Descriptive Catalogue* (1809) in which he claims that 'stupendous originals now lost', but once to be found in Asia, were copied by Greek artists (E530/K565). But in any case, Blake's ideas about the difference between good and bad art, however expressed, have a certain consistency, early and late. There are, as we have seen, two figures in Blake's mythology who owe something to the figure of the Demiurge: Urizen, the reasoner, and Los, the imaginative prophet. One of the most important things they do is to differentiate good and bad art and the two opposed notions of artistic form which encourage them: the Mathematic and the Living. Blake's more discursive treatments of these two notions, as I shall now go on to show, also owe something to Platonism.

ART AND TRUTH

Urizen's name, which comprises the idea of 'setting bounds', provides a useful way into Blake's theory of art. The 'bounded' for him is an ambiguous concept which may be associated either with negative or with positive notions. 'The bounded is loathed by its possessor' is a charcteristic assault on limitation, from *There is No Natural Religion*

(E2/K97). But equally characteristic is the epigram 'Truth has bounds. Error none' from *The Book of Los* (plate 4:30; E92/K258). The bounds of Truth are not limiting, and neither are those which the good artist imposes – or perhaps one should say, sees. Because of his training as an engraver Blake was always conscious of the value of outline, what he calls 'the bounding line' in his *Descriptive Catalogue*:

> The great and golden rule of art, as well as of life, is this: That the more distinct, sharp, and wirey the bounding line, the more perfect the work of art; and the less keen and sharp, the greater is the evidence of weak imitation, plagiarism, and bungling . . . The want of this determinate and bounding form evidences the want of idea in the artist's mind, and the pretence of the plagiary in all its branches. How do we distinguish the oak from the beech, the horse from the ox, but by the bounding outline? How do we distinguish one face or countenance from another, but by the bounding line and its infinite inflexions and movements? (E550/K585)

The bounding-line has two functions here: it is a distinguishing line imposed by a strong artist with clear conceptions; and it is the means by which an individual identity expresses itself. But in both these cases the line is devoid of the negative connotations of a limit. Blake's preference accords with the fashionable Romantic Neoclassicism: with the work of his friends Flaxman and Fuseli, and the theories of Winckelmann, whom Fuseli translated. Winckelmann asserts that Nature,

> never could bestow the precision of Contour, that characteristic distinction of the ancients.
>
> The noblest Contour unites or circumscribes every part of the most perfect Nature, and the ideal beauties of the Greeks; or rather, contains them both.[22]

It seems likely that Blake would have associated such descriptions of outline in Greek art with what he had read about the Intelligible World in Taylor's editions of Plotinus. Thus Taylor refers to 'those regions of mind, where all things are *bounded* in intellectual measure; where every thing is permanent and beautiful, eternal and divine' (emphasis added).[23] This paradoxical co-existence of boundedness and infinity in the Intelligible World is profoundly influential on Blake. R. T. Wallis ascribes Plotinus' conceptions to the problem 'of reconciling the mystical desire to transcend form and limit with the Classical Greek view of them as the essence of perfection'.[24] It was a

22 [J.J.] Winckelmann, *Reflections on the Painting and Sculpture of the Greeks*, trans. Henry Fuseli (London, 1765), p. 22.

23 Plotinus, *An Essay on the Beautiful*, [trans. Thomas Taylor] (London, 1792), p. ix.

24 R.T. Wallis, *Neoplatonism* (London, 1972), p. 6.

problem, and a solution, which Blake could understand. Yet, to look now above the Intelligible World, he had no time for a conception analogous to the One: Blake never allowed the slightest value to the ineffable or inconceivable. On the other hand, descending beneath the Intelligible World, he regarded the idea that in this world Forms supervened upon matter as based on an illusion: the illusion that matter existed. Blake may use the word 'Non-Entity', but unlike Plotinus he means this absolutely, as respects anything outside a mind: the idea of matter is simply a delusion for Blake. So his Eternal, or Living, Forms are both bounded, and at the same time exist in a mode of infinity, like those in the Plotinian Intelligible World. And as in so many artists' versions of Platonism (if this can indeed be called such) Blake's Eternal Forms are perceived in vision, so that when he speaks in his later work of perceiving them by means of 'Intellect', we must qualify that unexpected word with another usage of his: 'intellectual vision' (letter to Hayley, 23 October 1804: E757/K852). The aesthetic implications of such a position are well put by Pater in his essay on Winckelmann in *The Renaissance*: 'The mind begins and ends with the finite image, yet loses no part of the spiritual motive. That motive is not loosely or lightly attached to the sensuous form . . . but saturates and is identical with it' (see Varty, pp. 257–67 below).[25] Whatever one's opinion of the philosophical coherence of Blake's position, it would be understandable to think of him as a monist in respect of what he takes to be the true character of experience. Yet he spends so much time describing and analysing the power and threat of those who perceive wrongly, that illusion comes to take on the solidity of fact: Urizen may be self-deluded, but he often seems to have most of the battalions. Pondering this, one may feel that Blake is better described as a kind of dualist despite himself. One is speaking here not merely of the specific question of the mind–body distinction, but of Blake's apparently depicting a malign principle which creates this distinction. So much of his work depicts the conflict of visionary experience with its immemorial and persistent antagonist. As Leopold Damrosch says, 'Blake's monism wars with his dualism because he strives unceasingly to reconcile the desires of the heart with the facts of experience'.[26]

In view of Blake's celebrated trenchancy, combativeness, and insistence on originality, it may seem strange that he should adopt

[25] Walter Pater, *The Renaissance* (New York, 1959), pp. 139–40.

[26] Leopold Damrosch, Jr, *Symbol and Truth in Blake's Myth* (Princeton, 1980), p. 243.

any of the terms and ideas of Plato and Plotinus when it is clear that he saw Platonism as having fostered error. Yet the fact that he does borrow such terms may serve, finally, to illustrate a general condition of his work: that, believing error to be a concealment or misapprehension of the truth, rather than its negation, he wrenches notions from their original contexts in the works of his antagonists, and attempts to restore to them the visionary meaning which he believes they once possessed. This he does, for instance, with Newton's 'Ratio' and with Descartes' 'Vortexes'. He had a phrase for this tactic: 'Striving with Systems to deliver individuals from those Systems' (*Jerusalem*, plate 11, l.5, E154/K630).[27] There is a characteristically brilliant shrewdness about the endeavour.

It may tie up a few loose ends to suggest how the tactic is deployed in the present case. What Blake dislikes about Platonism can be broadly summed up in the word 'abstraction'. In his early works he uses Platonic motifs to represent his own conception of how the world of illusory limitation nevertheless seems real to unfortunates such as Thel. In his later works he continues to dramatise the powerful world of illusion and employs a Platonic vocabulary to describe it, with the understanding that only deceived states of mind are being described. As for his own sense of what is true: he feels able to take the works of the Neoplatonists, in particular Plotinus, and sift out both the One and Matter, and much else that goes with them, as representing the malign principle of 'abstraction' and the divided consciousness which Blake feels this encourages. What is left is a visionary version of the Intelligible World capable of being perceived here and now by Imagination and not by Memory. If it be Neoplatonic to believe such things, then Blake is a Neoplatonist.

[27] Cf. Steven Shaviro, '"Striving with Systems": Blake and the Politics of Difference', *Essential Articles*, ed. Hilton, pp. 271–99.

PART V

The nineteenth century

CHAPTER 18

Introduction

Richard Jenkyns

'Aristotle is dead, but Plato is alive' – so Benjamin Jowett (1817–93) used to say.[1] A man is not on oath in an epigram, but it may still be worth asking why Jowett should have said it and his pupils remembered it. He cannot have meant that Oxford undergraduates ignored Aristotle (most of them, throughout the nineteenth century, studied the *Ethics*), or that scholars were neglecting him (one might think of Grote and Alexander Grant), and it is unlikely that Jowett thought him of small intrinsic value. Rather he felt (as one can see from his private notebooks) that Plato could still aid the moral life of a Christian in the nineteenth century and, more generally, that Plato was a creative influence on the cultural and intellectual life of the age. That belief seems justified. Grote's *Plato and the Other Companions of Socrates* (1865) was a sign of the times, notable in that a radical and utilitarian, hostile to much of Plato's thought, believed it worth his while to engage with the philosopher, sifting those parts of his work which he considered of permanent value from those which were to be rejected.[2] Jowett for his part translated all Plato's dialogues, providing them with extended introductions which sought to bring out their usefulness for the modern world; his own work not only reflected Plato's continuing influence but helped to sustain it.

It had not been ever thus. As Pat Rogers indicates (see above, pp. 181–5), for much of the eighteenth century Plato was rather neglected (Aristotle too, for that matter). But between 1759 and 1780 Floyer Sydenham tried to give him wider currency by translating nine Platonic (or pseudo-Platonic) dialogues, and in 1792 the industrious Thomas Taylor began translating the rest, with more zeal than skill; he published the first complete English version of Plato's

[1] E. Abbott and L. Campbell, *The Life and Letters of Benjamin Jowett* (London, 1897), I, p. 261.
[2] William Whewell's *The Platonic Dialogues for English Readers* (1859–61), of no scholarly importance, is perhaps another sign of the times in its concern to reach a wider audience.

works, incorporating Sydenham's translations, in 1804.[3] These signs of a quickening interest were not immediately reflected in English universities. The belief of F.D. Maurice (1805–72) that Cambridge in the earlier nineteenth century had a Platonist flavour (and was therefore superior to Oxford, with its undiluted Aristotelianism) seems a half-truth at best.[4] At Oxford Aristotle was invariably studied by undergraduates reading Literae Humaniores at least from 1807; William Sewell began lecturing on Plato in the thirties, it is said to large audiences, but in the early years of the century he does seem to have been neglected.[5] 'Must I care about Aristotle?' the undergraduate Shelley asked his tutor. 'What if I do not mind Aristotle?'[6] His friend T.J. Hogg observed in 1821, 'Plato is unfortunately little read even by scholars'.[7] Peacock, three years before, had said that Plato 'certainly wants patronage in these days, when philosophy sleeps and classical literature seems destined to participate in its repose.'[8] Or to turn from life to fiction, Dr Folliott, in Peacock's *Crotchet Castle* (1831), declares, 'You must remember that, in our Universities, Plato is held to be little better than a misleader of youth; and they have shown their contempt for him, not only by never reading him (a mode of contempt in which they deal very largely) but even by never printing a complete edition of him'.[9] But through all these remarks we catch the condescending tone of self-confident youth, assured that it has the future on its side.

Shelley's revolt against Aristotle was part and parcel of his Platonism. But if we share the view of Plato and Aristotle as polar opposites, we may be falling into a nineteenth-century trap. Coleridge (1772–1834), the leading influence in disseminating transcendental and idealist philosophy in England, maintained, 'Every man is born an Aristotelian or a Platonist. I don't think it possible that any one born an Aristotelian *can* become a Platonist, and I am sure no born Platonist *can* ever change into an Aristotelian. They are the two classes of men beside which it is next to impossible to conceive a third'[10] (Though his immediate inspiration was Kant, there could be

[3] M.L Clarke, *Greek Studies in England 1770–1830* (Cambridge, 1945), p. 244.
[4] D. Newsome, *Two Classes of Men* (London, 1974), p. 8 etc.
[5] F. Turner, *The Greek Heritage in Victorian Britain* (New Haven and London, 1981), p. 373.
[6] T.J. Hogg etc, *The Life of Shelley*, ed. H. Wolfe (London, 1933), I, 70.
[7] [Jane Lady Shelley], *Shelley and Mary*, 4 vols ([London], 1882), I, 642.
[8] Peacock to Shelley, 30 Aug. 1818, in *The Works of Thomas Love Peacock*, ed. H.F.B. Brett-Smith and C.E. Jones, 10 vols (London, 1924–34), VIII, p. 203.
[9] T.L. Peacock, *Crotchet Castle*, ch. 7.
[10] Coleridge, *Table Talk*, 2 July 1830, ed. C. Wooding, 2 vols (Princeton, 1990), p. 118. (*The Collected Works of Samuel Taylor Coleridge*, 14.)

no doubt in which class he placed himself.) This outlook may not have been original to Coleridge, but it does appear to have a specially nineteenth-century character (one might contrast Raphael's fresco of the Schools of Athens (see frontispiece), where Plato and the younger Aristotle stand together in the centre of the picture, allies at the apex of classical thought). Coleridge was wrong. Plato and Aristotle are no doubt the greatest Greek philosophers, as well as the only two from the classical period to have survived in bulk, but the one was the pupil of the other, and for all their differences, they were agreed on the scope and method of philosophy, on what questions should be asked, and sometimes on the answers too (both, for example, give an intellectualist explanation of moral weakness). In radical contrast was the materialism of Epicurus, who rejected metaphysics altogether and argued that philosophical theory, ethics included, should derive from a scientific investigation of the nature of the physical world.

The nineteenth-century polarisation between Plato and Aristotle encouraged a stress upon the transcendent, even mystic element in Plato's philosophy. And for romantic poets, with their taste both for grand abstractions and for the particularities of the natural world, there was a special charm in what we may call the Platonic paradox. Plato holds that *ta polla kala*, the many individual beauties of the perceptible world, are only pale shadows of the everlasting and immutable forms which they embody. From one point of view this may seem to devalue the perceptible world, while from another it exalts it, for it is not only full of its own beauties but also our means of access to the transcendent, the eternal, the divine. In *Adonais* (1821) Shelley expressed this paradox in an image inspired by Plato's Myth of Er, where the physical universe is conceived as a series of concentric and diversely coloured whorls, like vessels fitting into one another:

> The One remains, the many change and pass;
> Heaven's light for ever shines, Earth's shadows fly;
> Life, like a dome of many-coloured glass,
> Stains the white radiance of Eternity,
> Until Death tramples it to fragments
>
> *Adonais*, stanza 52

He could also enlist Plato as an ally in his moral rebellion: in *Epipsychidion* (1821) the doctrine of the *Symposium* is adapted to become a defence of free love, while his unfaithfulness to his wife receives the loftiest justification: in his mistress's body he seeks the divine, eternal beauty which it incarnates. (see Wallace, pp. 229–41 below).[11]

Wordsworth's 'Immortality Ode' (1802–6), the most famous poetic expression of romantic Platonism, is an embarrassment to the historian, since it is unclear that Wordsworth knew Plato when he wrote it (see Price, pp. 217–81 below). Perhaps the issue may be approached through a later poet of Platonist tendency. Hopkins (1844–89) thought that 'Wordsworth's particular grace, his *charisma*, as theologians say, has been granted in equal measure to so very few men since time was – to Plato and who else? I mean his spiritual insight into nature'. And he compared Plato and Wordsworth as two of the very few men in history 'whom common repute . . . has treated as having had something happen to them that does not happen to other men, as having *seen something*, whatever that really was'.[12] That is a Platonist account of Wordsworth's Platonism: there is something 'out there' which both men have 'seen'. More prosaically, we may suppose an interaction between the poet's personal vision and a loose Platonism that was in the air at the time. Wordsworth's 'Ode' was 'falsely called Platonic' in John Stuart Mill's view, but ironically it may have influenced a more philosophical Platonism: it is hard to think that Maurice would have held 'All little children are Platonists, and it is their education which makes men Aristotelians', without the Wordsworthian fusion of the Platonic idea of *anamnesis* with the romantic sense of the child's peculiar purity of vision.[13] As for Hopkins, in him we meet an idea of the relation between the transcendent God and the diverse beauties of the natural world both more rigorous and more rhapsodic than in any other poet. Hopkins himself would have attributed a great deal of this to Duns Scotus, but it is likely that it owes as much to his direct encounter with Plato.

Plato's political thought did not attract much close scrutiny in the nineteenth century. People as diverse as Macaulay, Gladstone and Mill praised his political wisdom.[14] This may remind us of the authoritarian or paternalist streak that runs through much Victorian political thought, but we should also remember that the nineteenth century had no experience of Leninism or National Socialism, which were to inspire the assaults upon Plato by Crossman and Popper. To

[11] *Epipsychidion*, e.g. lines 149ff., 115f., 77ff.

[12] Hopkins to R.W. Dixon of 7 August and 23 October 1886 in *Gerard Manley Hopkins: Selected Letters*, ed. C. Phillips (Oxford, 1990), pp. 235, 240.

[13] Maurice quoted by Newsome, *Two Classes*, p. 8.

[14] For chapter and verse, see R. Jenkyns, *The Victorians and Ancient Greece* (Oxford, 1980), pp. 244–6.

be sure, no one could agree with everything that Plato said, but this in a way protected him: he seems to have been regarded more as a moralist than as an exact political thinker. The religious Plato, however, fascinated the Victorians. For agnostics the attraction was that he could be treated as a sort of alternative scripture. Mill (whose theory of mathematics was in fact radically anti-Platonist) pronounced him the greatest moralist of antiquity and compared him to Christ in his capacity for inspiring the love of virtue.[15] This attitude was enhanced by the cult of Socrates. Mill again compared his martyrdom to the passion of Jesus, and Matthew Arnold declared that though Socrates is dead, every man carries a possible Socrates in his breast – as it were, a secularised Holy Spirit (it is this sense of Socrates as pattern and mentor that is perhaps Plato's largest influence on Arnold)(see Rowe, pp. 242–56 below).[16] Such analogies were attractive to Christians too. Some theologians argued for Platonist elements in St John's doctrine of the incarnation. B.F. Westcott (1825–1901), the saintly Bishop of Durham, wrote, 'Plato is an unconscious prophet of the Gospel. The Life of Christ is, in form no less than in substance, the Divine reality of which the Myths were an instructive foreshadowing'.[17] This puts Plato on a par with Isaiah. Jowett joined in comparing Socrates to Christ, and Connop Thirlwall (1797–1875), a bishop of Liberal Anglican stamp, refused to meet a German scholar who had justified Socrates' death.[18] In this sphere, Plato seems less the property of one class of men than a common ground upon which different classes of men might meet.

Not everyone cared for a Platonising Christianity. Jowett's detractors suspected that his Platonism was a dodging of the issues or a cloak for a covert agnosticism.[19] This was the basis for W.H. Mallock's savage satire upon him in *The New Republic* (1877), where 'Dr Jenkinson', preaching a sermon, takes his text from the Psalms, plunges into a discourse on Plato, stressing his 'Christian' elements, dissolves Christianity into a vague beneficence, and ends by inviting everyone present, whatever his beliefs, to recite the Apostles' Creed.[20] This was unfair on Jowett; but it could more plausibly be claimed that Walter Pater (1839–94) (see Varty, pp. 257–67 below), approaching the issue from an agnostic standpoint, did present a spiritualised

[15] *Mill's Ethical Writings*, ed. J. Schneewind (New York, 1965), pp. 77.
[16] J.S. Mill, *On Liberty*; M. Arnold, *Culture and Anarchy*, 'Conclusion'.
[17] *Essays in the History of Religious Thought in the West* (London, 1891), p. 48.
[18] *The George Eliot Letters*, 7 vols, ed. G. Haight (London, 1954–6), VI, 407.
[19] Jenkyns, *Victorians*, p. 250.
[20] W.H. Mallock, *The New Republic*, bk 2, ch. 1.

Platonism which he almost assimilated to a watered-down Christianity, free of dogma. We meet this in his philosophical novel, *Marius the Epicurean* (1885), set in the second century AD.[21] His *Plato and Platonism* (1893) is predominantly concerned to blend the Platonic paradox with another idea: that Plato's philosophy, for all its abstraction, is visibly the product of a highly distinctive personality, one that has had to struggle between spiritual and sensuous impulses. There may be an insight here, but the book is vitiated by a self-indulgence that licenses wilful misinterpretation.[22] In an early essay on Coleridge Pater had asked who would give up the colour and curve of a rose-leaf for the colourless, formless and intangible being which Plato put so high; now he sees Plato as a poet and aesthete, cultivating a sensuous austerity: the spirit of the ideal state is to be compared to Gregorian music or the architecture of an early Gothic monastery.

One does not immediately think of Ruskin in this context, but his judgement of Plato may bring out what the philosopher meant to his age:[23]

> He is profoundly spiritual and capacious in all his views, and embraces the small systems of Aristotle and Cicero, as the solar system does the Earth. He seems to me especially remarkable for the sense of the great Christian virtue of Holiness, or sanctification; and for the sense of the presence of the Deity in all things, great or small, which always runs in a solemn undercurrent beneath his exquisite playfulness and irony; while all the merely moral virtues may be found in his writings defined in the most noble manner, as a great painter defines his figures, *without outlines.*

This account gives Plato the exuberance and diversity of a Gothic cathedral or a Victorian novel. At the same time it suggests that there was someting in Plato for everybody: he is prophet, artist, humorist, moralist, aesthete. Plato had his denigrators in the nineteenth century, such as Bentham and Herbert Spencer, while Macaulay's feelings were mixed: in his essay on Lord Bacon he praised the nobility of Plato's thought, while censuring its uselessness for practical life – indeed, the uselessness of Greek philosophy altogether. But on the whole the last century was a time of triumph for a philosopher who seemed able to appeal to aesthete and man of action, conservative and radical, agnostic and Christian alike.

[21] W. Pater, *Marius the Epicurean*, especially ch. 3.
[22] For detailed analysis, see Jenkyns, *Victorians*, pp. 253–61.
[23] J. Ruskin, *The Stones of Venice*, II, ch. 8, §49.

CHAPTER 19

Recollection and recovery: Coleridge's Platonism

Keith Cunliffe

The influence of Platonic thought on Coleridge is felt in almost every area of his work. In this chapter I shall consider only the way in which Coleridge used Plato's theory of ideas, and his theory of knowledge as recollection. He re-defined these in the light of his reading of the German transcendental idealist philosophers, notably Immanuel Kant. The intensive study of Kant which he undertook in the years following 1800 confirmed Coleridge in his opposition to the British empiricist tradition. It supplemented, but did not supplant, the study of Plato and the Neoplatonists. Plato and Kant both provided him with ammunition which he could use against the 'mechanical philosophy' as he generally called the complex of ideas centring upon the associationist psychology of David Hartley and the epistemology of impressions and ideas developed by Locke and Hume. Coleridge had two main objections to this system. It treats the mind as essentially passive; and it reduces the mind to a collection of disparate ideas loosely tied together by association and memory. Plato was central to the shaping of Coleridge's response to these perceived limitations of the empiricist position. Coleridge saw in him, as Shelley did also, the supreme example of the philosopher as poet. Plato's writings are in themselves 'poetry of the highest kind'.[1] As such, I shall argue, their value for Coleridge lay not in any specific Platonic doctrine, important though these were. It consisted rather in their ability to elicit an imaginative and creative response from the reader. The active nature of this response differs radically from the eighteenth-century empiricist model which conceived the mind as a *tabula rasa*, able only to receive the impressions made on it by objects in the external world. Platonism by contrast implicates its students in a process; the 're-production of states of Being', as Coleridge calls it in

[1] *Biographia Literaria*, II, ch. 14, in *The Collected Works of Samuel Taylor Coleridge*, general editor, Kathleen Coburn (London and Princeton, 1983), VII, p. 14.

a notebook entry of 1810.[2] Like poetry, which Coleridge defines in *Biographia Literaria* as bringing the 'whole soul of man into activity', this process engages all the mind's faculties, not merely the discursive understanding.[3] I shall argue that the Platonic idea, reinterpreted in the light of Coleridge's reading of Kant, is central to this conception of mind. More specifically I shall try to show that the Platonic concept of *anamnesis* or recollection supplied Coleridge with a metaphor, recurrently invoked, for the process by which the idea is 'awakened' into active life.

The direct influence of Plato during Coleridge's early years is frustratingly hard to gauge. It is not until 1801, in a letter to Thomas Poole, that Plato is proclaimed unambiguously as a 'great and astonishing' genius.[4] This awareness of Plato's full significance thus appears to emerge from the same period of intense metaphysical study, undertaken during 1800–1801, which also established the importance of Kant for Coleridge. It marks a resolution of the tension between Coleridge's earlier intellectual adherence to various empiricist philosophies and his instinctive, experiential exploration of a more active and organically unified conception of mind. He had been feeling his way towards this in the poetry of the 1790s. Many of the themes and images which are first developed there are later taken up in a more explicitly philosophical context. Plato and Kant thus enabled him to formalise, and to ground philosophically, insights which had been slowly forming for several years.

This does not mean that Coleridge simply remodelled Plato in the image of Kant. Coleridge adopted the Kantian distinction between reason and understanding, but he did not accept the limitations which Kant imposed on reason in the *Critique of Pure Reason*. In particular he rejected the circumscribed role of the ideas in Kant's philosophy. It is for this reason that Coleridge in *The Statesman's Manual* aligns Kant with Aristotle rather than with Plato and Plotinus.[5] Coleridge sided more with the last two. In his view the

[2] *The Notebooks of Samuel Taylor Coleridge*, ed. K. Coburn (London and Princeton, 1957–), III, §3935).

[3] *Biographia Literaria*, II, ch. 14, in *Works*, VII, pp. 15–16. The poet is defined as bringing the 'whole soul of man into activity, with the subordination of its faculities to each other, according to their relative worth and dignity'. It is revealing that this definition has close verbal parallels with Coleridge's summary of Plato's *Republic* as 'a description of an individual, all of whose faculities are in their proper subordination and interdependence'. *The Statesman's Manual*, edited by R.L. White, in *Collected Works*, VI, p. 62 and note.

[4] *Collected Letters of Samuel Taylor Coleridge*, ed. E.L. Griggs, 6 vols. (Oxford, 1956–71), II, 675, §380.

[5] *Lay Sermons, The Statesmans Manual*, in *Works*, VI, p. 114.

understanding itself presupposes the presence and the reality of the ideas. The idea is distinct from our common perceptions of reality though it is implicitly present working in and through them. It cannot however itself become an object of perception. Nor can it be expressed in words. The inadequacy of logic to grasp the ideas is demonstrated, Coleridge suggests, by the frequency with which Plato's dialogues end inconclusively, as in the *Theaetetus*, or by Plato's use of arguments leading to contradictory conclusions, as in the *Parmenides*. This was a method adopted also by Kant in the *Critique of Pure Reason*. Kant uses it to show that pure reason, and its ideas, transgress the bounds of what we can know through the understanding. Plato, Coleridge suggests, used this method for a radically different purpose. He presented arguments leading to opposite conclusions precisely in order to demonstrate the inadequacy of the discursive understanding and to show the need for something beyond it:

> the understanding is indirectly and by negation the organ of the reason, and the exercise of logic for this purpose by the understanding to prove the inadequacy of the understanding constitutes the Platonic dialectic which the divine philosopher calls the wings by which philosophy first raises herself from the ground.[6]

Whether Plato would have agreed that this was his purpose is arguable. But for Coleridge the important point was that the very absence of sharply defined conclusions in so many of the dialogues in itself suggested or showed more than could be said. It acted as a stimulus to the mind of the reader and implied the presence of the ideas working in and behind the discursive logic of the text.

Coleridge thus draws on elements of both Kant and Plato. He agrees with Kant that ideas cannot be known directly. The 'idea' in Coleridge's sense is not a transcendent object of knowledge. On the other hand it is not a concept like the Kantian 'categories'. Coleridge explicitly sought to 'establish the reality of ideas as contradistinguished from notions and perceptions'.[7] Moreover the idea is 'not merely formal but dynamic'; it is a latent 'power' or presence in the human mind which can be awakened.[8] This is quite different from Kant's concept of the 'categories' of the understanding. Coleridge envisages a process of mental development which refers as much to empirical psychology as to the logical forms of cognition.

For this reason the Socratic emphasis on self knowledge was

[6] *Logic*, in *Works*, XIII, p. 139.
[7] A.D. Snyder, *Coleridge on Logic and Learning*, p. 70.
[8] Coleridge's annotation on his own copy of *The Statesman's Manual*, *Works*, VI, p. 61.

important to Coleridge. In the philosophical lectures which he gave in 1819 he stresses the fact that both Socrates and Plato began by 'meditating' on the 'goings-on' of their own minds.[9] They refer us to a self which is not merely a logical pre-condition of experience, like the Kantian 'transcendental unity of apperception'. Equally however this self is not limited, as it was by Hume for example, to the internalised representation of impressions or ideas. As late as the *Phaedrus* Plato makes Socrates assert the primacy of the Delphic injuction to 'know yourself'. It is 'laughable', he says, to pursue 'other kinds of knowledge' so long as he is 'not yet able to know himself'. Such knowledge can only be acquired through the study of, and in conversation with, other people. The Socratic pursuit of self knowledge thus had a practical, and moral, orientation. Coleridge was deeply in sympathy with this, though as we shall see he took a far more positive view of nature than Socrates allows in this passage. It is a recurring theme in Coleridge's treatment of Platonism and one of the great advantages which it had in relation to other philosophies:

> One excellence of the Doctrine of Plato, or of the Plotino-platonic Philosophy, is that it never suffers . . . its Disciples to forget themselves, lost and scattered in sensible objects . . . It is impossible to understand the Elements of this Philosophy without an appeal, at every step & round of the Ladder, to the fact within, to the mind's Consciousness. (*Notebooks*, III, §3935)

This philosophy does not just transmit isolated conclusions or products of thought. Its value, Coleridge goes on to say, is that it implicates us in the process of 'creative Thought'. Significantly, he associates this with what he calls 'Recognition'. He conceives this as not simply the 'indolence of mere attention' but as the 're-production of states of Being'. Platonism here is presented as helping to recall the mind from the 'lost and scattered' existence which the empiricists had forced upon it by treating 'ideas' as internal pictures.

The energy and 'acts' of mind which Platonism 'rouses' were enormously important to Coleridge, and valuable in themselves, rather than for their results. It is an emphasis intimately connected with his own persistent sense of inadequacy in just this respect. The idiom is recognisably akin to that of 'Dejection: An Ode'. Here Coleridge analyses the poet's inability to make a creative response to nature, and the means by which that imaginative paralysis is overcome, in a way which can fruitfully be described in terms of this

[9] *The Philosophical Lectures of Samuel Taylor Coleridge*, ed. K. Coburn (London and New York, 1949). See Lecture III, p. 137, and V, p. 186.

dichotomy between 'mere attention' and re-creative reproduction of 'states of Being'. The poet attends to nature, but cannot recognise or respond to nature; the details of the world around him are meticulously noted, but 'with how blank an eye' (l.30). The 'state of Being' in which the poet responds to nature as well as attending to it finds expression in one of Coleridge's most powerful images:

> And would we aught behold, of higher worth,
> Than that inanimate cold world allowed
> To the poor loveless ever-anxious crowd,
> Ah! from the soul itself must issue forth
> A light, a glory, a fair luminous cloud
> Enveloping the Earth.
>
> (ll.50–5)[10]

The poet's present state of spiritual desolation forces him to externalise this state of being, to present it as an object in itself desirable and whose loss is to be lamented. Yet the very act of mourning this lost creative power compells the poet to recollect it, an act of recall which is also a reproduction, however fleeting, of his former 'state of Being'.

Coleridge had already explored this economy of loss and recovery in an earlier poem, 'This Lime Tree Bower My Prison'. There the poet's spiritual malaise is actually imaged on the physical level by the injury which has kept him at home and separated him from his friends, depriving him of the pleasures which he knows they are enjoying. The tone is infinitely lighter than that of 'Dejection', but the pattern is similar; the release and recovery of the mind from its 'prison' is effected by an act of imaginative empathy which consciously seeks to reproduce the 'states of Being' experienced by the poet's friends:

> and sometimes
> Tis well to be bereft of promis'd good
> That we may lift the soul, and contemplate
> With lively joy the joys we cannot share.
>
> (ll.64–7)

Imaginative projection necessarily bases itself here upon recollection, for the pleasures which Coleridge imagines for his friends are of course those which he has himself enjoyed on previous excursions. But the poem acquires an additional dimension in that the act of imaginative

10 All verse quotations are from Coleridge's *Poetical Works*, ed. E.H. Coleridge (Oxford, 1921). This image is strikingly and significantly anticipated in a notebook entry of November 1799, in which Coleridge refers to 'the sunny mist, the luminous gloom of Plato'. *Notebooks*, I, § 528.

recollection/reproduction which enables the poet to participate in the experience of his friends inevitably elicits a parallel act of imaginative reproduction from the reader of the poem. It is precisely this ability to elicit an imaginative as well as an intellectual response, to stimulate 'Creative thought', which Coleridge singles out as a distinctive feature of Platonism and which he finds lacking in his philosophical contemporaries.

The imaginative impoverishment of what he calls 'modern Philosophy' is sharply criticised by Coleridge in the same notebook entry which defines Platonism in terms of its capacity to engage the mind of the reader in 'Creative thought'. The highly charged language in which he defines the limitations of modern philosophy tells us, by implication, a great deal about the effect which he thought philosophy and poetry should have on the reader. Modern philosophy appeals to the 'mere understanding'

> without exciting or awakening any interest, any tremulous feeling of the heart, as if it heard or began to glimpse something which had once belonged to it . . . even as a man recovering gradually from an alienation of the Senses or the Judgement on beginning to recollect the countenances of his Wife, Mother, Children, or Betrothed. (*Notebooks*, III, §3935)

Words like 'awakening', 'recovering' and 'recollect' suggest that the Platonic Doctrine of Recollection supplied a scheme for this way of representing intellectual and imaginative growth. Plato originally developed this theory, in the *Meno*, as a way of accounting for the soul's ability to acquire knowledge. The soul does not really learn something new, according to this model. Rather it recollects knowledge which it had acquired in an antenatal existence and had subsequently forgotten, confused by its incarnation in matter (*Meno* 82b–85b; *Phaedrus* 250a–c). Coleridge did not of course take this literally.[11] Nor did he think that Plato meant us to take it literally. But it did supply him with a metaphor for the way in which the mind's latent faculties are awakened or elicited by and through experience. And, as this passage indicates, he could interpret it widely, to include the 'tremulous feeling of the heart'. Here the Platonic concept of Recollection, originally applied to knowledge, becomes emotionally and imaginatively charged. Coleridge is not talking about the recovery of some objective content of knowledge but about the recovery of the senses themselves from 'alienation'. Recollection or 'recovery' becomes a process which restores the mind to its original and true nature. Coleridge sees the

[11] *Biographia literaria*, II, ch. 22, p. 147.

'awakening' or 'exciting' of this process as one of the principal functions of both poetry and philosophy.

Coleridge's concern with the soul's 'alienation' from its true nature emerges still more strikingly in another notebook entry of this period, in which the metaphor of shipwreck is invoked to suggest both the soul's existentially isolated predicament and the possible means of its recovery:

I would compare the human Soul to a Ship's Crew cast on an unknown Island . . . the moment, when the Soul begins to be sufficiently self-conscious, to ask concerning itself . . . is the first moment of its intellectual arrival into the World – Its Being . . . is posterior to its Existence – Suppose the shipwrecked man stunned, & for many weeks in a state of Ideotcy or utter loss of Thought & Memory-& then gradually awakened . . . (*Notebooks*, III, §3593)

This passage is resonant with themes and images explored elsewhere in Coleridge's work. The Platonic associations are heightened here by parallels with Wordsworth's 'Immortality Ode' (see Price, pp. 217–18 below). But Coleridge uses the Platonic structure of pre-existence and recollection to a very different end. Like the infant in Wordsworth's poem the shipwrecked mariners have come over the sea, 'from afar'. Coleridge's 'shipwrecked man' resembles the child in the Immortality Ode, who is subject to a 'sleep and a forgetting'. Similarly the shipwrecked soul suffers an 'utter loss of thought and memory'. But this loss is followed by a recovery. The soul is 'gradually awakened'. (Cf. *Timaeus* 44b) This recalls rather Coleridge's own ancient mariner whose isolation and alienation from nature is followed by a gradual recovery. The process, like his journey home, is a long one. The moment of return is a climactic point in the poem, marked by the shock of recognition:

> Oh! dream of joy! is this indeed
> The light-house top I see?
> Is this the hill? is this the kirk?
> Is this mine own countree?
> (ll.464–8)[12]

Significantly this 'dream' leaves the mariner suspended uncertainly on the threshold of sleep and waking:

> O let me be awake, my God!
> Or let me sleep alway.
> (ll.470–1)

[12] The mariner's odyssey can also be read in a Neoplatonic context. See John Beer, *Coleridge the Visionary* (London, 1970), pp. 150–1.

Even more directly, the terms in which Coleridge defines the soul's alienated condition in his notebook recall the very end of the poem. The wedding guest, overwhelmed by the impact of the mariner's narrative, goes 'like one that hath been stunned / And is of sense forlorn' (l.622). He can no longer participate in the social celebration of the marriage feast; his very different participation in the traumatic narrative of the mariner has set him apart. But this suggests also that the condition of imaginative or spiritual desolation may in itself be a necessary stage in the process through which the soul is awakened. Although alienated from the mundane celebration of the wedding feast the wedding guest is directed by the mariner to the celebration of a higher reality, conceived here in terms of a communal act of Christian worship. It is far 'sweeter', we learn, to walk 'together to the 'kirk' and 'all together pray'. Although transposed into a Christian context, this recalls Plato's allegory of the Cave (*Republic* VII). Viewed in this perspective the sense of alienation or estrangement from mundane realities is a necessary condition for the overcoming of that more radical alienation which is the plight of the soul incarnated in matter. Thus the wedding guest is certainly awakened as well as 'stunned' by the mariner's narrative. He rises the 'morrow morn' a 'sadder and wiser man' (l.624).

But this emphasis on the awakening of the soul never implied for Coleridge, as at times it did for Plato, the rejection of nature. The mariner, trapped alone on a becalmed ship, is cut off both from the springs of his own humanity and from the nature which surrounds him. Only when he recognises the beauty of the water snakes which play around the ship can he begin the process of recovery and spiritual convalescence. Although the value of Plato for Coleridge was in part that he directs the mind inwards to its own sources of power, Coleridge never abandoned his early belief that that power should be awakened by, though not confined to, nature. The educative function which Coleridge ascribes to nature marks clearly the point of his divergence from Plato, or rather the point at which he feels the need to supplement and correct Plato. This becomes apparent as early as *The Destiny of Nations*, an uncompleted neo-Miltonic epic of 1796. Here Coleridge links the growth of the mind closely to a Platonic schema of the soul's gradual enlightenment and significantly modifies that schema while doing so. God is manifested through 'secondary things' as 'through clouds that veil his blaze'. Nature becomes 'symbolical'

one mighty alphabet
For infant minds; and we in this low world
Placed with our backs to bright Reality,
That we may learn with young unwounded ken
The substance from its shadow.

(ll. 19–23)

This development of the cave analogy from book VII of *The Republic* subtly alters the values attached to the terms of the Platonic allegory. For Plato the prisoners in the cave are far more in the dark. Their backs are turned not to 'bright reality' but to the fire which casts their shadows on the wall. They are the victims of an illusory phenomenal world in which they are seen as imprisoned and which is interpreted in a sense almost entirely negative (*Republic* 514 sq.). Coleridge endorses their gradual liberation from the tyranny of the senses but he suggests that that liberation can be achieved partly through the agency of the natural world itself, which is represented as a language, the self expression of the creator for 'infant minds'.

Coleridge was still syncretising Plato with this Berkeleyan conception of nature as the language of God when he gave his philosophical lectures more than twenty years later. Plato, Coleridge suggests, conceived the phenomenon as only 'a language by which . . . the invisible communicates its existence to our finite being'.[13] This ascribes a higher value to the natural world than Plato ever allowed. For Plato nature is at best, as in the *Timaeus* (30–1), a copy of the transcendent realm of the ideas. But the value of both nature and language for Coleridge was that they could stimulate the recovery or 'recollection' of the idea already latent within the mind. The doctrine of Recollection supplies Coleridge with a pattern which is valid imaginatively, if not logically, for this recovery, and which he approaches from the standpoint of his own experience:

In looking at objects of Nature while I am thinking . . . I seem rather to be seeking . . . a symbolical language for something within me that already and forever exists, than observing anything new. Even when the latter is the case, yet still I have always an obscure feeling as if that new phaenomenon were the dim Awaking of a forgotten or hidden Truth of my inner Nature. (*Notebooks*, II, §2546)

The 'forgotten' truth to be recalled or awoken has been transposed from the eternal realm of the Platonic ideas to 'my inner Nature'. The idea is thus naturalised and internalised. 'Is a word intelligible of

[13] *Philosophical Lectures*, V, p. 187.

itself', Coleridge asked in a notebook entry, or only 'by virtue of an idea in the soul of him that hears it, which the word awakens?' (*Notebooks*, IV, §5280).

Nature, as Coleridge had found in 'Dejection', cannot in itself recall us from that alienation, that sense of 'utter loss' which is the condition of the existentially shipwrecked soul. But it can act upon us as a catalyst for that process of recovery and growth which we have been examining. The locus of the ideal reality which it adumbrates is not the transcendent eternal realm of the Platonic ideas, but the human mind. Coleridge's 'modernised', or modified, Platonism thus exploits what we may perhaps call a transcendental version of the Doctrine of Recollection and the Platonic concept of awakening. These become a means to liberate the self from that vision of alienation, fragmented and forgetting, which haunts so much of his writing.

CHAPTER 20

Wordsworth's Ode on the Intimations of Immortality

A.W. Price

Platonism has left no more manifest imprint upon English poetry than within Wordsworth's Ode finally subtitled 'Intimations of Immortality from Recollections of Early Childhood': it takes up the idea that each human soul exists before conception and birth for which Plato argues, most familiarly, in the *Phaedo* (72e–78b). And yet there is no proof that at the times of writing the Ode (March and June 1802, and early 1804) Wordsworth had any direct acquaintance with any work by Plato. At Cambridge in his day Plato was neglected.[1] The sale catalogue of his library at Rydal Mount included both Forster's 1765 edition of the *Phaedo* and Thomas Taylor's 1793 translation,[2] but we do not know when these came into his possession.[3] It may be that he had already become acquainted with certain writings after Plato: the 'sack full of books' which Coleridge brought over on 10 June 1802, exactly a week before Wordsworth resumed his Ode,[4] may have contained a compendium of excerpts edited by Ficino in 1578 from Proclus and others which Coleridge acquired in 1796;[5] possibly it also contained a work by Thomas

[1] Cf. Ben Ross Schneider, *Wordsworth's Cambridge Education* (Cambridge, 1957), pp. 230–1n. E.K. Chambers quotes Charles Le Grice recalling evenings in Coleridge's Cambridge rooms, 'when Aeschylus, and Plato, and Thucydides were pushed aside, with a pile of lexicons, &c.', *Samuel Taylor Coleridge: A Biographical Study* (Oxford, 1938), p. 20. But that rather suggests an elementary and philological than a reflective and philosophical interest.

[2] Cf. Chester L. Shaver and Alice C. Shaver, *Wordsworth's Library: A Catalogue* (New York, 1979), p. 202.

[3] He very likely possessed one or the other by 1817, or whenever precisely he composed the Sonnet 'I heard (alas! 'twas only in a dream)', published in 1819. This alludes to the *Phaedo*, as a note announces, with a precision and condensation – bringing together Socrates' descriptions of swans as singing before they die as befits creatures of Apollo, 84e–85b, and of our world as a dim 'hollow', 109c–d – that prove a familiarity wholly unevidenced within the more profoundly but also vaguely derivative Ode.

[4] *Journals of Dorothy Wordsworth*, edited by E. de Selincourt, 2 vols (Oxford, 1941), I, p. 156.

[5] Cf. John D. Rea, 'Coleridge's Intimations of Immortality from Proclus', *Modern Philology*, 26 (1928), 206–7.

Burnet, *The Sacred Theory of the Earth* (1681–9), which Coleridge admired.[6] However, a letter that Dorothy wrote to De Quincey on 7 July 1809 warns us against assuming much of William's Grasmere library: 'This Library is in fact little more than a chance collection of old books (setting aside the poets and a few other Books that are to be found everywhere)'; she continues by requesting any cheap editions of Burnet and of 'translations from the Classics, mostly historical' including Thucydides but not Herodotus, whom he had already.[7] Further, it may be symptomatic that, in a note to *Excursion* III l.112, Wordsworth introduces a long passage of Burnet's (presumably from the copy of the original Latin version that was listed in his library in 1829, but had been borrowed from Coleridge since about 1810)[8] with the remark, 'Since this paragraph was composed, I have read with so much pleasure, in Burnet's "Theory of the Earth", a passage expressing corresponding sentiments. . .':[9] the Ode may rather have prompted relevant reading than have been inspired by it.[10] If we want to identify the Ode's 'onlie begetter' (as Plato put it, 'the father of the *logos*', *Symposium* 177d), we do not have to look beyond poems by, and conversations with, Coleridge himself.

The feelings of a father inclined Coleridge towards Platonic thoughts of prenatal experience. The birth of his son Hartley in September 1796 gave life to the fancy of 'some unknown Past', and to the supposal 'We lived ere yet this fleshly robe we wore' (Sonnet 'Oft o'er my brain does that strange fancy roll').[11] It was in the context of family life that he wrote a month later, in pursuit of Ficino's compendium of excerpts from Proclus, 'Now, that the thinking part of man, i.e. the soul, existed previously to its appearance in its present body, may be very wild philosophy; but it is very intelligible poetry.'[12]

[6] Cf. G.W. Meyer, 'A Note on the Sources and Symbolism of the Intimations Ode', *Tulane Studies in English*, 3 (1952), 33–45.

[7] Alexander H. Japp, *De Quincey Memorials*, 2 vols (London, 1891), I. p. 203.

[8] Shaver and Shaver, *Wordsworth's Library*, p. 320.

[9] *The Poetical Works of William Wordsworth*, eds E. de Selincourt and H. Darbishire, 5 vols (Oxford, 1940–9), V, p. 420.

[10] Thus Burnet may have been the source (cf. Meyer, 'A Note on the Sources', p. 39) of an allusion to Archimedes in the notes that Wordsworth dictated to Isabella Fenwick (reproduced in *Poetical Works*, IV, pp. 463–4) only many years later; it is also worth remarking that the 1697 edition of Burnet's *The Sacred Theory of the Earth* listed in the Rydal Mount catalogue (Shaver and Shaver, *Wordsworth's Library*, p. 42) was presumably acquired after Wordsworth had quoted from the Latin edition in his note to the *Excursion*. For doubts about any debt to Thomas Vaughan, cf. Helen N. McMaster, 'Vaughan and Wordsworth', *Review of English Studies*, 11 (1935), 313–25.

[11] Manuscript version of the poem. Coleridge, *Poetical Works*, ed. E.H. Coleridge (Oxford, 1912; reprinted 1969), p. 153.

[12] *Collected Letters of Samuel Taylor Coleridge*, 6 vols, ed. E.L. Griggs (Oxford, 1956–71), I, p. 278.

He was to enter in his *Notebooks* in December 1804, 'To deduce instincts from obscure recollections of a pre-existing state – I have often thought of it – Ey! have I said, when I have seen certain tempers and actions in Hartley, that is *I* in my future State / so I think oftentimes that my children are my soul.'[13] Striking here, and anticipatory of Wordsworth's Ode, is the use of pre-existence of the soul as a pointer towards its life to come. The death of his second son, Berkeley, in February 1799 provoked an ambiguous question, 'What a multitude of admirable actions . . . it learnt even before it saw the light?', which may be asking about cognitions in the womb, or before conception.[14] He at least put enough faith in such fancies to resist Christian doctrine: asked to write an epitaph 'On an Infant, who Died before its Christening', he called it 'Of the kingdom of the Blest / Possessor, not Inheritor' (ll. 5–6).[15] The Platonic idea of prenatal existence became for him a poetical expression of a doting conception of the intelligence and integrity of neonatal life.

On 20 March 1802, exactly a week before Wordsworth started his Ode, Coleridge and he 'talked about various things – christening the children, etc. etc.'[16] This is one of a series of entries in Dorothy's *Journals* linking William's composition of 'The Rainbow' and part of the Ode to conversations with Coleridge, readings aloud of poems ('The Pedlar', 'To the Cuckoo'), and relevant remarks. These last indicate that William's mind was already turning to the content of the central stanzas 5–8. The thought 'that it would be so sweet thus to lie in the grave, to hear the peaceful sounds of the earth, and just to know that our dear friends were near' (29 April) already justifies four lines that he was later to remove in deference to Coleridge's objections (in *Biographia Literaria*, ch. 22):

To whom the grave
Is but a lonely bed without the sense or sight
Of day or the warm light,
A place of thought where we in waiting lie.
(ll. 121–4)

Stanza 5 is less precisely suggested by an observation, 'that the full moon, above a dark fir grove, is a fine image of the descent of a superior being' (13 June). These connections have suggested to some

[13] *The Notebooks of Samuel Taylor Coleridge*, ed. Kathleen Coburn, vol, 2. *1804–1808*, 2 parts (New York, 1962), §2332.
[14] *Collected Letters*, I, p. 482.
[15] Cf. Rea, 'Coleridge's Intimations', p. 203n.
[16] *Journals of Dorothy Wordsworth*, I, p. 127.

that Wordsworth must have been wrong when he claimed much later, in his notes dictated to Isabella Fenwick, that about two years passed between the composition of stanzas 1–4 and of the remainder.[17] All that is certain is that stanzas 1–4 existed in something like their present form before 4 April (probably on 27 March, when Dorothy recorded, 'At breakfast William wrote part of an ode');[18] for Coleridge's 'A Letter to . . .' (written on 4 April, and later revised and published as 'Dejection: An Ode') is in part a reply to them.[19] It follows that it is likely that when 'William added a little to the Ode he is writing' on 17 June he was already embarking on the rest. Yet given his preference for recollection in tranquility, it would be rash to insist that the composition of stanzas 5–8 must have stretched only over two intervals of seven days within 1802 (from 20 until 27 March, and again from 10 until 17 June), and not over the two years or so which he himself later recalled – though his mismemory of working on the Ode from 1803 until 1806 reduces his authority. We can both ascribe the Ode to the personal impact of Coleridge, and envisage that the effect was germinating until shortly before Coleridge left for Malta, with a copy of the complete Ode, in the spring of 1804. An extended chronology does not itself exclude John Rea's most striking conclusion: 'The hand is the hand of Wordsworth, but the voice is the voice of Coleridge.'[20] I wish to agree that the Ode must indeed be understood in relation to Coleridge, but as a response, not an echo.

Thus, for freely putting Plato to poetic use, Wordsworth may have had the advantage of knowing no Platonic texts to tighten the free rein left him by his informant. Sciolism has its privileges: as Walter Pater commented, 'Skirting the borders of this world of bewildering heights and depths, he got but the first exciting influence of it, that joyful enthusiasm which great imaginative theories prompt, when the mind first comes to have an understanding of them.'[21] Coleridge testified to the freedom at once of his reading of Plato, and of Wordsworth's reception of it, when he predicted that sympathetic readers, 'will be as little disposed to charge Mr. Wordsworth with

[17] Cf. Rea, 'Coleridge's Intimations', pp. 209–11; he is followed by Herbert Hartman, 'The "Intimations" of Wordsworth's Ode', *Review of English Studies*, 6 (1930), 143–5.

[18] *Journals*, I, p. 129. Jonathan Wordsworth makes nice use of the sentence that follows: 'He was interrupted not by a man from Porlock, but by Mr Olliff with the dung, and went out to work in the garden'; *William Wordsworth: The Borders of Vision* (Oxford, 1982), p. 423 n. 1.

[19] Most obviously, Coleridge's lines 232–42 reply to Wordsworth's lines 1–9; but further, if Coleridge's 'A Light, a Glory, and a luminous Cloud' (l. 303) echoes Wordsworth's 'the visionary gleam' and 'glory' (ll. 56–7), Wordsworth must have completed his stanza 4.

[20] 'Wordsworth's intimations of Palingenesis', *Review of English Studies*, 8 (1932), 83.

[21] Walter Pater, *Appreciations, With an Essay on Style* (London, 1889), p. 56.

believing in the Platonic pre-existence in the ordinary interpretation of the words, as I am to believe, that Plato himself ever meant or taught it' (*Biographia*, ch. 22). After some ambivalent remarks half-defending the idea of 'a prior state of existence' as neither advanced in nor contrary to revelation, Wordsworth said much the same, years later, to Miss Fenwick: 'I took hold of the notion of pre-existence as having sufficient foundation in humanity for authorising me to make for my purpose the best use I could as a poet.'[22] It is not merely that Plato the philosopher believed, *pace* Coleridge, what Wordsworth the poet exploits: they describe the human situation quite differently. R.D. Archer-Hind put it nicely: 'According to Wordsworth we are born with the antenatal radiance clinging about us and spend our lives in gradually losing it; according to Plato we lose the vision at birth and spend our lives in gradually recovering it.'[23] For Plato, incarnation is a sudden catastrophe (imagined just like the fall of Icarus, *Phaedrus* 248c), productive of a massive amnesia whose slow cure begins with those perceptions that stimulate metaphysical recollection and reflection (*Phaedo* 74a–76a, *Republic* v. 523b–524d); for Wordsworth, it brings the gradual dissipation (imaged in the rising sun) of recollections of glory by common-day perceptions (*Ode*, stanza 5). Plato infers the need of theoretical training in arithmetic, geometry and astronomy (*Republic* 525a–530c), Wordsworth the harm of practical projects (as if within a progressive education) of invention and imitation (stanzas 6–7). The structure of Platonic recollection is, in fact, less respected in Wordsworth's rapturous evocation of childhood instincts than in his sober recognition of adult consolations: Socrates stresses in the *Meno* that 'the path of recollection' starts from an experience of perplexity and the discovery of one's ignorance (84a–c), and a realisation of what is lost through the years must precede 'soothing thoughts' in a 'philosophic mind' (*Ode*, stanza 10). Of that closer parallel Wordsworth was unaware; he owes to Plato an idea and not a doctrine.

What emerges within the Ode is a myth within a myth: Platonic Recollection goes hand in hand with an idealisation of infancy. It is no coincidence that stanzas 1–4 are free of both: the time there was is not yet specified as infancy,[24] and the glory that has passed away is

[22] Cf. a remark to Aubrey de Vere (cited by Rea, 'Coleridge's Intimations', p. 212) that he held the doctrine 'with a poetical, not a religious, faith'.

[23] R.D. Archer-Hind, *The Phaedo of Plato* (London, 1883), p. 85.

[24] This is noticed by Paul Magnuson, 'The Genesis of Wordsworth's Ode', *The Wordsworth Circle*, 12 (1981), 24.

assigned no origin. Then stanza 5 suddenly transports us back to birth, and beyond. As I have noted, Wordsworth thus simultaneously echoes Plato, and humours Coleridge. He admitted this double departure from reality to his nephew Christopher Wordsworth, who recalls him as stating, 'In my Ode on the "Intimations of Immortality in Childhood", I do not profess to give a literal representation of the state of affections and of the moral being in childhood. I record my own feelings at the time – my absolute spirituality, my 'all-soulness', if I may so speak.'[25] And yet it would be an error to hear in this a mere echo of alien voices, for we can trace elsewhere how it is a recurrent and confusing tendency of Wordsworth's to speak of inspired boyhood as if it were infancy. Even in his remarks to his nephew, the phrase 'at the time' is tellingly ambiguous: grammar would refer it to his childhood, which logic forbids; an impossible apparent reference leaves the actual reference indeterminable. Already in stanza 4 of the Ode, the 'happy Shepherd-boy' is addressed as 'Thou Child of Joy' (ll. 34–5). Similarly, the 1799 *Prelude* dates fructifying 'spots of time' especially to 'our first childhood', 'the twilight of rememberable life', but recalls a riding expedition when the poet was five or six years old (I. ll. 288–304); and the 1805 *Prelude* extols 'the might of souls . . . while yet / The yoke of earth is new to them' (III. ll. 178–80), although the context is not infancy, but 'the glory of my youth' (l. 171).[26] Thus there can be no certainty about the age of the dear 'child' and 'girl' apostrophised in the 1802 Sonnet 'It is a beauteous evening, calm and free', and described as lying 'in Abraham's bosom' and worshipping 'at the Temple's inner shrine'. The Ode is virtually summarised in a passage of the 1805 *Prelude* (v. ll. 531–46), which begins as follows:

> Our childhood sits,
> Our simple childhood, sits upon a throne
> That hath more power than all the elements.
> I guess not what this tells of being past,
> Nor what it augurs of the life to come,
> But so it is.
>
> (ll. 531–6)

[25] Christopher Wordsworth, *Memoirs of William Wordsworth*, 2 vols. (London, 1851), II, p. 476.

[26] It is an irony, but not a coincidence, that Wordsworth may himself have preserved few or no truly infantile memories (i.e., psychoanalytically, memories predating the onset of latency at five or six); cf. Mark L. Reed, *Wordsworth: The Chronology of the Early Years, 1770–1799* (Cambridge, Mass., 1967), pp. 43–4.

The temporal reference of 'childhood' is vague, but is extended back until birth in order to adjoin 'being past'. An association of the times before birth and after death then admits the suggestion that the 'all-soulness' of boyhood is a natural state which man can hope to recover. And yet it seems that Wordsworth actually believed that childhood develops rather than diminishes: 'infant sensibility' is a 'great birthright of our being', and yet to be 'augmented and sustained' (1799 *Prelude*, II. ll. 315–17); our human soul is to be built up, the elements of feeling and thought purified and sanctified (1805 *Prelude*, I. ll. 407–12). Of course Plato's tenet that we advance through learning as recollecting is no contradiction of this belief, but Wordsworth's Ode translates philosophy into poetry, and possible fact into evident fiction: recollection is recast not as an achievement but as an instinct, so that development becomes diminuendo, as the boy who learns is imaged in the infant who forgets.

Wordsworth inserts the contrast between real and ideal childhood into the Ode itself, and with an abruptness that compels attention. Instead of sitting comfortably, the reader is jolted into an awareness of the gap between metaphor and meaning. At the one extreme, the infant is the 'best Philosopher', an 'Eye among the blind' (ll. 111–12), a 'mighty prophet' and 'seer blest' (l. 115); at the other, infancy has a 'simple creed' of 'delight and liberty' (ll. 137–8). Within Wordsorth's thinking, death can be denied at either extreme, but the Ode's intimations of immortality are positive, and distinctive of ideal infancy. This kind of simplicity contrasts with the 'simple childhood' of 1805 *Prelude* (V. l. 532), which is characterised not by insight but by innocence, that of 'We are Seven' (ll. 1–4):

> A simple Child,
> That lightly draws its breath,
> And feels its life in every limb,
> What should it know of death?

The jubilee that is common to animal creation and children (*Ode*, stanza 4), and the liberty that the infant can share imaginatively with 'sunbeams, shadows, butterflies and birds' (*Home at Grasmere*, l. 31), yield illusions that are not intimations: as Wordsworth was to write in 1810 in his 'Essay upon Epitaphs, I', 'Forlorn, and cut off from communication with the best part of his nature, must that man be, who should derive the sense of immortality, as it exists in the mind of a child, from the same unthinking gaiety or liveliness of animal spirits with which the lamb in the meadow, or any other irrational Creature is endowed.'[27] One thinks at once of the lambs bounding and the babe leaping up in stanzas 3–4 of the Ode, and these contain no mention of immortality. That follows only as the Babe gives way to the Best Philosopher. What is his philosophy? It has to be distinguished both from the unthinking gaiety of the 'happy Shepherd-boy' (*Ode*, l. 35), and from 'the philosophic mind' that only the years can bring (l. 187). Coleridge's objection is magnificently obtuse:

> In what sense can the magnificent attributes above quoted be appropriated to a child, which would not make them equally suitable to a bee, or a dog, or a field of corn; or even to a ship, or to the wind and waves that propel it? The omnipresent Spirit works equally in them as in the child, and the child is equally unconscious of it as they. (*Biographia*, ch. 22)

He is mistaking metaphorical for literal childhood (and that in forgetfulness of his own paternal fancies), and hence reducing its philosophy to a mere delight and liberty. His final assertion is dubiously just anyway: perhaps the philosophy of inexperience is conscious, without theory or reflection, of the omnipresent Spirit that links lamb and babe. He clearly has in mind his early pantheism; alternatively, one could think of communion with the Christian god (cf. *Excursion*, IV. ll. 83–6). 'The eternal mind' (*Ode*, l. 114) could denote either, and may be meant to.

The Ode further contains, and the Fenwick note confirms, a different philosophy again. What are 'those obstinate questionings / Of sense and outward things, / Fallings from us, vanishings' (ll. 142–4)? Speaking to Miss Fenwick, Wordsworth associated with 'the indomitableness of the spirit within me' which made it difficult to apply the notion of death to himself a spontaneous tendency to a solipsistic idealism:

> With a feeling congenial to this, I was often unable to think of external things as having external existence, and I communed with all that I saw as something not apart from, but inherent in, my own immaterial nature. Many times while going to school have I grasped at a wall or tree to recall myself from this abyss of idealism to the reality.[28]

'The shadowy recollections' that are 'a master-light of all our seeing' (*Ode*, ll. 150–4) disclose to him a world that is 'a dream, / A prospect in

[27] *The Prose Works of William Wordsworth*, eds W.J.B. Owen and J.W. Smyser, 3 vols (Oxford, 1974), II, pp. 50–1.

[28] Cf. 'Letter from Professor Bonamy Price on the Ode of Immortality', *Transactions of the Wordsworth Society*, 2 (1883), 26; also C. Wordsworth, *Memoirs*, II, p. 480.

my mind' (1799 *Prelude*, II. ll. 400–1), 'an unsubstantial, faery place' (1802 'To the Cuckoo', l. 31). This might imply not that the world and oneself are eternal, but that both are equally transient. Yet it would seem that the human effect of such an egocentric experience of the world is rather to suggest the omnipotence of thought than the transience of matter.

Thus the Ode's philosophy is a web of protean suggestion. One nice variation is in the sources of light. Near the beginning and the end we read of casting the light that one sees: it is with her own projected light that the moon looks round the heavens (ll. 12–13); sunset clouds take on 'a sober colouring' from the adult observing eye (ll. 197–9). For an expansion, we can turn to the 1799 *Prelude* (II. ll. 417–23):

An auxiliar light
Came from my mind, which on the setting sun
Bestowed new splendour; the melodious birds,
The gentle breezes, fountains that ran on
Murmuring so sweetly in themselves, obeyed
A like dominion, and the midnight storm
Grew darker in the presence of my eye.

In the context of stanzas 1–4, 'the visionary gleam' (l. 56) must be supposed to be cast by the child, and lost by the adult. Coleridge offered the natural comment in his reply: 'We receive but what we give' ('A Letter to . . .', l. 296).[29] Then Platonic realism irrupts in stanza 5: 'The growing Boy / . . . beholds the light, and whence it flows, / He sees it in his joy' (ll. 68–71). Thus a statement of realism within the Platonic myth is balanced on either side by indications of projectivism within the real world.

Even the Ode's central theme is elusive. It took on its present subtitle, 'Intimations or Immortality from Recollections of Early Childhood', only in 1815. Writing to Mrs. Clarkson in December 1814, Wordsworth conjoined its ideas as follows: 'The poem rests entirely on two recollections of childhood, one that of a splendour in the objects of sense which is passed away, and the other an indispostion to bend to the law of death as applying to one particular case.'[30] The myth of stanza 5 permits a marriage between these two ideas. The immortality implicit in its symbolism is well explicated by Charles Sherry: 'What remains unspoken is that when 'life's Star' sets

[29] Wordsworth echoes that in the 1805 *Prelude*: 'From thyself it is that thou must give, / Else never can receive' (XI, ll. 332–3); cf. XII, ll. 376–9, XIII, ll. 93–5.

[30] Cited in *Poetical Works*, IV, p. 464.

on earth it will once again rise in the immortal skies of its eternal home. The soul is like a little immortal sun circling about its earth. Its rising and setting are the boundaries of its life on earth, but only moments in the course of its eternal life, where rising is setting, and setting, rising.'[31] Thus, as in Plato himself, pre-existence points to post-existence: the light that recedes promises a light that returns. But again, a clear indication is clouded by a mythical setting, so that the true nature of the immortality that 'broods like the Day' over the child (ll. 119–20) remains in obscurity. There is some easy invocation of Christian comfort, as in 'the faith that looks through death' (l. 186), and yet it seems that it was only after the death of his brother John in February 1805 that Wordsworth relapsed securely into the orthodoxy expressed suddenly in two lines of the 1805 *Prelude*:

> The feeling of life endless, the one thought
> By which we live, infinity and God.
> (XIII. ll. 183–4).[32]

The Ode rather permits than invites such a definite understanding. The only promise of immortality that it redeems is of a life that we can give rather than receive: we came 'trailing clouds of glory . . . / From God, who is our home' (ll. 64–5), but our own glory is to illumine with the colouring of our own experience 'the Clouds that gather round the setting sun' (l. 197).

The Ode is a story of loss and gain for a soul who knows no religious conversion. The loss is mitigated by 'those shadowy recollections' which 'are yet the fountain-light of all our day' (ll. 150–2). They take us back to 'spots in time' which retain 'a fructifying virtue' to nourish and repair our imaginative powers (1799 *Prelude*, I. ll. 288–94). The fertility of such memories lies not in any Proustian immediacy of a recaptured past, but in a vague suggestion of future possibilities:

> The soul –
> Remembering how she felt, but what she felt
> Remembering not – retains an obscure sense
> Of possible sublimity, to which
> With growing faculties she doth aspire,
> With faculties still growing, feeling still
> That whatsoever point they gain they still
> Have something to pursue.
> (1799 *Prelude*, II. ll. 364–71)

[31] C. Sherry, *Wordsworth's Poetry of the Imagination* (Oxford, 1980), p. 31.
[32] Cf. J. Wordsworth, *William Wordsworth*, pp. 33–4.

In the Ode, the poet receives the winds from 'the fields of sleep' (l. 28), and hears 'the mighty waters rolling evermore' (l. 168) – powerful images of the 'how' without the 'what' (that perfectly imprecise expression of imprecision), of depth without definition. Among the obscure objects of memory is

> the primal sympathy
> Which having been must ever be.
> (ll. 182–3)

Half-recollections of an oceanic feeling of being at one with the created world nourish the conscious – one may feel, self-conscious – atonement of felt sympathy with both thoughtless happiness and unhappy thought (*Ode*, stanza 10). Loving communion with the forms of nature develops into a 'kindred love' of 'fellow-natures' (*Excursion*, IV. ll. 1207–17). A deep distress humanises the soul so that it bids farewell to 'the heart that lives alone, / Housed in a dream, at distance from the Kind' ('Elegiac Stanzas suggested by a Picture of Peele Castle', ll. 53–4). After the 'dizzy raptures' of sight without thought comes an ear for 'the still, sad music of humanity' ('Lines composed above Tintern Abbey', ll. 85, 91). 'The innocent brightness of a new-born Day' (*Ode*, l. 195) makes way for 'a sober colouring' that comes of a harmony between 'the setting sun' and 'an eye / That hath kept watch o'er man's mortality' (ll. 198–9). By a parallel with the morning light of the myth of stanza 5, evening light becomes a promise of the future: as dawn reflects pre-existence, so twilight prefigures the life to come. But this new life will not re-enact the mythical pre-history: it is rather Christian than Platonic, characterised by perfect love and not by abstract knowledge. Whether it will be lived just here or also hereafter, and what form it will take other than that of an ode, remain unanswered questions. Restored to a life that is alive, the poet need not yet worry about death.

When William Blake remarked in 1825, 'Wordsworth is no Christian, but a Platonist',[33] he was missing the point: Wordsworth's goal was not to discard one doctrine for another, but to escape from doctrine into myth, where there is none abiding. His poetry of allusion pursues a strategy of elusiveness that respects the nature of emotion coloured but uncaptured by thought; he weighs a vague depression against a vague hope, both (to borrow from Byron) 'hushed into depths beyond the watcher's diving'. For Wordsworth,

[33] I quote from J. Wordsworth, *William Wordsworth*, p. 435, n. 18.

listening to Coleridge, the philosophy of Plato had a power that Christianity lacked: the power to illumine the recesses of the psyche, behind the veil of conscious belief, that can come to ideas, like a resurrection from the dead, when they are no longer believable.

CHAPTER 21

Shelley, Plato and the political imagination

Jennifer Wallace

Shelley (1792–1822) has traditionally been considered the most 'Platonist' of all the Romantic poets. Indeed, James Notopoulos devoted a whole book to Platonism in Shelley, arguing for a natural affinity between the ancient philosopher and the Romantic poet and claiming that 'Shelley is the most outstanding Platonist in the Platonic renascence of the Romantic period'.[1] And Edward Dowden, the poet's first authorised biographer, spoke for many later critics when he wrote that Shelley 'felt the radiance and breathed the air of Plato's genius as though he were himself a scholar in the garden at Colonus'.[2]

Shelley has been hailed as the Romantic poet most influenced by Plato partly because, unlike the others, he not only read Plato extensively but actually translated him.[3] Some of his translations are only fragmentary. Scattered lines from *Republic* II and III appear in his notebooks, as well as short passages from the *Menexenus* and the *Phaedo*. These constitute working translations conveying ideas which particularly arrested him in his reading and which chimed with his own thoughts. Other translations, however, are complete and obviously intended for publication. He translated the *Ion* in 1821. And three years earlier he produced a complete version of the *Symposium*, together with a lengthy preface to explain the strange Greek custom of homosexuality to the Greekless reader:

1 J.A. Notopoulos, *The Platonism of Shelley; A Study of Platonism and the Poetic Mind* (Durham, North Carolina, 1949), p. 145.

2 E. Dowden, *The Life of Percy Bysshe Shelley*, 2 vols. (London, 1886), I, 74–5. Dowden's biography was commissioned by Lady Jane Shelley, the daughter-in-law of the poet.

3 Shelley read Plato at school and at Oxford, but his most concentrated reading of Plato began after 1817, as the entries in Mary Shelley's journal testify: see *Mary Shelley's Journal*, ed. P.R. Feldman and D. Scott-Kilvert (Oxford, 1987). Mentioned specifically in the journal are the *Phaedo*, the *Phaedrus*, the *Republic* and the *Symposium*, but in his letters Shelley also referred to the *Apology of Socrates*, the *Gorgias* and the *Ion*.

There is no book which shows the Greeks precisely as they were; they seem all written for children . . . But there are many to whom the Greek language is inaccessible, who ought not to be excluded by this prudery to possess an exact and comprehensive conception of the history of man.[4]

Neither of these texts, the *Ion* or the *Symposium*, was published in Shelley's lifetime, as with so much of his *oeuvre*, but the pioneering, disseminating purpose behind the translation is clear.

Shelley has also been particularly associated with Plato because of the idealising tendencies of his modern critics, behind whose critical comments lies the notion that the Romantic movement was an apolitical, semi-religious upheaval and Platonism a mystical, religious progression to an unworldly divinity. Thus what they interpret as the ethereal, dreamlike writing of Shelley can be associated with their Neoplatonic understanding of Plato, which is concerned only with the notion of mystic transcendence to a world of greater reality, greater beauty, greater unity. Neville Rogers, for example, argues that Shelley adopts symbols similar to those used by Plato – veils, boats, caves – in order to represent metaphorically the mind's ascent beyond the world of particulars to the realm of the eternal and the universal.[5] Moreover, he presents his own attempt to understand Shelley's thinking as itself a quest for ultimate truth, a journey along what he terms the 'Platonic path'. In this way he risks accepting uncritically the terms of his reading and revealing the idealising purpose behind his own interpretation. Other critics also reveal their idealism by linking their depiction of Platonism with what they consider 'poetical' or beautiful. C.E. Pulos announces in his otherwise excellent chapter on Shelley's Platonism that 'it is generally agreed that the main feature of Shelley's Platonism is his pursuit of Beauty'.[6] Finally critics associated Platonism with a vague notion of synthesis, of the gathering together of disparate parts. So Carl Grabo can write of Shelley's early poem *Queen Mab*, without troubling to define his terms: 'This is sheer Platonism . . . which was destined to become the solvent which, in Shelley's matured philosophy, bent these seemingly recalcitrant materials to a unity'.[7] The 'recalcitrant materials' are

[4] Shelley, 'A Discourse on the Manners of the Antient Greeks Relative to the Subject of Love', in J.A. Notopoulos, *The Platonism of Shelley*, p. 407. All Shelley's translations from Plato are contained in Notopoulos's work.

[5] N. Rogers, *Shelley At Work: A Critical Inquiry* (Oxford, 1956). For a similar interpretation of Shelley's imagery, see P. Butter, *Shelley's Idols of the Cave* (Edinburgh, 1954).

[6] C.E. Pulos, *The Deep Truth: A Study of Shelley's Scepticism* (Lincoln, Nebraska, 1954), p. 77.

[7] C. Grabo, *The Magic Plant: The Growth of Shelley's Thought* (Chapel Hill, 1936), p. 118. For other idealising interpretations of Shelley's Platonism, see J. Barrell, *Shelley and the Thought of his Time: A Study in the History of Ideas* (New Haven, 1947); S. Rogers, *Classical Greece and the*

ideas from such philosophers as Baron d'Holbach and William Godwin, radical thinkers whose early influence upon Shelley, Grabo and others claim was thankfully tamed by the apolitical reveries of Plato.

What has been forgotten by these critics is that Shelley was first and foremost a political poet. Throughout his short life, from his rebellious adolescence right up to his last years in Italy, he stressed the importance of political reform, of the responsibility of the poet to change society radically in order to alleviate the poverty and injustice suffered by the people. 'I consider Poetry very subordinate to moral and political science, & if I were well, certainly I should aspire to the latter', he wrote to his friend Thomas Love Peacock only three years before he died.[8] Poetry was used as a means to an ultimate political end. Every source, every idea was to be put to political use.

It is therefore imperative to set Shelley's Platonism in a political context as well. There were obvious, specific political ideas to be drawn from Plato. Shelley showed interest in the question of the corrupting process of civilisation addressed in the *Republic*. He reflected to his friend Thomas Jefferson Hogg after reading *Republic* VI that Plato's 'speculations on civil society are surely the foundations of true politics, & if ever the world is to be arranged upon another system than that of the several members of it destroying & tormenting one another for the sake of the pleasures of sense, or from the force of habit & imitation; it must start from such principles'.[9] Shelley also derived moral and social instruction from the depiction of ancient Greek society in the *Symposium* announcing in the preface that 'whatever tends to afford a further illustration of the manners and opinions of those to whom we owe so much . . . were infinitely valuable'.[10] More generally, the two main strands of philosophic thought in Plato, the sceptical and idealising, could also be drawn upon and applied politically. Both Plato's questioning of established opinion and the argument that political change could come about

Poetry of Chenier, Shelley and Leopardi (Indianapolis, 1974). Sir Kenneth Dover has added a further dimension to the question of the idealising of Shelley's Platonism since his death. In 'Expurgation of Greek Literature', *Entretiens sur l'Antiquité Classique*, 26 'Les Etudes Classiques aux XIX et XX siècles' (1980), 55–82, he writes of the posthumous bowdlerisation of Shelley's translation of the *Symposium* and considers the extent to which this reveals the editors' interpretations of Classical Greece.

8 Shelley to Thomas Love Peacock, *The Letters of Percy Bysshe Shelley*, ed. F.L. Jones, 2 vols. (Oxford, 1964), 23–4 January 1819.

9 Shelley to Thomas Jefferson Hogg, 22 October 1821, *ibid.*

10 Shelley, 'A Discourse on the Manners', p. 407. A sensitive account of the historical interest of the *Symposium* for Shelley can be found in R. Holmes, *Shelley: The Pursuit* (London, 1974; Harmondsworth, 1987), pp. 430–4.

peacefully through education and awakened perception captivated Shelley's imagination. Through an examination in particular of Shelley's essay *A Defence of Poetry* (1821) and his poetic drama *Prometheus Unbound* (1820), we shall consider how the fluctuations between scepticism and idealism in Shelley's own political thinking and writing were supported by the paradoxical influence of Plato.

SCEPTICISM

Throughout his life it seemed important to Shelley to maintain a sceptical position. Certainty only seemed to augment the binding dogmatism which he believed oppressed society. In *A Defence of Poetry*, he explained this concern in terms of language. The language of poets, he argued, was

> vitally metaphorical; that is, it marks the before unapprehended relations of things and perpetuates their apprehension until the words which represent them become, through time, signs for portions or classes of thoughts instead of pictures of integral thoughts; and then if no new poets should arise to create afresh the associations which have been thus disorganised, language will be dead to all the nobler purposes of human intercourse.[11]

Once the association between thought and word was taken for granted, the liberating power of words was lost and replaced by a repressive rigidity. In the same way, according to Shelley, once philosophy had been codified into a system, it became narrowing for the mind. But philosophical thinking – what James Notopoulos calls the 'mind in process' – was as enlightening and liberating as political active reform. Shelley mused in the 'Essay on Life':

> [Philosophy] leaves, what it is too often the duty of the reformer in political and ethical questions to leave, a vacancy. It reduces the mind to that freedom in which it would have acted but for the misuse of words and signs'.[12]

'Vacancy' here is a boon, a freedom from crabbing prejudice and deep-rooted system. Just as philosophical inquiry can produce this liberating result so can poetry, which 'awakens and enlarges the mind itself by rendering the receptacle of a thousand unapprehended combinations of thought'. (*Defence*, p. 487).

[11] Shelley, *A Defence of Poetry*, in *Shelley's Poetry and Prose*, edited by D.H. Reiman and S.B. Powers (New York, 1977), p. 482. Hereafter page numbers from this edition will be given in the text.

[12] Shelley, 'Essay on Life', *Shelley's Poetry and Prose*, p. 477.

When Shelley was seeking sources which could 'awaken and enlarge the mind', he was attracted both by the recent sceptical tradition of David Hume and by the sceptical questioning of Plato's early Socratic dialogues. Early dialogues such as the *Laches* and the *Protagoras*, which Shelley read at Oxford in the Dacier translation, followed a pattern in which a common assumption or definition was broken down under fierce questioning by Socrates, and all the participants in the dialogue were left in a state of 'aporia', or uncertainty about the original definition.[13] No positive answer or alternative philosophical theory was suggested, but the error of existing definitions was revealed. There was an established tradition of drawing upon this dialogue form for radical writing. Most influential for Shelley was the work of William Drummond. His *Academical Questions* (1805) significantly alluded in its title to the Academy set up by the followers of Plato, and used the sceptical questioning form to refute philosophical dogmatism of the past. Following this tradition, Shelley composed 'A Refutation of Deism', a dialogue between Eusebes and Theosophus which discussed the relative merits of faith and atheism. Christian faith was associated with the Establishment, because of the close link between the Church of England and the government, and thus the paganism of Plato's early Socratic dialogues, as well as their free dialectic form, added to the subversive effect of Shelley's pamphlet. The Socratic dialogue must also lie behind his later poem, *Julian and Maddalo* (1818), which narrates the encounter between a Shelleyan and a Byronic figure and their debate over the best approach to life. Julian, the Shelleyan figure, displays an optimistic attitude to life: people and society can be changed for the better. By contrast, Maddalo, the Byronic figure, adopts a pessimistic stance, despondently arguing that life will always remain the same. Through the encounter, both dogmatic positions are questioned, disrupted.

[13] The first text of Plato which Shelley read was the *Symposium*, which he studied while he was at Eton. At Oxford he read a number of dialogues, mostly in the English version of a French translation of Plato by Dacier: M. Dacier, *The Works of Plato abridged, with an Account of his Life, Philosophy, Morals and Politics, together with a Translation of his choicest Dialogues*. Translated from the French (London, 1701). The 'choicest dialogues' included the *Apology*, *Phaedo*, *Laches* and *Protagoras*. Plato was little studied in the original at schools or university at this time, so Shelley was not unusual in reading the dialogues in translation. For details of the study of Plato during Shelley's time, see M.L. Clarke, *Greek Studies In England 1700–1830* (Cambridge, 1945), pp. 112–22.

VISIONARY IMAGINATION

However, the sceptical, questioning mode was not the only way to write politically, to encourage political change. An alternative to the use of scepticism as a means of ridding the mind of dogmatism was the use of idealism. A visionary imagination could see beyond the daily stalemate of society, could realise that the existing system was not a 'given' but a deadening convention which could be replaced. Shelley's *A Defence of Poetry* elevates the poet who displays a visionary imagination almost to prophetic status. This is partly explained by the particular background of the essay. It was composed at speed in reply to an attack on poetry by Peacock, *The Four Ages of Poetry*.[14] Thus an assertion of the exalted status of the poet was needed to counter Peacock's depressing arguments about the anachronism of poetry in the climate of scientific progress, arguments which Shelley possibly half believed himself at a time of industrial revolution and urban development.

However, there is more behind the excessive idealism of the *Defence* than a reply to Peacock, and it seems likely that he was also replying to Plato himself. Plato's views on poetry were highly contradictory, as Anne Sheppard has described (see pp. 12–18 above). In the *Republic*, he had rejected poetry, initially because it immorally misrepresented 'the nature of gods and heroes'. This rejection of poetry must have seemed controversial at the time, because Plato apparently felt it necessary to add a final book to the *Republic*, amplifiying his views. Art by its very nature could never give an accurate picture, he explained, because it imitated the visible world and thus produced 'images at the third remove from reality'. In contrast, the *Ion* circumvented the problem of the distance of art from reality by arguing that the poet was divinely inspired and that his art proceeded directly from the divine. Essentially it was a question of whether as an artist one should proceed by means of reason and knowledge, or by inspiration and vision, in order to produce a true depiction. Reason involved the active participation of the artist; inspiration used the artist as a passive mouthpiece.

Some ideas in the *Defence* clearly stem from the *Ion*. 'Poetry is indeed something divine' (*Defence*, p. 503), Shelley writes, and 'it acts

[14] Thomas Love Peacock, *The Four Ages of Poetry*, in *The Works of Thomas Love Peacock*, ed. H.F.B. Brett-Smith and C.E. Jones, 10 vols (London, 1924–34), VIII, 3–25. Peacock's essay first appeared in the first and only number of Charles Ollier's *Literary Miscellany* in 1820.

in a divine and unapprehended manner' (p. 486), recalling the divine origins claimed for poetry in the *Ion*: 'beautiful poems are not human nor from man but divine and from the Gods' (534e; *Defence*, p. 473).[15] Shelley chooses to ignore the irony which may be discerned in Socrates' tone, and echoes the irrational quality of divine inspiration. 'Poetry is not like reasoning, a power to be exerted according to the determination of the will', he argues, 'for the mind in creation is as a fading coal which some invisible influence, like an inconstant wind, awakens to transitory brightness'. (*Defence*, pp. 503–4) This argument is forced upon Shelley in order to explain the emergence of poets when the society around them seems not conducive to poetry. It is impelled by his need to separate and idealise the poet in the face of Peacock's criticisms, and by his wish to encourage fresh poetic voices through this proselytising essay. However, these depictions of the irrational, irresponsible poet in the *Defence* have been emphasised at the expense of the other more politicised strand of thinking, the influence of Platonic reason.

Shelley inverted Plato and the *Republic* by substituting imagination for reason. In the sixteenth century, Sidney, influenced by the Neoplatonic replacement of reasoned dialectic with emotional, semi-religious intuition, had argued for the creative power of the poet in his *Defence of Poetry*: 'Only the poet, disdaining to be tied to any such subjection, lifted up with the vigour of his own invention, doth grow in effect another nature, in making things either better than nature bringeth forth, or, quite anew, forms as never were in nature'.[16] But Shelley mirrored Plato's arguments more closely than Sidney, and made a direct link between the poet's imagination and Plato's reason. He attempted to cite the object of imagination not in the poet's own created world, as Sidney had done, but in an external reality which the poet entered through a Platonic ascent of the soul. Whereas Plato had argued in the *Republic* that the mind was enlightened by moving from a reasoned contemplation of particular things to abstract ideas, in the *Symposium* he had depicted this progression in terms of love: 'Love is indeed universally all that earnest desire for the possession of happiness and that which is good' (205d; *Defence*, p. 444). Shelley

[15] All quotations from the *Ion* and the *Symposium* are from Shelley's translations in Notopoulos, *The Platonism of Shelley*. Original Platonic pagination and page numbers from Notopoulos are given in the text.

[16] Sir Philip Sidney, *A Defence of Poetry*, ed. J.A. Van Dorsten (Oxford, 1966), p. 23. See Roe, pp. 103–7 above. Shelley was reading Sidney at the time of writing his own *Defence of Poetry*. See *Mary Shelley's Journal*, 1, 11 and 12 March 1821; and endpaper, p. 426.

picked up the language of love when he transferred the force behind this enlightenment to imagination: 'Poetry enlarges the circumference of the imagination by replenishing it with thoughts of ever new delight, which have the power of attracting and assimilating to their own nature all other thoughts, and which form new intervals and interstices whose void for ever craves fresh food' (*Defence*, p. 488). Once the poet, through his imagination, has risen beyond the narrow circumference of quotidian existence, he also participates in 'the eternal, the infinite, and the one' (*Defence*, p. 483). This is the world inhabited by the true philosopher in the *Republic*: 'the philosophers are those who can apprehend the eternal and unchanging, while those who cannot do so, but are lost in the masses of multiplicity and change, are not philosophers' (484b).

Shelley does not only coincide with Plato on the ascent of the soul and the existence of two worlds, but also, most importantly, on turning such ideas to political use. Plato's philosopher had a responsibility to society:

> It is for us, then, as founders of a commonwealth, to bring compulsion to bear on the noblest natures. They must be made to climb the ascent to the vision of Goodness, which we called the highest object of knowledge; and when they have looked upon it long enough . . . [they] must go down, then, each in his turn, to live with the rest'. (519c, 520c)

For Shelley too, once the philosopher-poet had experienced 'the Good', which includes the true and the beautiful, it was his responsibility to communicate this to the benighted people of his society. Once the poet had stripped 'the veil of familiarity from the world' (*Defence*, p. 503), he could recognise the ultimate good in the universe and reveal it to his readers. Thus for all of society 'the great instrument of moral good is the imagination' (*Defence*, p. 488).

So while the methods of Plato and Shelley differed, one proceeding by reason and the other by imagination, their aims were similar. Both saw political change occuring as a result of a change of perception. As a result, Shelley's claims about the importance of the poet resonate with the claims of Plato about the philosopher. Since for Shelley the poet possesses the heightened sensitivity to the unchanging world beyond this world, since he is gifted with the imagination which can apprehend the Good which must be brought back to society, he is the most important person in society. 'But poets, or those who imagine and express this indestructible order, are not only the authors of language and of music . . . they are the institutors of laws and the founders of civil society and the inventors of the arts of life and the teachers' (*Defence*, p. 482). Plato's philosopher must be king; Shelley's poets are the 'unacknowledged legislators of the world' (*Defence*, p. 508). Indeed Shelley's argument about the poet's ability to see beyond the corruption of this world to a purer understanding of how the world could be ordered leads him even to claim the superior moral fibre of the poet: 'the greatest poets have been men of the most spotless virtue' (*Defence*, p. 506).

So the apocalyptic vision which Shelley bestows upon the poet, the ability to witness 'veil after veil' of this world 'withdrawn', becomes, through the resonances from Plato, revolutionary. Plato is not interested in the prisoner's ascent from the cave for its own sake, but for what it can mean for the ordering of the republic, the education and government of its citizens. And Shelley's analysis of the power of poetry has one aim: the awakening of the people from oppression and misery. A new political voice is found, not in the sceptical rejection of theories, but in the vision of a brighter future and in the understanding of the contingency of the daily world of division and conflict.

PROMETHEUS UNBOUND

But how was the new political voice used? How could the theories about the prophetic or legislative powers of the poetic voice be put into practice? The most revolutionary of Shelley's poems is *Prometheus Unbound* (1819), which dramatises the liberation of Prometheus and with it the escape from all manner of oppression. In the course of this change, the poem charts a virtual Platonic Ascent to the world of Reality and universality. The gradual replacement of Aeschylus by Plato as the main source of the poem is recognised widely by critics. Even a contemporary reviewer, writing in Gold's *London Magazine*, described the poem in Platonic terms:

> The subject is so treated, that we lose sight of persons in principles, and soon feel that all the splendid machinery around us is but the shadow of things unseen, the outward panoply of bright expectations and theories, which appear to the author's mind instinct with eternal and eternally progressive blessings.[17]

The reviewer here is admiring the ineffable, unworldly associations of

[17] Gold's *London Magazine*, II (October 1820), in T. Redpath, *The Young Romantics and Critical Opinion 1807–1824* (London, 1973), p. 355.

Plato. I would contend that it is for his political vision that Plato is appropriated for this revolutionary poem. The revolution can be seen taking place partly in the figure of Prometheus himself and partly in the constitution of the world around him and in the language of the poem. At first Prometheus is a lonely rebel, locked into his unremitting conflict with Jupiter and his own state of Platonic illusion, in which he worries about individual division and is unable to take a wider perspective, like the man who is obsessed with only one beautiful woman in the *Symposium*. But the first change in his attitude comes about after he has heard the curse he had shouted at Jupiter repeated back to him; he then realises his error. Once he replaces hatred with the bond-breaking power of pity, 'I wish no living thing to suffer pain', the imprisoning duel with Jupiter is ended.[18] Prometheus turns to love, and at this point the ascent of the soul through the power of love described in the *Symposium* becomes important. He extends his love to Ione and Panthea, two messenger nymphs who thus become intermediaries lifting his thoughts still higher. Finally he unites with his greatest love, Asia, and loses his divisive individuality altogether. The Earth sings at the end:

> Man, oh, not men! a chain of linked thought,
> Of love and might to be divided not . . .
> Man, one harmoious soul of many a soul.
> (IV. ll. 394–5, 400)

Just as Plato's philosopher-king can realise the correct political path through his education, so Prometheus can engineer his release not through action but through the change in his attitude and his new understanding.

A similar revolution takes place in the world around Prometheus, apparently prompted by his change of attitude. The opening act adopts the harsh, violent vocabulary of tragedy, with tormenting furies and monologues of pain and isolation. But the mood and the setting of the poem change. As Shelley said in the *Defence*, when the initial referential language becomes increasingly inadequate, the poet makes new connections between words and what was previously beyond expression. Demogorgan replies to the questions of Asia: 'The deep truth is imageless' (II. iv. 116), and the chorus sing 'In the world unknown / Sleeps a voice unspoken' (II. i. 190–1). 'Veil after veil' is lifted as the known world of referential language, which has

[18] Shelley, *Prometheus Unbound*, in *Shelley's Poetry and Prose*, Act I, ll.305. Hereafter line references from this edition will be given in the text.

degenerated into 'signs', gives way to the evocation of a vital new world beyond the range of ordinary human perception or expression. As Plato cannot describe the Good itself in the *Republic* but relies upon analogies and myths, so Shelley can only suggest the paradisic new world with the suggestive vocabulary of shadows, dreams, negatives. In the new world the imprisoning duel between Prometheus and his antagonist is replaced by a paean of many singers, expressing synthesis by their plurality and unity through the one voice which paradoxically lies behind all their utterances.

Yet the words in Act IV, which should form a hymn of triumph and celebration, are bland and empty. They lack the tension and vitality of Act I. They are negligible, replaceable. Chorus after chorus answers each other in a song which adds nothing to our understanding or interest. Moreover the revolution that Prometheus is supposed to have brought about through his renunciation of hatred seems insubstantial. The Earth's optative, 'Man, oh, not men', suggests that the world of unity and egalitarianism is desired rather than achieved; and Demogorgon's final speech leaves the question of the possible return of the old wrangling world of violence and hatred wide open:

> Gentleness, Virtue, Wisdom, and Endurance,
> These are the seals of that most firm assurance
>   Which bars the pit over Destruction's strength;
> And if, with infirm hand, Eternity,
> Mother of many acts and hours, should free
>   The serpent that would clasp her with his length;
> These are the spells by which to reassume
> An empire o'er the disentangled Doom.
>
> (IV. 562–9)

The 'if' here, emphasised by the pause created by the parenthesis succeeding it, is telling, highlighting the fragility of the revolution. This is all part of the limits of idealism, the distance between the ideal and the practicable. Plato noted the difficulty of realising his *Republic* in actuality: 'Can theory ever be fully realised in practice? Is it not in the nature of things that action should come less close to the truth than thought?' (473a). Shelley admitted in the *Defence* that 'the most glorious poetry that has ever been communicated to the world is probably a feeble shadow of the original conception of the poet' (p. 504). The attempt to express the ideal world, to act as the legislative poet and communicate to the readers a sense of the beautiful and eternal, produces only a 'feeble shadow'.

The limitations of *Prometheus Unbound* are not confined to the difficulty of expressing the ideal world of Reality only, but also extend, perhaps more seriously, to the complete working through of the Platonic revolution. Whereas Plato's revolution involves not only the recognition and participation in the world of the Good, but also its communication to the world below, in *Prometheus Unbound* there is no such communication. Once Prometheus has glimpsed Asia, he does not return with the good news he has learnt. Instead he retreats with Asia into a cave (not the Platonic one) and disappears from the final act of the poem. Thus the ideal world, the world of Reality, which in Plato is vital to the world of plurality and illusion, becomes impossibly distant in Shelley.

It is in this respect that Shelley departs from Plato. The substitution of imagination for reason, which aspires to invest the poet with as much political vision and power as the philosopher-king, ultimately leaves the poet with no connection between this world and the next. The ascent of the soul from the world of illusion to the world of truth and order is based ultimately not on dialectic, which may be taught and repeated, but on faith, which is drawn upon only when knowledge fails. Despite Shelley's attempt to ground his imagination in Plato's reason, the assumptions of his age about the effect of the surrounding world upon knowledge mean that assertions about an alternative world can come only as flashes of divine, irrational inspiration. According to the empirical philosophical tradition, in which Shelley is steeped, the poet is influenced by his experience, by the climate in which he lives. He cannot gain knowledge of an alternative world through his experience, through rational methods. Therefore glimpses of the alternative world cannot rest on processes of reason, but only on mysterious and unrepeatable acts of inspiration.

It is clear, then, that in Shelley's writing the sceptical voice and the visionary voice are directly linked.[19] Scepticism questions established notions of society; idealism then asserts the answer. But there are no solid grounds for this assertion, only the fleeting image of a spark of inspiration, a fading coal. A vision of the Good is suggested to fill the gap left by the sceptical questioning. But as there can be no return from the vision without rational understanding, the vision of the Good increasingly seems distant and irrelevant. This is why Prometheus does not return to the unenlightened world. Since his former being, bound by the world of experience, could never participate in the ideal

[19] For a discussion of the connection of Platonic idealism with scepticism, see C.E. Pulos, *The Deep Truth*, pp. 67–88.

world of Reality, he had to dissolve his identity or, in other words, die in order to reach it. It is noticeable that, after writing *Prometheus Unbound*, Shelley increasingly found himself linking the ideal world of Reality, which should have proved vital to this world, with death, annihilation and escape.[20]

Thus Platonism is an ambiguous resource for Shelley. On the one hand it provides an expression of revolutionary change, whether that means drawing upon the democratic political associations of Socratic dialogue or remodelling Plato's account of the soul's ascent to the Beautiful and Good in order to suggest a revolutionary, moral vision. On the other hand it disappoints the political imagination as Shelley was forced to recognise the limits of idealism. Just as he perceived the early hopes of the French Revolution fade with the onset of the violence which must always accompany social upheaval, he discovered the difficulty of putting into practice the political idealism expressed in such works as *A Defence of Poetry*. He also encountered the distancing effect of idealism, because of the necessary gulf between the world of scepticism and the world of vision in his interpretation of Plato. There was therefore a danger that the political motivations behind his idealism would be misinterpreted, and of course this has subsequently happened with the de-politicising of Shelley's Platonism by critics. But this is just one of the dangers of idealism, part of the tension and difficulty of all dynamic and visionary political writing.

[20] The most extreme example of Shelley's increasing association of idealism with the death wish occurs at the end of *Adonais* (1821), the poem commemorating the death of Keats:

> The One remains, the many change and pass;
> Heaven's light forever shines, earth's shadows fly;
> Life, like a dome of many-coloured glass,
> Stains the white radiance of Eternity,
> Until Death tramples it to fragments. – Die,
> If thou wouldst be with that which thou dost seek! (ll. 460–5)

CHAPTER 22

Arnold, Plato, Socrates

M.W. Rowe

EARLY WRITINGS

Tracing the evolution of Plato's influence on Matthew Arnold (1822–1886) allows us to see the whole of Arnold's intellectual development more clearly. Plato is a central figure in Arnold's prose work,[1] but up until the age of thirty-five Arnold saw himself as primarily a poet, and here the Platonic influence is minimal. 'Quiet Work' contains hints of Plotinus, and 'In Utrumque Paratus' explores the Plotinian idea of the world as an emanation from the one all-pure; 'To Critias', the dedication of 'The World and the Quietist', is probably derived from the *Eryxias**,[2] and the story of 'The Scholar-Gipsy' is taken from the Oxford scholar Glanvill, who was associated with the Cambridge Platonists.[3] Only 'Self-Deception', based upon the Myth of Er, shows direct and major Platonic influence, but of that poem Arnold said, '[It is] not a piece that [at] all satisfies me' (*Poems*, p. 292).[4]

Arnold at this period was not ignorant of Plato. His diaries from the years 1845–7 have survived and show him to have read – in Greek

I would like to thank Margaret Howatson, Peter Smith, Philip Highley, Marie McGinn, A.W. Price, Alan Heaven and the editors for comments on earlier versions of this paper.

[1] I therefore disagree with Warren Anderson when he writes, 'Plato is a useful source of quotation and illustration. No deeper dimension appears nor was any intended'. (*Matthew Arnold and the Classical Tradition* (Ann Arbor, 1965), p. 125). Despite our differences, I have learned a great deal from Anderson's detailed and authoritative study.

[2] An asterisk indicates a work whose authenticity is now thought to be doubtful.

[3] Although I do not have a chance to explore the matter here, the Cambridge Platonists continued to influence Arnold, particularly his religious thought, long after he ceased to think of himself as primarily a poet. See Arnold's essay, 'A Psychological Parallel' (*Prose*, VIII, pp. 111–47), and Ruth apRoberts, *Arnold and God* (California, 1983), pp. 11 and 220.

[4] All verse quotations are from *The Poems of Matthew Arnold*, ed. Kenneth Allott, 2nd edn revised by Miriam Allott (London, 1979). All prose quotations are from *The Complete Prose Works of Matthew Arnold*, ed. R.H. Super, 11 vols (Ann Arbour, 1960–77).

– the *Republic* and *Phaedrus*, together with five early works, the *Menexenus*, *Lysis*, *Greater Hippias**, *Lesser Hippias*, and *Ion*.[5] As Arnold's first volume of poetry appeared in 1849, there should have been plenty of time for the Platonic influence to filter through to his verse. The fact that it did not, suggests that Arnold's imaginative preoccupations at the time could not make use of Plato, and if we consider the philosophical outlook of his poetry it is not difficult to see why.

Arnold is the supreme poet of isolation, loss and alienation: nature is cold and indifferent (it 'hath really neither joy, nor love, nor light . . . nor help for pain' (*Poems*, p. 256); personal relationships only increase one's sense of isolation ('we mortal millions live *alone*' (*Poems*, p. 130)); and society, with 'its sick hurry, its divided aims' (*Poems*, p. 366) is a source merely of anxiety and enervation. Only 'he / who finds himself, loses his misery', and the desire to 'be thyself' is associated with a self-poised indifference to the external world: like the stars we should not 'pine with noting / all the fever of some differing soul' but be 'bounded by [our]selves, and unregardful / in what state God's other works may be' (*Poems*, p. 150). The drive towards self-knowledge is gloomily introspective ('there rises an unspeakable desire / after the knowledge of our buried life') and also, ultimately, doomed to failure: 'and many a man in his own breast then delves, / but deep enough, alas! none ever mines . . . hardly have we, for one little hour, . . . been ourselves') (*Poems*, pp. 289–90). It is impossible not to feel that, at this stage of his development, Arnold could not assimilate Plato's influence because Plato's philosophy, even in its literary form, is pre-eminently social, public and political: it is concerned, especially in the early dialogues, with parents, friends, education, love, the good citizen, the *polis*. Arnold only approaches even the most personal of these offices and relationships through death, failure or estrangement.

The preface to the collection of poems Arnold published in 1853 reflects the sense of aridity and self-disgust his introspective search for self-knowledge caused, by explicitly condemning exactly the kind of poetry at which he excelled. No poetical enjoyment, he tells us, can be derived from poems 'in which the suffering finds no vent in action; in which a continuous state of mental distress is prolonged, unrelieved

[5] Kenneth Allott, 'Matthew Arnold's Reading Lists in Three Early Diaries', *Victorian Studies*, 11 (1959), 254–66.

by incident, hope or resistance; in which there is everything to be endured and nothing to be done. In such situations there is inevitably something morbid . . .' (*Prose*, I, pp. 2–3). The solution proposed was to write objective classical poems of action and incident, and in three of his next major poetic productions he attempted to follow his own precepts. The results were not encouraging. *Sohrab and Rustum* is saved by the subjective concerns of its magificent coda, but *Balder Dead* makes dull reading, and the 'classical' drama *Merope* was received from the first as a frigid failure. That success did not attend these projects was due, as Trilling puts it, to 'Arnold's failure to see that subjectivism in romantic poetry had its roots in historical reality, that it could not be dismissed by turning away to its seeming opposite, "classical" objectivity... Arnold does little more than direct our taste from the romantic to the classic; the problem goes beyond mere taste'.[6]

It is striking that at least three of the major generalising essays which followed the 1853 preface have, as one of their themes, the intimate relationship a writer has, and must have, with his society. In 'The Function of Criticism at the Present Time', for example, Arnold argues that, 'the exercise of the creative power . . . is not at all epochs and under all conditions possible' (*Prose*, III, p. 260). The English Romantics produced no more than moments of sporadic brilliance, he continues, because society at that time was not sufficiently suffused by ideas and lacked 'a national glow of life,' whereas 'in the England of Shakespeare the poet lived in a current of ideas . . . society was in the fullest measure, permeated by fresh thought, intelligent and alive' (*Prose*, III, p. 262). By the time *Culture and Anarchy* was written, about four years later, the right kind of social conditions are not only necessary for great creative epochs but for the very existence of a cultivated individual:

> Perfection as culture conceives it, is not possible while the individual remains isolated. The individual is required, under pain of being stunted and enfeebled . . . to carry others along with him in his march towards perfection. (*Prose*, V, p. 294)

If it is impossible to ignore contemporary 'historical realities' and write objective classical poetry, and if the subjective poetry of elegiac withdrawal only leads to inertia and self-disgust, then these early prose writings urge the only other course. They no longer try and ignore society, indeed the social nature of individual culture and

[6] Lionel Trilling, *Matthew Arnold* (Oxford, 1982), p. 156.

creativity could not be more strongly acknowledged, and they mark the beginning of an effort to change the nature of society itself that would occupy the remainder of Arnold's life.

SOCRATES

It is only when Arnold begins to think seriously about society that Socrates makes his first important appearance, and this is in the essay 'Democracy' published in 1861. Here, Socrates is as much a symptom, an effect, of the kind of society Arnold wished for as he is a cause and creator of it:

> It was the *many* [in Athens] who relished those arts, who were not satisfied with less than those monuments. In the conversations recorded by Plato, or even by the matter-of-fact Xenophon, which for the free yet refined discussion of ideas have set the tone for the whole cultivated world, shopkeepers and tradesmen of Athens mingle as speakers . . . this is why a handful of Athenians of two thousand years ago are more interesting than the millions of most nations of our contemporaries. (*Prose*, I, p. 25)

Interestingly, the reference to Plato turns out to be a mistake. Although the conversations recorded by Plato often take place in the market or outside the law courts, he does not show Socrates talking to 'shopkeepers and tradesmen', this, as Warren Anderson points out, is only to be found in Xenophon.[7] The Socrates of Xenophon's *Memorabilia* is a slightly prosaic popularist: he shows craftsmen how they can improve their work by understanding the precise purpose of their task; he emphasises the importance of self-control and acquired skills; he offers homely but shrewd moral advice. The Socrates found in Plato's early dialogues is recognisably the same figure (as Arnold's slight confusion would suggest) but is altogether sharper and more elusive. He is a much greater dialectician; he prefers to advance by refuting others rather than offering theories himself; and he is more prone to confessions of ignorance and the use of irony. Plato, unlike Xenophon, does not generally claim to be recording what the historical Socrates actually said, but the nature of Xenophon's intelligence was practical rather than philosophical and it therefore seems quite likely that Plato's imaginative reconstructions bring us closer to the historical Socrates than Xenophon's not always comprehending attempts at literalness. Arnold had been familiar

[7] Warren Anderson, 'Matthew Arnold and the Classics', in K. Allott (ed.), *Matthew Arnold*, 'Writers and their Background' (London, 1975), p. 281.

with Xenophon's works since his schooldays, and it is notable that his early diaries show him concentrating – apart from the *Republic* and *Phaedrus* which were of constant interest throughout his life – on five early Platonic dialogues.

The character called 'Socrates' who speaks in the dialogues of Plato's late and middle periods continues to exhibit many of the amenities of the earlier character, but he differs from the earlier figure in at least the following respects: he is not exclusively a moral philosopher; he holds elaborate theories of the forms, recollection, and the soul; he has mastered mathematics; he seeks deductive knowledge and, when he feels he has found it, is quite prepared to expound it to others. Most importantly for our purposes, he is emphatically elitist rather than popularist in his view of philosophy, and he has a complex theory of government in which democracy ranks very low. Because of these marked differences, generations of scholars have identified this 'Socrates' with Plato himself.[8] I shall follow them in this practice.

Arnold's interest in Socrates and Plato reflects his own central concern: what relationship should a man devoted to disinterested thought and contemplation have with his society which must, of necessity, be largely practical and commercial? Although he changed his mind several times about the exact relationship between Plato, Socrates and Xenophon, the general progression of his interest is clear enough. In what follows, I shall show Arnold moving away from an identification with the popularist Socrates towards the more embittered, aristocratic, and reactionary Plato. Up to, and culminating in, *Culture and Anarchy* in 1869, Arnold is largely fascinated by Socrates' personality. In *Culture and Anarchy*, however, he is also influenced by the political theories of the *Republic*, and after this date one can see him grow increasingly disillusioned, elitist and Platonic in his attitude towards the society around him.

If we look at Arnold's reading lists which exist, with odd gaps, from 1852 until the end of his life, we can see that although he read a good deal of philosophy, no Plato is recorded between 1852 and 1867.[9] However, he did note down Xenophon's *Memorabilia* as one of his 'books for the summer' in 1860. As we might expect from this, Plato

[8] Here I rely on Gregory Vlastos, *Socrates: Ironist and Moral Philosopher* (Cambridge, 1991), pp. 45–131.

[9] *The Note-Books of Matthew Arnold*, edited by Howard Foster Lowry, Karl Young, and Waldo Hilary Dunn (London, 1952).

exerted little influence on the writings eventually published as *Essays in Criticism* in 1865; in fact, he is discussed only once, and that is in the 1864 Joubert essay. Although Arnold offers qualified praise, what he has to say about Plato's actual doctrines (presumably those found in the *Republic* and *Phaedrus*) is not flattering:

Joubert was all his life a passionate lover of Plato; I hope other lovers of Plato will forgive me for saying that their adored object has never been more truly described than he is here:-

'Plato shows us nothing, but he brings brightness with him; he puts light into our eyes and fills us with a clearness by which all objects afterwards become illuminated. He teaches us nothing; but he prepares us, fashions us, and makes us ready to know all. Somehow or other, the habit of reading him augments in us the capacity for discerning and entertaining whatever fine truths may afterwards present themselves. Like mountain air, it sharpens our organs, and gives us an appetite for wholesome food.' (*Prose*, III, p. 203)

CULTURE AND ANARCHY

In *Culture and Anarchy*, Arnold is still drawn to Xenophon's Socrates:

'The best man is he who most tries to perfect himself, and the happiest man is he who feels that he *is* perfecting himself', – this account of the matter by Socrates, the true Socrates of the *Memorabilia*, has something so simple, spontaneous and unsophisticated about it, that it seems to fill us with clearness and hope when we hear it. (*Prose*, V, p. 167–8).

But by this stage the influence of Plato is coming to be felt. We know from his reading lists that Arnold read the *Phaedo*, *Symposium*, *Theages** and *Erastae** in 1868, and several of these are quoted and discussed in the book. Arnold never had any time for metaphysics, and the arguments in the *Phaedo* for the soul's immortality are dismissed as 'sterile' (*Prose*, V, p. 171), but many of the most important phrases in *Culture and Anarchy* – and the argumentative weight placed on phrases is a feature of Arnold's thought – have their origin in Plato. 'Seeing things as they really are' and 'the firm intelligible law of things' are explicitly acknowledged as Platonic (*Prose*, V, p. 178) but 'best self' also seems to come from the *Republic* 591. 'Doing as one likes' alludes to Roebuck's, 'Is not every man in England able to say what he likes?' but it is used in the *Republic*'s criticism of democracy ('And has not every man license to do as he likes?' 557b) and Arnold would certainly have heard Roebuck's remarks thrown into ironic relief by the Platonic background.

Plato's doctrinal influence, however, is largely subterranean and not overtly signalled. W. David Shaw has pointed out that Arnold, like Plato, is attracted by analogies between self and state, and that the three classes of the ideal republic, each with its characteristic virtue, are similar to Arnold's Barbarians, Philistines and Populace.[10] This is true, but Plato's damning description of democratic society in decline is even closer in spirit to Arnold's analysis. For Plato, the democratic man is utterly lacking in depth, direction and fixed principles:

> And frequently he goes in for politics and bounces up and says and does whatever enters his head . . . and there is no order or compulsion in his existence, but he calls this life of his the life of pleasure and freedom and happiness and cleaves to it to the end. (*Republic* 561d)

The mainspring of action in a democracy is a craving for unrestricted liberty (562c and d) and the pursuit of wealth (564e). The result is 'anarchy' (563e): no awe is felt for established authority, no child respects his father, teachers fawn on their pupils and pupils ignore their teachers (563).

Plato also divides a degenerating democracy into three classes: firstly, 'the dominating class . . . the fiercest part of it makes speeches and transacts business . . . the remainder keep up a buzzing . . .' (564d). Secondly, the 'capitalistic class' who are 'orderly and thrifty' and therefore become the wealthiest (564e). Lastly, 'the people', who own no property but are 'the largest and most potent group in the democracy when it meets in assembly' (565). Although this is not the same classification as Arnold's – one could hardly expect that in two such distant societies – it is possible to recognise in these descriptions nearly all of the characteristics of Victorian England which Arnold singled out for criticism: the desire for untrammelled liberty and the pursuit of happiness; a craving for material wealth that obliterates all other values; a noisy, hurrying, thrifty, speechifying middle class; and a threat of anarchy from an underlying populace which, at the time Arnold wrote, was beginning to make its power felt in minor riots and huge public meetings.

For Arnold as for Plato the remedy is the same. The state must be strong and centralised; it must deal firmly with disobedience and lawlessness; it must answer to the best self in each of its citizens; and it

[10] W. David Shaw, *The Lucid Veil: Poetic Truth in the Victorian Age* (London, 1987), p. 219. Anderson, in *Matthew Arnold*, draws attention to the similarity between Arnold and Plato's criticisms of democracy. See p. 122.

must model each of its future citizens by means of a state-controlled education. This education was to be achieved by feeding the soul upon the fine arts because, 'no one could ever become a good man unless from childhood his play and all his pursuits were concerned with things fair and good' (558b), and a major proportion of Books II and III of the *Republic* is given over to discussing exactly which kinds of literature and music are suitable for this purpose. When the political vision is achieved then Plato's 'divine governing principle' (590d) and Arnold's 'reason and the will of God' (*Prose*, v, p. 91) will prevail. Thus Plato unites literary criticism, education, politics, and even to a certain extent religion, in exactly the same way as Arnold.

But it is only at the very end of *Culture and Anarchy* that the really important link with Plato's work is established, and this has nothing to do with Platonic doctrine and everything to do with identifying with the character and social role of Socrates. Sidgwick and Harrison had both noted Arnold's Socratic pretensions in the mid-1860s;[11] now Arnold makes the identification explicit:

> Socrates has drunk his hemlock and is dead; but in his own breast does not every man carry about with him a possible Socrates, in that power of disinterested play of consciousness upon his stock notions and habits, of which this wise and admirable man gave all through his lifetime the great example, and which is the secret of his incomparable influence? And he who leads men to call forth and exercise in themselves this power, and who busily calls it forth and exercises it in himself, is at the present moment, perhaps, as Socrates was in his time, more in concert with the vital workings of men's minds, and more effectually significant, than any House of Commons' orator, or practical operator in politics. (*Prose*, v, pp. 228–9)

Culture and Anarchy is not centrally concerned with proposing a list of political improvements, or with suggesting a method which would allow such a list to be arrived at; rather, its whole tone and manner gives each reader an example of an ideally supple amenity on which he can model himself. Just as Arnold formed his literary persona by meditating on the character of Socrates, so each reader can now model himself on Arnold; and it is in the interaction of such ideally reasonable persons that the perfect society consists. As a prelude to realising this vision, each man must ask, 'How should a man live?' and follow the injunction, 'Know thyself'; he must bring a disinterested

[11] Henry Sidgwick, 'The Prophet of Culture', *MacMillan's Magazine*, 16 (August 1867), 271–80; Frederic Harrison, 'Culture: A Dialogue', *Fortnightly Review*, 11 (November 1867), 603–14. Both reprinted in *Matthew Arnold: Prose Writings*, edited by Carl Dawson and John Pfordresher (London, 1979), pp. 209–37.

play of consciousness to bear on his stock notions and habits; he must bring his powers of mind – the love of industry, of things of the mind, and of beautiful objects – into harmonious co-operation; he must cultivate sweetness, light, and flexibility, and avoid noise, dogmas, disputatiousness and rhetoric; finally, he must aim at a harmonious expansion of his powers, avoid all onesidedness, be willing to recognise his own ignorance, and realise that culture is not a 'having and a getting but a growing and becoming'. (*Prose*, v, 94). Arnold's important legacy, like Socrates', is not a body of doctrine but a style and manner of thought.[12]

LATER WRITINGS

Culture and Anarchy marks the high-point of Arnold's identification with Socrates. In the writings after 1870, we can discern a diminishing interest in the figure of Socrates and an increasing involvement with the moral outlook of Plato. In *Literature and Dogma*, published in 1873 and his most important work on religion, we can see the beginning of this process: 'Plato sophisticates somewhat the genuine Socrates; but it is very doubtful whether the culture and mental energy of Plato did not give him a more adequate vision of the true Socrates than Xenophon had.' (*Prose*, vi, pp. 372–3) By the time we reach *God and the Bible* in 1875, Plato has become an 'idealising inventor' (*Prose*, vii, p. 307) with regard to Socrates. Plato and Socrates are as far apart as they were in *Culture and Anarchy* but this time it is to Plato's advantage.

This shift in attitude is partly to be explained by a general darkening of Arnold's personality as he grew older. Two of his sons died in 1868 followed by a third, his favourite, in 1871. This series of personal tragedies initiated a more profound interest in religion than he had shown hitherto and a notable hebraising of his character. In *Culture and Anarchy*, the Hellenic ideal of 'spontaneity of consciousness' and the Hebraic ideal of 'strictness of conscience' are both held up as the twin poles of human ethical aspirations, but there can be no doubt that Arnold, in Collini's words, would rather have 'loll[ed] on Parnassus than crawl[ed] up Calvary',[13] although Arnold would no doubt defend his treatment by arguing that the British public stood in greater need of the Hellenic ideal. But by the 1870s the emphasis is less

[12] This paragraph is only the barest sketch. I shortly hope to complete a paper examining the influence of Socrates' character on Arnold's literary *persona* and style.

[13] Stephan Collini, *Arnold* (Oxford, 1987), p. 84.

on disinterested thought and the free play of consciousness than on righteousness and conduct, the latter of which, he reminds us endlessly, is 'three fourths of life' (e.g., *Prose*, VI, p. 173).

However, two other factors must be taken into account when considering the shift from Socratic populariser to Platonic elitist. Firstly, up until the mid-century, Plato was little read in England, but after the publication of Grote's *Plato, and the Other Companions of Socrates*, in 1865, discussion of his philosophy not only became widespread but also intensely politicised. Grote was a radical, democratic, nominalist utilitarian who divided Plato's dialogues into 'dialogues of search' and 'dialogues of exposition'. Plato's work is valuable and correct, Grote argues, when it exemplifies the power of rational analysis in the dialogues of search, false and retarding when, in the dialogues of exposition, it relies on intuition – the metaphysics and politics of the *Republic* being the most egregious examples. In contrast to this, Jowett's commentaries on his complete edition of Plato, which first appeared in 1871, favoured what might be termed the high-Anglican interpretation that found its deepest sympathies most fully engaged with the more mystical, authoritarian elements of the *Republic*. Arnold knew both these approaches: he frequently mentions Jowett's commentaries and translations in later years, and he certainly read Caird's long article on Grote's Plato in the *North British Review* the year after it was published.[14] Faced with a choice between Grote's utilitarian radicalism and his friend Jowett's traditionalism which defended what Coleridge termed the 'Platonic old England' against the 'new commercial Britain',[15] there can be no doubt where Arnold's loyalties lay.

However, the power of Grote's scholarship was not to be denied. Frank Turner has described Grote's book as 'longer, more thorough, and more deeply influenced by general European scholarship than any other study of Plato in English, and remained so for over half a century'.[16] Whatever his opinion of Grote's politics, Arnold cannot fail to have been impressed by a portrait of the historical Socrates he

[14] E. Caird, 'A Review of G. Grote: *Plato, and the Other Companions of Socrates*', *North British Review*, 43 (1865), 351–84. A star by the 1866 Notebook entry indicates that Arnold fulfilled his intention to read this review. He indicates his familiarity with Grote's earlier *History of Greece* (where Socrates is also discussed) in the first instalment of his review of Curtius's *The History of Greece* (*Prose*, V, p. 259).

[15] S.T. Coleridge, *Anima Poetae*, edited by E.H. Coleridge (Boston, 1895), p. 128. Quoted in Frank M. Turner, *The Greek Heritage in Victorian Britain* (Yale, 1981), p. 21.

[16] Turner, *The Greek Heritage*, p. 384.

would have found intensely unsympathetic. Socrates, for Grote, was an ardent rationalist who was driven to question all established custom, religion and authority; and yet he was motivated in this task by a religious fanaticism which ultimately led him to seek his own death. Given Arnold's opinion of both rationalism and religious fanaticism, it is no wonder that the figure of Socrates plays a much less commanding role in his later writings.

The second factor required to explain the Socrates–Plato shift was Arnold's reading of Curtius' *The History of Greece*. Arnold wrote a substantial five-part review of this work which appeared between 1868 and 1876 in the *Pall Mall Gazette*, the last part of which discusses Curtius' portrayal of the character and influence of Plato. Arnold quotes with approval Curtius' remark:

> In proportion as Plato in his ideal demands rose above the data of the circumstances and principles around him, it became impossible to expect that he would exercise a transforming influence upon the body of the people. He was by his whole nature far more aristocratic than Socrates, the simple man of the people; and his teachings and aims could only become the possession of a circle of elect. (*Prose*, v, pp. 292–3)

Curtius' portrayal of Plato's opposition to an outwardly thriving but actually corrupt and pleasure loving Athens exercised a decisive influence on Arnold, as we can see from his explicit discussion of the German historian in 'Numbers', written seven years later (*Prose*, x, p. 146). The reason is not hard to see. In the 1860's Arnold had a touching faith that, eventually, clear disinterested thought would prevail over commercialism and clap-trap. If thought would only disavow immediate practical purposes, he wrote in 'The Function of Criticism' then '[criticism] may perhaps one day make its benefit felt [even in the sphere of practice] . . . in a natural and thence irresistible manner'. (*Prose*, III, p. 275). Similarly, distinction, including distinction of thought, is a quality of which 'the world is impatient; it chafes against it, rails at it, mocks it, hates it; – [but] it ends by receiving its influence, by undergoing its law' (*Prose*, III, p. 106). At the end of *Culture and Anarchy*, Arnold had deliberately set himself up in competition with more pragmatic, rhetorical, political contemporaries, and claimed that he, the Socrates of his time, would ultimately exert the greater influence. But in Arnold's later work there is clear evidence that he was disappointed in his expectations. His protests against Lowe's Revised Code in education, and his criticisms of government policy in Ireland had not been effective, and it is hard to hear a note of irony when, in *Discourses in America*, he remarks, 'I have produced so little effect on [my countrymen]' (*Prose*, x, pp. 143–4). The preface to *Irish Essays* contains one of his few genuinely bitter passages as he contemplates, with lively satisfaction, how helpless the pragmatic, practical man feels when faced by ultimate philosophical issues. Taking up Plato's account of the matter in the *Theaetetus*, he quotes, with some relish, the following:

'Then, indeed', says Plato, 'when that narrow, vain, little practical mind is called to account, above all this, he gives the philosopher his revenge. For dizzied by the height at which he is hanging, when he looks into space, which is a strange experience to him, he being dismayed and lost and stammering out broken words is laughed at, not by Thracian handmaidens such as laughed at Thales, or by any other uneducated persons, for they have no eye for the situation, but by every man who has been brought up a true free man'. (*Prose*, IX, p. 315)

Arnold's identification with Plato at this point is significant. In 'Democracy', Arnold had held up the Athens in which Xenophon's Socrates flourished as the ideal society. In 1869, in an attempt to further the cause of disinterested thought, he made a bid to become the Socrates of his own time despite the apparently unpropitious circumstances. He began to be aware of this project's failure at the same time as Curtius was showing him that Plato's position in his society was analogous to his own situation in Victorian England, and both Grote and Curtius were demonstrating that his ideal Socrates was a historically invalid illusion. Consequently, by the time he came to publish *Irish Essays* in 1882, he had come to identify with the later Plato's lonely endurance of society's superficiality, worldliness, and corruption.

It is in the 1870s and 80s that Plato's writings become most important to Arnold. The *Protagoras*, *Gorgias*, *Meno*, *Ion*, *Phaedrus*, *Parmenides*, *Republic*, *Philebus* and *Statesman*, are all mentioned on his reading lists, and it is worth remarking that most of these, in contrast to the Plato he recorded reading in the 1840s, are late and middle period works. The influence of this reading shows up clearly in *Discourses in America*, the last work to be published in his lifetime and, Arnold thought, the finest. The book consists of three extended lectures – 'Numbers: or the Majority and the Remnant', 'Literature and Science', and 'Emerson' – and Plato plays a major role in all of them. He no longer suggests phrases or supplies a background influence, or exemplifies an attitude towards enquiry, he is now the major intellectual influence and his works are discussed explicitly and at length. In 'Emerson' he is ultimately the standard by which Emerson is weighed and found wanting:

> The Platonic dialogues afford an example of exquisite literary form and treatment given to philosophical ideas. Plato is at once a great literary man and a great philosopher . . . Emerson cannot, I think be called with justice a great philosophical writer. He cannot build; his arrangement of philosophical ideas has no progress in it, no evolution. (*Prose*, x, p. 174)

In 'Literature and Science' Plato inspires both the long introduction and a crucial turning point in the argument. The lecture is a defence of literary education against some of its more forceful scientific and technological opponents. Arnold's basic strategy is to argue that science, however comprehensive and interesting, can never supply more than mere knowledge, and that the cognitive faculty is neither the only nor the most important power of mind. Arnold suggests that there are in fact four fundamental powers to which education must address itself – the powers of intellect, beauty, manners and conduct – and argues, with reference to the views of Diotima (*Symposium* 201d–212b), that it is natural for human beings to try and combine them harmoniously together. It is here, Arnold thinks, that a literary education is most effective. Poetry, unlike mere knowledge, appeals to our sense of beauty, and because of this it touches our emotions. These in their turn, affect our manners and conduct. By way of opposition to the limited scientific conception of what education is, Arnold quotes Plato's remark, 'An intelligent man will prize those studies which result in his soul getting soberness, righteousness, and wisdom and will less value the others', and comments, 'I cannot consider *that* a bad description of the aim of education' (*Prose*, x, pp. 54–5).

However, it is in the first of the *Discourses*, 'Numbers: or the Majority and the Remnant' that Plato plays his most significant role. This is the later Arnold at his darkest and most moralistic, and Plato's condemnation of Athens is invoked as the model for Arnold's condemnation of the immorality and superficiality of his own civilisation – particularly the 'lubricity' of the French. The basic theme of the lecture is that ancient societies were very small; consequently their wise men and clear thinkers were too few and scattered to combine into an effective force and therefore exercised little influence on their societies. The same is true of the states of modern Europe; but in a vast modern society such as the USA this minority or remnant would, if sufficiently inspired and motivated, be numerous enough to influence the tone of the nation very much for the better.

It is not the amenity of Socrates or the political arguments of the *Republic* that influence 'Numbers', but Plato's execration of sexual licence and his condemnation of the multitude. The remnant's unhappy position in most societies is illustrated with a long quotation from the *Republic*. It ends as follows:

> They may be compared to a man who has fallen among wild beasts: he will not be one of them, . . . and before he can do any good to society or his friends, he will be overwhelmed and perish uselessly. When he considers this, he will resolve to keep still, and to mind his own business; as it were standing aside under a wall in a storm of dust and hurricane of driving wind; and he will endure to behold the rest filled with iniquity, if only he may live his life clear of injustice and of impiety, and depart, when his time comes, in mild and gracious mood, with fair hope. (*Prose*, x, pp. 145–6)

In *Culture and Anarchy*, Plato and St Paul are the embodiments of Hellenism and Hebraism respectively, and represent the opposite poles of human perfection. In 'Numbers', spurred on no doubt by the biblical echoes of Jowett's translation, Plato's account of the remnant is linked with Isaiah's, and Plato himself is set alongside St Paul as a lover of 'Righteousness and making one's study of the law of the eternal' (*Prose*, x, p. 152). Plato and the saints are also at one in imploring us to think only of whatsoever things are pure, and Arnold repeats Plato's warning that if we indulge in dissoluteness, 'we feed and strengthen the beast in us and starve the man' (*Prose*, x, p. 160). Finally, the 'aliens' of *Culture and Anarchy*, the individual thinkers who transcend their place in the social order, now have their separate identities obliterated by being placed under a single mass term 'the remnant', and far from glorying in their remoteness from practice, Arnold appears to think of them as a crusading force in the cause of moral rearmament, 'A remnant of how great numbers, how mighty strength, how irresistible efficacy!' (*Prose*, x, p. 163) The Socrates of Xenophon and Plato's early dialogues could stand in opposition to the saints and prophets as an emissary of sweetness and light, but the later Arnold's Plato is so dark-hued that no strain is felt as he is quietly assimilated into the Hebraic conception of perfection.

It is unlikely to be Arnold's late social criticism which most appeals to the modern reader – it is too moralistic, too horrified by sex, too reliant on racial equations. The voice which speaks to us most clearly is the Arnold of the 1860s at the height of his identification with Socrates. This is the Arnold who puts light into our eyes and fills us with a clearness by which all objects afterwards become illuminated; who teaches us nothing, but prepares us, fashions us, and makes us ready to know all. It is no coincidence that the quality which, at this period, Arnold most valued in Plato's writings, should be the very quality which we most value in Arnold himself.

CHAPTER 23

Flux, rest, and number: Pater's Plato

Anne Varty

'The imagery in which [Plato's] philosophy is conveyed often touches on subjects which are revolting to Christian and manly feelings', wrote Benjamin Jowett in his notes for a lecture series on Plato and Pre-Socratic philosophy.[1] These began by outlining the difficulties that an Oxford student of the 1860s might have encountered. Walter Pater, an undergraduate reading for Greats at Queen's College from 1858–62, was amongst Jowett's potential audience as his student and afterwards, from 1864 until his death thirty years later, as his colleague. But those features of Plato's work which Jowett saw as obstacles to contemporary appreciation in fact secretly confirmed the character of Pater's dissent, which was atheist and homosexual. And they became central to his influential position as aesthetic critic. The young Pater found himself unwittingly constructed by Jowett as Plato's ideal reader, the inverse of the bewildered student who, Jowett thought,

> supposed himself to be studying philosophy & finds that he has been reading a poem. He cannot understand why ~~the Republic~~ Plato should be at once so ideal & yet so sensual . . . he objects to arguing from the arts to the virtues . . . neither does harmony in music appear to be the same as harmony in life.[2]

Gripped rather than alienated by these obscurities, Pater found in Plato authority for the style and substance of his most famous exhortations about how to live, from the display of 'moral expressiveness' in whosoever 'has treated life in the spirit of art' to the dictum 'all art

[1] Oxford, Balliol College, Jowett Papers, Box B[1], Bk. 5, p. 27. All quotations from Benjamin Jowett are from his unpublished papers held in The Jowett Papers in Balliol College, Oxford. Copyright remains with the Jowett Copyright Trustees, and I am grateful for their permission to quote from this source. Examination of these papers suggests that Jowett's influence as a teacher was rather different from that of his published writings which has been investigated by Ian Small in 'Plato and Pater: Fin de Siècle Aesthetics', *British Journal of Aesthetics*, 12 (1972), 369–83.

[2] The Jowett Papers, Box B[1], Bk. 5, pp. 23–6.

constantly aspires towards the condition of music' (which includes the art of life).[3] This becomes clear in 'Plato's Aesthetics', the tenth and closing chapter of Pater's last monograph, *Plato and Platonism* (1893), which mirrors Book x of *The Republic*:

> It is life itself, action and character, he proposes to colour; to get something of that irrepressible conscience of art, that spirit of control, into the general course of life, above all into its energetic and impassioned acts. (p. 282)

Given Pater's lifelong engagement with the philosopher, it is no surprise that this Plato sounds more like an auto-epitaph for the author himself, than an account of the ancient Greek.

Pater's manipulation of Plato is manifest throughout his published writing, from the earliest prose piece 'Diaphaneitè' (1864) to the lecture series *Plato and Platonism*. At first sight the latter seems to be a conventional portrayal of Plato's work, setting it in the context of the various schools of Presocratic thought, as Jowett did in his own lectures on this subject, and as other nineteenth-century authorities on Plato such as the German scholar Eduard Zeller and the British authority George Grote had also done. However, Pater's concern with the sources of Plato's vision is not primarily exegetical: it is an early instance of the modernist quest for origins and new beginnings. First Pater presents the teachings of Heraclitus, Parmenides and Pythagoras before addressing how Plato transformed their doctrines. These introductory chapters are anything but conventional. Each is rounded off with a religious poem (Shadwell's translation of Canto vi of Dante's *Purgatory*, an anonymous prayer to Zeus the One God from Mullach's *Fragmenta Philosophorum Graecorum*, and Henry Vaughan's 'The Retreat'), to illustrate the perennial tendencies of human need to think in terms of the doctrines of motion, rest and number; and in this way, Pater implied that contemporary 'aestheticism' was similarly nothing new. Pater's presentation of these three distinct schools and their assimilation by Plato depends equally on temperament: the attractions held for him by the Heraclitean doctrine of motion are as undisguised as his emotional dislike of the Parmenidean doctrine of rest, while Pythagorean thinking offers, in Pater's view, the richest

[3] See 'Diaphaneitè', *Miscellaneous Studies* (first published 1895; London, 1910), p. 249; 'Conclusion', 'Winckelman', 'The School of Giorgione' in *The Renaissance. Studies in Art and Poetry*, ed. Donald Hill (London, Berkeley and Los Angeles, 1980), pp. 189, 183, 106. All quotations from Pater's work except *The Renaissance* are taken, unless otherwise stated, from the ten-volume Library Edition edited by Charles L. Shadwell (London, 1910). *The Renaissance* was first published 1873 as *Studies in the History of the Renaissance*.

intellectual anticipations of both nineteenth-century science, and aestheticism.

Unlike Jowett, and unlike Grote, Pater never emphasised the distance which the metaphysical imagination had to travel in order to meet Plato; he always wrote of the philosopher's proximity and in 1893 even claimed him as a contemporary,[4] aligning him with the aesthetic movement by putting unattributed statements by its proponents into his mouth. Alluding amongst others to Gautier, Swinburne and even himself, Pater states, '[Plato] anticipates the modern notion that art as such has no end but its own perfection, – "art for art's sake"'. He clinches this by quoting in Greek out of context from *Republic* 341d, 'and the interest of each of the arts is the perfection of each of them; nothing but that';[5] alluding to Gautier again, '[t]he author of this philosophy of the unseen was one, for whom . . . 'the visible world really existed'.[6] There are many allusions to Wilde's Platonic dialogue *The Critic as Artist* (1890), which had sharpened much of what Pater had already written. One such allusion is a link between Arnold and Yeats, and justifies Pater's habitually polyvocal presentation of the philosopher:

> From the first to last our faculty of thinking is limited by our command of speech . . . [T]he essential, or dynamic, dialogue, is ever that dialogue of the mind with itself, which any converse with Socrates or Plato does but promote. (*Platonism*, p. 142)

This in turn enables Pater's launch into the present tense for the final rally of the book, a deftly Platonic apologia for the Aesthetic Movement: '[w]e, then, the founders, the citizens, of the Republic have a peculiar purpose. We are here to escape from . . . a certain vicious centrifugal tendency in life' (p. 273). This is made more resonant by his portrayal of Oxford University as a latter day version of Plato's Academy throughout the volume. Yet while some of Pater's

[4] See for example, the review by Edmund Gosse in *New Review* (April 1893) quoted in *Walter Pater. The Critical Heritage*, ed. R.M. Seiler (London, 1980), p. 254.

[5] *Plato and Platonism*, p. 268. The wording is that of Jowett's 1876 translation, and Pater plays on the failure of the Greek to distinguish between fine arts and crafts.

[6] *Plato and Platonism*, p. 126. For Gautier as 'un homme pour qui le monde visible existe', see Edmond and Jules de Goncourt, '1 mai 1857', *Journal: Mémoires de la vie littéraire, 1851–1863*, ed. Ricatte (Paris, 1956), I, 343. Pater cites or alludes to this statement several times throughout his corpus, e.g. *Marius the Epicurean* (1885), I, p. 32. Compare *Platonism*, p. 119, where Pater may also be referring to Rossetti. See R. Hall, *Recollections of Dante Gabrielli Rossetti* (London, 1882), p. 249.

central tenets are unthinkable without Plato, his appropriation of the philosopher for the aesthetic avant-garde was not unproblematic.

The problems are twofold. First, while the erotic dialogues *Symposium* and *Phaedrus* provided a rationale for Pater's love of the sensuous world and of youthful male beauty, his very affinity with these texts set him at serious odds with prevailing public morality. Pater, unlike Jowett, never wished to argue that Plato would have transposed his love of men to women had he lived 'in our own times'.[7] And while, like his fellow historian of the Renaissance, John Addington Symonds, Pater saw analogies between the Platonic ascent to the 'divine' and the Dantesque, he had no interest in exploring these in the fashion of 'The Dantesque and Platonic Ideals of Love' which Symonds published in *The Contemporary Review* in 1890. This would have entailed some concession to attempts to harmonise Platonic with Christian thought, and Pater made his view of such attempts clear in his 1871 essay 'Pico della Mirandola'.[8] Furthermore, Symond's efforts to place serious discussion of homoeroticism on the intellectual agenda were at once more covert and more blatant than Pater's meliorating approach. Concurrently with his christianising efforts, Symonds was preparing for private circulation in pamphlet form an apologia for male homosexuality, first published as *A Problem in Modern Ethics. Being an Inquiry Into The Phenomenon Of Sexual Inversion* in 1896, the year following Wilde's conviction, and revised in 1901 as *A Problem in Greek Ethics*, both of which draw heavily on ancient Greek and Platonic models.

Second amongst Pater's problems in the appropriation of Plato is the fact that there are features of his thought which he found uncongenial and which appear to undermine the sanction otherwise granted to the aesthete's deployment of the figure and significance of Eros. The father of the British Art for Art's Sake movement, and exponent of the 'relative spirit' in criticism, had to contend with the fact that Plato banished the artists from the ideal city, and that he retained a Parmenidean dimension to his theory of Ideas. Analogue and allusion therefore provide the habitual structures for Pater's statements of homoerotic intent, while expressions of dismissive contempt or wilful reinterpretation characterise his address to the Eleatic realism of Plato's thought.

Pater's abiding admiration for Plato can be seen in a comparison

[7] Jowett, quoted by Richard Ellmann, *Oscar Wilde* (London, 1987), p. 58.
[8] See, for instance *Renaissance*, p. 35.

between one of his first and last compositions, 'Diaphaneitè' in which he outlined an ideal type of man who is neither the 'artist' nor the 'saint', but the 'scholar', and chapter VI of *Plato and Platonism*, 'The Genius of Plato':

> Plato was . . . one of the great scholars of the world . . . possessed of the inborn genius...a certain defiance of rule, of the intellectual habits of others, he acquires, by way of habit and rule, all that can be taught and learned; what is thus derived from others by docility and discipline, what is *rangé*, comes to have in him, and in his work, an equivalent weight with what is unique, impulsive, underivable. (pp. 146–7)

This classification of Plato as 'scholar' is Pater's highest accolade, and is reminiscent of the terms in which Carlyle's 'Hero as Man of Letters' and Fichte's related lectures on *Der Gelehrte* (The Scholar) inform 'Diaphaneitè' with their versions of Plato's philosopher-king who sees beyond the shadow play of ephemeral appearances and is the type most fit to govern. Pater's portrayal of the scholarly type, capable of effecting 'the regeneration of the world' in 'Diaphaneitè' may also have been inspired, aptly, by Jowett's view of Plato (potentially amongst the first things Pater heard on his arrival in Oxford). Jowett's terminology recurs in 'The Genius of Plato':

> All writers are under the influence of their age; no one is exempt from this natural law of the human mind. But great genius has the privilege of freeing itself from the more superficial tendencies of an age to embrace the deeper ones; of creating anew & casting in a mould the elements which serve its use . . . It is this sort of transmutation which the previous philosophies have undergone at the hands of Plato.[9]

Plato's ideas, and contemporary Oxford teaching about him provide the substance of 'Diaphaneitè', while the man himself exemplified the ideal type. Yet both were to remain unidentified for thirty years.

Pater's first published essay, 'Coleridge's Writings' (*Westminster Review*, 1866) displays, however, a more contradictory view of Plato. Here Pater makes his first statement of the value of the relative spirit, which we have already seen to be implicit in Jowett's teaching.[10] Heraclitus and Darwin combine to make Pater dismiss any attempt to 'apprehend the absolute' as an 'effort of sickly thought'.[11]

[9] Jowett Papers, Box B [iii], Bk. 5, p. 85. When, as in most cases, Jowett has not dated his notes, the papers are nearly impossible to date accurately. In my view, however, this statement was written for delivery during the autumn of 1858.

[10] 'Coleridge', in *Appreciations with an Essay on Style* (1889), p. 66.

[11] 'Coleridge', p. 68.

Who would change the colour or curve of a roseleaf for that *οὐσία ἀχρωματος, ἀσψημάτιστος, ἀναφὴς*. A Transcendentalism that makes what is abstract more excellent than what is concrete has nothing akin with the leading philosophies of the world.[12]

Although Pater only glanced at Plato here, he was directly opposed to what he saw as Coleridge's excess of seriousness by which theories were his captors rather than his servants (see Cunliffe, pp. 207–16 above), and jealously corrective, declared: 'Plato, whom Coleridge claims as the first of his spiritual ancestors, Plato, as we remember him, a true humanist . . . holds his theories lightly, glances with a blithe and naive inconsequence from one view to another'.[13] In *Plato and Platonism* he argued that Plato did not value the abstract at the expense of the concrete: in Plato's conception of love, 'it was as if the faculty of physical vision . . . were still at work at the very centre of intellectual abstraction' (p.170). This view of Plato was indebted to ideas which Pater had formulated twenty-five years earlier in relation to the archaeologist and art historian Winckelmann (see Larissey, pp. 196–7 above). Plato becomes 'a seer who has a sort of sensous love of the unseen', and as such wields the power which Marius in *Marius the Epicurean* (1885) had longed for in his plea for 'knowledge which . . . was like sensation'.[14] Pater's Plato becomes the conduit between Keats' desire for a life of 'Sensations' rather than 'Thoughts' and T.S. Eliot's admiration for the undissociated sensibility of the metaphysical poets. Pater resisted any dualist interpretation of Plato's Theory of Ideas, and reserved his opprobrium for the Eleatics whose work, after all, Plato had transformed. Reviewers of *Plato and Platonism* of course took issue with Pater's efforts to rescue Plato from the Immutable Being of Parmenides.[15] But the whole of Pater's enterprise as an aesthetic critic turns on personal and authentic response, the transforming power of temperament. This vision of reciprocating signification between particular and universal is fundamental to his thought. The argument is played out in narrative form in the Imaginary Portrait, 'A Prince of Court Painters' (1885).[16] The Ionian-Eleatic (Heraclitean-Parmenidean) division in Pater's evaluation of Plato is dramatised again in the companion portrait to this, 'Sebastian van Storck' (1886).[17] 'Winckelmann' (1867), his next published essay after 'Coleridge's Writings', betrays the fact that his

[12] 'Coleridge's Writings', *The Westminster Review*, n.s. 29 (1866), 108.
[13] 'Coleridge's Writings', p. 111. Revised and replaced in *Appreciations*, p. 69.
[14] *Platonism*, p. 143; *Marius*, II, p. 22.
[15] See for example, Richard H. Hutton's review *Spectator* (April, 1893), in *Critical Heritage*, p. 265.
[16] *Imaginary Portraits* (1887), pp. 32–4. [17] *Imaginary Portraits*, 110; *Appreciations*, p. 104.

hostility towards the immutable realm of Ideas is generated in part by attraction towards it. It is in search of something fixed where all is moving that Pater turns, with Winckelmann's help, to salvation through art.

WINCKELMANN

Johan Joachim Winckelmann (1717–1768) provided Pater with a historical example by which homoerotic desire was refracted through an enthusiasm for the writings of Plato to aesthetic appreciation of ancient Greek sculpture. As he wrote in *The Renaissance*,

> Enthusiasm – that, in the broad Platonic sense of the *Phaedrus*, was the secret of his divinatory power over the Hellenic world. This enthusiasm, dependent as it is to a great degree on bodily temperament, has the power of reinforcing the purer motions of the intellect with an almost physical excitement. (*Renaissance*, p. 152)

Winckelmann is presented as a kind of case study illustration of the Platonic ascent from love of beautiful male youth to love of Beauty and the Good which does not neglect the means once the end is reached, and which ascent is possible in virtue of the soul's reminiscence of its origin. He begins his ascent by a series of fervent friendships with men, setting the pattern for a number of friendships in Pater's fiction, such as Marius and Cornelius in *Marius the Epicurean* or Prior John and Apollyon in 'Apollo in Picardy' (1893), all of which lead to higher enlightenment. Here Plato's (Pythagorean) Doctrine of Reminiscence is incorporated as a feeling of temperamental affinity with the culture of ancient Greece, and explains Pater's insistence that the Renaissance is not to be understood as a definable historical period but as a habit of mind. Winckelmann's affinity with the ancient art which he studies is so strong that, 'he is *en rapport* with it; it penetrates him, and becomes part of his temperament'.[18] The provocative sexual imagery here asserts the enabling participation of Eros in Winckelmann's endeavour, while Pater is quick to point out that Winckelmann's union with his object of study restores him to a state of primal, if pagan, innocence: 'he fingers those pagan marbles with unsinged hands, with no sense of shame or loss' (*Renaissance*, p. 177).

The Doctrine of Reminiscence shades, in Pater's hands, into that of imitation. It borders on the risky ground of Plato's banishment of representational or mimetic artists in the *Republic*. But Winckelmann's

[18] 'Winckelmann', *The Westminster Review*, n.s. 31 (1867), 88. Revised in *Renaissance*, p. 154.

recovery of a state of unfallen innocence in relation to ancient statuary indicates as least the influential importance of the work of art, and suggests that Pater would revise the artists' expulsion, Pater's account of Plato's theory of imitation, as he explains it in the last chapter of *Plato and Platonism*, was taken by some contemporary reviewers as a concession to Ruskin's moral aesthetic. 'Art can never be a morally indifferent thing if, as Ruskin says after Plato, every work of art tends to reproduce in the beholder the state of mind and temper that brought it forth', wrote one reviewer.[19] But Pater's interpretation of Plato's theory was more radical than anything offered by Ruskin.

Pater never quotes Winckelmann's famous paradox, 'the only way for us to become great and, if possible, even inimitable, is through imitation of the ancients', but his technique as a critic of the arts was learned from what Winckelmann meant by this. The German neoclassicist was an exponent of an emotive form of art criticism, which did not seek to describe, but to evoke feeling akin to the projected 'intellectual and spiritual ideas sunk by [the artist] in sensuous form', thereby creating a fresh work of art (*Renaissance*, p. 176). Winckelmann therefore imparted not knowledge but technique. Pater cites with approval Goethe's statement about Winckelmann, '[o]ne learns nothing from him . . . but one becomes something' which had anticipated Jowett's summary of what one learns from Plato, '[h]is system is . . . a movement towards true being – not a book but a conversation, not a result but a process . . . he disputes with us . . . creating rather than imparting'.[20] The regenerative technique of Winckelmann's criticism, imitated by Pater's own style, anticipates the theme of 'The Child in the House' (1878), Pater's autobiographical allegory of the development of the soul in the body in which, 'the sense of harmony between his soul and its physical environment became . . . like perfectly played music'.[21] In *Plato and Platonism* Pater attributes human susceptibility to the physical environment not to some alien theory of ancient metaphysics, but to up-to-the-minute determinism, '[l]ike those insects . . . of which naturalists tell us, taking colour from the plants they lodge on, they will come to match with much servility the aspects of the world about them' (p.272). And because of this habitual servility, Pater, like

[19] Paul Shorey, *The Dial* (1893) in *Critical Heritage*, p. 261.
[20] *Renaissance*, p. 147. Jowett Papers, Box B[III], Bk. 1, p. 38.
[21] *Miscellaneous Studies* (1895), p. 180.

Plato, wishes to discriminate amongst the arts: 'Let us beware how men attain the very truth of what they imitate' (p. 272). The musical imagery provides the analogy by which Pater unifies his uneasy dualism of body and soul, form and content. Like Plato who sought to forge perfect individuals by education in gymnastics and music in his idealised Spartan state of Lacedaemon, Pater declares, 'art comes to you proposing frankly to give nothing but the highest quality to your moments as they pass'.[22]

He thus incorporates a Parmenidean quality in his aestheticism. Zeno's paradox, about the flying arrow that mysteriously moves from A to B while at every instant that we try to measure its progress is stationary, and which therefore proves that 'perpetual motion is perpetual rest', was one of the popular tenets of Eleatic thinking (*Platonism*, p. 30). Pater argues similarly that the vanishing point of the present moment, the imperceptible watershed between past and future, can be fixed, by aesthetic contemplation. Here the infinite touches the finite, and contemplative sensibility is regenerated or penetrated by the work of art. Pater learned to turn Heraclitean flux into Parmenidean stasis, as every moment was expansively structured by the imitative response to art.

In 1873 Pater placed 'Winckelmann' as the closing essay of *The Renaissance*. The book as a whole, with this finale, calls for the rebirth or palingenesis of the Greek spirit in modern culture, and offers simultaneously evidence of its rebirth. In the light of disintegrating Christian faith, and advancing empirical sciences, Pater began to see this renaissance as a real possibility for the future. 'Hermione melts from her stony posture, and the lost proportions of life right themselves', he declares, in the present tense, extending the description of Winckelmann's sentiments to an assertion about the potential awakening of contemporary culture (p. 147). The winter's tale of medieval puritanism was over; Hermione, sensuous perception incarnated by the artist in the work of art, life transfigured to art and revivified by the spectator's mimetic responsiveness into a new, chastened order, represents the metempsychosis of the Greek spirit itself into the modern world. He recast this notion of cultural palingenesis as fiction in the Imaginary Portrait, 'Duke Carl of Rosenmold' (1887). Appended to 'Winckelmann' as a 'Conclusion' to the book, came the second part of the notorious 1868 review of

[22] 'Conclusion', *Renaissance*, p. 190.

'Poems by William Morris', in which not Hermione but 'all' melts 'under our feet' (*Renaissance*, p. 189). Here the plangent but strictly materialist evocation of Heraclitean flux makes the arresting power of the aesthetic sensibility an urgent necessity.

In the chapter on what Plato took from Pythagoras in *Plato and Platonism*, 'The Doctrine of Number', Pater explains how the theories of metempsychosis and reminiscence retain their explanatory value in an age of unbelief, when Christianity was overshadowed by the teaching of Hegel and Darwin. He rehearses arguments from 'Coleridge's Writings', but sets them now in proper context. Citing Wordsworth's 'Ode on the Intimations of Immortality', he argues that we do indeed come 'not in nakedness', nor, however, trailing clouds of glory, but (in a grim parody) 'fatally shrouded' by the forces of naturalist determinism: genetic inheritance, language and culture all shape the lives we lead (p. 72). These forces constitute the transmigrating soul of the species, which uses, and does not respect, the individual. Again, Pater looks to artistic creativity as the only possible form of personal salvation within this bleak scheme:

> To create, to live, perhaps, a little while beyond the allotted hours, if it were but in a fragment of perfect expression:– it was thus his [Marius'] longing defined itself for something to hold by amid the 'perpetual flux'. (*Marius*, I, p. 155)

For in doing this the artist adds to the language that is passed from generation to generation, and by investing some personal connotation in the heritage of words, turns determinism into control. Language, as Wilde had argued, is the parent not the child of thought. Pater, a 'lover of words for their own sake' treats language as though it were a living thing, as indeed it is, in his metempsychotic view.[23] His choice of vocabulary reflects his interest in semantic transmigration and control. His favourite words parade their etymological origins, but also display a knowing mischievousness about how their meaning has changed. The use of words like 'virtual', 'insane', 'obliterate', or 'method'[24] to carry simultaneously their root and current meanings is a way of throwing linguistic flux into sharp relief; it is the art of the palimpsest at the miniature level of the word, as ghosts of meaning cluster around the new coinage which is really old. The most Platonic

[23] 'Style', *Appreciations*, p. 20.

[24] For an interesting account of Pater's etymological understanding and use of the word 'method' in *Plato and Platonism*, see William F. Shutter, 'Pater's Reshuffled Text', *Nineteenth Century Literature*, 43 (1988–9), 518.

of these coinages is Pater's favoured use of the words 'charm' or 'charming', which are resonant with the Latin *carmen* and the Middle English notion of 'occult spell', both of which point back to Plato's Lacedaemonian significance of music.

The means by which Pater idealised the figure of Plato, as a scholar, or master, of a significant body of thought which preceded him, who yet had a transforming contribution to make, fashion Plato as a precursor for the Modernist movement whose exponents were burdened by their sense of belatedness in the tradition. Behind Pound's battle cry of 'make it new' stands Pater's Plato whose achievement was in the debonair handling of tradition. And during the first ten years of Pater's publishing career he had formulated the extensive responses to Plato's thought and style which would colour his own work, from the polyphonic quality of the essay style, to the contemporary signification of the great myths; the way was also prepared for the debts of Joyce, Woolf, T.S. Eliot and Yeats to this transmigrating figure.

PART VI

The twentieth century

CHAPTER 24

Introduction

Angela Elliott

Platonism in the twentieth century has undergone many challenges and transformations while continuing as a major reservoir of the imagination in English letters. Though attitudes have run a course from Late Romantic enthusiasm to Postmodernist detachment, many leading writers and thinkers have steadily acknowledged the Platonic tradition as an important heritage – one not easily defined, yet perhaps the more compelling on that account.[1] The attraction of Platonism for such writers springs from the value they attach to the role of reason and spirit in a period when events of Western history have posed a serious threat to the survival of humanism. The quest for the just society has foundered, and philosophy has rebelled against rationalism. Yet in the face of social fragmentation, many modern Platonists believe that eternal realities such as the Good, love and truth still give meaning and value to human life – even if 'Things fall apart', as W.B. Yeats perceived in 'The Second Coming', or 'The scientists are in terror', as Ezra Pound declared in *The Cantos* (115/794).

Since 1900, classical studies have advanced greatly, resulting in the establishment of the canon of Plato's writings and new English translations of the Platonic corpus. The standard Greek text of Plato dates from the turn of the century, being the edition of Ioannes (John) Burnet, *Platonis Opera*, 5 vols. (1900–7, reprinted 1973). Benjamin Jowett's English translation of the major works (4 vols., 1871) is still, in its latest revisions, highly esteemed. All of Plato's writings, constituting the canon in Greek and English, are available in the Loeb Classical Library. The many modern translations of Plato's works include the selection of dialogues published in the Penguin Classics and the complete collection edited by Edith Hamilton and Huntington Cairns in the Bollingen Series.

[1] For extended definitions of 'Modernism' and 'Postmodernism' based on English and American literary history, see David Perkins, *A History of Modern Poetry*, 2 vols, vol. II, *Modernism and After* (Cambridge, Mass. and London, 1987), especially pp. 331–4.

A few works by Neoplatonists have been translated into English during this century. Stephen MacKenna's translation of *The Enneads of Plotinus* (1917–19) influenced British and American intellectuals, including the philosophers Alfred North Whitehead and George Santayana, as well as the poets W.B. Yeats and Ezra Pound. MacKenna's text was revised by B.S. Page (1917–30; 1956; 1962) and then superseded by A.H. Armstrong's new translation for the Loeb Library (7 vols., 1966–88). Works by Proclus, Julianus and Iamblichus have also appeared. Current scholarship shows that the revival of Neoplatonism in the last two centuries has owed a great deal to the translations and pagan commentaries of the prolific Thomas Taylor, called 'the Platonist' (1758–1835), who presented the Romantics and the moderns with his versions of Plato, Aristotle, Plotinus, Porphyry, Iamblichus and others. Like Coleridge and Shelley, W.B. Yeats owned copies of Taylor's works, which were promoted by the Theosophical Society.[2] Helena P. Blavatsky (1831–91), the oracular founder of the society, and George R.S. Mead (1863–1933), its scholar secretary, also contributed to the lively literature of Neoplatonism that was a source of Hermetic images and symbols for the Modernist poets W.B. Yeats, Ezra Pound and T.S. Eliot.

Plato's works were taught and promoted early in the twentieth century by distinguished British scholars such as G.R. Levy, A.E. Taylor and F.M. Cornford. Platonic themes of literary significance since then have been the government of the self and of the state, analogically conceived in relation to each other (*Republic*); the theory of the Forms, with knowledge as virtue and recollection (*Phaedo*) and with the soul composed of reason, appetite and will (or spirit) as distinct parts (*Republic*); the ascent of the soul to a vision of the Good, through human love and the desire for beauty (*Phaedrus*, *Symposium*); the use of myths, images and symbols of the processes of creation and the cycles of the soul, derived from the pre-Socratics or early religion (*Symposium*, *Timaeus*, *Parmenides*, *Republic*), especially the metaphor of the sun as the Good, along with the myth of the Cave (*Republic*); and the notion of art and poetry as mimesis – as imitation of nature's imitation of a Form (*Republic*).

Distinguishing Plato from Socrates has been another focus of interest. Gregory Vlastos has tentatively isolated an historical Socrates, an 'ironist and moral philosopher' for whom reality 'is in the

[2] Kathleen Raine and George Mills Harper (eds), *Thomas Taylor the Platonist: Selected Writings* (Princeton, 1969), pp. 10–11, 296, 322–42.

world in which he lives'. On the other hand, Plato, known to Vlastos through the 'Socrates' of the middle and later dialogues plus the witness of Aristotle and Xenophon, appears a 'profoundly other-worldly' philosopher of 'Form-mysticism' and 'ecstatic contemplation'. To this day, according to Vlastos, the hallmark of the Platonist has remained 'the postulation of an eternal self-existent world, transcending everything in ours, exempt from the vagaries and vicissitudes that afflict all creatures in the world of time'.[3]

The sceptical side of Plato, however, remains in view. Scholars still speculate about the significance of the *Parmenides*, where the theory of Forms is questioned by raising the problem of the relationship between a particular thing and a Form: how, exactly, do the Many 'share' in the One? Another perennial debate concerns the *Seventh Letter*. If the letter is genuine as most scholars believe, then Plato denies philosophical validity to written works, endorsing only live conversation as the proper vehicle for philosophy.[4] Were there unwritten teachings of an oral tradition for a privileged elite? Did Plato discourse on the Mystery rites to which he occasionally alludes? Ambiguities in the *Gorgias* are also receiving attention. Although this work has traditionally been taken as a blatant attack on rhetoric, it has recently been read as a sophisticated dialogue through which Plato emphasises rhetoric's importance, particularly for 'its role in refutation' rather than 'its utility in pragmatic discourse'.[5] Many such paradoxical features of Plato's work are being viewed by literary theorists as subtleties of an agile intellect capable of various perspectives.[6]

In the twentieth century, Platonic thought has faced challenges traceable to Freud, Marx, and the demoralising impact of two world wars. Freud, inspired by classical studies, explored the complex role of *eros* as an ineluctable force in the unconscious and in culture. His views are implicated in new interpretations of Platonic *eros* and love by modern writers. Marx's critique of imperialism has been extended, in modern literature, to a general critique of republicanism that includes the reassessment of Plato's ideal state in light of twentieth-century totalitarianism and militaristic technocracy.

[3] Gregory Vlastos, *Socrates: Ironist and Moral Philosopher* (Ithaca, NY, 1991), pp. 78–80.

[4] G.R. Levy and A.E. Taylor, among others, inferred the authenticity of the *Seventh Letter*. According to I.M. Crombie, it has come to be 'almost universally thought genuine' *An Examination of Plato's Doctrines* (London, 1962), p. 14.

[5] See James L. Kastely, 'In Defense of Plato's *Gorgias*', *PMLA*, 106 (1991), 96–109.

[6] For some newly posed problems in reading Plato, see Charles L. Griswold, Jr. (ed.), *Platonic Writings, Platonic Readings* (New York, 1988).

European existentialists and philosophers of language, notably Sartre and Wittgenstein, have instigated renewed critical scrutiny of dualistic rationalism, basing objections to it on their conviction of the inseparability of thought from feeling, mind from body, or discourse from its presumed referent, the world. The French philosopher of Deconstruction, Jacques Derrida, pointed out that Western thought tends to rely on binary oppositions (light/dark, masculine/feminine) to interpret texts such as Plato's *Phaedrus*, which he considered to defy logic's law of non-contradiction. Recently, feminist and liberal critics have been deconstructing Platonic texts to reveal androcentric, authoritarian values passed down through the generations.[7]

On the whole, however, the appeal and relevance of Platonism have been enhanced in prospects gained from anthropology, psychology, and mythology. J.G. Frazer's study of pagan culture, *The Golden Bough* (1890–1915), was instructive to T.S. Eliot and Ezra Pound. Frazer's analysis of the primal mind formed a bridge back to the ambience of pre-Christian Europe with its fertility rites, dying gods and Eleusinian Mysteries. Carl Jung and other students of depth psychology and symbology described the role of myth and archetype in the unconscious and in culture. In addition, scholarship in religion, including the discovery of the Dead Sea Scrolls, has heightened the pertinence of Platonism by inviting a broader view of the rise of Christianity from a more complex cultural matrix than was visible earlier. In that view, Christianity and paganism draw closer to one another, tending to merge in some areas, so that Neoplatonic studies become crucial for reconstructing the history of religious and philosophical thought in European culture.[8]

In this milieu, 'kulchur' – as Ezra Pound called it – becomes increasingly international and interdisciplinary. Many writers live cross-culturally in a time of unprecedented travel and communications. The English language is more widely used than ever before. Consequently, British, Irish and American writers share a communality of culture that is reflected in the heightened intertextuality of their English works. Such international figures as America's Ezra Pound and T.S. Eliot, and Ireland's W.B. Yeats and Iris Murdoch have

[7] Derrida, *Writing and Difference*, trans. Alan Bass (London, 1981). Luce Irigaray views Platonism as 'male theory' in *Speculum of the Other Woman*, trans. Gillian C. Gill (Ithaca, NY, 1985). Natalie Harris Bluestone offers a critique of feminist readings of Plato in *Women and the Ideal Society: Plato's 'Republic' and Modern Myths of Gender* (Amherst, Mass., 1987).

[8] See Angela Elliott, 'The Word Comprehensive: Gnostic Light in *The Cantos*', *Paideuma*, 18.3 (1989), 7–57.

participated in a literary 'tradition' that, as T.S. Eliot averred, 'cannot be inherited', since 'you must obtain it by great labour'.[9] An essential part of that labour has often been the study of Platonism.

A centre of intellectual tradition and change was London's Bloomsbury Group, which was influenced by the young philosophers Bertrand Russell and G.E. Moore. Moore influenced Russell in the direction of a Platonic realism, which holds that in addition to the physical world there are abstract domains of numbers and values, which constitute the subject-matter of mathematics and ethics.[10] These views were famously propounded in a pair of works, both published in 1903, Russell's *Principles of Mathematics*, and Moore's *Principia Ethica*. In the latter, Moore not only propounds a Platonist conception of the Good as the supreme abstract value, but he also follows Plato in celebrating the value of Love itself.[11]

The novelist and liberal humanist E.M. Forster also moved in the Bloomsbury circle. In *A Room with a View* (1908), *Howards End* (1910) and other novels, he treated love and passionate friendship as essential to personal fulfillment and to the social solidarity that forms the basis of civilisation. His views are linked to the influence of Moore's ethics and the ideals of Plato's *Symposium*, which helped to inspire Bloomsbury's quest for a comprehensive vision of eros in all its dimensions. For him this included homosexuality, in his fiction as well as in his personal experience. He circulated privately his novel on a homosexual theme, *Maurice*, which did not see publication till 1971.

Virginia Woolf, at the centre of Bloomsbury, related her work strongly to Plato. She had read the dialogues in Greek in her youth, tutored by Clara Pater, sister to Walter, and Jane Ellen Harrison, fellow and lecturer at Newnham College, Cambridge. Woolf adapted elements from the *Phaedrus*, the *Symposium*, the *Republic* and other works of Plato in her mature feminist writings of fiction, literary criticism and social commentary. She made frequent use of such motifs as the Cave, light and mimesis. Her novels *To the Lighthouse* (1927) and *The Waves* (1931) reflect the permutations of consciousness in lives that participate Platonically in the mystery of one continuity of Being (See Lyons, pp. 290–7 below).

Platonic motifs appear in works by other major British novelists.

[9] 'Tradition and the Individual Talent', *Selected Prose of T. S. Eliot*, ed. Frank Kermode (New York, 1975), p. 38.

[10] See A.J. Ayer, *Russell and Moore: The Analytical Heritage* (Cambridge, Mass., 1971), pp. 3–4, 188.

[11] G.E. Moore, *Principia Ethica* (Cambridge, 1903), p. 204.

Joseph Conrad in *Heart of Darkness* (1902) ironically inverted a Platonic myth to explore the European conscience and its justification of colonialism in what was called 'darkest Africa'. The Congo, like Plato's Cave, appeared to many to represent a primal ignorance that civilisation and its knowledge should ideally illumine. Conrad, however, exposed the European trading station as not 'a beacon' for 'instructing' the native peoples but a despotism for exploiting them. The narrator's nearly unspeakable tale of that discovery, based on Conrad's African travels, constitutes a tragic illumination carried back to the real cave, the moral darkness enveloping the colonialist consciousness.

After the Great War and the Communist Revolution, novelists attacked the idealisation of Platonic republicanism and the modern bureaucratic state, by imagining totalitarian dystopias of the future. In the ironic turnabout of Aldous Huxley's *Brave New World* (1932), a caste system based on science erodes the possibility of Platonic spiritual freedom and moral choice. In George Orwell's *Nineteen Eighty-Four* (1949), truth is nullified by Big Brother's corruption of language and constant revision of history; real speech and dialectic vanish. The Canadian novelist Margaret Atwood, in *The Handmaid's Tale* (1986), puts a feminist twist on Platonic notions of restructuring the social reproductive order. She projects the reproductive enslavement of women on a grand scale. All these nightmare fables in effect have exorcised subliminal fears of the hazards lurking in would-be utopian governments of the twentieth century. In a more realistic vein, and with comedy, Iris Murdoch engages Platonic themes in her novels of contemporary society. A professional philosopher, Irish-born, educated at Oxford, Iris Murdoch has lectured on philosophy in Oxford and London (See Conradi, pp. 330–4 below). *In Metaphysics as a Guide to Morals* (1992) her interpretation of Plato's idea of the Good is central to her discussion of modern philosophy, religion and politics.

Poets, too have adapted the Platonic heritage. W.B. Yeats, steeped in Celtic lore and Irish nationalism, began as one of 'the last Romantics' and served in the Senate of the Irish Free State. Yet, sojourns in London and Sussex brought him into international circles that included the Russian Blavatsky and the American Ezra Pound. Neoplatonism he encountered in his early study of Blake and of Hermetic literature. He read Plotinus in MacKenna's translation, and by the mediumship of his wife Georgie Hyde-Lees made contact with spiritual 'communicators' who gave him the material for *A*

Vision (1937), his essay on history and human possibility. The gyres of his polar dynamic are derived, he tells us, from Plato's *Timaeus*, and throughout *A Vision* he discusses Plotinus and other Neoplatonists.[12] W.B. Yeats's *Anima Mundi* is the World Soul of Plotinus, mediating – like a Jungian collective unconscious – between the individual soul and the One[13] (see Arkins, pp. 279–89 below).

As a young admirer of W.B. Yeats, Ezra Pound left his native land for London in 1908, progressing to a three-year residency with 'the great man' at Stone Cottage in Sussex from 1913 to 1916. The poets read Neoplatonism and collaborated as cultural activists.[14] Ezra Pound had attended Theosophical meetings in London at which G.R.S. Mead encouraged his Neoplatonic studies of Provençal literature. In 1911 he heard T.E. Hulme's lectures on Henri Bergson's intuition-based, Platonistic philosophy of 'duration' and the 'élan vital' (life force). Like W.B. Yeats, he sought a broad symbology to encompass a grand vision of history and of human individuality. The emanationist philosophy of Neoplatonism suggested his concept of the *nous*, the universal mind, as 'the sea crystalline and enduring . . . that envelops us, full of light'.[15] In 1927 Ezra Pound wrote to his father that he intended *The Cantos* to evoke a transcendental 'moment of metamorphosis, but thru from quotidien [sic] into "divine or permanent world". Gods, etc.'[16] (see Moody, pp. 308–18, below).

In America as in England, Platonism flourished in the early twentieth century, and it flowed in cross-currents between the two nations. At Harvard T.S. Eliot (see Brown, pp. 298–307 below) studied modern philosophy under Santayana, then a Platonic aesthetician and a writer on Dante. *The Sense of Beauty: Being the Outline of Aesthetic Theory* (1896) was Santayana's justification of Plato's teaching on the role of beauty in the religious life. T.S. Eliot began a dissertation at Harvard which he continued at Oxford, on

[12] See W.B. Yeats, *A Vision*, 1937 edn (New York, 1966), pp. 66–80, and 'The Gyres' in *The Collected Poems of W. B. Yeats* (New York, 1956), p. 29.

[13] See W.B. Yeats, 'Anima Mundi' in *Mythologies* (New York, 1969), pp. 343–66.

[14] See James Longenbach, *Stone Cottage: Pound, Yeats and Modernism* (New York, 1988), esp. pp. 228–30.

[15] Ezra Pound, *Guide to Kulchur* (New York, 1970), p. 44.

[16] Ezra Pound, *The Selected Letters of Ezra Pound, 1907–1941* (New York, 1971), p. 210. See Angela Elliott, 'The Eidolon Self: Emerson, Whitman and Pound' in *Ezra Pound and America*, ed. Jacqueline Kaye (London, 1992), pp. 43–54. On Ezra Pound's use of Neoplatonic 'Light philosophers' see Sharon Mayer Libera, 'Ezra Pound's Paradise: A Study of Neoplatonism in the *Cantos*' (Diss., Harvard, 1972); Angela Elliott, 'Light as Image in Ezra Pound's *Cantos*', (Diss., Drew, 1978).

the Platonist F.H. Bradley, author of *Appearance and Reality* (1893). Persuaded by Ezra Pound to settle in England in 1914, by 1927 he had become a British subject and joined the Anglican church. With *Four Quartets* (1936–43) T.S. Eliot succeeded in transmuting his experience of Christian faith into a religious poem for a sceptical age. Dame Helen Gardner recognised that this work ponders, through Julian of Norwich, the Platonic question of the Good in relation to the prevalence of sin in the world.[17] The poem turns on the eternal moment of human moral choice, and the ultimate triumph of love and beauty.

While Ezra Pound and T.S. Eliot enacted the hieratic function they ascribed to poets, the younger, English-born W.H. Auden (see Turner, pp. 319–29, below) shunned any suggestion of a priestly role. Even as he rejected Modernist and Romantic modes, however, he sustained a Neoplatonic idealism and an incantational lyric power. With T.S. Eliot's assistance in getting published, W.H. Auden proved highly successful with the public, not just in England but in America, where he became a citizen in 1946, at times living in Berlin and Austria. Congenially didactic, he delighted readers with his wit and moved them with his acute social consciousness, which was based on his cosmopolitan experience. W.H. Auden was not formidable. He did not present the authoritative pose or puritanical austerity that cloaked Ezra Pound or T.S. Eliot. With his realism, irony and urbanity, W.H. Auden was an intermediate presence between the Modernist and Postmodernist poets. Since the 1950s, the British poets Philip Larkin, Geoffrey Hill and Charles Tomlinson, and the Irish poet Seamus Heaney, have sought to avoid entirely the grandiosity associated with High Modernism, restricting themselves by uncompromising realism and severe introspection. Nevertheless, the moralist tradition intrinsic to their work engages ideals and themes that are related to Plato. W.H. Auden, contrastingly, involved Plato directly. By such preoccupations do our authors reveal that Platonism in the twentieth century continues to be a force in the English imagination – a steady current, transformative, interacting with the realities of historical change.

[17] *The Art of T. S. Eliot* (New York, 1950), pp. 167ff.

CHAPTER 25

Yeats and Platonism

Brian Arkins

While Yeats refuses to be categorised, it is clear that Platonism is the philosophical tradition with which he is most closely aligned;[1] as Robertson Davies has said, reviewing a book on Yeats and Jung, 'If we do not agree that Yeats and Jung are wholly Platonists, we must agree that they fit better into that honorable assembly than any other'.[2] For Platonism provided Yeats with three key doctrines in which he himself believed: a transcendent reality, the immortality of the soul, and reincarnation. And while Yeats is the sort of Platonist who strongly endorses the material world, his theism is simultaneously a means of countering reductive empiricism, of which he sees Locke as the archetypal exponent. So in his philosophical correspondence with T. Sturge Moore, Yeats asserts in May 1926 that, 'the three provincial centuries' of reductive, mechanical thought engineered by Locke and others have come to an end and that our task now is to 'deduce all from the premises known to Plato'.[3]

Yeats was attracted to Platonism from the beginning, for while still at school he 'stood with Plato and with Socrates'.[4] But Yeats came to Platonism, as it were, backwards, beginning with late-nineteenth-century versions, proceeding to the Cambridge Platonists (see Scott, pp. 139–50 above) about 1914, and reaching Plato and Plotinus, pure and unadulterated, only in the last two decades of his life, the 1920s and 30s. So in Yeats's early life Platonism presented itself to him

[1] For Platonism in Yeats see the seminal article by K. Raine, 'Yeats and Platonism', *Dublin Magazine*, 7 (1968), 38–63; F.A.C. Wilson, *W.B. Yeats and Tradition* (London, 1968); J. Olney, *The Rhizome and the Flower: The Perennial Philosophy – Yeats and Jung* (Berkeley, 1980); B. Arkins, *Builders of My Soul: Greek and Roman Themes in Yeats* (Gerrards Cross, 1990), 24–69.

[2] R. Davies, reviewing Olney, *Rhizome*, 'Jung, Yeats and the Inner Journey', *Queen's Quarterly*, 89 (1982), 476.

[3] *W.B. Yeats and T. Sturge Moore – Their Correspondence 1901–1937*, ed. U. Bridge (Westport, Con., 1978), pp. 92–3.

[4] W.B. Yeats, *Memoirs*, edited by D. Donoghue (London, 1972), p. 65.

through curious channels such as the theosophy of Madame Blavatsky, which was so thoroughly syncretistic that, by definition, it had to contain a good deal of popular Platonism, and the Order of the Golden Dawn, which can be viewed as an extremely late revival of Renaissance Platonism.

After Yeats completed the first version of *A Vision* in 1925, he began to read an elaborate list of books on philosophy, two of the central figures in which were Plato and Plotinus. So Yeats told Sturge Moore in a letter of March 1926: 'I read for months every day Plato and Plotinus',[5] and, in the introduction to the second version of *A Vision*, elaborated upon this in connection with his wife's reading in philosophy: 'I read all MacKenna's incomparable translation of Plotinus, some of it several times, and went from Plotinus to his predecessors and successors whether on her list or not. And for four years now I have read nothing else except now and then some story of theft and murder to clear my head at night'.[6] Clearly, Yeats had now reached back to the foundations of Platonism and the rich harvest from this can be found in the second 1937 version of *A Vision* and in the volumes of poetry from *The Tower* of 1928 onwards.

PLOTINUS

The central Platonic philosopher in Yeats is Plotinus.[7] For Yeats, Plotinus provided the sort of metaphysical exposition he longed for; as Kathleen Raine has written, 'Yeats came to Plotinus because in him more than in any other philosopher he discovered a cosmology, a metaphysics, consistent with the nature of man as he had come to understand it'.[8] Which is not surprising, given Yeats' beliefs that the confusion of modern philosophy derives from the fact that we have renounced 'the ancient hierarchy of beings from man up to One',[9] that there is 'Nothing in mind that has not come from sense except mind',[10] and that 'We, who are believers, cannot see reality anywhere but in the soul itself'.[11]

5 *Yeats and Sturge Moore*, p. 83. 6 *A Vision* (London, 1962), p. 20.

7 Three doctoral theses deal with Yeats and Plotinus: J.D. Easterly, 'Yeats, Plotinus, and Symbolic Perception' (Cambridge, 1972); M.R. Motes '"Plotinus for a Friend"; MacKenna's Translation of Plotinus and W.B. Yeats' "A Vision" and Later Poetry' (Miami, 1973); R.P. Ritvo, 'Plotinistic Elements in Yeats' Prose Works' (Fordham, 1973).

8 K. Raine, *Death-in-Life and Life-in-Death: 'Cuchulain Comforted' and 'News for the Delphic Oracle'* (Dublin, 1974), p. 20.

9 *The Letters of W.B. Yeats*, ed. A. Wade (London, 1954), p. 74.

10 W.B. Yeats, *Essays and Introductions* (London, 1961), pp. 414–15.

11 W.B. Yeats, *Explorations* (London, 1962), p. 170.

So in the 1937 version of *A Vision*, Yeats employs Plotinus' hierarchical system to enunciate his own metaphysical beliefs and applies his own special terminology to it. So in the metaphysical or Intelligible World, Plotinus' Hypostases are translated into Yeats' Principles as follows:[12] Plotinus' One becomes Yeats' Ultimate Reality, which is 'symbolised as the Sphere' (*A Vision*, p. 187), an image of perfection. His *nous* or Intelligence becomes, when considered as Being, Yeats' Celestial Body, and, when considered as Act, Yeats' Spirit; and his *psyche*, Soul or *anima mundi*, becomes Yeats's Passionate Body. Following Plotinus (*Enneads* v. 1.10), Yeats predicates Real Being – which he calls (after Stephen MacKenna) Authentic Existence – of Celestial body, Spirit, and Passionate body, which are his equivalents of the second and third hypostases, Intelligence and Soul. Real Being, like everything else, cannot be predicated of the first hypostasis. Yeats' fourth Principle Husk cannot be fully identified with Plotinus' hypostasis, but must represent the lower part of Soul which Plotinus calls *physis* or Nature and which operates as an immanent principle of life.

Yeats' view of Matter is also indebted to Plotinus. In a crucial letter of 27 May 1926, to Sturge Moore, Yeats emphatically rejects the mechanistic model of the world and endorses Plotinus' doctrine that matter is a non-entity, 'a phantom' (*Enneads* II. 5.5), that it possesses 'neither colour, scent, nor magnitude' and that it is 'indeterminate', requiring to be shaped by the power of Soul (*Enneads* II.4 3.6).[13] It is significant that Yeats concludes his attack on 'the three provincial centuries', which have succeeded to such a remarkable extent in persuading European man that Matter and the objects of sense-perception are alone real, by advising Sturge Moore to go to the Platonists for the opposite view, to Plato, Plotinus, and that modern Platonist, Alfred Whitehead: 'Read Whitehead, and from that go to Stephen MacKenna's *Plotinus* and to the *Timaeus*. What Whitehead calls 'the three provincial centuries' are over: Wisdom and poetry return'.[14] Mind, not Matter, rules the world.

THE PLATONIC WORLD-VIEW

Yeats' prose usually endorses the Platonic world-view as put forward by Plotinus and other Platonists; his poetry is much more ambivalent,

[12] R.P. Ritvo, 'A Vision B: the Plotinian Metaphysical Basis', *Review of English Studies*, 26 (1975), 38.
[13] *Yeats and Sturge Moore*, pp. 91–3. [14] *Ibid.*, p. 93.

accepting, rejecting, modifying, vacillating. We begin with acceptance. What lies behind the poem 'A Meditation in Time of War',[15] written just after the First World War broke out in 1914, is Plotinus' doctrine that at the pinnacle of the two-world system is the One, ultimate source of all Being. As Yeats sits in one of the desolate places conducive to mystical inspiration, for one moment, Blake's 'pulsation of the artery', he is granted the knowledge that the sole animating force in the *kosmos* is the One, that, in comparison, human beings lack soul or *anima* and so belong to a world of unreality, *phantasia*:

> For one throb of the artery,
> While on that old grey stone I sat,
> Under the old wind-broken tree,
> I knew that One is animate,
> Mankind inanimate fantasy.

It is, however, the poem 'Under Ben Bulben' (NCP, pp. 325–28), written towards the end of Yeats' life in 1938 and now the initial poem in the volume *Last Poems*, which encapsulates Yeats' Platonism. As Kathleen Raine has rightly said, it is 'his most Platonic of all poems'.[16] And this, I believe, affords us a proper entry to the poem Yeats entitled originally 'His Convictions', for, if read as Platonic, 'Under Ben Bulben' becomes much more satisfactory and its apparent rant, meaningful. The spiritual authority invoked in the first stanza is Platonic because early Christianity in Egypt was consciously Platonising; because Shelley, whose Witch of Atlas is referred to, was deeply inbued with Platonism; and because the spirits who ride on the mountain Ben Bulben and so mediate between heaven and earth are the *daimones* long known to the Platonic tradition, and especially to later Neoplatonists like Iamblichus and to the Cambridge Platonist, Henry More. To this authority is later added another Platonising Romantic, Blake, and Michelangelo, deeply influenced by the Florentine Platonists of the Renaissance.

In the remaining five sections of the poem Yeats gives us 'the gist of what they mean': reincarnation; constant strife in this material world; the necessity for artists in general and Irish artists in particular to mirror the beauty of the Intelligible world; and, in consequence of that, the triumphant acceptance of life and death by Yeats, the Platonist who has provided this world with so much beauty. In

[15] *Collected Poems of W.B. Yeats* (London, 1950) (hereafter CP), p. 214. *W.B Yeats, The Poems – A New Edition*, edited by R.J. Finneran (London, 1984) (hereafter NCP), p. 190.

[16] Raine, 'Yeats and Platonism', p. 44.

following the Platonic tradition, Irish poets must sing of the Marriage of Heaven and Earth as exemplified by holy monks who seek God in heaven and celebrate Him on earth, by peasants devoted both to the land and to the unwritten tradition of the spirit, by aristocrats who ride horses to the full, by men given to sex and drink. For what all these disparate groups have in common is a devotion to beauty, whether sacred or profane, and as they cultivate various forms of Eros in seeking that beauty, they, unlike 'the unremembering hearts and heads' of the modern world, preserve the Platonic memory or *anamnesis* of the Intelligible world. In keeping to these Platonic themes which were honoured in the past, Irish poets will ensure that they take their proper place in the great European tradition. And the Irish, freed from the ravages of British empiricism, will be, like the Greeks, 'indomitable'. So in the final analysis Yeats cannot accept the orthodox Christian view of the resurrection of the body and soul, and consequently rejects those eighteenth-century epitaphs that enjoin the traveller to stop and contemplate his mortality. Instead, Yeats opts for Platonic reincarnation, not of spirit only, not of body only, but of the two eternally intertwined: the process of life, death and rebirth winding continually and continuously on its journey. Thus, the human aristocratic horseman of section VI, who mirrors, of course, the divine *daimones*, must pass Yeats' tomb regardless, as he seeks forever the Beauty of the Intelligible world through Eros:

> Cast a cold eye
> On life, on death,
> Horseman, pass by!

PLATONISM MODIFIED

Yeats' Platonism is not always so clear-cut and can be severely modified. What often happens is that Yeats exploits the tensions within Platonism – how far does the material world resemble the Intelligible world, how far has it fallen from it? – to set up his own tensions, between body and soul, heaven and earth, either within a group of poems such as *Words for Music Perhaps* or within individual poems such as 'The Tower'. In thus exploring Platonic dualism, Yeats is conducting a debate about what in an early essay he calls 'the only controversy in which it is greatly worth taking sides, and . . . the only controversy which may never be decided'.[17]

[17] Yeats, *Essays and Introductions*, p. 152.

The most famous example of Yeats' vacillation about and rejection of Platonism comes in the great poem 'The Tower', written in 1925. Now sixty and raging against old age, Yeats considers how to cope. In Section I, one apparent possibility is to devote himself to the study of Plato and Plotinus, conceived of as hostile to the imagination of the Romantic poet because they are constructors of abstract systems. But in Section III, Yeats decides to opt instead for the imagination and the concrete, and so asserts in his swan-song:

I mock Plotinus' thought
And cry in Plato's teeth
(ll. 146–7)

What Yeats is attacking, with Plato and Plotinus as scapegoats, is a view of the Intelligible world that ascribes to it an extreme transcendence, totally and utterly independent of this irredeemable, material world. From one point of view this is, of course, a strand of thought in Platonism, but it can be considerably modified, depending on *how much emphasis* is put on the doctrine that this world derives from the Intelligible world. The nuances here are delicate, as indicated by Yeats himself in his well-known note to this poem, written three years later and quoting Plotinus, *Enneads* V.1.2, to show that the philosopher does in fact endorse created matter (CP, p. 533/NCP, p. 596): 'When I wrote the lines about Plato and Plotinus I forgot that it is something in our own eyes that makes us see them as all transcendence'.

A less acute form of this tension is found in another great poem from *The Tower*, 'Among School Children' (CP, pp. 242–5/NCP, pp. 215–17). Written a year later than 'The Tower' in 1926, 'Among School Children' continues the theme of old age, but now moves on to dwell on the fact that great philosophers also grow old and become – like Yeats – scarecrows: 'Old clothes upon old sticks to scare a bird'. And yet these men have constructed marvellous systems which remain indispensable to the human condition. The result is that although Platonism (together with other systems) is expounded, only to be denigrated, in stanza VI, it is also utilised in various ways in stanzas II, V and VII.[18]

The nature of Platonic dualism of the world of Forms and the world of Becoming is brilliantly summed up in the first two lines of stanza VI:

Plato thought nature but a spume that plays
Upon a ghostly paradigm of things
(ll. 31–2)

[18] Compare Olney, *Rhizome*, p. 285.

The kosmos is only a model or copy of what is real, 'things' that exist in the Intelligible World, and consequently has only an attenuated form of existence like a ghost, while the material world of everyday sense-perception, 'nature', is even more attenuated, merely an adjunct to the kosmos as foam is to the sea. The official doctrine of stanza VI is that Plato – together with Aristotle and Pythagoras – are to be dismissed as scarecrows. But both previously and subsequently in the poem Platonic doctrine is invoked. To begin with, in stanza II Yeats wants to indicate the unity that at times existed between himself and Maud Gonne, conceived of as Leda's daughter, Helen of Troy. To do so he uses not only the Platonic symbol of the sphere, but also – in explicitly naming Plato – adapts Aristophanes' fable in *Symposium* 189e–190c for his own purposes. Whereas in Plato each human being was originally a rounded whole and Zeus then cut them in half like eggs which are cut with a hair, Yeats puts across his idea of lovers' unity by adding the vivid, concrete detail of 'the yolk and white of the one shell'. This neatly encapsulates the view in Plato that 'love is simply the name for the desire and pursuit of the whole' (*Symposium* 192e) and gains added force from the fact that Helen/Maud Gonne herself came out of an egg.

In stanza V, Yeats again manipulates Platonic material – here Porphyry's *On the Cave of the Nymphs*, ll. 16–17, a Neoplatonic exegesis of *Odyssey* XIII – to deal with the painful nature of human life. For the new born baby boy must leave behind pre-natal bliss and what betrays him into this is sexual intercourse, in particular semen, termed 'honey of generation' because intercourse is sweet and honey 'indicative of the pleasure which draws souls downwards into generation'. If the baby possesses *anamnesis* (recollection) of his previous state, he will object strenuously to being born, but if he does not, he will acquiesce – and it is in the assertion that 'the drug' or 'honey of generation' causes such acquiescence that Yeats deviates from Porphyry, as he himself admitted:

> I have taken the 'honey of generation' from Porphyry's essay 'On the Cave of the Nymphs', but find no warrant in Porphyry for considering it the 'drug' that destroys the 'recollection' of pre-natal freedom. He blamed a cup of oblivion given in the zodiacal sign of Cancer. (CP, p. 535/NCP, p. 597)

These two examples show Yeats using Platonic doctrine as a frame of reference in a rather cavalier way. But the Platonism of stanza VII is both clear-cut and orthodox: the 'Presences' worshipped by lovers, nuns and mothers are clearly akin to Platonic Forms, Forms that, unlike human beings, are self-begotten, that symbolise the Form of the Good in the transcendent world, and that consequently deride the entire human enterprise. Plato may grow old, but Platonism remains immutable.

Platonism is a dynamic force in the twenty-five poems that constitute the sequence *Words for Music Perhaps*, written between 1929 and 1932, and described by Yeats as sometimes coming 'out of the greatest mental excitement I am capable of'.[19] The opening of the sequence is dominated by the marvellous, extravagant figure of Crazy Jane, who features in the first seven poems, and who is of course not 'crazy' at all. Her vision of life is complex, granting a place to soul and God, and so avoiding a reductive materialism, but it is fair to say that Crazy Jane is essentially a champion of the self or body, especially as exemplified in sexuality and completely opposed to 'that sweet extremity of pride / That's called platonic love' (CP, p. 277/NCP, p. 228). At the end of the sequence we have the counter-figure of Old Tom who features directly in poems XXII–XXIV, these being bracketed by two other poems with a similar vision, XXI called 'The Dancer at Cruachan and Cro-Patrick' and XXV called 'The Delphic Oracle Upon Plotinus'. Though called a lunatic, Old Tom is no more a 'lunatic' than Crazy Jane is 'crazy'. He is equally extravagant, and his vision of life is also complex and not reductive. But whereas Crazy Jane stresses the body, Old Tom stresses the soul (CP, pp. 304–07/NCP, pp. 268–70).

Nevertheless, Old Tom is the sort of Platonist who has no problem in endorsing this created world and in the poem 'Tom the Lunatic' is clearly well versed in the passages of Plotinus that do the same, like *Enneads* V. 1.2, for in the face of apparent change and death he splendidly affirms the permanence both of God and his creation. Old Tom's relationship to the Moon of mutability is therfore complex. Labelled a lunatic (from Latin *luna*), in his last line he echoes Villon and so becomes one of the select band like Villon and Verlaine who, Yeats tells us, 'with impediments plain to all . . . sings of life with the ancient simplicity'. And he does so by reconciling the central paradox of Platonism which can be, as here, turned into its central glory. The material world, what Yeats calls 'the circle of the moon / That pitches common things about' (CP, p. 233/NCP, p. 207) is sanctified

[19] *Letters*, p. 814.

precisely because it 'Stands in God's unchanging eye'. Old Tom yields to no one in his ability to save the phenomena.

In the poem 'Old Tom Again' Tom looks at things from the other angle, that of the Intelligible World:

> Things out of perfection sail,
> And all their swelling canvas wear,
> Nor shall the self-begotten fail
> Though fantastic men suppose
> Building-yard and stormy shore,
> Winding-sheet and swaddling-clothes.
> (ll. 1–6)

From the world of Platonic Forms and Plotinian hypostases which constitute perfection, created, material things sail down along the sea of generation in the full glory that naturally belongs to their exalted origin. But that Intelligible World is not itself created and is therefore something absolutely permanent and unchanging. As in a sense human beings must be, because they possess immortal souls which derive from the third hypostasis, Soul, and will return to it. Since that is so, human birth and death have no real existence. The deluded empiricists who think they do have real existence enjoy, in Plato's terms (*Sophist* 263d), neither knowledge (Greek *dianoia*) nor even opinion (Greek *doxa*), but are reduced to what is only the purest illusion (Greek *phantasia*) and can therefore be properly called 'fantastic'.

The poem 'The Delphic Oracle Upon Plotinus', which ends the series, brilliantly encapsulates the body/soul tension exemplified by Crazy Jane and Old Tom. This is a paraphrase of the verse oracle given to Plotinus' disciple Amelius who consulted Delphi to find out where Plotinus' soul had gone after his death; preserved in Porphyry's *Life of Plotinus* 22, it is described by Yeats as 'the last great oracle at Delphi commemorating the dead Plotinus' and as one of his 'favourite quotations'.[20] In the first stanza of Yeats' poem Plotinus is clearly on the way across the sea of generation to the Intelligible World, but his journey is very difficult as he struggles with the waves that symbolise the flux and conflicts of life.[21] He is summoned to Heaven by the judge of the dead, Rhadamanthus – described as 'bland', which seems to hover between meaning 'coaxing' (cf. Latin

[20] *Essays and Introductions*, pp. 278 and 409.

[21] This stress may derive from Henry More's poem about the oracle on Plotinus, 'The Oracle' in *Philosophical Poems of Henry More*, edited by G. Bullough (Manchester, 1931), 159–62.

blandus) and 'unsullied'.[22] But Plotinus is able to perceive the inhabitants there, 'the Golden Race', only in a very imperfect way, since his eyes are blocked by the salt water of the sea, termed 'blood' to indicate that it functions as a symbol of human life. Furthermore and crucially, the poem fails to establish that Plotinus actually reached heaven and is thus far from Porphyry's assertion that 'you enter at once the heavenly consort'. So the stress is almost entirely on Plotinus' struggle with 'the bitter waves of this blood-drenched life' (*Life of Plotinus*, 22).

In the second stanza, on the other hand, the entire stress is on the idyllic, pastoral landscape of the Intelligible World. This is peopled by the three categories of men Plotinus tells us (*Enneads* I.3. 1–3) are most capable of cultivating the Intellectual Life and arriving at visionary experience: the metaphysician 'takes to the path by instinct' and is represented here by Plato. The musician and lover 'need guidance' and are represented here by Pythagoras and 'the Choir of Love' respectively. They are joined in Heaven by the judges of the dead, Rhadamanthus and Minos, described by the oracle as 'great brethren of the golden race of mighty Zeus'. They were, in fact, the sons of Zeus and the mortal woman Europe, and their exalted role here contrasts with the scorn poured on Europa by Crazy Jane in Poem II of the sequence. For the wheel has come full circle and we end with Love that does, precisely, 'take the whole/Body and Soul', when Time is gone.

But we will not leave Yeats' Platonism there. A final, crucial poem remains, 'What Then?' (CP, pp. 347–8/NCP, p. 302), written towards the end of his life in 1936 and now part of the *New Poems* (1938). Here Yeats recounts in simple language the achievements of his life and work: his unceasing efforts for the Irish Literary Renaissance and the Abbey Theatre, his happy marriage, his unequalled collection of friends – 'my glory was I had such friends' (CP, p. 370/NCP, p. 321) – his paradigmatic plays, his brilliantly eloquent prose, and, above all, the greatest body of poetry written in English in this century. Truly, he had, as much as any man, 'something to perfection brought'. And yet, as he lists these achievements, Yeats is confronted, inevitably, with the spirit of Plato: an exemplar of unrelenting devotion to his work, the man who has done so much to inspire, in various guises, subsequent European philosophy and art, the man who, as we have seen, lies

[22] For the meaning of 'bland' see W.C. Barnwell, 'The Blandness of Yeats's Rhadamanthus', *English Language Notes*, 14 (1977), 206–10.

behind Yeats' lifelong attachment to Platonism. It is essential to the human condition that there is always something more to strive for, and so Yeats is haunted by the refrain which concludes the first three stanzas of the poem: '*What Then?' Sang Plato's Ghost. 'What Then?*'. And this even more, when perfection is obtained in old age:

> 'The work is done', grown old he thought,
> 'According to my boyish plan'
> Let the fools rage, I swerved in naught,
> Something to perfection brought';
> *But louder sang that ghost, 'What then?'*
> (ll. 16–20)

It is, then, the spirit, the *daimon* of Plato that presides over the eternal hankering for more, because Yeats, in the final analysis, does choose Plato for a friend and so endorses the sentiments of his fellow Celt Edwin Muir in the poem 'I have been taught', the last of his *Collected Poems* and one of the last poems he wrote towards the end of his life in 1959:

> And now that time grows shorter, I perceive
> That Plato's is the truest poetry,
> And that these shadows
> Are cast by the true.[23]

[23] Edwin Muir, *Collected Poems* (London, 1963), p. 302.

CHAPTER 26

Virginia Woolf and Plato: The Platonic background of Jacob's Room

Brenda Lyons

Virginia Woolf was a serious Platonic scholar and her writings allude to Plato and the dialogues, but to call her a Platonist would be a mistake. Woolf's work does not conform to any '-ism', and Platonism is no exception; her philosophy is of the 'rag-bag' sort, not adopting or promoting any system, but transferring philosophical metaphors and ideas into the contexts of real and fictive experiences.[1] Her writings do not engage with Platonic arguments, but rather draw from the dialogues to inspire, complicate, and support her own aesthetic ends. Woolf's poetic expresses a neoclassical delight in formal unities of design, rhythm, and imaginative human purpose, alluding parodically to Plato and subsequent academic pursuits of philosophy, while metaphors of the cave, darkness/illumination, and mimesis, for example, reimagine Platonic motifs in twentieth-century contexts. She was aware of the complex religious traditions suggested by these allusions, but her own anti-religious sentiment was closer to the Heretic Society than to doctrinal, especially Christian, Platonism. This essay will explore what exactly Plato meant to Woolf and how her Platonic allusions operate, particularly in the context of non-realistic parodic fiction.

It is clear that Woolf felt the importance of Plato very strongly. In the essay 'Is This Poetry?' she declared that the works of Hogarth Press were 'addressed to no public save that which has in it the ghosts of Plato.'[2] Seven of her nine novels, along with short stories and two volumes of essays, were included in the more than 400 titles Hogarth

[1] T.S. Eliot, 'Introduction', G. Wilson Knight, *The Wheel of Fire: Interpretations of Shakespearian Tragedy* (London, 1956), p. xiii.

[2] Virginia Woolf, *The Essays of Virginia Woolf*, ed. Andrew McNeillie, 3 vols. (London, 1986–8), III, *1919–24* p. 54.

published during her lifetime,[3] and her haunting remark invites readers to ponder what she really meant. For Woolf, the dialogues inspire a love of knowledge; on the construction of Plato's arguments, she wrote, it is 'not so much the end we reach as our manner of reaching it. That all can feel – the indomitable honesty, the courage, the love of truth which draw Socrates and us in his wake to the summit where, if we too may stand for a moment, it is to enjoy the greatest felicity of which we are capable.'[4]

But truth, she argued in *A Room of One's Own*, was a male domain until the birth of fiction. Her imaginative projection of a feminine aesthetic was expressed in Platonic tropes: 'For if Chloe likes Olivia and Mary Carmichael knows how to express it she will light a torch in that vast chamber where nobody has yet been. It is all half lights and profound shadows like those serpentine caves where one goes with a candle peering up and down, not knowing where one is stepping.'[5] From her borderline position as an upper-middle-class Victorian woman ideologically within and outside the Oxbridge and Apostolic 'intellectual aristocracy',[6] Woolf sought to inspire and empower women, and she employed Platonic allusion as a supportive resource. She credited Plato's high regard for Sappho as evidence of women's superiority in 'The Intellectual Status of Women', an argument deliberately countering Arnold Bennett's denigrating attack on female intellectual capacity in the *New Statesman*.[7]

In Woolf's day Plato was the paragon of elevated heights, marking a divisive boundary of lower and upper intellectual spheres. Her late work continued to accord him this status, used to feminist purposes. The imaginary speech by Nicholas in her novel *The Years* and its precursive speech to the London National Society for Women's Service (21 January 1931) implicitly call for a humanist utopia reminiscent of Plato's *Republic*.[8] She is, however, under no illusion about the impracticality of egalitarianism in her day, and imagines the master's horrified reaction to finding his kitchen maid in the library reading Plato.[9] Woolf's argument links patriarchal essentialism,

[3] J. Howard Woolmer, *A Checklist of the Hogarth Press* (London, 1976).
[4] Virginia Woolf, 'On Not Knowing Greek', *The Common Reader* (1925; London, 1933), p. 51.
[5] Virginia Woolf, *A Room of One's Own* (1929; New York, 1957), p. 88.
[6] Jane Marcus, 'Liberty, Sorority, Misogyny', *Virginia Woolf and the Languages of Patriarchy* (Bloomington, Indiana, 1987), p. 92.
[7] Virginia Woolf, 'The Intellectual Status of Women', *The Diary of Virginia Woolf*, ed. Anne Olivier Bell (London, 1988), II, *1920–24*, pp. 339–42.
[8] John Batchelor, *Virginia Woolf: The Major Novels* (Cambridge, 1991), p. 144.
[9] Virginia Woolf, *The Pargiters: The Novel-Essay Portion of The Years* (London, 1978), p. xlii.

or the argument that man is naturally superior to woman, to the modern problems of economics and education. She counsels that although this particular man considers the education of servants and women worse than unnatural – indeed sinful – generous and humane men exist with whom women can live in 'perfect freedom'; her concluding advice for a just and good society is that patience and humour over anger are preferred strategies in the campaign to liberate women through education and economic accomplishment. Woolf proffered the notion that a room where Plato could be freely read had been paid for; the door was open to a future of exciting dialogues.[10] Her concerns are aligned with Socratic goals for an ideal state, but her plan emphasizes the educational and economic success of women, ignoring such contradictions as that between sexual equality and political/philosophical hegemony in the *Republic*.

The knowledge of Greek that her classicist cousin J.K. Stephen had identified as a key to fraternal power was denied to most women,[11] so choosing Plato signaled the acquisition of cultural power, an act replete with associated biological, economic and pedagogical controversies. Virginia Woolf herself was familiar with most of the dialogues and her study notes on the *Euthyphro*, *Phaedrus*, *Symposium*, and *Republic*,[12]though cursory outlines, indicate special attention to questions of creativity, love, and truth. She prefaced her summary of *Symposium* with a list of various Greek terms for loving: 'εραστος = beloved. εραστης = a lover. εραω = to love. ἡ ερωμενη = the beloved woman. εpατος = beloved.'[13] However, whereas Socrates was always searching for truth in discourse, and Plato wrote myths which postulate its real existence, to Woolf truth was always subjective. This belief invades the very structure of her work, partly explicated in the argument of *A Room of One's Own*, which states the controversial, impossible purpose of a lecture as the contribution of an eternal 'nugget of pure truth', in this case on the 'true nature of woman . . . and fiction.' The slippery problem of truth is parodically extended as the subjective object of her discourse; she recounts the disappearance of assumptions founded on lost knowledge and failed attempts to find authentic facts about women in history, concluding that 'a spot the

[10] Woolf, *The Pargiters*, p. xliv.

[11] Jane Marcus, 'Liberty, Sorority, Misogyny', *Virginia Woolf and the Languages of Patriarchy* (Bloomington, Indiana, 1987), p. 92.

[12] Brenda R. Silver, *Virginia Woolf's Reading Notebooks* (Princeton, 1983).

[13] Virginia Woolf, 'Plato. Symposium!', Monks House Papers (Oxford, Bodleian Library Films 1425, reel 1, A21, p. 53). Quoted by kind permission of the Bodleian Library.

size of a shilling at the back of the head' must be described by a woman before a 'true picture of man as a whole can 'ever' be painted.'[14] Relations of truth to forms of loving are central, interrelated problems explored in most of Woolf's fiction through the imaginary experiences of characters. An early journal entry, which states her belief in an integrated universal unconscious, that is, 'how any live mind today is .. of the very same stuff as Plato's',[15] is metaphorically repeated in the fiction, serving to construct a global, eternal ideal 'mind' that links antiquity to modernity. The potential of recollection exists, then, in an intimated, immortal unconsciousness, but historical amnesia inhibits truth, equality, and human development.

Nowhere is Woolf's longing for, yet mistrust of, the Platonic verities more visible than in the third novel, *Jacob's Room*, whose structure questions traditional, formal assumptions. Here Woolf aims for the first time to present 'character without realism',[16] recognised by most critics as an important moment in feminist/modernist *avant-garde* fiction; it should also be seen, however, as a watershed in Woolf's attitude to the Platonic past. Written between April, 1920, and November, 1921,[17] its shadow texts are *Phaedrus* and, indirectly, other dialogues that address problems of love, idealism, body/spirit duality, and the soul. Jacob's ghostly presence was partly a reincarnation of Thoby Stephen, her brother and first classics mentor who died unexpectedly early from typhoid fever contracted in Greece. *Jacob's Room* is a radical departure in form and content from her first two novels, *The Voyage Out* (1915) and *Night and Day* (1919), which treat philosophical inquiries in general and Platonic subjects in particular with a much simpler ridicule, for example, to express disenchantment with G.E. Moore's quasi-Platonic philosophy. The quests for truth, goodness, beauty, and friendship that characters figuratively undertake in these early novels indicate their differing positions on the ladder of Platonic scholarship, a male domain to which women aspire. In *The Voyage Out*, an emotive, Mrs. Clarissa Dalloway debuts as a figure desiring 'Plato', dreaming of an anthropomorphic androgynous alphabet whose Greek letters stalk about and pass 'from one brain to

[14] Virginia Woolf, *A Room of One's Own* (1929; New York, 1957), p. 94.

[15] Virginia Woolf, 'The Country in London', Brenda R. Silver, *Virginia Woolf's Reading Notebooks* (Princeton, 1983), p. 5.

[16] Virginia Woolf to David Garnett, 20 October 1922, *The Question of Things Happening: The Letters of Virginia Woolf*, eds. Nigel Nicolson and Joanne Trautmann, 6 vols. (London, 1975–82), vol. 2, *1912–22* (1976), p. 571.

[17] Virginia Woolf, *Diary*, II, *1920–24*, 30, 141.

another'. Here, as in *Jacob's Room*, the use of Plato through direct and indirect allusion does not produce a Platonic scheme; the references are, rather, a way of complicating the fictive texture to question contemporary issues at a time when, on the one hand, classical and philosophical studies were still denied to most women and, on the other hand, Plato was a sign of ultimate intellectual achievement, while classical studies were under fire as representing an elite and socially irrelevant pedagogical discipline.

Jacob's Room is a deeper, poetical exploration of Platonic fissures; into the gaps within language, nation, and cultural politics Woolf inserts the *Phaedrus* as a metaphorical touchstone by which to measure twentieth-century definitions of love, the soul, knowledge, identity, and idealism. In *Jacob's Room* the parody is not operating simply in the sense of ridicule, but rather that of intimate relations, or what Linda Hutcheon has called 'a bitextual synthesis', 'a formal or structural relation between two texts' applicable to any codified discourse.[18] As with irony, Hutcheon explains, parody operates on at least two levels, the primary surface, or foreground, and the secondary, implied background. The parodic edges of Platonic experience in *Jacob's Room* reside ambiguously in a spacial distance between Plato's Greece and the lights of London and Cambridge, which Woolf referred to as a cave when she was writing *Jacob's Room*: 'I lay in the shallow light, which should be written dark . . . Perhaps Cambridge is too much of a cave.'[19]

Her commemoration of Thoby is neither autobiographically realistic nor eulogising; and Plato is no more sanctified than Jacob portrayed as a scholar. Initially, Jacob rejects 'cloisters and classics', frustrated by the trap of a body harnessed to a brain, a contemporary restatement of the ancient Platonic dualism between body and mind. Since Jacob himself, for all his mistrust of ideas, is dead, a knowledge of what his existence means is ironically only possible through ideas – in the memories of others. In fact, there is a kind of parody of the Platonic ascent from body to mind, as Jacob is transformed during the course of the novel from experience to idea. A shallow bed of knowledge, Greek or Platonic, was the unlikely ground preceding his pilgrimage to the Acropolis; at its peak he embraced a solitary

[18] Linda Hutcheon, *A Theory of Parody: The Teachings of Twentieth-Century Art Forms* (New York, 1985), pp. 22–33.

[19] Virginia Woolf, *Diary*, II, 49. Virginia Woolf, *Jacob's Room* (1922; London, 1991), p. 93.

moment of great happiness, an emotional and spiritual breakthrough associated with the ability to experience mortal love.

The transition in Jacob's consciousness occurs after a day at the British Museum, where Plato, readers are informed, has been preserved as part of the 'enormous mind . . . hoarded beyond the power of any single mind to possess it.'[20] That night he read Plato, who continued 'imperturbably'; the Platonic dialogue is foregrounded as an undisturbed force against which more transient realities of rain, cab whistles, and the cries of a drunken woman locked out of her house fade into the background. Meanwhile, Jacob contemplates:

> The *Phaedrus* is very difficult. And so, when at length one reads straight ahead, falling into step, marching on, becoming (so it seems) momentarily part of this rolling, imperturbable energy, which has driven darkness before it since Plato walked the Acropolis, it is impossible to see the fire.
>
> The dialogue draws to its close. Plato's argument is done. Plato's argument is stowed away in Jacob's mind, and for five minutes Jacob's mind continues alone, onwards, into the darkness. Then, getting up, he parted the curtains, and saw, with astonishing clearness.[21]

Woolf's irony derives partly from the knowledge that Jacob's new, extraordinary vision of ordinary reality is produced from conditions of exile and solitude. His 'presence' is that of a ghostly protagonist in an elegiac anti-war novel, realised only through a multivocal weave of memories in which existence as incorporeal reality merges with the vestigial Platonic subject he becomes in fantasy, intimating complex questions about the nature of the human and divine soul. In the *Phaedrus* the explication of immortal soul as ever-changing form is part of the Socratic defence of passion as love's blessed madness, divinely inspired creativity, and the power of healing (244a–246d). Jacob enacts in fiction the problem of (non)existence as a Platonic trope, that is, his identification with Plato alludes to an internalized Socratic unconscious, implying the interrogation of 'immortality' as fancy. Thus engendered as a Socratic/Platonic subject, Jacob/Thoby also enacts the fourth and best form of divine possession, the madness of a lover of worldly beauty, recalling what Socrates described as the 'blessed vision' of wholeness and pure light, 'without taint of that prison house which now we are encompassed with, and call a body' (*Phaedrus* 250c).

All that remains of the body are memories recollected in 'Jacob's

[20] Woolf, *Jacob's Room*, p. 93. [21] Woolf, *Jacob's Room*, p. 95.

room', a neoclassical chamber that serves as an allusive double for the cave, containing in its darkness questions of mortality and immortality. There the source of true light, albeit ironised, comes from the Greek, science, and philosophy, where 'the lamp of learning' is 'not simple, or pure, or wholly splendid'.[22]

Woolf's references to Plato in *Jacob's Room* foreground a central 'character' as the ghost of an average Oxbridge classics student; the episodic movements of Jacob's transformation include an implied range of contemporary controversies, the status of classical studies and women's intellect as well as more complex aesthetical and ethical questions in the texture of Western philosophical/literary history. 'Jacob' expresses an accord with Clive Bell's hypothesis of 'significant form', which S.P. Rosenbaum has explicated as a synthesis of Moore's idealism and Platonic love.[23] Bell asserts an aesthetic essence, a common qualifier in the visual arts, or significant form, which means an emotive combination of lines and colours that are apprehended through a mystical, spiritual, or religious experience.[24] The solution to the dilemma that Woolf considered in literary critical terms to be one of conveying 'character without realism' was effected as an allusive Platonic riddle of ideality and love. *Jacob's Room* sketches ideality as an (in)(di)visible spirit/body, filled with problems of *a priori* knowledge versus definitions of love and truth.

But *Jacob's Room* also undercuts the Platonic certainties by its very structure, its destruction of the familiar notions of character (soul) and realism. Woolf's fictive representation of 'Jacob' as relations between temporality and non-identity are in line with Price's definition of the Platonic 'mind' as 'a bundle of episodes and dispositions', episodes being synonymous with 'mental stages'.[25] While Woolf's fiction does not engage with argument, it sets a philosophical stage resonant with Platonic texts as its parodic unconscious. The ghost of Jacob Flanders as a Platonic scholar is deeply ironic: he is real and not real; he is not really a scholar; he is and is not Plato. Jacob's egotistical claims to knowledge of the Greeks countered Woolf's own that:

[22] Virginia Woolf, *Jacob's Room* (London, 1991), p. 31.

[23] S.P. Rosenbaum, *Victorian Bloomsbury. The Early Literary History of the Bloomsbury Group* (London, 1987), I, 235.

[24] Clive Bell, *Art*, ed. J.B. Bullen (Oxford, 1987), pp. 3–37.

[25] A.W. Price, *Love and Friendship in Plato and Aristotle* (Oxford, 1990), pp. 21–3.

it is vain and foolish to talk of knowing Greek . . . since we do not know how the words sounded, or where precisely we ought to laugh . . . and between this foreign people and ourselves there is not only difference of race and tongue but a tremendous breach of tradition.[26]

His rudimentary ability to read Greek would have sufficed only to 'stumble' through the *Phaedrus* and he blamed governesses for starting 'the Greek myth', considering the elevation of 'Greek this, that, and the other' over Shakespeare an illusion. The end of the novel is its beginning, however: a dramatic empty finale, which has occasioned the critical pursuit of an answer to the incorporeal riddle of a 'character without realism', leaves readers with the memory of Jacob, perceived through the author's and readers' creative vision. Only the Room remains, Jacob himself disappears, leaving only a Form, recalling Plato in the *Phaedrus*,

There let it rest then, our tribute to a memory that has stirred us to linger awhile on those former joys for which we yearn. Now beauty, as we said, shone bright amidst these visions, and in this world below we apprehend it through the clearest of our senses, clear and resplendent. (*Phaedrus* 250d)

[26] Virginia Woolf, 'On Not Knowing Greek', *The Common Reader* (London, 1933), p. 39.

CHAPTER 27

Plato and Eliot's earlier verse

Dennis Brown

Critics of T.S. Eliot's poetry have frequently cited a Platonic influence.[1] This is scarcely surprising since Eliot not only studied Plato, in the Greek, at Harvard, but also wrote essays on Platonic thought while commencing his doctoral work on F.H. Bradley at Oxford.[2] Overall, Eliot's poetic career strangely replicates Plato's own progression from dramatised dialogue to a more monological commitment to the Real: the earlier verse is dialogical and sceptical; *Four Quartets* is affirmatory and declarative.[3] In effect, the earlier verse of Eliot, which will be the main focus here, calls into question the nature of Platonism itself. It queries whether Plato's own philosophical contribution should be regarded as an elaboration of ideal truths (as Neoplatonism often represents it) or as a quasi-sceptical[4] journey into ultimate mystery. Eliot's earlier poetry suggests the

[1] See, for instance, Kristian Smidt, *Poetry and Belief in the Work of T.S. Eliot* (London, 1967, p. 158: Eric Thompson, *T.S. Eliot: The Man and his Works* (Toronto, 1969), p. 81; A.D. Moody, *Thomas Stearns Eliot: Poet* (Cambridge, 1979), p. 131.

[2] Eliot to J.H. Woods, 28 January 1915; Eliot to Professor L.B. R. Briggs, 28 January 1915; Eliot to Professor L.B.R. Briggs, 10 July 1915; Eliot to J.H. Woods, 28 December 1915, in *The Letters of T.S. Eliot*, ed. Valerie Eliot, vol. 1–, continuing (London, 1988), I, *1898–1922*, pp. 84, 85, 109, 124.

[3] I am drawing partly on distinctions between monology and dialogy elaborated by Mikhail Bakhtin in *Problems of Dostoevsky's Poetics*, ed. and trans. Caryl Emerson (Manchester, 1984) and *The Dialogic Imagination*, ed. Michael Holquist and trans. Caryl Emerson and Michael Holquist (Austin, Texas, 1981). For Platonic influence in *Four Quartets*, see Maud Ellman, *The Poetics of Impersonality: T.S. Eliot and Ezra Pound* (Brighton, 1987), pp. 119–20.

[4] 'If Platonism from age to age has meant, for some, a doctrine of "being", or the nearest attainable approach to or substitution for that: for others, Platonism has been in fact only another name for scepticism, in a recognisable philosophical tradition': Walter Pater, *Plato and Platonism* (New York, 1969), p. 194. On Pater and Plato, see Anne Varty, pp. 257–67, above. In his essay of 1930, 'Arnold and Pater', Eliot shows himself familiar with Pater's text – see T.S. Eliot, *Selected Essays* (London, 1958), p. 440. I am grateful to my colleague Beverley Southgate, for information that both Montaigne and Hegel entertained the notion of Plato's possible scepticism.

latter. The exercise of questioning will be a strong theme in this essay: Socrates, Plato and Eliot are alike in deeming the 'unexamined life' not worth living. And while, this end of twentieth-century cultural history, Eliot's career can easily be construed as an end-directed pilgrimage towards Christian faith (where both Plato and Aristotle make a contribution), his inquiry was always rooted in Socratic humility ('"I can connect / Nothing with nothing"')[5] and Socrates' unceasing interrogation of any asserted knowledge: 'Are these ideas right or wrong?'[6]

It is well known that the foundation of Eliot's poetic style was formed through an absorption in the verse of Jules Laforgue between the years 1908 and 1912. Eliot would later discuss Laforgue (along with Tristan Corbière) as a 'metaphysical' poet, because his verse 'acquires emotional colouring by entertaining metaphysical beliefs'.[7] Stylistically, however, it is the ironic treatment of intellectual abstractions rather than any entertainment of belief which Eliot appropriated from the French symbolist. By adapting the mock-sceptical stance and liltingly ironic tone, Eliot was able to transfer Laforgue's suburban cabaret (with its Pierrots and Shakespearian *poseurs*) into an urban, interiorised symposium where what is at issue, finally, is always a quasi-Socratic interrogation of reality. In 'Poems Written in Early Youth' a Socratic self-consciousness emerges abruptly from the Laforguean pastiche – 'Logic a marionette's all wrong / Of premises' ('Humouresque'); 'Your shadow leaping behind the fire against the red rock' ('The Death of Saint Narcissus'); 'On the doorstep of the Absolute' ('Spleen').[8]

In the earliest-written of the poems published in *Prufrock and Other Observations* (1917) the image-realm of urban alienation is subjected to thorough-going metaphysical questioning. 'Preludes'[9] is initially constructed out of a plethora of metonymic urban details characterised as 'masquerades'. Eliot's questioning concerns what the day's 'consciousness' consists in, whether the 'soul' here is anything more than 'sordid images' and what the 'notion' of infinite gentleness and suffering might mean. The poem ends with a dismissive laugh and an

5 *The Waste Land*, ll. 301–2, *The Complete Poems and Plays of T.S. Eliot* (London, 1969), p. 70. All reference will be to this volume. 6 'Portrait of a Lady', *ibid.*, p. 20.

7 Quoted from Eliot's eighth Clark Lecture in Ronald Bush, *T.S. Eliot: A Study in Character and Style* (Oxford, 1985), pp. 173–4. 8 *Complete Poems and Plays*, pp. 587–606.

9 *Ibid.*, pp. 22–3.

evocation of endless cosmic flux: yet already here the method of Plato – as the search for higher meaning in a realm of insubstantial phenomena – is given haunting realisation as an initiation into poetic quest. Laforguean irony has enabled Eliot to establish a self-questioning philosophical verse akin to Platonic dialogue. As R. Peacock has suggested: '[Eliot's] theory of voices could also be said to be influenced by Plato's basic poetic forms. Plato distinguished forms according to the 'direct' or 'indirect' address of the poet . . . Eliot's address is to himself, neither direct nor indirect but neutral.'[10] And, just as importantly, Plato's writings provided a negative vision of the demotic, sensual world and a key privileging of the 'shaft' of light over 'shadows' which would animate all Eliot's work,[11] together with an ideal, in the form of the Absolute, towards which the earlier poems aspire in anguished contention.

PRUFROCK

The most accomplished of Eliot's earliest poems is 'The Love Song of J. Alfred Prufrock'.[12] It is in the form of a modified dramatic monologue, set against an epigraph from the *Inferno*, and is reminiscent of a Shakespearian soliloquy, as well as Browning's studies of 'action in character'. However, it is a more philosophically dialogical poem than precedents would suggest. For all its early-modern setting and the psychological curiosity of its spokesman, the intellectual specificity of the poem is produced by Eliot's 'address to himself' which is elaborated as an ironic collation of hypotheses, rhetorical questions and partial declarations, always under the shadow of some Socratic *elenchus*[13] involving fearful realisation: 'To lead you to an overwhelming question' (l. 10). As in Plato's earlier dialogues, we have a dramatised debate where, in the manner of the dramatic monologue, responses are imagined rather than 'externally' voiced – '"That is not what I

[10] R. Peacock, 'Eliot's Contribution to Cricism of Drama, in *The Literary Criticism of T.S. Eliot: New Essays* (London, 1977), p. 101.

[11] See 'Falls the Shadow', in Dennis Brown, *The Modernist Self in Twentieth-Century English Literature: A Study in Self-Fragmentation* (London, 1989), pp. 149–58. For 'shaft', see *Republic* 616e.

[12] *Complete Poems and Plays*, pp. 13–17.

[13] '"Elenchus" in the wide sense means examining a person with regard to a statement he has made, by putting to him questions calling for further statements, in the hope that they will determine the meaning and the truth-value of his first statement'; 'The *elenchus* changes ignorant man from the state of falsely supposing that they know to the state of recognising that they do not know.' Richard Robinson, *Plato's Earlier Dialectic*, 2nd edn (Oxford, 1953), pp. 7 and 11.

meant at all"'. (l. 97) The poem represents an appropriation (in modern dress) of Platonic dialogue and Socratic irony to express an intellectual's radical alienation in the *agora* of contemporary city life. And two of its key images – the 'etherised' patient on the table (l. 3) and the 'magic lantern' throwing patterned nerves 'on a screen' (p. 105) – remind us powerfully of the condition of Plato's chained prisoners in the Parable of the Cave (*Republic* 514 sq.).

At the core of the poem is a thirst for ultimate Reality – for some higher meaning within or behind or above those urban images which merely 'drop a question on your plate' (l. 30). The voices of others – characterised typically as women's voices – utter the words of Sophistry as opposed to inquiry: 'fix you in a formulated phrase' (l. 56). At the same time, as in Plato's dialogues, the issue concerns virtue as well as truth. Self-understanding is a matter of how one should be and what one should do: 'And would it have been worth it, after all . . .?' (l. 99). The *elenchus* ('of insidious intent'), leading at least to a knowledge of one's error, is studiously avoided throughout. This is perhaps out of a fear of intellectual demolition – it is in 'human voices' that 'we drown' (l. 132). Yet although no resolution to problems is offered – and in this too there is a touch of the Socratic[14] – the pressure of self-investigation, the rehearsal of tantalising questions and the constant interrogation of terms, themselves, is essentially Platonic. The young philosophy student who wrote the poem has utilised the dialogical method of the founding father of the 'mind of Europe'[15] to express and assess a finally-personal (and modern) quest for the Real.

The somewhat uncharacteristic quatrain poems which Eliot wrote between *Prufrock* and *The Waste Land* (1922)[16] are not very directly in pursuit of 'τό ἕν' (being)[17] despite ironic evocation of the Neoplatonic 'Word'. Through the likes of Burbank and Bleinstein, Pipit and the low-life Sweeney, they are mainly concerned to satirise the increasingly democratised world of 'the many' – where appetite, profit and sloth are the main motives. The Platonic impulse here, as in some of Eliot's political commentary later, comes from that 'aristocratic' disdain for the unphilosophical common man which informs such key texts as the

[14] 'Whatever he says in any place has an element of the provisional already built into it': C.J. Rowe, *Plato* (Brighton, 1984), p. 53.

[15] Eliot's phrase in 'Tradition and the Individual Talent', *Selected Essays*, p. 16.

[16] See Dennis Brown, *Intertextual Dynamics Within the Literary Group – Joyce, Lewis, Pound and Eliot: The Men of 1914* (London, 1990), pp. 73–7.

[17] 'Mr Eliot's Sunday Morning Service', l.6, *Complete Poems and Plays*, p. 54.

Republic and the *Laws*. Heightened by the bitterness of World War, these satires 'Kodak'[18] the sensual legatees of the European collapse:

> The red-eyed scavengers are creeping
> From Kentish Town and Golder's Green;
>
> Where are the eagles and the trumpets?
> 'A Cooking Egg' (ll. 27–9)

It is a vision which will recur in 'Gerontion' and *The Waste Land*: but in the latter it will be balanced by a still-Socratic pursuit of Reality. In the quatrains, the mode is comedic exposure of unexamined lives, Platonically-sanctioned since 'the acquisition of virtue requires us to recognise buffoonery, in order that we can avoid it ourselves'.[19] These poems boast their philosophical superiority through coldly-assumed deployment of rarified terminology and arcane allusion. They implicitly assert the intellectual integrity of a modern soul – as *The Waste Land* will manifest the same soul in near-terminal breakdown.

THE WASTE LAND

The chief clue to a Platonic intent in *The Waste Land* surfaces from the manuscript drafts prior to Ezra Pound's editing of the poem. In section III, 'The Fire Sermon', between the apparition of the 'demotic' Mr. Eugenides in the 'Unreal City' and Tiresias' sordid vision of a suburban seduction, there is a clear reference to the effective conclusion of Plato's argument in the *Republic*: 'Not here, O Glaucon, but in another world'.[20] This cancelled line is implicitly connected with the reiterated 'burning' metaphor from Augustine's *Confessions*, since the passage in the *Republic* helped inspire *The City of God*.[21] However, in the early twenties Eliot was far from committed to the Christian faith and the satiric vision of contemporary London in *The Waste Land*, as a whole, is genuinely Platonic in its depiction of 'democratic' man who 'teems with . . . pleasures and appetites, and who is governed by his unnecessary desires' (*Republic* 359) in a world of mere appearance and flux. Another passage from the *Republic* concerns the 'wise man' who seeks: 'the city whose home is in the ideal, for I think that it can be found nowhere on earth' (*Republic* 592).

[18] Wyndham Lewis's term, see my *Intertextual Dynamics*, p. 76. [19] Rowe, *Plato*, p. 47.

[20] See T. S. Eliot, *The Waste Land: a Facsimile and Transcript of the Original Drafts Including the Annotations of Ezra Pound*, ed. Valerie Eliot (London, 1971), p. 128.

[21] See the discussions in Grover Smith, *The Waste Land* (London, 1983), pp. 52–3 and Erik Svarny, *The Men of 1914: T.S. Eliot and Early Modernism* (Milton Keynes, 1988), pp. 198ff.

The remoteness of the ideal city from the contemporary metropolis is precisely what *The Waste Land* laments. Stephen Spender aptly termed his chapter on the poem: 'The Temporal City of Total Conditioning.'[22] Hence:

> Jerusalem Athens Alexandria
> Vienna London
> Unreal
> (*The Waste Land* ll. 373–5)

The Waste Land is characteristically Socratic in its basic stance of self-aware ignorance. Another cancelled line reads: 'And if Another knows, I know not'.[23] This is quite directly an echo of Socrates' key avowal in *Apology* 21d 'he thinks that he knows something which he does not know, whereas I am quite conscious of my ignorance . . . I do not think that I know what I do not know'. The authorised and published text of Eliot's poem retains the stance of the cancelled line; it is full of declarations of ignorance: '"and I knew nothing"' (l. 40); '"Do / You know nothing?"'; (ll. 121–2); '"I can connect / Nothing with nothing"' (ll. 300–1); 'These fragments I have shored against my ruin' (l. 430). In commenting on his own essays on Plato, Eliot had confessed his 'fatal disposition toward scepticism'.[24] However, as in 'Prufrock', scepticism in *The Waste Land* is based on a Socratic honesty of enquiry and is fully Platonic in so far as it is persistently in pursuit of a higher Reality than is evident in the image-world of the mundane realm – which is the poem's chief subject matter. The personae in the poem are all 'chained prisoners' entranced by shadows – but the text shows this to be the case and so it presupposes some 'heart of light' (l. 14) where true awareness might occur. *The Waste Land* is in pursuit of this although it fails to find it. It constitutes radically dialogic heteroglossia and concludes, like some of Plato's earlier dialogues, leaving the key issues very much open. In its quest for meaning, two Platonic precedent texts seem especially relevant: the *Republic*, as suggested, with its prolonged debate about the possibility of establishing a just city within the actual world; and also the *Phaedo*, the dramatised interrogation of the nature of the soul in the immediate shadow of death.

The *Republic* opens with a brief disquisition by the ageing Cephalus, who quotes Sophocles to the effect that sexual desire is a form of savage tyranny. This is a major theme of *The Waste Land* too, with its public house innuendo and sordid seduction scene and with Tiresias

[22] Stephen Spender, *Eliot* (London, 1975), pp. 90–119. [23] *Facsimile and Transcript*, p. 69.
[24] Eliot to J.H. Woods, 28 January 1915, *Letters*, p. 84.

(fittingly, since he is a key figure in Sophoclean drama) as its aged (and ageless) spokesperson. What the whole poem expresses is an imperfect society presided over not by a philosopher king but by a sickly Fisher King. In place of the rational voices of philosophical debate, *The Waste Land* exposes its readers to the neurotic babble of distracted citizens ('"O keep the Dog far hence"' (l. 74); '"Do you see nothing?"' (l. 122); '"my heart / Under my feet"' (ll. 296–7); 'Hieronymo's mad againe' (l. 431)). And instead of some manifestation of 'that essence which is eternal' (*Republic* 485b) the poem expresses only 'a heap of broken images'. Nevertheless, *The Waste Land*, like the *Republic*, inscribes a development toward some point of enlightenment. The thunder's commands suggest an ordered awareness such as is hoped from Plato's 'guardians' – even if the voiced responses imply the inability of the waste-landers to attain this. Similarly, the Fisher King wonders whether he should set his lands 'in order' – a conformity to Platonic justice as defined in *Republic* Book 443d, and translated in the Penguin version as: 'in the truest sense set his house in order, and be his own lord and master and at peace with himself.'[25] And, finally, the poem concludes, if ironically, with a reiterated 'Shantih', just as the *Republic* ends in divine consummation ('at peace with God and with ourselves', as the Penguin version again renders it, and 'all will be well with us' (621c–d).[26] It will not be until the conclusion of *Four Quartets* that Eliot will affirm, with Julian of Norwich too, that 'all shall be well'. Nevertheless, along with Sir James Frazer's *The Golden Bough* and Jessie L. Weston's *From Ritual to Romance*, Plato's *Republic* is surely one of the founding texts in dialogue with which *The Waste Land* effects its manner of meaning.

The influence of the *Phaedo* is less obvious – but perhaps as significant. *The Waste Land*, like the *Phaedo*, is a dramatised meditation set against the horizon of death: 'He who was living is now dead' (l. 328). Eliot's first choice for the poem's epigraph was the utterance of Conrad's dying Kurtz: '"The horror! the horror!"'; his second, was the published (and untranslated) quotation from Petronius, in which the salient words are the caged and wizened Sybil's cry: '"I want to die"'. The themes of death-in-life and life-in-death have long been

[25] Plato, *The Republic*, translated by H.D.P. Lee (Harmondsworth, 1965), p. 96. This translation, of course, may have been influenced by Eliot's own phraseology. Paul Shorey translates the Greek: 'he should dispose well of what in the true sense of the word is properly his own, and having first attained to self-mastery and beautiful order within himself . . .' *Collected Dialogues*, ed. Hamilton and Cairns, p. 686.

[26] Lee's translation, *The Republic*, p. 401. Shorey gives: 'that we may be dear to ourselves and to the Gods . . . we shall fare well', *Collected Dialogues*, p. 844.

critically acknowledged in accounts of *The Waste Land*. The Platonic precedent for such dialogue between Being and Nothingness is embedded centrally in the *Phaedo*:

the living have come from the dead no less than the dead from the living. But I think we decided that if this was so, it was a sufficient proof that the souls of the dead must exist in some place from which they are reborn. (72a)

Such fructive reciprocity between death and life has become broken down in *The Waste Land*: this lies at the heart of its crisis ('That corpse you planted last year in your garden, / Has it begun to sprout?' (l. 71–2). Yet the poem exhibits one watchful soul from that other 'place' – Tiresias, the Greek prophet, in whom both male and female, death and life, co-mingle. *The Waste Land* dramatises a world which denies the Platonic doctrine of the immortality of the soul – and hence has no meaning. So the central figure of Phlebas enters 'the whirlpool'. Yet the poem's overall implication is that its personae are radically self-deceived and hence fit only for limbo. That this was Eliot's own conviction is attested in a coded reference by Pound to the holiday in France he shared with Eliot in 1919:

And the tower with cut stone above that, saying:
'I am afraid of the life after death'.
and after a pause:
'Now, at last, I have shocked him.'[27]

'The Hollow Men' (1925) also expresses that fear. The inhabitants of 'death's other kingdom' think of the contemporary 'many' as 'stuffed men' – nonentities. The poem is built up out of a range of influences, yet the precedent of the Parable of the Cave seems, again, particularly pertinent to section I, which was originally written separately. The 'many' here are chorically expressed as 'Old Guys', yet their situation is very much the same as Plato's prisoners in 'a sort of subterranean cavern' ('our dry cellar'), shackled together ('paralysed force'), aware only of shadows ('Shape without form, shade without colour') and discussing illusions ('We whisper . . . meaningless'). Throughout the poem, and partly with reference to Dante's *Vita Nuova*, there is a strong contrast between antithetical realms of awareness – as in the Parable. Sunlight (in the poem 'on a broken column') is the absolute opposite to the shadow-play, and eyes, as the vehicle of sight and hence understanding, are key metonymic figures.

27 Ezra Pound, *The Cantos* (London, 1986), p. 145. For the identification of 'Arnaut' with Eliot here, see Hugh Kenner, *The Pound Era* (California, 1973), pp. 336–8.

In the *Republic*, also, modes of seeing (hence awareness) are central:

But a sensible man, I said, would remember that there are two distinct disturbances of the eyes arising from two causes, according as the shift is from light to darkness or from darkness to light, and, believing that the same thing happens to the soul too, whenever he saw a soul perturbed and unable to discern something, he would . . . observe whether coming from a brighter life its vision was obscured by the unfamiliar darkness, or whether the passage from the deeper dark of ignorance into a more luminous world and the greater brightness had dazzled his vision. (518 a)

Jacques Derrida has asserted that 'the metaphor of darkness and light (of self-revelation and self-concealment)', which he centres on Plato, constitutes 'the founding metaphor of Western philosophy as metaphysics'.[28] It is certainly central to Eliot's verse, and to this poem in particular. Thus in section v 'the shadow' mediates between a varied (and semi-ironic?) list of quasi-Socratic entities:

Between the idea
And the reality
Between the motion
And the act
Falls the Shadow.[29]

It can be said, then, that the earlier poetry of T.S. Eliot was written in agonistic relation to Platonic precursor texts. Eliot pursued his contention with the Neo-Hegelian F.H. Bradley in his doctoral dissertation and article in the *Monist*.[30] In the poems, his struggle is with the founding father of philosophy.[31] Yet although he turns the dialectical method into a mode of self-questioning (and can evoke the threat of *elenchus*) it is typical of the poet that he seems to owe more to Plato's rhetorical figures than to his logic. The notion of an ideal city transcending the sensual *agora* of metropolitan life, the image of direct sunlight in contrast to the shadow-realm of the world's 'cave', and the heroic figuration of the intellectual who owns to his final ignorance yet still pursues truth – these are key influences in the poetry Eliot wrote from 1908 to 1925. Thereafter occurs the 'turn' of 'Ash-

[28] 'More than any other philosophy, phenomenology, in the wake of Plato, was to be struck with light. Unable to resist the last naïveté, the naïveté of the glance, it predetermined Being as object'. Jacques Derrida, *Writing and Difference*, trans. Alan Bass (London, 1981), pp. 85 and 27.

[29] 'The Hollow Men', *Complete Poems and Plays*, p. 85.

[30] 'Leibniz' Monads and Bradley's Finite Centres', *The Monist* (1916), reprinted in T.S. Eliot, *Knowledge and Experience in the Philosophy of F.H. Bradley* (London, 1964), pp. 198–207.

[31] See Harold Bloom, *The Anxiety of Influence: a Theory of Poetry* (New York, 1973), *passim*.

Wednesday' and the development of a kind of Christian Neoplatonism which will seek the 'still point' through the 'figure' of music.[32]

In earlier Eliot the Ideal, the Beautiful and the Good cannot be invoked without irony: in this respect he is both influenced by Plato and in contention with him. Or put another way, he accepts Plato the sceptic but refuses Plato the idealist. At the same time, he uses poetry not logic in pursuit of the truth, thus turning Plato's own figural powers against his teased-out definitions and distinctions, and denying Plato's low opinion of the poetic. As Eric Thompson writes about the later 'Burnt Norton': 'as a defense of poetry . . . it is written by a poet who grants in advance . . . the validity of Plato's indictment . . . Eliot's defensive tactics are to show that the soul which falls by the imagination rises by the imagination'.[33] Eliot the one-time philosopher thus uses poetry to challenge the discursive terrain on which blindness and insight are to be contested. So reading Eliot makes us rethink Plato, as reading Plato opens up key implications of Eliot's earlier verse.

[32] See Maud Ellmann, *The Poetics of Impersonality*, pp. 119–20.
[33] Thompson, *T.S. Eliot*, p. 81.

CHAPTER 28

The Cantos *of Ezra Pound: 'To build light'*

A.D. Moody

In Pound's *Cantos*, as in Platonism generally, the generative energy of the universe is conceived as germinal intelligence, as *nous*. The light of intelligence manifests itself in every living thing, thus, 'oak leaf never plane leaf' (87/573), and, 'there is something intelligent in the cherry stone' (113/788); thus 'bull by the force that is in him – / not lord of it, / mastered' (113/789).[1] But the workings of *nous* are most effectively grasped when the mind penetrates such particular manifestations and conceives its governing conceptions, the universal Ideas and all-shaping Forms. Then, moreover, it becomes possible for the divine conceptions to enter into and to govern human existence and society. This is humanity's part in the making of the Cosmos, to realise the light of the divine intelligence in the form of the Republic, or the 'paradiso *terrestre*' as Pound preferred to call it.

The Cantos are one man's effort to conceive the governing ideas of the process of which we are part, so that we might participate in it more effectually. That is to say, *The Cantos* are not about the Platonic idea of *nous*, but are an attempt to practise it – to be, as Spinoza put it, a human mode of the divine intelligence. The poem is an attempt 'To make Cosmos – To achieve the possible' (116/795), and to do 'our job' which is, as Ocellus said, 'to build light' (98/684). The reader, it should be said, is necessarily involved in the work.

Platonism, in its Neoplatonic form, is referred to in *The Cantos* by way of allusions to and citations of a dozen or so philosophers. The earliest, (to set them in chronological order, which is not their order of appearance), is Pythagoras (fl. *c.* 530 BC), who was before Plato (*c.* 427–347 BC), but whose teachings became an important component of Neoplatonism. Next come two followers of Pythagoras, Ocellus who

[1] References to *The Cantos* are to *The Cantos of Ezra Pound* (New York and London, 1975). The first number indicates the canto, and the second the page in that edition.

flourished in the fifth century BC, and Apollonius of Tyana, a near-contemporary of Jesus Christ and in the eyes of some his pagan counterpart. Then come the Neoplatonists proper, Plotinus (AD 205–270), who, in the opinion of Longinus his contemporary in Rome, 'set the principles of Pythagoras and of Plato in a clearer light than anyone before him'; Porphyry (AD 234–*c*.305), his disciple and editor of his *Enneads*; and Iamblichus (d. AD *c*.330), a student of Porphyry and known as both a Platonist and a Pythagorean. Those philosophers all wrote in Greek. After them come certain Christian Neoplatonists whose working language was Latin but who knew Greek well enough to translate and to draw on their Greek predecessors: John Scotus Eriugena (AD *c*.810–*c*.877), the first to unite Greek philosophy and Christian thought in a single system; Anselm of Canterbury (1034–1109), the next systematic thinker after Erigena, but more of a theologian and less of a speculative philosopher; and Richard of [the abbey of] Saint-Victor in Paris (d. 1173), who combined Neoplatonic and Christian ideas in his writings on the theory and practice of contemplative mysticism. (Robert Grosseteste (1175–1253), Oxford scholar and Bishop of Lincoln, is not named in *The Cantos*, but from his treatise on light is drawn the formulation of a key concept of Neoplatonic cosmology). Two Neoplatonists associated with the Renaissance in Italy are mentioned – Gemistus Pletho (1355?–1450?) and Marsilio Ficino (1433–99) – less for any original contribution than for their passing on the tradition. The last of the line is John Heydon (b. 1629?), an English astrologer, alchemist and visionary, thought a charlatan in his own time, and exposed as a plagiarist in ours.

It should not be thought that Neoplatonism as such looms large or figures as a major subject in *The Cantos*. Most of those philosophers are represented by little more than their names and a tag or an anecdote. There is no substantial treatment of their particular ideas, nor of Neoplatonic thought in general. What we are explicitly given amounts to no more than a number of points and references. It is true that these can be seen to make up, when sorted into chronological order, an outline history of the Neoplatonic way of thinking the Cosmos. And it would appear that this cosmology is being affirmed. Yet it is left quite undefined, indeed virtually unstated. This frugality of reference can tempt commentators to provide what has been withheld, and to insert, for example, Grosseteste's *De Luce* into their reading of *The Cantos*, on the strength of the citation from it of the single phrase 'per plura diafana' (through the many diaphonous [degrees of being]). I rather think that this is a distraction from the process of intelligence and not a contribution to it. The Neoplatonism is being practised, not expounded.

Consider the case of Iamblichus, who gets a brief mention early in *The Cantos*, as one of the 'outstanding representatives of the early phase of the school of Plotinus', as a Pythagorean, and for his influence on later Neoplatonism.[2] Much might be made of Iamblichus. But we are given only the terse phrase, 'Iamblichus light'. The *Companion to the Cantos of Ezra Pound* pertinently tells us that in his thought Light denoted the One, 'the single principle from which the plurality of things derive'[3]. But to make anything of the allusion we need to read it in context:

> Measureless seas and stars,
> Iamblichus' light,
>   the souls ascending,
> Sparks like a partridge covey,
>   Like the 'ciocco', brand struck in the game,
> 'Et omniformis': (5/17)

If Iamblichus' light is indeed the source of all things then *measureless* seas and stars would not be in apposition to it, but would be opposed. For in Pythagorean terms it is the *measured* which manifests the primal light, while the unmeasured is what is not informed by it. But then again 'measureless' might imply only that the perceiver is unable to measure the 'seas and stars'. What is in question is not simply the objective situation but also the capacity of the observer: and the apparently measureless might, if it could only be seen in the light of Iamblichus, be numbered within the cosmos. The images which follow are a variation upon this miniature drama of the mind. In Dante's *Paradiso* (XVIII, 100), the individual souls in their ascent assume a single form as they become subject to the all-comprehending and all-generating divine light. That at least is the idea; but what we actually see in these lines are the separate lights, not the one light – just as we see 'Measureless seas and stars' rather than 'Iamblichus' light'. The Latin phrase, a gloss of Ficino upon Porphyry, makes the point: our intelligence is omniform, it is inevitably drawn into the plurality of things. And thus it may be 'wrecked in the multiplicity of

[2] J.O. Urmson and Jonathan Rée (eds), *Concise Encyclopaedia of Western Philosophy and Philosophers* (London, 1989), p. 220. See also Sheppard p. 5 above.

[3] Carroll F. Terrell (ed.), *A Companion to the Cantos of Ezra Pound* (Berkeley, 1980), I, p. 17.

the Universe' (*Enneads* II, 3. 8). The reader's mind, struggling to make coherent sense of the discrete fragments, is caught up in this drama of the mind which would perceive the intelligible universe and be at one with the *nous* but which actually perceives and feels itself lost in a multiplicity of detail. Thus the passage neither gives nor asks for an exposition of Neoplatonic doctrine, but is a direct experience of mind struggling for enlightenment.

Plotinus figures relatively extensively in *The Cantos*, first in its hell and later in the approaches to its paradise. 'Hell' and 'paradise', it should be noted, are states of mind, not places. Hell is the state of minds deprived of the light of intelligence; and paradise is the state in which the apparently incomprehensible becomes intelligible. The latter state is not easily attained. Before Herakles, in Pound's version of Sophocles' *Women of Trachis*, attains it and exclaims 'SPLENDOUR! IT ALL COHERES', he has suffered extreme anguish and agony. Neither the poet, nor the reader in his wake, can expect to reach it without mind-cracking effort.

In Canto 15 Plotinus shows the poet the way out of hell. He does this in the figure of Perseus, armed with the mirror-shield of Minerva and the severed head of the Medusa, and not by any explicit reference to his philosophy. Just the same, his treatise 'The Nature and Source of Evil' (*Enneads* I. 8) would provide the most helpful commentary on Pound's hell. Eliot, in the well-known passage in *After Strange Gods*,[4] objected to Pound's presenting only types of evil-doing while omitting the drama of individual damnation. His objection assumes that the individual soul is of primary significance. But for Plotinus the individual is real only to the degree in which it participates in the Universal. Evil is that which is formless and shapeless, without order or measure, unstable, deliquescent, falling away 'in gloom and mud' (*Enneads* I. 8. 13) into endless dissolution and darkness. Individual identity, therefore, is precisely what is lost with the loss of the universal principle. This is the essence of Pound's hell, a place deprived of all light ('"d'ogni luce muto"', 14/16), 'last cess-pool of the universe', 'The soil a decrepitude, the ooze full of morsels, / lost contours, erosions', 'The slough of unamiable liars, / bog of stupidities', 'melted ossifications, / slow rot, foetid combustion' (14/62–3). The poet feels himself being sucked into the bog, and Plotinus/Perseus tells him 'Keep your eyes on the mirror', while he petrifies the soil by the

[4] T.S. Eliot, *After Strange Gods* (London, 1934), pp. 42–3.

shield on which the Medusa's head has been mounted, 'The serpents' tongues . . . Hammering the souse into hardness' (15/66). This is myth, not philosophy, but it dramatises the philosophy. In the mirror-shield of Minerva the mind sees things as they are reflected in the divine Mind, that is, it beholds their forms and is protected from the dissolving accidents.

But how are Pound's readers to get out of his hell? Our experience is of 'DECOMPOSITION', and perhaps over-whelmingly so. Yet what Pound was after was 'the idea of mental ROT'.[5] His writing seems not to be mirroring that idea, but to be giving us only its particulars. Those particulars, however, are intelligible, and when they are comprehended the mind discovers in them a certain vision of unenlightenment. Their governing idea is not spelt out in an abstraction or a generalisation; but then, if the universal is to be grasped at all, it can be grasped only in and by the mind confronting the data. That, in the end, has to be the reader's own mind. It is our getting the idea, 'the idea of mental ROT', which liberates us from the 'DECOMPOSITION'. In practice the only mirror of Minerva is the mind itself.

In Pound's approaches to paradise in the final sections of *The Cantos*, *Thrones* (1959) and *Drafts & Fragments* (1969), Plotinus figures in a number of snippets and brief extracts. These make little sense on their own and can seem to be at best mere fragments in a mosaic. Upon careful consideration, however, they can be found to function as organic components in very complex and high-powered passages of meditation. At the end of canto 100 (100/721–2) we come upon these impenetrable lines:

come in subjecto
lisses
amoureuses
a tenir
EX OUSIAS . . . HYPOSTASIN
III, 5, 3 PERI EROTAS

Then there is a hieroglyph, three columns on a base, representing the façade of a temple, and beside it the word 'hieron', the Greek word for a temple as a place dedicated to and under the protection of a divine power. The passage goes on to speak directly of the *nous* -

[5] Brita Lindberg-Seyersted (ed.), *Pound/Ford: The Story of a Literary Friendship* (New York, 1982), p. 134.

nous to ariston autou
as light into water compenetrans
that is pathema
ouk aphistatai'
thus Plotinus
per plura diafana
neither weighed out nor hindered;
aloof.

The fragmentariness is reinforced by the shifts from Italian to French to Greek (transliterated), to English and to Latin, with the hieroglyph adding another kind of language altogether. The mind that would comprehend this without being shattered must be just a bit 'omniformis', able to move freely through the various languages, in order to pick up the idea of it all.

The Greek is from Plotinus. 'Ex ousias . . . hypostasin' is the gist of the first proposition of section 3 of the fifth tractate of the third Ennead – 'III, 5, 3' gives the reference. 'Peri Erotas' ('about love') is the title of this tractate. Plotinus argues that Love really and substantially exists, that it is a 'hypostasis' or real being born of a real being. His explanation is part mythical theology and part mystical psychology:

Aphrodite, [daughter of Heaven, that is, of the Intellectual Principle], concentrated her being upon her father and felt affinity with him, and filled with passionate love for him brought forth Eros, and through this child of hers she gazes upon him . . . [Eros or Love has] its being in this, that it is an intermediary between desiring and the desired; it is the eye of desire, the power by which the lover sees the object of desire. (*Enneads* III. 5. 3)[6]

A similar view of Love is to be found in Dante and his Tuscan contemporaries. Pound studied it most closely in the poetry of Guido Cavalcanti, from whose philosophical *canzone* on the nature of love, 'Donna mi prega' – given in translation in canto 36 – comes the phrase '*come in subjecto*'. In his essay on Cavalcanti he discussed the phrase in a way to connect it with Plotinus' view that the soul as knower (or subject) has two phases, the receptive and the resplendent.[7] That is to say, whoever knows and loves the light of the intellect, and those in whom the light is manifest as beauty and intelligence, are as '*diafana*', infused with light and spreading light about them. The Cavalcanti phrase seems to function here as a tag to recall Plotinus'

[6] Based on Armstrong, III, 177 and MacKenna, p. 193.
[7] *Make It New* (London, 1934), pp. 388–9.

account of how *nous* is mediated by love.

But first Villon's 'la belle heaulmière' is briefly recalled, the once-beautiful woman remembering, in crabbed age, that in her youth she was 'lissom and loving to hold'. How is her realism and pathos to be related to the idealism of Cavalcanti and Plotinus? Her life too has had its two phases, and her beautiful and bitter song is as real a manifestation of soul as was her diaphanous loveliness. The interactions of the fragment of her song with the philosophical fragments go beyond irony, and reveal her as a real-life and challenging instance of the mystical ideas. She serves to bring them down to earth, and to bring them to proof.

That thought prompts another about the temple hieroglyph. Its three pillars, based upon the plinth of earth, are open to the light raining from heaven. That light is *nous*, the intellectual principle which is supreme in the cosmos, as we can read at the start of the fourth Ennead, 'nous to ariston autou' ('Intellect is the best part of it', IV. 2[1]. 1). 'As light into water compenetrans' puts into an image Plotinus' account (*Enneads* IV.2) of how the *nous* enters into the muliplicity of beings while itself remaining undivided. 'That is pathema' implies the effect of it as felt by the individual soul or lover – *la belle heaulmière*, for example; while 'ouk aphistatai' indicates that Love itself, the hypostasis of the primal source of light, like it stands 'distinct and aloof' (III. 5. 3: McKenna, p. 194). The dictionary yields 'neither weighed out nor hindered' as further glosses upon 'ouk aphistatai'. 'Compenetrans' – penetrating the whole, in every direction – could have come from any one of a number of philosophers in the Neoplatonic tradition, Grosseteste of the multiple '*diafana*' among them.

The arcane passage thus turns out to be an intensely concentrated gist of Plotinus on the action of *nous* in the form of Eros. The mind is moved very swiftly from one point of reference to another, with each fragmentary detail interacting with the rest to create, not an argument, but an intellectual field of force; one in which, just here, Plotinus and his hypostases and the temple and La Belle Heaulmière co-exist as if each applied equally to the other. The light penetrates in all directions. But to comprehend it the reader must not only have gathered the materials, as I have been doing here, but must then swiftly perceive their relations. That heightened level of intellectual activity, the swift perceiving of relations, is, in Pound's view, the essence of the mind's genius or *nous*. In this passage he has been doing the work of *nous*, and involving the reader in it. The poetry is, as ever, practising the philosophy, not simply referring to what Plotinus thought.

We have been looking there at just half of one page of one canto. No total revelation is to be had from it. The reading, the perceiving of relations, needs to go on to take in the whole canto; and the full sequence of *Thrones de los Cantares:* XCVI–CIX; and ultimately the totality of *The Cantos of Ezra Pound.* But the half-page yields some insight into how the whole poem works, and specifically into how it works in its Neoplatonic reaches. One striking feature is how rarefied the intellectual atmosphere has become, compared with the *Pisan Cantos* where memory was dominant, or with the first half of the epic where history was dominant. In *Thrones*, history and personal experience have been refined into references and allusions which function as symbols, as in mathematics or logic, symbols which presuppose a body of knowledge and which serve for very advanced thinking about it. The purpose of that thought, as it was the purpose of Plotinus's and of Plato's, is to attain certain concepts, the concepts which 'make Cosmos' (116/795). And the only way to attain them, Pound was convinced, is 'via intellect'. It makes for a shocking kind of poetry.

Now in order to make Cosmos the ideas must go into action, as Pound frequently affirmed. Whether the concepts formed in the mind of its readers by *The Cantos* themselves will make a difference to the way the world is going, is a question for future historians to resolve. But it is certain that the measure by which Pound would have his own and all Platonic concepts judged, is their effectiveness. Their virtue is not in their logic or their rhetoric but in their action. By their fruits you shall know them. This shows very clearly in his relative valuations of Plato and Apollonius of Tyana.

One would have expected Plato to be accorded a place of honour in *The Cantos.* In *Guide to Kulchur* (1938) Pound wrote: 'even the most rabid anti-platonist must concede that Plato has repeatedly stirred men to a sort of enthusiasm productive of action, and that one cannot completely discount this value as life force'.[8] Yet in *The Cantos* he is merely mentioned in passing, on just four occasions, and by philosophers and statesmen who put him in the shade. There is an anecdote of Gemistus Plethon speaking in Florence about Plato's efforts to hitch his philosophy to the power of the Tyrant of Syracuse,

[8] *Guide to Kulchur* (London: Peter Owen, 1952), p. 347.

'But he was unable to persuade Dionysius / To any amelioration' (8/31). This shows Plato not as the ideal intellect of the Socratic dialogues, but in the less flattering light of the *Epistles*, unsuccessfully trying to get his ideas put into practice. The point is rubbed in by the contrast with Gemistus Plethon himself, who had a remarkable effect upon Cosimo de' Medici. Under his influence, Cosimo founded the Platonic Academy of Florence, set Ficino to translating the Greek Neoplatonists, and thus 'set off a renaissance'[9].

In other cantos Pound has Plato put down by John Adams and Thomas Jefferson, founders and early presidents of the American republic. Jefferson had written that he could not take *The Republic* seriously. Adams agrees, devastatingly. There was just one thing he had learnt from him: 'that sneezing is a cure for the hickups' (33/162). In a later canto Pound cites Adams's reflection that 'some parts of Plato and Sir Thos More are as wild as the ravings of Bedlam' (68/395). Again we have the practical statesman weighing the philosopher and finding him wanting. Ten cantos are devoted to the life and works of John Adams. Plato gets about ten lines.

The reason for his being virtually banished from the poem is his failure to give his thought the precise definition necessary for it to communicate its energies effectively. His 'purple patches', high on god and infinity, appealed to emotion rather that to *nous*.

> Socrates tried to make people think, or at any rate the Socrates 'of Plato' tried to make 'em use their language with greater precision and to distinguish knowledge from not-knowledge.
>
> And the Platonic inebriety comes to readers and Platonism when Plato's Socrates forgets all about logic, when he launches into 'sublimity' about the heaven above the heavens, the pure light of the mind, the splendour of crystalline lastingness.[10]

Against such rhapsodising mystification Pound calls for 'factual study'; the 'discipline of real theology' so far as it demands the clear definition of terms; and the discipline of verse technique for the sincere expression of dynamic emotion. Judged by the demands Pound made upon himself in *The Cantos*, Plato was not enough of a poet to secure a place in its paradise.

Apollonius of Tyana is hardly remembered as a philosopher (see

[9] *Ibid.*, p. 45. See also pp. 224–5.

[10] *Ibid.*, p. 33. For the rest of the paragraph see pp. 31–3, 40, 44–5, 128, 222–3; and 'On Criticism in General', *Criterion*, 1, 2 (1923), 156.

Sheppard, p. 16 above), yet he is given a larger place in *The Cantos* than any other Pythagorean or Platonist. He believed, as Plato did, that kings, to rule well, should be lovers of wisdom; and he devoted his long life, as Plato did not, to persuading rulers to rule wisely, and to the amelioration of civic order. He was a practising sage who carried through into the conduct of daily life the conviction that all of life should be in accord with the divine ordering. He brought philosophy down to earth, hence his throne in *The Cantos*.

More than half of canto 94 is devoted to a digest of Philostratus' *Life of Apollonius of Tyana*.[11] He is presented not as a thinker, but as someone who travelled the world and became wise through knowing the ways and the wisdom of all its nations; and who then put his knowledge at the service of others. He gave forth the light which he had received, in practical ways. He helped many cities bring law and order into their civic affairs, and, most importantly, he advised the Emperor Vespasian. For example, he persuaded him that rather than exploit his people to increase the empire's riches he should use the wealth to improve their lives. But when Vespasian deprived the Greek cities of their independence Apollonius withdrew from his service. His influence, however, (such is the implication), continued through Vespasian's relatively enlightened successors down to the Empress Julia Domna, who comissioned Philostratus to set down his *Life*. Many of the fragments making up the mosaic of Pound's digest of the life are given in the original Greek, as if to remind us that it was the culture of Greek philosophy that was exerting a civilising influence upon the Roman Empire. But certain of Apollonius' sayings are transposed into Chinese ideograms, which turn out to be equivalent sayings of Mencius and Confucius, and here the implication is that just as the governing ideas of those sages held together Chinese civilisation for some thousands of years so Apollonius was behind the Roman order for a century and more.

Canto 94 ends with '"To build light"' (94/642), a key statement of *The Cantos*, attributed to the earlier Pythagorean Ocellus; and with two Chinese ideograms, associated with the great Shang emperor Ch'eng T'ang, which can be translated as *renew the day*. The sign for 'day' is a representation of the sun, so that an idea of light is present, and of the sun as the source of the day and of what each day brings. In the sign for 'renew' the root idea is of pruning away dead wood to

[11] Pound's source was the Loeb edition, Philostratus, *The Life of Apollonius of Tyana*, ed. and trans. F.C. Conybeare, 2 vols. (Cambridge, Mass. and London, 1912).

allow the fresh growth to come through. The Chinese phrase not only parallels the Pythagorean motif, but adds a particular emphasis, presenting the constructive process of enlightened government as a wholly natural one. The 'mandate of heaven', the Chinese equivalent of the *nous*, is conceived, not as primarily intellectual energy, but as the same energy which operates in phyllotaxis and all natural process. Justice is therefore a natural product like any other, requiring only that those responsible for it observe due natural process. Its pattern is in the nature of things, not 'laid up in heaven'.

There is then a necessary connection between observing the law (or *logos*) and observing the nature of things. Justness of perception becomes the basis of Justice. 'To make Cosmos' implies, not having control over the world, but perceiving how it shapes itself, and acting in accord with it. In the same way, 'To build light' implies an eye, and a mind's eye, that has first been enlightened. (Ocellus' very name, a form of *oculus*, or 'eye', seems to underline this: it is with the eye that one builds.) In canto 93, following another mention of Ocellus – 'and the soul's job? (Ocellus) / '"Renew"', as in *renew the day* – Pound adds 'Plus the luminous eye' (93/629). He accompanies this with the Chinese ideogram for 'to see; to observe; to perceive', a sign which can be read as an eye in motion, an active eye. The 'luminous eye' acts justly by giving out the light which it receives. Hence the exhortation, 'God's eye art 'ou, do not surrender perception' (113/790). This is Plotinus, and Platonism, made new.

CHAPTER 29

Platonism in Auden

Daphne Turner

'I would rather,' wrote Auden, 'if I must be a heretic, be condemned as a pantheist than as a Neoplatonist'.[1] This is typical of Auden's attitude to Plato: writing about him casually in poems and at some length in essays, he is usually critical. One such essay is his preface to *The Portable Greek Reader*, which contains his own selections from Plato. His main criticisms are that Plato's *Republic* was a tyranny and his philosophy dualist. But one argues earnestly only against ideas that one takes very seriously. In fact, Auden seems to define himself against Plato, Christian sacramentalist against classical transcendentalist.

But there are other ways of reading Plato, which connect rather than oppose Christian and classical. Iris Murdoch reads his work as a religious vision based on love of good, on the energy of Eros and on purifying Eros from the blurring projections of ego by constantly attending to reality. Auden is secretly much closer to this version of Plato than to his own, enough for G.T. Wright to write that, 'his way of thinking is at times remarkably Platonic'.[2] When one compares him to Beckett, another great modern writer who is deeply read in theology, one can see how true this is. Auden uses a Platonic vocabulary totally alien to Beckett: the Good, beauty, justice and the Just City, desire for truth, intelligence, love (which Auden often calls Eros); even *anamnesis*, *polis* and the Socratic sign. Auden was close to Plato in the four issues I shall be covering in this essay: the transcendent and the material, the vision of Eros, the Just City and the role of the artist in it. In this essay I shall look at his continuing quarrel with Plato on these topics and how it fuels the complex feeling and technique of some of his best poems.

[1] W.H. Auden, 'The Shield of Perseus' ('Postscript'), *The Dyer's Hand and Other Essays* (London, 1963; first published 1948) (hereafter, *DH*), p. 460.
[2] G.T. Wright, *W.H. Auden* (New York, 1969).

TRANSCENDENT AND MATERIAL

Auden's central objection is to Plato's dualism: his picture of an impersonal, unchanging Good totally separate from the world.[3] Here he would have in mind such passages as *Phaedrus* 250 and *Phaedo* 66e, where Socrates claims, 'no true knowledge is possible in the company of the body'. Auden objects to this splitting of body and soul, as it devalues the world and fails to make love central, unlike the personal god of Christianity. He writes as a Christian incarnationalist, believing that the body and the material world manifest God and will be, as a totality, redeemed. In his long poem, 'For the Time Being', a Christmas meditation on the Incarnation, Herod assents to the massacre of the innocents out of fear of the shift from Platonic to Christian values: 'Reason will be replaced by Revelation', knowledge and 'Rational Law, objective truths perceptible to anyone who will undergo the necessary intellectual discipline', by a 'riot of subjective visions' and 'the statesman and philosopher will become the butt of every farce and satire'.[4] But Simeon welcomes the incarnation: 'We may no longer . . . with the philosophers, deny the Multiplicity, asserting that God is One who has no need of friends and is indifferent to a World of Time and Quantity and Horror which he did not create' (*CLP*, p. 183). Auden's own sympathies lie with Multiplicity. His relish of the variety of the material world shows poetically in the witty lists found in such poems as 'Spain 1937', 'Vespers', and 'The Cave of Nakedness'; his relish of the material of language shows in his constant technical display. So far, it would appear he rejects the transcendent for the multiplicity of the body and of the created world.

Yet Auden can himself write as a dualist. There are moments when he opposes a transcendental vision to human experience. There is in him a tension between the transcendence he attacks in Plato and the Incarnation, a tension which is of course historically part of Christianity, with its own absorption of Platonism. The gap between flesh and spirit is constantly present: in comic terms at the end of 'The Sea and the Mirror', where a glimpse of transcendence is distanced as 'Wholly Other' (*CLP*, p. 250), soberly in 'Lullaby' (*CSP*, p. 107).

[3] E. Mendelson, editor, *The English Auden: Poems, Essays and Dramatic Writings 1927–1939* (London, 1977) (hereafter, *EA*). Auden, p. 345; 'Augustus to Augustine', *Forewords and Afterwords* (London, 1973; first published 1943) (hereafter *FA*), pp. 35–6.

[4] 'For the Time Being', W.H. Auden, *Collected Longer Poems* (London, 1968) (hereafter *CLP*), pp. 188–9.

Auden writes about the implications of being flesh in such terms as 'we are corporal contraptions',[5] made of the same physical material as animals and bound by the same physical laws: 'in anamnesis / Of what is excellent / Yet a visible creature'.[6] He uses the Platonic word and the language of dualism. And how can one verbalise these perceptions without using such a language? When he *affirms* 'Soul and body have no bounds', he is *writing* as if they are dual; if he unifies the dualism, it is by making verbal paradoxes.

'The Quest', a sequence of twenty poems (*CSP*, pp. 178–188), with its prologue, 'The Dark Years' (*CSP*, pp. 176–8), hopes that such dualism can be healed. Indeed, Auden hopes for more: 'embrace and encourage' is how he wishes the positive way of the incarnation and the negative way of the mystics to relate to each other. In fact, the sequence sways between the two. The incarnationalist asserts everywhere could be the place the quester seeks; there are sonnets warning about trying to be a spiritual hero and asserting the need to be ordinary. Particularly, 7 and 9 are critical of idealism. One begins with a tower like Yeats's; the other sends the quester up a winding stair to lose himself in uncreated being until the flesh, in a darkly comic way long fed-up with him, takes this as permission to destroy itself and him.

Yet the prologue, 'The Dark Years', speaks of God in the Platonic language of St John's Gospel, dualistically setting Him apart from the flesh and its contrasting 'shabby structures'. The opening poem of 'The Quest' is a vision of the quester's transcendental goal, glimpsed once, marvellous and totally inaccessible. Alice's wonderland is the symbolic notation for it, and the whole sequence draws on children's archetypal stories, at once concrete and magically remote, to suggest what is elusive beyond definition. The desire for this vision issues in the grief of the poems ('cry', 'grief', 'long', 'wish', 'thirst' are dominant words in them). Finally, in sharp opposition to poems 7 and 9 of the sequence, 17 and 18 are positive about the negative way. The questers set off into the 'blank and dumb' to their Nameless and Absconded God: the irony is turned on the commonsense world of the sane.

The poems are characteristically Auden's in their blend of longing for the visionary Good, their compassionate acceptance of human

[5] 'The Cave of Nakedness', *About the House* (London, 1966; first published 1959), p. 44.

[6] 'Bucolics' '1, Winds', Auden, *Collected Shorter Poems, 1927–57* (London, 1966) (hereafter, *CSP*), p. 256.

mediocrity and the wit with which the fairy-tale material is adapted to these:

> Enormous Alice (saw) a wonderland
> That waited for her in the sunshine and,
> Simply by being tiny, made her cry.
> ('The Quest', I, ll. 12–14)

THE VISION OF EROS

Auden and Plato both try to bridge the gap between the material and transcendent by what Auden calls 'the Vision of Eros'.[7] By this he means an experience of sacredness and glory through the experience of human love. This is absolutely central in his verse, and is, I think, close to the experience Diotima describes in the famous passage in *Symposium* 210–211. Again, Auden criticises Plato's version of the vision for having to leave the particular person behind and for creating a distance of 'many rungs' between the erotic vision and the Good, instead of Dante's 'one step'.[8] Yet he also says that Plato and Dante give the 'classic' and 'the two most serious' accounts of it, and are the only two who 'give a religious explanation of the Vision'.[9] So does Auden himself. They share an understanding of romantic love, and how it may be a means of access to divine love by providing a glimpse of God or Good. They both understand its longing and incompleteness (Diotima calls Eros 'son of poverty'; such a voice speaks as Ariel to Caliban), the need to purify Eros and transmute it into Agape, and Eros as the energy that leads to building the Just City (*New Year Letter* passim).

Again, Auden is divided. The Christian incarnationalist in him wants to keep human love close to divine love, but poem after poem admits how far it falls short. Though Plato writes perceptively on the terrible obsessiveness of Eros in the myth of the charioteer in *Phaedrus*, Auden, well-read in psychoanalysis, gives even more attention to its dangers and deceits ('Aphrodite's garden / Is a haunted region').[10] Even the pre-Christian Auden assumes '*The desires of the heart are as crooked as corkscrews*'.[11] People's ability to love is shaped by family history

[7] 'The Protestant Mystics', IV, 'The Vision of Eros', *FA*, p. 63.
[8] 'Shakespeare's Sonnets', *FA*, p. 102, 'The Vision of Eros', *FA*, p. 68.
[9] 'Shakespeare's Sonnets' and 'Protestant Mystics', *FA*, pp. 101, 65, 102.
[10] 'Twelve songs', VIII, *CSP*, p. 162. [11] 'Poems 1936–1939', IV, *EA*, p. 206.

Before this loved one
Was that one and that one
A family
And history.[12]

Ability to love is also shaped by the deficiencies of their culture which breed fear and denial. Human love is selfish (a 'two-faced dream "I want"') and deluded by fantasies and projections ('no one but myself is loved in this').[13] This is a long way from the love which is a knowledge of God.

Some later poems push the distance between the two loves to more comic lengths. 'The Love Feast' (*CSP*, p. 310), a title ironically evoking Ficino's Symposium as well as Plato's, sets up an extreme contrast between divine love and sexuality at a drunken New York party:

In an upper room at midnight,
See us gathered on behalf
Of love according to the gospel
Of the radio-phonograph.
(ll. 1–4)

The title suggests the Christian eucharist. 'In an upper room at midnight' reminds us of the Last Supper, when the eucharist was instituted; 'according to the gospel' is the language of liturgy. Then the stanza plunges into bathos. The extreme linguistic contrasts continue: 'The Love that rules the sun and stars' and the 'enthusiastic eyes' which 'Flicker after tits and baskets' (ll. 10–11). The contrast is both comic and indicative of the extreme distance between them.

However, he manages to keep the two loves so close in 'The Prophets (*CSP*, pp. 147–8); that it can be read both as a religious and as a love poem. It is a poem about the glimpses of the Good Place which a child had through his passion for machines and lead-mines, and ends,

And now I have an answer from the face
That never will go back in any book
But asks for all my life

He wrote it at the time when he returned to the church and met Chester Kallman. God's face or Chester's? Finally, the much more

[12] 'Poems 1927–1931', xv, *EA*, p. 31.
[13] *Ibid.*, I, p. 21, and 'Poems 1931–1936', XVII, *EA*, p. 145.

complex 'Lullaby' (*CSP*, pp. 106–7), one of the great poems on the Vision of Eros, combines both the antithesis between and the closeness of the human and divine. The Platonic words 'vision' and 'beauty' are repeated as the lover contemplates his 'grave' vision of 'the entirely beautiful'. Yet the hermit and the lovers, vision and sexuality are rhetorically set in opposition and he accepts that the vision is transient, subjective only, and that Venus' slope is 'enchanted', an ambiguous value. The poem is Neoplatonic in that the erotic experience leads to the religious vision (the knowing post-Freudian Auden adds that the reverse happens to the hermit, who experiences sensual ecstacy), but qualified in that there is no suggestion that the lovers must rise above being 'human' and 'mortal'. The prayer at the end to 'find the mortal world enough' wishes to preserve the human as well as the divine Eros.

These poems see romantic love as a manifestation of our longing for a lost and absolute Good, a fact that leads Auden to write that 'something like what we mean by romantic love' is found in Plato.[14] Yet Auden is also sceptical about whether such longing is an *anamnesis* of the Good. He knows that it is usually regressive, a child's wish for the lost Eden of the mother: the 'promiscuous pastures where the minotaur of authority is just a roly-poly ruminant and nothing is at stake'.[15] One of his best poems, 'In Praise of Limestone' (*CSP*, p. 238), owes its complex mixture of tones to a combination of this scepticism and longing. With amusement and wit, the voice describes a back-to-the-womb landscape whose inhabitants never have to grow up; then soberly admits that neither the greatly bad nor the greatly good are at home there. Finally, it addresses a lover, admitting that its love is inadequate and that a 'faultless love' is unimaginable, except by means of the human landscape that is both comically flawed and much desired. His sense of the absurdity of flawed human desire with its parody of *anamnesis* and his compassion towards it fuel the complex verse and are typical of Auden's love poetry.

THE JUST CITY

Auden's sad awareness of the flaws and selfishness of personal love leads him to acknowledge that it cannot build the Just City. It is too concerned with itself and its object; too little concerned with the rest

[14] 'The Greeks and Us', *FA*, p. 22.
[15] 'Caliban to the Audience', in 'The Sea and the Mirror', *CLP*, p. 243.

of the world: ('... business shivered in a banker's winter / While we were kissing').[16] But the Just City is one of his central concerns. Again, he attacks Plato. His Republic is a tyranny: 'We have seen with our own eyes the theory . . . put into practice, and the spectacle is anything but Utopian'.[17] Throughout his career, he attacks the closed and authoritarian society in both comic and horrific terms in such poems as 'The Unknown Citizen' (1939) and 'City without Walls' (1967).

Here again Auden defines himself against Plato and is farthest from him. Auden was as interested in the historical formation of society as of the individual: 'we are conscripts to our age'.[18] Although he agrees that Plato's proposed population of 5040 is 'about right',[19] conditions in the twentieth century are such that we know about other cultures and are faced with a whole world that must be transformed. The war in China is a 'local variant'.[20] The scale of his historical and cultural survey is necessarily much greater than Plato's. Further, Auden all through his career insisted on the unique value of every individual and on the necessity of free will. (He comments that choice is the weakest part of Greek ethics).[21] These are Christian values, and opposed to

> Plato's lie of intellect
> That all are weak but the Elect.[22]

Now, everyone has to be a hero, even the Chinese soldier who died ignorant of the Good.[23] Finally, he is aware that demands for law and order may spring from dubious motives,[24] and he would certainly disagree with *Laws* 797 that 'change – except when it is change from what is bad – is always highly perilous'.

Yet there is common ground: they both see the necessity for law. Auden recognises that man is a social being. The question is how to reconcile private and public, law and freedom. Auden's solution is to propose the law of love, a paradox commonplace in Christianity but quite different from Plato's literal idea of law. As early as 1932, long before he returned to the Christian church, he was writing of 'disciplined love'[25] as a solution to social injustice, though the phrase

[16] 'Poems 1931–1936', XVI, *EA*, p. 142. [17] 'The Greeks and Us', *FA*, p. 29.
[18] 'New Year Letter', *CLP*, p. 115. [19] 'Reading', *DH*, p. 7.
[20] 'In Time of War': 'Commentary', *EA*, p. 264. [21] 'The Greeks and Us', *FA*, p. 28.
[22] 'New Year Letter', *CLP*, p. 121. [23] *Ibid.*, p. 126; 'In Time of War', XVIII, *EA*, p. 258.
[24] Also 'Letter to Lord Byron', part 2, *EA*, p. 181.
[25] 'Poems 1931–1936', XVI, *EA*, p. 144.

is a vague one. 'September 1, 1939' diagnoses the cause of war as warped, selfish love. The Christian Auden proposes a 'Law like Love' (1939). At the end of 'Vespers' (1954) freedom and order are reconciled by Christ: 'For without a cement of blood (it must be human, it must be innocent) no secular wall will safely stand' (*CSP*, p. 333). Auden's Just City is by now both an image of the perfection which man should strive towards and use to judge actuality, and a perfection not to be gained through human activity, a state of grace, Augustine's City of God.

By 1933, Auden, like Plato, was struggling to reconcile his vision of love with practical realities. Auden included part of *Letter Seven* in his selection from Plato. Plato was brave – and rash – enough to suggest a system. At least, Auden, after real experience of fascism, took it seriously as a system, though he admitted that *The Republic* can be read as 'playful'.[26] He himself invented systems only in play ('Under which Lyre'; 'Vespers'; 'Reading': *DH*, p.6). His Edens – perhaps he is cocking a snook at Plato? – are emphatically not places of law and order. He has serious objections to the law that is not love, but he knows that his Eden is regressive and comic. However, the difficulty is seriously treated in 'A Summer Night' (1933). The opening stanzas of the poem describe an experience of love shared by a group. Auden calls it 'the Vision of Agape' in his prose account of it (*FA*, p. 69), and it was one of the formative moments of his life. Yet most of the poem is about private joy ignoring what is going on in the world, where the flood is preparing to break over Europe and destroy it, and it is vulnerable to criticisms of its liberal guilt and wish to retain selfish cosiness. Auden's dilemma is that the vision may need 'excuse', and the poem ends with a prayer, a wish, not an assertion, that the vision of Agape may be part of a new 'strength' after the world has fallen in pieces and begun to grow again.

New Year Letter also tackles the problem of building the Just City 'now' at the point of time to which our history and cultural development has brought us. Again, his solution is Eros – he uses Plato's word – whose 'legislative will' is to build it. Since the poem sketches the development of Western culture from the Renaissance to the present and outlines various philosophical and theological positions, it is necessarily analytic and discursive, the short couplets often epigrammatic. Yet repeatedly the sentences slip on and on for

[26] 'The Greeks and Us', *FA*, p. 29.

long paragraphs, accumulating association and suggestion, until at the end less has been defined than a vision suggested, and the poem ends with an invocation of God. Again, the complexity of the poem comes from the tension between Agape and the material world.

THE ROLE OF THE ARTIST

I would like to end with Auden specifically exploring how the tension between material and transcendent affects poetry. Auden did not share Plato's conviction that poetry is necessarily dangerous: 'Poetry makes nothing happen'[27] was his conclusion by 1939. Like Plato, however, he thought that the demands of truth and good were paramount. Plato sacrificed poets to the Republic; Auden wrote: 'To a Christian, unfortunately, both art and science are secular activities, that is to say, small beer'.[28] They share concern about the truthfulness of art. 'The Sea and the Mirror' is the poem in which Auden examines the dilemma of the Christian artist. It is subtitled 'A Commentary on Shakespeare's *The Tempest*'. In it, one character from the play after another speaks: Prospero is the poet, Ariel his imagination, and Caliban his carnal being. Auden's concerns here are also Plato's: poetry as magic (*Republic* 601), without serious claims to truth (*Republic* 608); language as inadequate to express the nature of reality (*Letter Seven* 342–343).

Auden questions the truth of poetry on these same three grounds. First, it is a kind of magic. Poets, in this poem, are conjurers (Preface): that is, they entertain with deceptions and illusions and so are morally suspect. The source of this desire for illusion, shared by writer and reader, is the wish to deny reality and create a world suited to the self. Auden draws on metaphors from dream and fairy story to suggest a childish world rather than an adult grip on reality. Children fantasise to 'ride away from a father's imperfect justice' (Prospero), adults to hold their fear of mortality at bay. Desirable as the magic is, it is a source of sin: childish dreams ('where each believed all wishes wear a crown' (Sebastian)) survive in the murderous adult Sebastian and make his brother seem so unreal that he is prepared to murder him.

Further, the 'autonomous completed state(s)'[29] that a poem is makes it totally different from human experience. Ariel is 'unanxious'; he and Auden's poem sing 'lightly'. To Auden the human condition is

[27] 'In Memory of W.B. Yeats', II, *CSP*, p. 142.
[28] 'The Shield of Perseus' ('Postscript'), *DH*, p. 456. [29] 'New Year Letter', *CLP*, p. 81.

characterised by necessary freedom and necessary anxiety. Music (and poetry) can 'only play'[30] and consequently 'Art is not life and cannot be / A midwife to society'.[31] In the Epilogue, Ariel, 'Elegance, art, fascination', longs to be completed by Caliban, the flesh, 'drab mortality'. By playing with the syntax, which makes the word ambiguous, Auden unites them in the 'I' of the refrain. But this reconciliation happens only in the poem, not in the real world.[32]

Finally, poetry falsifies. It cannot express the unassimilable. (Caliban represents this, but is paradoxically assimilated into the pattern of the poem.) Language itself falsifies: 'In whose booming eloquence / Honesty became untrue' (Gonzalo) (*CLP*, p. 215). 'I never suspected the way of truth / Was a way of silence', says Prospero (*CLP*, p. 209). It is at the moment when 'there is nothing to say' that we glimpse the 'real Word' (Caliban)(*CLP*, p. 249). That ultimate truth cannot be spoken is familiar from the mystics, and is the central dilemma of the Christian poet.

However, faced with these Platonic doubts, Auden does not banish the poets. He preserves them both as a mirror in which we see the distance between what we are and what we should be, and as an inadequate reflection of the real, an extension of the Platonic Eros. The honesty of art is to acknowledge that it is 'tall tales' only and that truth is found in silence:

> What but tall tales, the luck of verbal playing,
> Can trick his lying nature into saying
> That love, or truth in any serious sense,
> Like orthodoxy, is a reticence[33]

This provides a justification for Auden's playfulness and inventiveness, and is where for him the moral and aesthetic combine. 'The Sea and the Mirror' exemplifies what it says. It is teasingly about another work of art (*The Tempest*) about art; it playfully modernises Prospero; Caliban's monologue is absurdly inappropriate: an extraordinarily elaborate parody of late Henry James; it handles one difficult lyric form after another; it puns and plays with the material of language. And it asks

> Can I learn to suffer
> Without saying something ironic or funny
> On suffering?
>
> (Prospero, *CLP*, p. 209)

[30] 'Anthem for St. Cecilia's Day', II, *CSP*, p. 174. [31] 'New Year Letter', *CLP*, p. 81.
[32] 'The Virgin and the Dynamo', *DH*, p. 71.
[33] 'The Truest Poetry is the Most Feigning', *CSP*, p. 317.

I would like to suggest that in this fine poem about poetry the struggle between Platonist and poet in Auden leads to some of his most characteristic poetry: a playful, witty display of technical mastery, which actually produces haunting sadness, because it emphasises the gap between its own surface and the painful longing for an elusive and perfect truth.

CHAPTER 30

Platonism in Iris Murdoch

Peter Conradi

Iris Murdoch poses two questions that link her intimately to Plato: what is goodness or what is a good man like? And what is the place of love and desire within the quest for goodness? These questions recur throughout her twenty-four (to date) novels and her few, sometimes slender and yet very influential works of moral philosophy. The nature of goodness and its relationship with love: these are preoccupations in her philosophy and her fiction alike.

The West owes to Plato the invention of the soul, and thus also the idea of morality as *aspiration*. Just as Plato's picture of man as possessing a soul was a revolutionary one,[1] so to argue for the soul today has once again become a radical move. Unlike Plato, Murdoch certainly does not wish to argue for the soul's immortality: rather she wishes to insist that human life concerns a mysterious battle between good and evil, and that we are essentially spiritual beings.

This distinguishes her from other twentieth-century writers who are Plato-haunted. The Modernists – Eliot, Pound, Yeats – often turn to Plato for an *aesthetic* rationale. They variously find in Plato ways of under-writing the authority of the separate and other-worldly realm of art. Art is to occupy a zone beyond either history, contingency or messy individuality, and beyond, indeed, democracy too. The Modernists and Symbolists 'refuse to conceive of perfection in human terms';[2] which is to say that they seek to redeem the horrors of contingency – of chance and necessity, or, as a Neoplatonist might put it, of multiplicity – through a resort to myth and symbol. They attempt a literature of the 'metaphysical task',[3] to whose stylistic self-consciousness and narcissism, and whose tendencies towards abstraction and integration, Murdoch's early essays are hostile.

[1] See F.M. Cornford, *Before and After Socrates* (Cambridge, 1932).
[2] Iris Murdoch, 'The Sublime and the Beautiful Revisited', *Yale Review*, 49 (1959), 247–71.
[3] Murdoch, *Sartre, Romantic Rationalist* (London, 1953), p. 30.

Modernism is marked by an apocalyptic hatred of the present and a disdain for ordinary consciousness; and by a conception of the artist borrowed from Romanticism as an aristocrat doomed to exile in an inhospitable age. Eliot's work, for example, is marked alike by a fear of sexuality and an elegiac mistrust of the contemporary. Joyce simultaneously exalts and demeans the characters of *Ulysses* through his mock-epic, mock-heroic and essentially *comedic* Homeric correspondences. Woolf holds out a distant promise that the flux in which we are immersed might be redeemed by symbol, by art, and by love. Murdoch, by contrast – and perhaps in this echoing Auden – argues for a greater patience with this flux, with the difficulties of knowing other people, which can happen only through the agencies of love and attention. Art is for her an imperfect realm, even at best. Yet it is precisely because art is necessarily wounded, in her view, that it can help to heal the imperfect human world it must reflect and serve.

Perhaps this is to say that there have always been two Platos, not one. The authoritarian Plato feared by Popper never constituted the whole story.[4] In 1866 Walter Pater attacked Coleridge's 'lust for the Absolute' and chose a more relaxed and sceptical position (see Anne Varty, pp. 261–2 above). Against Coleridge's remorseless idealism with its coercion of human difference, Pater argued for a liberal Platonism, and for the habit of 'tentative thinking and suspended judgement'.[5] For this Platonism the novel has always been an apt vehicle, as D.H. Lawrence pointed out, mercifully incapable of the Absolute. Julia Kristeva has noted the resemblance between Socratic dialogue and the ambivalent word of the novel;[6] and Bakhtin too saw how the Dialogues subvert any claims to ready-made truth, a subversion he admires in fiction too.[7] As Iris Murdoch has put this herself, the novel is 'the most imperfect of art-forms'.[8]

In her own fiction, the idea of provisionality itself has always had some special power. In her first novel *Under the Net* (1954) with its rapidly changing and collapsing scenery, the artist-narrator Jake, who 'hates contingency'[9] is taught by the plot and by his foil Hugo Belfounder, to move towards some healing surrender to the picaresque

[4] K. Popper, *The Open Society and its Enemies*, 2 vols (London, 1962), vol. 1 'The Spell of Plato'.
[5] Pater's article in *Westminster Review*, 85 (1866), 49–50 was published anonymously. See also his *Plato and Platonism* (London, 1893), and Anne Varty's essay in this volume.
[6] Julia Kristeva, *Desire in Language*, trans. L. Roudiez *et al.* (Oxford, 1980), pp. 80ff.
[7] Mikhail Bakhtin, *Problems of Dostoevsky's Poetics*, trans. and ed. C. Emerson (Manchester, 1984).
[8] Murdoch, 'Force Fields', *New Statesman*, 3 Nov. 1978, p. 586.
[9] Murdoch, *Under the Net* (Harmondsworth, 1954), p. 24.

sea of contingency in which he, like everyone, is immersed. Hugo has the instructive gift of being able to love and honour particulars, as well as to renounce a selfish love. The different modes of being and seeing embodied by Jake and Hugo mark the first of Murdoch's recurrent oppositions between artist and saint.[10] Her rapid supercession of one novel by another, her throw-away imagery and migrating themes and motifs, pick up this aspect of Platonism. In the *Theatetus* Plato dismisses one of his own arguments. In the *Parmenides* and *Sophist* he dismantles earlier imagery to replace it with new imagery in the *Timaeus* where, however, he warns his readers against looking for more than a likely story. Since the Good itself is indefinable and cannot be inscribed, her work, like Plato's, is in pursuit of imperfection,[11] 'an investigation that never ends, rather than a means of resolving anything',[12] as she has put it.

THE MORAL ENQUIRY

As for the nature of this enquiry, it is of course a moral one. Two of Iris Murdoch's early lovers were, one directly in 1944, the other indirectly in 1952, victims of Hitler and died young.[13] Moreover Murdoch spent the period 1944–6 working as Administrative Officer with the United Nations Relief and Rehabilitation Administration in England, Belgium and Austria, working with victims of concentration camps and deportations. Yet philosophy, in the very period of Hitler and Stalin, had emasculated itself and become the whore of a Rationalism at once 'scientistic' and romantic, incapable of interestingly addressing the moral. Existentialism had then at least the apparent attraction of continuing to speak of consciousness and of value at a time when Anglo-Saxon philosophy was bankrupt of ability to speak interestingly of either. Murdoch explored Existentialism and wrote a notable early book on Sartre.[14] Yet both Existentialism and Anglo-Saxon philosophy came, in the end, to seem equally facile. Both evacuated inwardness through dignifying a romantic voluntarism or cult of the will. Both falsely divided man between an image of total freedom and determinism. Indeed Murdoch came to see the Anglo-Saxon tradition as crypto-Existentialist.

[10] See Peter J. Conradi, *Iris Murdoch: The Saint and the Artist*, 2nd edn (London, 1989), *passim*, from which the present essay borrows freely.

[11] See Lorna Sage, 'The Pursuit of imperfection', *Critical Quarterly*, 19 (1977), 67–87.

[12] J. Barrows, 'Living Writers, 7', *John o'London's*, 4 May 1961, p. 495.

[13] S. Summers and F. Hauptfuhrer, 'The Lost Loves of Irish Murdoch', *Mail on Sunday: You Magazine*, 5 June 1988, pp. 17–21.

[14] See note 3.

Murdoch's philosophy and fiction alike are thereafter in strong revolt against this world-view and of the popular 'hero-of-the-will' to whom Existentialism had given birth in mid-century fiction.[15] In the 1950s she found a valuable ally in this battle in the work of Simone Weil, whose thought helped deepen her moral address, and also enabled her the better to understand Plato, whom she had been routinely taught at Oxford, and was herself teaching. At Oxford 'there was no wide consideration of [Plato], he was simply misunderstood. I learnt nothing of value about him as an undergraduate (he was regarded as 'literature') . . . Simone Weil helped me very much'. Having read 'Greats' herself as a student, Murdoch was able to return to him in the original Greek – 'his voice sounds in Greek'.[16]

Weil, drawing on Plato, on the Christian mystics and on Buddhism, saw morality as a form of un-selfing through the discipline of attention. What this comes to mean, in Murdoch's re-interpretation, is that human beings inhabit a cloud of egoistic fantasy, designed to protect the psyche from pain. Such fantasy is not neutral but highly consequential – the 'gravity' in Weil's famous phrase, that prevents 'grace'.[17] The power of imaginative attention alone can – albeit with difficulty – cut through this fantastic reverie and start to reveal the world and its inhabitants more accurately. Real freedom is not in this view a jumping-about of the will but the total absence of concern for Self, the energy of which is burnt up in its strenuous effort to proceed towards the Good, which is to say the Real. Murdoch uses two myths as explanatory devices to describe this pilgrimage away from fantasy and towards the Real. Crucial to this enquiry is the Platonic myth of the Fire and the Sun. (To her use of myth of Apollo and Marsyas, I return later).

The Sovereignty of Good (1970) leads up slowly to an exposition of the first of these myths. Its austere project is to rescue a religious picture of man from the necessary and in some ways welcome collapse of all dogma, to attack all forms of false consolation, romanticism, and self-consciousness, and to address the degeneration of Good within morals. The disappearance of God is not for her an excuse for the intense metaphysical self-pity of so many twentieth-century writers. On the contrary, it poses an essential challenge. Without the childish bribes of 'God-the-Father' and the after-life, religion – if it neither disappears nor becomes demonic – could at last come into its own.

[15] See Murdoch's 'Existentialists and Mystics' in W. Robson (ed.), *Essays and Poems Presented to Lord David Cecil* (London, 1970). [16] Letter to the author, January 1992.

[17] S. Weil, *Gravity and Grace*, translated by E. Craufurd (London, 1952).

Man could at last, in a famous phrase, be good *for nothing*.[18] The idea of a reward for virtue appears to her, as to other mystics, blasphemous, and to call into question the idea of goodness itself in the first place. She is sustained in this quest to reinvent the spirit of morality and truth by Plato's discovery of the Form of the Good, and the 'ontological proof' which supports it.[19]

In *The Sovereignty of Good* Murdoch memorably reinterprets Plato's great myth of the Fire and the Sun, to make room for Freud and Existentialism within it. This myth shows the moral pilgrim progressing through a series of states of consciousness, each of which turns out to seem provisional, obsolescent, illusory, as it is seen through and discarded. The prisoners who manage to turn round at look at the fire are seen as having achieved the feat, of which so much fuss has been made in contemporary thinking, of *self-awareness*. The Fire, in other words, is seen as something like the Freudian Ego: a source of real heat and light which we may falsely mistake for that of the Sun. The victory of psychoanalysis (and perhaps Existentialism) is to teach us to turn round sufficiently to confront this energetic heat-and-light source. But this is a dangerous discovery by which we may be further distracted, fascinated, and delayed. Freud in other words gives us among the best and most 'up-to-date' pictures we have of life in the Cave, and of the Fallen man who lives there, enslaved to fantasy and therefore doomed to relive the patterns of mechanical desire. He says nothing, on the other hand, about life in the Sun. Freud wanted to make men workable: Plato wanted to make men good.

Although I shall address Murdoch's fiction later on, its treatment of psychoanalysts and psychiatrists could be mentioned here, a treatment often satirical, if not hostile. Palmer Anderson in *A Severed Head* (1961) is typical in his pronouncements about the psyche being largely mechanical, 'and mechanical models are the best to understand it by'.[20] Palmer thus gives the best available description of the mechanics of the novel's *plot*, which was widely misunderstood by critics, and which turns upon a series of compensatory promiscuous love-affairs, each energised by individual life-myths. But Palmer is also a demon, and expresses this dangerous half-truth about the

[18] The phrase is oddly given to the demonic priest Carel Fisher in *The Time of the Angels* (St Albans, 1978), p. 165.

[19] Murdoch fully discusses this difficult idea in *Metaphysics as a Guide to Morals* (London, 1992), ch. 13, 'The Ontological Proof'.

[20] Murdoch, *A Severed Head* (Harmondsworth, 1963), p. 31.

psyche-in-the-Cave in order to further his own interests in terms of love and power. Psychoanalysis 'generates self-concern, it degrades Eros, it lacks and so cannot account for spiritual purpose, it is too abstract and crude to capture the complex thereness of persons'.[21] In *The Black Prince* (1973) the author campaigns against and equates Freudians and reductionists, and in the Dostoevskian failure and buffoon Francis Marloe, finds exactly such a fatuous misinterpreter of the novel's events. In the next novel *The Sacred and Profance Love-Machine* (1974), Blaise Gavender is a psychiatrist who is also a temporiser, a sexual cheat and a poor listener who reduces all experience to formula. Only in *The Good Apprentice* (1985) is there a 'good' psychiatrist in Thomas McCaskerville, and his virtue is in exact proportion to his disillusion with psychiatry and his adoption of a quasi-Buddhist philosophy of dying-into-life in its place.

'Freud more than once labels himself as a Platonist',[22] Murdoch tells us; and where she admires Freud, it is often when Freud's indebtedness to Plato can be elicited. The discovery of the unconscious can be related back both to the Cave and to doctrine of *anamnesis*, for example. But, above all, Freud vouchsafed that 'the enlarged sexuality of psycho-analysis coincides with the Eros of the divine Plato'.[23] Eros, to the Greeks, is a divine power driving us towards the world and linking us with others. Socrates speaks of love as the *only* thing he understands (*Symposium* 177d). And Weil, asking rhetorically for the name of the force that enslaves the prisoners within the Cave, and for the name of the force that liberates, gives the same answer to each question: Eros, or the doctrine of the continuity of apparently disparate and unlike desires.[24] Low Eros (blind, obsessive, mechanical desire) enslaves; High Eros (desire educated or purified) liberates. Like Plato and Freud, Murdoch gives to sexual love and to transformed sexual energy the central place in her thinking. The Erotic dialogues (*Symposium*; *Phaedrus*) *complete* the myth of the Fire and the Sun, by evoking the processes by which we learn to purify and educate this desire-stream. 'A purified sexual desire, the good Eros, could lead us to Enlightenment':[25] that is, could help start to move us away from fantasy toward a more accurate apprehension of the

[21] David Gordon, 'Iris Murdoch's Comedies of Unselfing', *Twentieth Century Literature*, 36 (1990), 123. [22] Murdoch, *Metaphysics as a Guide to Morals*, ch. 1.

[23] Freud, *Three Essays on the Theory of Sexuality* (London, 1977), p. 43.

[24] Simone Weil, *Notebooks*, vol. 2, trans. A. Wills (London, 1956), pp. 383–4.

[25] Murdoch, 'Art is the Imitation of Nature', *Cahiers du Centre de Recherches sur les Pays du Nord et du Nord-Ouest* (1978), 60.

contingency and variety of the world and of the uniqueness of the individuals it contains.

Love and goodness, in other words, are at the centre of Murdoch's thought and relate her moral philosophy to her fiction, if not always simply. Both her ethics and her fiction concern the understanding of *individuals*; and individuals have a way of cutting through theory, particularly in a good novel.

THE AESTHETIC ENQUIRY

As I have suggested, Murdoch refuses to separate the ideal, the transcendent, from the flux of actual life. Philosophy and art must have experiential dimensions for her, rather than act as an access to any other realm than the one we already share but fail, in her view, to see. Transcendence, in other words, means transcendence of the ego, not of the sublunary world itself. Like another recent Platonist, Hans-Georg Gadamer, Murdoch takes the Platonic myths not as an ecstacy that transports us to another world, but as ironic counter-images of the process by which we attain a more accurate perception of this one. Love and its purification provide one means to this end; the other – as for all Neoplatonists – is of course art. Love and art are paths towards the Good, which is to say that they may provide a means towards un-selfing.

In *The Fire and the Sun* (1977) she lucidly explicates Plato's distrust of art, contesting that distrust as if to a commentator on the contemporary scene, connecting Plato's objections to those other humblers of art, Kant and Freud. Plato wrote poetry which he later destroyed, and is himself a great artist so far as his invention and supercession of his own imagery is concerned. The figure of an anti-art artist who fears or suspects his own talent recurs in her early novels, in Hugo from *Under the Net* and Bledyard in *The Sandcastle*. Yet Plato 'never did justice to the unique truth-conveying capacities of art'.[26] She rejects the classic Neoplatonic sleight-of-hand by which art co-opts the Forms themselves, a view untruthful about the degree to which even great art is on terms not just with contingency but with muddle. Art is, on the other hand, 'at least more valuable to the moralist as an auxiliary than it is dangerous as an enemy'.[27] It is indeed the greatest of what Weil terms our *metaxu* or intermediaries, those messengers that either lead us towards the spiritual or point in its direction.

[26] Murdoch, *The Fire and the Sun* (Oxford, 1977), p. 85. [27] *Ibid.*, p. 77.

In *Metaphysics as a Guide to Morals* (1992), loosely based on her 1982 Gifford lectures, Plato is described as aware of current twentieth century problems. This is partly because, for her, we still live in a Greek light, partly because she finds in Plato an acute commentator on such contemporary issues as doubts about the empirical self, as well as doubts about the ontological and moral ambiguity of art, which makes of Plato a forerunner of the structuralists. Plato's interest in iconoclasm, demythologisation and morality takes on a special force since Plato, like us, inhabits an age in which our entire world-view, religion included, is undergoing systematic 'demythologisation' (a key word in this study), and the 'Noble Lies' by which we live become problematic. Plato is her hero because he champions transcendence and sees demythologisation as a route towards it (as in the Allegory of Fire and Sun). Structuralism is the enemy because it demythologises transcendence itself. This touches both religion and art. Christianity is to survive through being demythologised: Christ becomes the Buddha-of-the-West, a human not a divine figure whose life is in itself a kind of showing. And what is shown by a good life is the pilgrimage towards the sun, itself a process of demythologisation or discarding of specious and illusory goods. So far as art goes, a triumphalist view of great art is again rehearsed, through which the mysteries of good and evil can be re-explained in each generation. Though much of this book is detailed and technical and directed towards the professional philosopher, there is none the less some interesting literary criticism, notably of Shakespearian tragedy.

The most accessible account of Murdoch's conversation with Plato is to be found in *Acastos*, the two Platonic dialogues she published in 1986. In that each contains a group of characters, they recall the *Symposium*. But they are also imaginative treatises, within which Plato is depicted as an unbalanced twenty-year-old whose moral absolutism needs to be tempered by Socrates' wisdom. Both Plato and Socrates here are aspects of a single truth, and form two halves of the dualism I earlier noted. They may also be said to represent two aspects of Iris Murdoch herself.

These dialogues are to be performed in either 'period' or modern dress, with only one episode (concerning slavery) requiring adaptation in the former case. It is striking that an author should use the dialogue form successfully today, and the 'platform' performances (so-called) of *Art and Eros* at the National Theatre in 1982 were memorable and well-received. Both work not just as *pastiche* but are also filled with a fierce and contemporary moral urgency. Murdoch's Platonism has always been open to currents of contemporary thought. Rather than using him to levitate out of our condition, she has sought with his help the more zealously to engage with her time. Her Plato is our contemporary since he pioneers a way of thinking about the fate of spirituality, and the fate of art, in a post-religious age. The first dialogue – *Art and Eros* – centres on art; the second, *Above the Gods*, on religion. But the fate of spirituality figures in both. Both see the present age as a dangerous interim, with the survival of religion beyond mere superstition and magic in question. Both debate the need for a re-invention of religion, for its continual remaking into something we can believe. Both concern the place of Eros, in life and in art:

> Art comes from the deep soul where a great force lives, and this force is sex and love and desire – desire for power, desire for knowledge, desire for God – what makes us good or bad – and without this force there is no art, and no science either and no, no man – without Eros man is a ghost. But with Eros he can be – either a demon or – Socrates.[28]

EROS IN THE NOVELS

Murdoch's philosophy, on the one hand, points towards a 'higher' and more sublimated consciousness, associated with virtue. Her tragi-comic plots, on the other hand, are frequently chronicles of desublimation and of the punishment and even annihilation of puritans. The idea-play enjoins a slow unselfing ('We cannot suddenly change ourselves');[29] the action warns us, as does Weil in her study *The Need for Roots*, against a fast unselfing.

The depiction of Eros is necessarily complicated by the fact that art has its own roots in the unconscious, which is to say in the Cave, the realm of substitution and repetition; and, despite some priggish interpretations, Murdoch's fictional treatments of Eros are not narrowly moralistic but, at their best, generous, humane and above all comic. With these provisos, certain Platonic themes recur: the view of human life as a pilgrimage away from fantasy and towards imagination; the concern, from Hugo in *Under the Net* to Stuart in *The Good Apprentice* to depict a good person who is always – like Socrates in the *Symposium* – a *particular* good person, one whose idiosyncrasies and virtues necessarily interpenetrate; the conflict of saint and artist which I have discussed elsewhere.

[28] Murdoch, *Acastos: Two Platonic Dialogues* (London, 1987), p. 53.
[29] Murdoch, *The Sovereignty of Good* (London, 1970), p. 39.

Murdoch's fiction may be crudely divided into three phases: the early novels of the 1950s, in which she rehearses with great assurance different sub-genres of romance; a middle period during the 1960s during which she struggles with, and against, her own Platonism; and a mature phase starting in 1970 with *A Fairly Honourable Defeat*, where her desire to explore character, as well as tell an ingenious story, comes into its own. I shall look briefly at each phase.

In *The Bell*, her most achieved early novel, a background Platonism is already visible. It is the first in what is to become a series of novels that take a leading character with a spoiled religious vocation – a spoiled priest (*Henry and Cato*; *The Philosopher's Pupil*), monk (*The Nice and the Good*), or nun (*Nuns and Soldiers*). The novels witness her interest in the purifying of Eros. Michael Meade, failed priest and failed schoolmaster, gives up his family home, Imber Court, to become a place of religious retreat. There is a motto on the old house – AMOR VITA MEA – which echoes the inscription on the other-worldly bell of the title – EGO VOX AMORIS SUM: *Amor*, or Eros, rules everywhere. Michael is typical of many of Murdoch's fictional ascetics and would-be seekers who wish to levitate prematurely out of their condition and leave it behind: to be better than they should be. The way up, however, as for Heraclitus, turns out to be the way down. The actual plot forces Michael, like other aspirants, into a deeper and humbler apprehension of the energies that have shaped his life *as it already is*, an education that characteristically resembles a *katabasis* or descent into chaos or contingency. The chastening he movingly suffers is an encounter with the sublime, a purging descent into particulars.

The middle phase that followed *The Bell* could be termed her most 'mythological'. It coincided with the 1960s, that decade of a general rediscovery of Eros by so many in the West, for which her work can be read both as prophecy and as map. It now seems that she was, during the 1960s, struggling to transmute her Platonism into an intelligible public rhetoric. Reviewers were sometimes left unconvinced and she may temporarily have lost readers also. Her chief ambition as a novelist – to allow the expansion of character to occur against the 'myth' of the novel – was in this decade sometimes left half-realised. If there is a key to understanding a Murdoch plot of this vintage, it is given variously by Palmer Anderson when he pronounces on the essentially mechanical nature of the psyche;[30] by the yet more

[30] Murdoch, *Severed Head*, p. 31.

demonic Julius King when he sneers that, 'Human beings are essentially finders of substitutes . . . Anyone will do to play the roles;'[31] and by Bradley Pearson's insight that, 'the unconscious delights in identifying people with each other. It has only a few characters to play with.'[32]

We could translate this into Platonic-Freudian language by saying that human beings inhabit the Cave where, in being victims of blind and unconscious need, they *repeat* certain relationships, whose victims they then become. Many novels at this period employ a repeating plot, and show their characters as slaves or casualties of repetition or substitution. This 'insight' sometimes reads stylishly, sometimes schematically. As for 'goodness', and the chances of seeing and celebrating human 'otherness', many Murdoch characters undergo a crash-course in maturity and are inducted into the mysteries of our communal enslavement in ways which may – although the endings are often equivocal – augur slightly better for their future chances of transcending slavery.

One important enemy to goodness often lies in the power of the past. Among the most successful novels of the 1960s are *The Nice and the Good* (1968) and *Bruno's Dream* (1969). Plato is recalled in each title. *The Nice and the Good* points to what separates ordinary hedonism from virtue, taking a whole cast of characters variously and comically haunted by past misfortune, and exploring the ways very different temperaments move variously towards love, forgiveness, and reconciliation. As for Bruno's 'dream', it is also his *eikasia*, the lowest stage of Platonic illusion. The very elderly Bruno also wishes to make his peace with the past, and his dying is lovingly set against a symbolic city-scape of Fulham, Baron's Court and Battersea, between the Lots Road power-station, figuring the naked energies of Eros – and the Brompton Road cemetery (death), while the river Thames runs redemptively (or not) nearby. These Neoplatonic themes of love and death are worked out with a characteristic nerve and inventiveness and 'worked' also through the dance of the lovers that, as often, occupies the foreground. 'One isn't anything, and yet one loves people', is Diana's very moving *anagnorisis*, nursing the dying Bruno at the end, awoken to a vision of love purified or purged that echoes Bruno's own dying wisdom.

Such playful schematism, however, begins to look crude when set

[31] Murdoch, *A Fairly Honourable Defeat* (Harmondsworth, 1972), p. 233.
[32] *The Black Prince* (Harmondsworth, 1975), p. 195.

by the side of the best work of her latest phase, from 1970 onwards. Although *A Fairly Honourable Defeat* (1970), which inaugurates this mature phase, makes use of allegory, it is an enabling, not a determining use; and the escape from allegory is the rule from now on. The shape of her career has been towards a use of myth that is consciously disposable and provisional, subordinated to character. As she becomes surer of her own moral psychology and philosophy, she becomes less absolute, more dialectical and playful, patient and relaxed. Her explorations during the 1960s look like a necessary prelude to her mature phase, where she is able to combine atmospheric intensity and poetry, with a newly powerful grasp of character. And her best work from this date also often recalls Shakespeare, who offers a model to her desire to marry the pleasures of an unusual tale and a naturalistic use of character.

This mature phase begins, with triumphant confidence, with the superbly assured *A Fairly Honourable Defeat*, a Mozartian novel set in South Kensington, involving a *psychomachia* between a Christ-figure and a Satan-figure, and the destruction of the blandly optimistic Platonist Rupert Foster. He is destroyed not because his ethic is false – 'cosy Platonic uplift'[33] as the devilish Julius puts it – but because he is unable fully to inhabit it.

In *The Black Prince* (1973) the question of whether this philosophy is fully habitable by *anyone* gets addressed. If one had to single out one novel that, more than any other, bears the marks of Murdoch's absorption in Platonic thought, it would have to be *The Black Prince* (1973). A gripping thriller, a black book about marriage and about authorial rivalry, it is also a reflective book about the Platonic Eros, in all its darkness and ambiguous power. It is sub-titled 'A celebration of love', since, 'man's creative struggle, his search for wisdom and truth, is a love story' (p. 9). The novel is narrated by Bradley Pearson, but framed by Bradley's prison-friend 'Loxias' – one name of Apollo – and there are allusions, some jokey, throughout, to that greatest of Neoplatonic myths of ascesis, the flaying of Marsyas by Apollo.[34]

Bradley is first flayed by undergoing much that frightens him. He is a spinsterish, puritanical, selfish, blocked writer who fears women, betrayal, emotion, loss of control. He is waiting for the right conditions to write his masterpiece (the novel itself): but it is precisely

[33] *Defeat*, p. 222.

[34] See Edgar Wind, *Pagan Mysteries in the Renaissance* (London, 1968), ch. xi, 'The Flaying of Marsyas', pp. 173ff.

the 'wrong' ones which are to catalyse his writing. Despite his attempts to keep contingency at bay, the horror of the world keeps breaking in. His friend (who is also his rival), Arnolf Baffin, embroils him in his marriage difficulties; his predatory ex-wife reappears after years in America; his sister suffers the painful collapse of a disastrously unhappy marriage. Above all, Bradley suffers first the partial ascesis involved in falling desperately in love with Baffin's daughter, who is much younger than him. He then is further 'unselfed' by losing her, and by being falsely punished for a murder he may have willed but did not commit. He is obliged to make some healing surrender before his own end. Eros is necessary to his quest: without it there would have been no journey, and nothing learnt.

The myth of Apollo and Marsyas is partly a cautionary tale about an artist who competes with the divine, partly a tale of divinely inspired ascesis. Bradley is taught 'the pain and final joy gained from loss of self and loving attention to the world'.[35] He is flayed, if not into the truth, at least into starting to see the direction in which truth might lie, both as moral agent, and also as an artist. There are echoes of Dostoevsky, like whose novels this is both acutely distressing and wildly funny. There are allusions to *Hamlet*: a fast-paced story alternates with Hamlet-like soliloquies on the relations between art, consciousness, suffering and truth, meditations that often recall or directly name Plato. Through such meditations Murdoch voices more nakedly and movingly than elsewhere in her fiction (and by an implicit analogy, the novel suggests, with Shakespeare's *oratio recta* in *Hamlet*) her own concerns. Although the novel contains destruction, it also embodies a wise and moving and essentially comic vindication of Murdoch's triumphalist view of good art which, in its final words, and *contra* Plato, 'tells the only truth that ultimately matters. It is the light by which human things can be mended. And after art there is, let me tell you, nothing'.

No other contemporary thinker has better tended the flame of truth that Plato lit; and nor is the work of any other writer in our time better illuminated by the light that flame continues to give out.

[35] E. Dipple, *Iris Murdoch: Work for the Spirit* (London, 1980), p. 43. For an alternative view of Murdoch's Platonism, see W. Bronzwaer 'Images of Plato in *The Fire and the Sun* and *Acastos*', in *Encounters with Iris Murdoch*, ed. R. Todd (Amsterdam, 1988), pp. 55–67.

Bibliography

The following abbreviations are used:
PMLA Publications of the Modern Languages Association of America
JEGP Journal of English and Germanic Theology

TRANSLATIONS OF GREEK AND LATIN SOURCES

Unless otherwise indicated, the following translations of Plato and Plotinus have been used by all contributors:

Plato. *The Collected Dialogues of Plato.* Ed. E. Hamilton and H. Cairns. Princeton, 1961; second printing with corrections, 1963. (Bollingen Series, 71).
Plotinus. *Plotinus with an English Translation.* Ed. and trans. A.H. Armstrong. 6 vols. London and Cambridge, Mass., 1966–88 (Loeb Classical Library).

The following is a list of translations of seminal works in the Platonic corpus. They are not necessarily those used by contributors, but represent those which are most easily available.

Augustine of Hippo, St. *The City of God.* Trans. H. Bettenson. Harmondsworth, 1972.
Augustine of Hippo, St. *Confessions.* Trans. R.S. Pine-Coffin. Harmondsworth, 1961.
Augustine of Hippo, St. *Confessions.* Trans. Henry Chadwick. Oxford, 1991.
Boethius. *The Consolation of Philosophy.* Trans. V.E. Watts. Harmondsworth 1969.
Boethius. Ed. H.F. Stewart and E.K. Rand (1918), revised and trans. S.J. Tester. London, 1973, reprinted 1978.
Dionysius the Areopagite. *The Complete Works.* Trans. Colm Lubheid and Paul Rorem. Mahwah, N.Y., 1987.
Ficino, Marsilio. *Commentary on Plato's Symposium on Love.* Trans. Sears Jayne. Dallas, 1985.
Ficino, Marsilio. *Marsilio Ficino and the Phaedran Charioteer.* Trans. M.J.B. Allen. Berkeley, 1981.

Ficino, Marsilio. *Masilio Ficino: the Philebus Commentary.* Trans. M.J.B. Allen. Berkeley, 1979.

Hermes Trismegistus. *Hermetica: the Greek Corpus Hermeticum and the Latin Asclepius.* Trans. B.P. Copenhaver, Cambridge 1992.

Macrobius. *Macrobius' Commentary on the Dream of Scipio.* Trans. W.H. Stahl. New York, 1952.

Martianus Capella. *Martianus Capella and the Seven Liberal Arts*, translated by W.H. Stahl, R. Johnson and E.L. Burge. New York and London, 1977.

Philo. *Philo with an English Translation.* Ed. and trans. F.H. Colson and G.H. Whitaker. 12 vols. Harvard 1929–1953. (Loeb Classical Library).

Plato. *Plato with an English Translation.* Ed. and trans. N. Fowler et al. 13 vols. London and Cambridge, Mass., 1912–35 (Loeb Classical Library).

Plotinus. *Plotinus: the Enneads.* Trans. Stephen McKenna. Edited and abridged by John Dillon, London, 1991.

Proclus. *Commentary of the Republic.* French translation by A.J. Festugière. *Proclus sur la République.* 3 vols. Paris, 1970.

Proclus. *Elements of Theology.* ed. E.R. Dodds. 2nd edn. Oxford, 1963.

Proclus. *Platonic Theology.* Ed. H.D. Saffrey and L.G. Westerink. 5 vols. continuing. Paris, 1968–.

FURTHER READING

This list of books is not a definitive bibliography of Platonism and English Literature, but is intended as a guide to further reading. Details of primary sources are given in the notes of the studies in which they are discussed.

GENERAL

Bolgar, R.R. *The Classical Heritage and its Beneficiaries.* Cambridge, 1954.

Bolgar, R.R., (ed.). *Classical Influences on European Culture, 500–1500.* Cambridge, 1971.

Bolgar, R.R., (ed.). *Classical Influences on Western Thought, 1500–1700.* Cambridge, 1976.

Bolgar, R.R., (ed.). *Classical Influences on European Culture 1650–1870.* Cambridge, 1979.

Casey, J. *Pagan Virtue.* Oxford, 1991.

Clarke, M.L. *Classical Education in Britain 1500–1900.* Cambridge, 1959.

Inge, William R. *The Platonic Tradition in English Religious Thought.* London, 1926.

O'Meara, D.J. (ed.). *Neoplatonism and Christian Thought.* Albany, N.Y., 1982.

Panofsky, E. *Idea. A Concept in Art Theory.* trans. J.J.S. Peake, Columbia, 1968.

L.D. Reynolds and N.G. Wilson. *Scribes and Scholars. A Guide to the Transmission of Greek and Latin Literature.* 3rd edn Oxford, 1991.

Sandys, J.E. *A History of Classical Scholarship.* 3 vols. Cambridge, 1903–8.

Shorey, Paul. *Platonism Ancient and Modern.* Berkeley, 1938.

Tigerstedt, E.N. *The Decline and Fall of the Neoplatonic Interpretation of Plato.* Helsinki, 1974.
Tigerstedt, E.N. 'Interpreting Plato'. *Stockholm Studies in the History of Literature*, 17 (Stockholm 1974).

ANTIQUITY

Annas, Julia. *An Introduction to Plato's Republic.* Oxford, 1981.
Bundy, M.W. *The Theory of Imagination in Classical and Medieval Thought.* Urbana, 1927.
Dillon, J. *The Middle Platonists.* London, 1977.
G.M.A. Gruber. *Plato's Thought.* London, 1935.
Guthrie, W.K.C. *History of Greek Philosophy.* vols 4 and 5. Cambridge, 1975, 1978.
Hare, R.M. *Plato.* Oxford, 1982.
Irwin, T. *Classical Thought.* Oxford, 1989.
Melling, D.J. *Understanding Plato.* Oxford, 1987.
Price, A.W. *Love and Friendship in Plato and Aristotle.* Oxford, 1989.
Rist, J.M. *Plotinus; the Road to Reality.* Cambridge, 1967.
Rowe, C.J. *Plato.* Brighton, 1984.
Russell, D.A. *Criticism in Antiquity.* London, 1981.
Tigerstedt, E.N. *Plato's Idea of Poetic Inspiration.* Helsinki, 1969.
Watson, G. *Phantasia in Classical Thought.* Galway, 1988.

LATER PLATONISM AND THE EARLY CHRISTIAN PERIOD

Armstrong, A.H. (ed.). *Cambridge History of Later Greek and Early Medieval Philosophy.* Cambridge, 1987.
Bundy, M.W. *The Theory of Imagination in Classical and Medieval Thought.* Urbana, 1927.
Chadwick, Henry. *Boethius. The Consolations of Music, Logic, Theology and Philosophy.* Oxford, 1981, reprinted 1990.
Chadwick, Henry. *Augustine* (Past Masters). Oxford, 1986.
Coleman, Janet. *Ancient and Medieval Memories: Studies in the Reconstruction of the Past.* Cambridge, 1992.
Dodds, E.R. *Pagan and Christian in an Age of Anxiety.* Cambridge, 1965.
Fowden, G. *The Egyptian Hermes.* Cambridge, 1986.
Ivánka, E. von. *Plato Christianus.* Einsiedeln, 1964.
Lamberton, R. *Homer the Theologian.* Berkeley and Los Angeles, 1986.
Louth, Andrew. *The Origins of the Christian Mystical Tradition: from Plato to Denys.* Oxford, 1981.
Markus, R.A. *The End of Ancient Christianity.* (Cambridge 1990).
Markus, R.A. *Augustine. A Collection of Critical Essays.* New York, 1972.
Pépin, J. *Mythe et allégorie.* 2nd edn. Paris, 1976.
Rist, J.M. *Eros and Psyche; Studies in Plato, Plotinus and Origen.* Toronto, 1964.
Wallis, R.T. *Neoplatonism.* London, 1972.
Watson, G. *Phantasia in Classical Thought.* Galway, 1988.

MIDDLE AGES

Burnley, J.D. *Chaucer's Language and the Philosophers' Tradition*. Cambridge, 1979.

Butler, C. *Western Mysticism*. 2nd edn. London, 1927.

Dronke, Peter. *Fabula; Explorations into the uses of Myth in Medieval Platonism*. Leiden, 1974.

Dronke, Peter. (ed.). *A History of Twelfth-century Western Philosophy*. Cambridge, 1988.

Dronke, Peter and Jill Mann. 'Chaucer and the Medieval Latin Poets', in *Geoffrey Chaucer*, ed. Derek Brewer. (Writers and their Background). London, 1974.

Economou, George D. *The Goddess Natura in Medieval Literature*. Cambridge, Mass., 1972.

Gibson, Margaret, editor. *Boethius. His Life Thought and Influence*. Oxford, 1981.

Jefferson, B.J. *Chaucer and the Consolations of Philosophy of Boethius*. Princeton, 1919.

Klibansky, Raymond. *The Continuity of the Platonic Tradition during the Middle Ages*. London, 1939; reprinted Munich, 1981.

Klibansky, Raymond. 'Plato's *Parmenides* in the Middle Ages and the Renaissance', *Medieval and Renaissance Studies*, 1 (1943), 281–330. Reprinted in Klibansky, *Continuity* (1981).

Knowles, D. *The English Mystical Tradition*. London, 1961.

Lewis, C.S. *The Discarded Image*. Cambridge, 1964.

Louth, Andrew. *Denys the Areopagite*. London, 1989.

Marenbon, *Early Medieval Philosophy 480–1150; and Introduction*. London, 1983.

Minnis, A.J. *Chaucer and Pagan Antiquity*. Cambridge, 1982.

Minnis, A.J. *The Medieval Boethius. Studies in Vernacular Translations of* De Consolatione Philosophiae. Cambridge, 1987.

Otten, K. *König Alfreds Boethius*. Tübingen, 1964.

Riehle, W. *The Middle English Mystics*. London, 1981.

Steadman, John M. *Disembodied Laughter: 'Troilus' and the Apotheosis Tradition*. Berkeley and Los Angeles, 1972.

Wetherbee, Winthrop. *Platonism and Poetry in the Twelfth Century*. Princeton, 1972.

RENAISSANCE AND SEVENTEENTH CENTURY

Agar, M. *Milton and Plato*. Princeton, 1928.

Allen, M.J.B. *The Platonism of Marsilio Ficino: A Study of his Phaedrus Commentary, its Sources and Genesis*. Berkeley, 1984.

Baker-Smith, Dominic. *More's Utopia*. London, 1991.

Baldwin, E.C. 'Milton and Plato's *Timaeus*'. *PMLA*, 35 (1920), 210–217.

Bennett, Josephine Waters. 'Spenser's "Garden of Adonis"', *PMLA*, 47 (1932), 46–80.

Bennett, Josephine Waters. 'Spenser's Venus and the Goddess of Nature in the *Cantos of Mutabilitie*', *Studies in Philology*, 30 (1933), 159–92.

Bieman, Elizabeth. *Plato Baptized; Towards the Interpretation of Spenser's Mimetic Fictions.* Toronto, 1988.
Cassirer, Ernst. *The Platonic Renaissance in England.* trans. J.P. Pettigrove. London, 1953.
Cody, Richard. *The Landscape of the Mind: Pastoralism and Platonic Theory in Tasso's Aminta and Shakespeare's Early Comedies.* Oxford, 1969.
Copenhaver, Brian and Charles Schmitt. *Renaissance Philosophy.* Oxford, 1992.
Cragg, G.R. *The Cambridge Platonists.* New York, 1968.
Corrigan, Kevin. 'The Function of the Ideal in Plato's *Republic* and St. Thomas More's *Utopia*', *Moreana*, 27 (1990), 27–48.
Ellrodt, Robert. *Neoplatonism in the Poetry of Spenser.* Geneva, 1960.
Evans, Jessie M. *Paradise Lost and the Genesis Tradition.* Oxford, 1968.
Fallon, S. *Milton among the Philosophers.* Columbia, 1991.
Fiore, P.A. *Milton and Augustine.* Pennsylvania, 1921.
Gordon, Walter M. 'The Platonic Dramaturgy of Thomas More's Dialogues', *Journal of Medieval and Renaissance Studies*, 8 (1978), 193–215.
Guegen, John M. 'Reading More's *Utopia* as a Criticism of Plato', *Albion*, 10 (1978), 43–54.
Hankins, James. *Plato in the Italian Renaissance.* 2 vols. Leiden, 1990.
Hankins, John. *Source and Meaning in Spenser's Allegory; a Study of 'The Faerie Queene'.* Oxford, 1971.
Heninger, S.K. 'Sidney and Serranus' Plato', *English Literary Renaissance*, 13 (1983), 146–61.
Hunter, W.B. 'Milton and the Thrice-Great Hermes'. *JEGP*, 45 (1946), 327–336.
Hunter, W.B., Patrides, C.A., Adamson, J.H. *Bright Essence: Studies in Milton Theology.* Salt Lake City, 1971.
Hutton, Sarah. 'Lord Herbert of Cherbury and the Cambridge Platonists', in *Routledge Histroy of Philosophy*, vol v, *British Philosophy and the Age of Enlightenment*, ed. Stuart Brown (forthcoming).
Jayne, Sears. *John Colet and Marsilio Ficino.* Oxford, 1963.
Jayne, Sears. 'Ficino and English Platonism', *Contemporary Literature*, 4 (1952), 214–238.
Jayne, Sears. 'The Subject of Milton's Ludlow Masque'. *PMLA*, 74 (1959), 533–43.
Jayne, Sears. *The Pre-Tudor Revival of Plato in England (1423–1483).* forthcoming, 1994.
Levinson, R.B. 'Milton and Plato', *Modern Language Notes*, 46 (1931), 85–91.
Marcel, R. *Marcel Ficin.* Paris, 1958.
Marks, Carol L. 'Thomas Traherne's Commonplace Book', *Papers of the Bibliographical Society of America*, 58 (1964),
Marks, Carol L. 'Thomas Traherne and Hermes Trismegistus', *Renaissance News*, 19 (1966), 118–131.
Marks, Carol L. 'Thomas Traherne and Cambridge Platonism'. *PMLA* (1966), 521–534.

Marks, Carol L. 'Traherne's Ficino Notebook' *Papers of the Bibliographical Society of America*. 63 (1969), 73–81.
Marks, Carol L. and Guffrey, George R. 'Introduction' to Thomas Traherne, *Christian Ethicks*. Ithaca, 1968.
Martindale, C. & M. *Shakespeare and the Uses of Antiquity*. London and New York, 1990.
Miles, Leland. *John Colet and the Platonic Tradition*. La Salle, Illinois, 1961.
Nelson, J.C. *Renaissance Theory of Love*. New York, 1958.
Neumann, Harry. 'On the Platonism of More's *Utopia*', *Social Research*, 33 (1966), 495–572.
Patrides, C.A. *The Cambridge Platonists*. Cambridge, 1969.
Perella, N.J. *The Kiss Sacred and Profane*. Berkeley, Los Angeles and London, 1969.
Robb, Nesca. *Neoplatonism of the Italian Renaissance*. London, 1935.
Samuel, I. *Plato and Milton*. Ithaca, 1947.
Schmitt, Charles, and Skinner, Quentin (eds). *The Cambridge History of Renaissance Philosophy*. Cambridge, 1988.
Stirling, Brents. 'Spenser's "Platonic" Garden', *JEGP*, 41 (1942), 482–6.
Walker, D.P. *The Ancient Theology; Studies in Christian Platonism from the Fifteenth to the Eighteenth Century*. London, 1972.
White, Thomas I. 'Pride and the Public Good: Thomas More's Use of Plato in *Utopia*', *Journal of the History of Philosophy*, 20 (1982), 329–54.
Wind, Edgar. *Pagan Mysteries in the Renaissance*, 2nd edn. London, 1967.

EIGHTEENTH CENTURY

Beer, John. *Blake's Visionary Universe*. Manchester, 1969.
Clarke, M.L. *Greek Studies in England, 1700–1830*. Cambridge, 1945.
Damon, S. Foster. *William Blake; his Philosophy and Symbols*. London, 1924.
Evans, F.B. 'Platonic Scholarship in Eighteenth-century England'. *Modern Philology*, 41 (1943), pp. 103–110.
Harper, G.M. *The Neoplatonism of William Blake*. Chapel Hill and London, 1961.
Larrissy, Edward. *William Blake*. Oxford, 1985.
Hilton, Nelson (ed.). *Essential Articles for the Study of William Blake, 1970–1984*. Hamden, Conn., 1986.
Probyn, Clive T. *The Sociable Humanist: the Life and Works of James Harris 1709–1780*. Oxford, 1991.
Raine, K. *Blake and Tradition*. 2 vols. London, 1969.

NINETEENTH CENTURY

Anderson, Warren D. *Matthew Arnold and the Classical Tradition*. Ann Arbor, 1965.
Baker, Joseph E. *Shelley's Platonic Answer to a Platonic Attack on Poetry*. Iowa, 1965.
Caird, Edward. 'Mr. Grote's Plato'. *North British Review*, 43 (1865), 351–84.

Dover, Kenneth J. 'Expurgation of Greek Literature', *Entretiens sur l'antiquité classique*, 26 (1980), 55–81.
Dourka Kabitoglou, E. *Plato and the English Romantics*. London, 1990.
Evans, Frank B. 'Thomas Taylor, Platonist of the Romantic Period'. *PMLA*, 55 (1940), pp. 1060–1079.
Holmes, Richard. *Shelley on Love*. 1980.
Jenkyns, R. *The Victorians and Ancient Greece*. Oxford, 1980.
Jowett, Benjamin. *The Dialogues of Plato*. Translated and introduced by Benjamin Jowett. 3rd edn. 5 vols. Oxford, 1892. (First published, 1871).
McFarland, Thomas. *Coleridge and the Pantheist Tradition*. Oxford, 1969.
Meyer, G.W. 'A Note on the Sources and Symbolism of the Intimations Ode', *Tulane Studies in English*, 3 (1952), 33–45.
Mill, J.S. 'Grote's Plato'. In Mill, *Essays on Philosophy and the Classics*. Ed. J.M. Robson. *Collected Works of J.S. Mill*. Vol. 11. Toronto, 1978, pp. 377–440.
Mills, Harper, G. and K. Raine. *Thomas Taylor the Platonist*. London, 1969.
Muirhead, J.H. *Coleridge as Philosopher*. London, 1930.
Newsome, D. *Two Classes of Men: Platonism and English Romantic Thought*. London, 1972.
Notopoulos, J.A. *The Platonism of Shelley; a Study of Platonism and the Poetic Mind*. Durham, N.C., 1949.
Orsini, G.N.G. *Coleridge and German Idealism*. Carbondale and Edwardsville, Ill., and London, 1969.
Pulos, C.E. *The Deep Truth; a Study of Shelley's Scepticism*. Lincoln, Nebr., 1954.
Rea, John D. 'Coleridge's Intimations of Immortality from Proclus', *Modern Philology*, 26 (1928), 201–13.
Small, Ian. 'Plato and Pater: Fin de Siècle Aesthetics', *British Journal of Aesthetics*, 12 (1972), 369–83.
Turner, F. *The Greek Heritage in Victorian Britain*. New Haven and London, 1981.
Webb, Timothy. *English Romantic Hellenism*. Manchester, 1982.
Winstanley, Lilian. 'Platonism in Shelley', *Essays and Studies by Members of the English Association*, 4 (1913), pp. 72–100.

TWENTIETH CENTURY

Arkins, Brian. *Builders of My Soul: Greek and Roman Themes in Yeats*. Garrards Cross, 1990.
Bluestone, Natalie Harris. *Women and the Ideal Society; Plato's 'Republic' and Modern Myths of Gender*. Oxford, 1987.
Bronzwaer, W. Images of Plato in *The Fire and the Sun* and *Acastos*', in *Encounters with Iris Murdoch*. Ed. R. Todd. Amsterdam, 1988. pp. 55–67.
Conradi, Peter J. *Iris Murdoch: the Saint and the Artist*. 2nd edn. London, 1989.
Crisp, Peter. 'Pound, Leibnitz and China', *Paideuma*, 19 (1990), pp. 33–40.
Davies, R. 'Jung, Yeats and the Inner Journey', *Queen's Quarterly*, 89 (1982), 471–77.

Elliott, Angela. 'Pound's "Isis Kuanon": an Ascension Motif in *The Cantos*'. *Paideuma*, 13 (1984), 327–56.
Elliott, Angela. 'The Word Comprehensive: Gnostic Light in *The Cantos*'. *Paideuma*, 18 (1989), 7–57.
Esterly, J.D. *Yeats, Plotinus and Symbolic Perception*. Unpublished dissertation. Cambridge, 1977.
Gugelberger, Georg. 'The Secularization of 'Love' to a Poetic Metaphor: Cavalcanti, Centre of Pound's Medievalism'. *Paideuma*, 2 (1973), 159–73.
Libera, Sharon M. 'Casting his Gods back in the *NOUS*: Two Neoplatonists and *The Cantos* of Ezra Pound'. *Paideuma*, 2 (1983), 355–77).
Michaels, Walter B. 'Pound and Erigena'. *Paideuma*, 1 (1972), 37–54.
Miyake, Akiko. *Ezra Pound and the Mysteries of Love*. Durham, N.C., and London, 1991.
Moody, A.D. *Thomas Stearns Eliot: Poet*. Cambridge, 1979.
Motes, M.R. '"*Plotinus for a Friend*". MacKenna's Translation of Plotinus and W.B. Yeats's '"A Vision" and Later Poetry'. Unpublished dissertation. Miami, 1973.
Murdoch, Iris. *The Fire and the Sun; Why Plato Banished the Artists*. Oxford, 1977.
Murdoch, Iris. *The Sovereignty of the Good*. London, 1970.
Murdoch, Iris. *Metaphysics as a Guide to Morals*. London, 1992.
Neault, D. James. 'Richard of St Victor and *Rock-Drill*'. *Paideuma*, 3 (1974), 219–27.
Oderman, Kevin. "Cavalcanti' that the Body is not Evil'. *Paideuma*, 11 (1982), 257–79.
Olney, J. *The Rhizome and the Flower: the Perennial Philosophy – Yeats and Jung*. Berkeley, 1963.
Raine, Kathleen. 'Yeats and Platonism'. *Dublin Magazine*, 7 (1968), 38–63.
Raine, Kathleen. *Death-in-Life and Life-in-Death: Cuchulain Comforted' and 'News for the Delphic Oracle'*. Dublin, 1974.
Ritvo, R.P. *Plotinistic Elements in Yeats's Prose Works*. Unpublished dissertation. Fordham, 1973.
Ritvo, R.P. 'A Vision B: the Plotinian Metaphysical Basis'. *Review of English Studies*, 26 (1975), 34–46.
Santas, G.X. *Plato and Freud; Two Theories of Love*. Oxford, 1988.
Smidt, Kristian. *Poetry and Belief in the Work of T.S. Eliot*. London, 1961.
Thompson, Eric. *T.S. Eliot, the Man and his Works*. Toronto, 1969.
Wilhelm, James J. *Dante and Pound: the Epic of Judgement*. Orono, Maine, 1974.
Wilson, F.A.C. *W.B. Yeats and Tradition*. London, 1958.

Index

The following index lists names of historical figures, translators and scholars of Plato, literary and philosophical movements, Plato's Dialogues, Platonic and Neoplatonic concepts and themes.

Adams, John, 316
Aeschylus, 237
Aestheticism, 258–60, 265
Akenside, 184
Alain of Lille, 24, 26, 45, 50f., 127, 133
Alcuin, 38
Alfred, King, 23, 38–44
Ambose of Milan, 29
Amelius, 287
Anselm of Canterbury, 309
Antiochus of Ascalon, 53
Antisthenes, 91
Apollonius of Tyana, 15–16, 309, 315–17
Aquinas, Thomas, 121
Aristippus Henricus, 24, 39
Aristippus of Cyrene, 78
Aristophanes, 181
Aristotle/Aristotelianism, 4, 5, 12, 15, 16, 23–5, 25, 32, 67, 73, 86, 122, 166, 170–1, 182, 201, 202, 208, 273, 285, 299
Armstrong, A.H., 272
Arnold, Matthew, 205, 242–56, 259
Arnold, Thomas, 181
Art, 15, 24, 195, 234, 262–5, 330–1, 336–8, 342
Athenian Academy, 4, 53, 67, 233, 259
Atticus, 8
Atwood, Margaret, 276
Auden, Wystan Hugh, 278, 319–29, 331
Augustine of Hippo, St, 5, 24, 25, 27–37, 38, 39, 40, 52, 55–8, 68, 69, 71, 87, 90, 94, 153, 158–61, 176, 302

Bakhtin, Mikhail, 331
Basil of Caesarea, 29
Becket, Samuel, 319
Bell, Clive, 296
Bembo, Pietro, 72, 81–3
  Castiglione's Bembo, 100–2, 105, 106
Benivieni, Girolamo, 79
Bentham, Jeremy, 206
Bennett, Arnold, 291
Bergson, Henri, 277
Bentley, Richard, 182
Berkeley, George, 215
Bernard of Clairvaux, 32, 45, 48, 58, 60, 62
Bernardus Silvestris, 24, 45, 127, 135n
Bessarion, Cardinal Giovanni, 68, 75, 77, 78, 80, 82–3
Bible, 33, 142, 157
  Genesis, 24, 154
  Song of Songs/Solomon, 62, 77–8, 80, 83
  St John, 22, 321
  St Luke, 54
  St Matthew, 89
  Acts, 25
  Romans, 34
  Corinthians, 22, 91n
  Colossians, 22
  Hebrews, 54
Blake, William, 184, 186–98, 227, 276, 282
Blavatsky, Helena, 272, 276, 280
Boehme, Jacob (Behmen), 187
Boethius, Severinus, 5, 23, 25, 26, 38–44, 45, 46, 47, 50, 103, 127
Bolingbroke, Henry St John, First Viscount Bolingbroke, 185
Bonaventure, 59, 60
Boyle, Sir Robert, 75
Bradley, F.H., 278, 298, 306
Browning, Robert, 300
Bruni, Leonardo, 68, 69, 76
Bruno, Giordano, 85, 106, 127

Burnet, John, 271
Burnet, Thomas, 218
Butler (of Shrewsbury), 181
Byron, George Gordon, 227

Cabbala, Cabbalism, 80, 84, 193 *see also* Kiss (*mors osculi*)
Cairns, Huntington, 271
Calcidius, 24, 28, 38
Calvinism, 73, 143
Cambridge Platonists, 9, 73–4, 124, 139–50, 166, 177, 181, 242, 279, 282
Carlyle, Thomas, 261
Cartwright, William, 162
Casaubon, Isaac, 69, 74
Case, John, 71
Castiglione, Baldasar, 71, 83–4, 96, 100–2, 105, 107, 112, 114, 117, 127
Catullus, 105
Cavalcanti, Giovanni, 79, 313, 314
Chaldean Oracles, 4, 11
Chapman, George, 72, 100, 107, 110–12, 116, 119–20
Charles I, King, 72
Chartres, School of, etc., 24, 38, 45, 48, 50–1, 135n
Chaucer, Geoffrey, 23, 25, 26, 43, 45–51, 127, 133
Ch'eng T'ang, 317
Chester, Robert, 119
Childhood, 167, 176–7, 221–5
Christ, 22, 31, 32, 33, 34, 50, 54, 91, 134, 145, 150–7, 205, 309, 336, 337
Chrysoloras, Manuel, 68
Chubb, Thomas, 183
Cicero, Marcus Tullius, 4, 28, 29, 30, 33, 68, 93, 104, 159
Clarkson, Mrs, 225
Clement of Alexandria, 4, 22, 29
Clerke, Bartholomew, 71
Cleveland, John, 163
Cloud of Unknowing, 25, 56–8, 62–4
Coleridge, Berkeley, 219
Coleridge, Hartley, 218, 219
Coleridge, Samuel Taylor, 187, 202, 203, 206, 207–16, 217–22, 228, 251, 262–3, 272, 331
Colet, John, 70, 88
Collier, Arthur, 183
Confucius, 317
Conrad, Joseph, 276, 304
Corbière, Tristan, 299
Cornarius, Janus, 122
Cornford, F.M., 272
Corsi, Giovanni, 79n
Cudworth, Ralph, 73–5, 139, 140, 143–7, 149–50, 177
Culverwell, Nathaniel, 73, 75, 177

Dacier, André, 182, 233
Dante Alighieri, 49, 258, 260, 277, 300, 305, 310, 313, 322
Darwin, Charles, 156, 261, 266
Davenant, Sir William, 72, 119
Davies of Hereford, John, 71
Decembrio, Pier Candido, 70, 87, 93
Denys *see* Dionysius
De Quincey, Thomas, 218
Derrida, Jacques, 274, 306
Descartes, René, 73, 75, 141, 198
d'Holbach, Baron, 231
Diogenes of Sinope, 91
Diogenes Laertius, 76, 78
Dionysius (Denys) the Areopagite, 5, 22, 25, 52, 56–8, 60, 77, 88, 127, 154, 167
Dionysius of Syracuse, 96
Donne, John, 100, 107, 112–16, 163
Dorp, Maarten van, 89
Drayton, Michael, 72
Drummond, William, 233
Du Bellay, Joachim, 72
Duns Scotus, 204
d'Urfé, Honoré, 119

Ebreo, Leone, 84, 127
Eckhart, Meister, 88
Education, 27, 31, 33, 34, 36, 149, 249, 252, 254, 292, 294, 296
paideia, 31, 35
Greek Studies, 28, 68, 181–2, 292, 298
Eliot, T.S., 262, 267, 272, 274–7, 298–308, 311, 330–1
Elizabeth I, Queen, 39
Empiricism, 144, 190, 207, 210, 279
Epictetus, 91
Epicurus/Epicureanism, 4, 203
Erasmus, Desiderius, 70, 71, 73, 86–93, 98–9
Eriugena, John Scotus, 22, 25, 38, 47, 57, 154–9, 309
Estienne, Henri (Stephanus), 70, 130n
Existentialism, 274, 332–3
Everard, John, 74, 156, 169, 187

Fenwick, Isabella, 220, 221, 224
Ferrar, Nicholas, 74
Fichte, J.G., 261
Ficino, Marsilio, 69–70, 74, 78–83, 85, 87, 88, 92, 93, 99–102, 106–10, 112, 114, 118, 122–3, 127, 131, 132, 134, 135, 154, 156, 158, 163, 166, 169, 172–5, 177, 217, 218–20, 309, 310, 315, 323

Fielding, Henry, 182
Filelfo, Francesco, 68
Fisher, Robert, 88
Flaxman, John, 184, 196
Fludd, Robert, 154, 156, 157
Forster (editor of *Phaedo*), 217
Forster, E.M., 275
Fox, Richard, 71
Francis, St, 89
Freud, Sigmund, 273, 334–6
Frazer, J.G., 274, 304
Fuseli, Henry, 196

Gadamer, Hans-Georg, 336
Gallus, Thomas, 58
Gale, Theophilus, 75, 169–71
Gautier, Théophile, 259
George of Trebizond, 68, 69, 75, 77
Gibbon, Edward, 181
Gillis, Pieter, 95, 97
Gladstone, William Ewart, 204
Glanvill, Joseph, 242
Gnosticism, 193–4
God, 22, 27, 29, 31, 34, 35, 37, 39, 40, 44, 53, 54, 56, 62, 79, 133, 137, 141, 144, 154, 155, 156, 157, 159, 161, 173, 176, 321, 323, 333
  Trinity, 24, 75, 135 *see also* Christ
Godwin, William, 231
Goethe, Johann Wolfgang von, 264
Goncourt, Edmond and Jules de, 259
Gonne, Maud, 285
Grant, Alexander, 201
Gray, Thomas, 184
Gregory the Great, 60
Gregory of Nazianzen, 29, 159
Gregory of Nyssa, 29, 57, 62, 154
Grocyn, William, 94
Grosseteste, Robert, 309, 314
Grote, George, 201, 251, 258–9
Grotius, Hugo, 71

Halewijn, Joris van, 91
Hamilton, Edith, 271
Harris, James, 183
Harrison, Frederic, 249
Harrison, Jane Ellen, 275
Hartley, David, 207
Hayley, William, 194
Heaney, Seamus, 278
Hegel, G.W.F., 266, 298n
Hellenism, 183, 250, 255
Henrietta Maria, Queen, 72, 163
Heraclitus, 258, 261, 265, 339
Herbert, George, 74
Herbert of Cherbury, Edward, Lord, 163
Hermes Trismegistus, 4, 67, 69, 70, 74, 169, 172, 173, 194
Hermetica/Hermeticism, 5, 69, 154, 156, 166, 187, 192, 276
Hermias, 10n
Herodotus, 218
Heydon, John, 309
Hilduin of St-Denis, 57
Hill, Geoffrey, 278
Hilton, Walter, 25, 56, 61, 63
Hobbes, Thomas, 73
Hoby, Thomas, 72, 117
Hogg, Thomas Jefferson, 202
Homer, 12, 13, 16, 17, 45, 182–3, 189
Homosexuality, 76–81, 229, 257, 260, 275
  homo-eroticism, 85, 260, 263
Hopkins, Gerard, Manley, 204
Hulme, T.E., 277
Humanism, 68, 70–1, 77, 86–99, 138
Hume, David, 207, 210
Humphrey, Duke of Gloucester, 70
Huxley, Aldous, 276
Hyde-Lees, Georgie, 276

Iamblichus, 5, 8, 59, 272, 309, 310
Imagination, 12–17, 195, 236, 241, 309 *see also* Platonic and Neoplatonic concepts and themes
Irigaray, Luce, 274n

Jackson, Thomas, 74, 75, 166, 169, 170
James Henry, 328
Jean de Meun, 39
Jefferson, Thomas, 316
John of Salisbury, 57
John Scotus Eriugena *see* Eriugena
John the Saracen, 57
Johnson, Samuel, 185
Jonson, Ben, 72, 118–20
Jowett, Benjamin, 201, 205, 251, 257–61, 264, 267
Joyce, James, 267, 331
Judaism, 27, 29, 33 *see also* Philo of Alexandria, Cabbala
Julia Domna, Empress, 317
Julian the Apostate, 5, 272
Julian of Norwich, 25, 60, 278, 304
Justinian, Emperor, 67
Jung, Karl, 274, 277, 279

Kabbalah *see* Cabbala
Kallman, Chester, 323
Kant, Immanuel, 202, 207–9, 336
Keats, John, 262

Kingsley, Charles, 156
Kiss (*mors osculi*), 80, 83–4, 102, 105
Kristeva, Julia, 331

Laforgue, Jules, 299–300
Landino, Cristoforo, 93
Langland, William, 25
Language, 33, 34, 35, 215, 266–7
Larkin, Philip, 278
Lawrence, D.H., 331
Levy, G.R., 272
Lewis, Wyndham, 302n
Locke, John, 183, 207, 279
Longinus, 309
Lucan, 45
Lucian of Samosata, 93, 94
Luther, Martin, 97

Macaulay, Thomas Babington, First Baron Macaulay, 204, 206
MacKenna, Stephen, 272, 276, 280–1
Macrobius, 24, 26, 38, 45, 126
Manicheism, 28
Malebranche, Nicholas, 74
Mallock, W.H., 205
Malory, Sir Thomas, 107
Manutius, Aldus, 68, 87
Markland, Jeremiah, 182
Marsigli, Luigi, 68
Marston, John, 120
Martianus Capella, 24, 38, 45–7
Marvell, Andrew, 74, 163–7
Marx, Karl, 273
Maurice, F.D., 202
Maximus, 154
Mead, George R.S., 272, 276
Medicis, the, 92
Medici, Cosimo de', 316
Medici, Lorenzo de', 81
Mencius, 317
Michelangelo, 282
Middle Platonists, 4, 21, 53 *see also* Neoplatonism
Mill, John Stuart, 204–5
Milton, John, 67, 74, 151–62
Montaigne, Michel de, 298n
Moore, G.E., 275, 293, 296
More, Henry, 73, 75, 139, 140, 143–7, 149, 167, 169, 177, 282
More, Sir Thomas, 70, 71, 86–8, 92–9, 184, 316
Mornay, Philippe du Plessis, 70–1
Mosheim, J.L., 194
Muir, Edwin, 289
Murdoch, Iris, 274, 276, 330–42
Mysticism, 11, 22, 25, 52–64, 321, 333
  apophatic theology, 57–8

Neoplatonism, 3–18, 21–4, 27–9, 35–7, 39, 40, 41, 45–51, 53, 61, 67–71, 98, 100, 106–9, 112–16, 120, 127, 134, 137–8, 153, 163–4, 166, 167, 169, 177, 187, 198, 282, 308–10, 314, 315, 319, 342 *see also* Platonic and Neoplatonic concepts and themes
Newton, Issac, 198
Niccoli, Niccolo, 68
Nicholas of Cusa, 68, 69
Nobili, Flaminio, 84n
Norris, John, 74, 183
Numenius, 4

Ocellus, 308, 318
Olympiodorus, 19
Origen, 4, 22, 29, 30, 61, 62, 87, 99, 145–6, 166
Orpheus, 67, 68, 70, 130n, 182
Orwell George, 276
Ovid, 45, 81, 108, 110–12
Owen, John, 75

Panormita, Antonio, 77
Paracelsus, 187
Parmenides, 258, 260, 262, 265
Paracelsus, 187
Parker, Samuel, 75
Pater, Clara, 275
Pater, Walter, 205, 206, 220, 257–67, 331
Paul, St, 28, 33–5, 90
Peacock, Thomas Love, 231, 234
Pearl, 25
Petrarch, Francis, 32, 68, 81, 86, 106
Petronius, 304
Pheidias, 14, 16
Philo of Alexandra, 4, 21, 22, 29, 57, 60, 154n
Philostratus, 15, 16, 317
Pico della Mirandola, Giovanni, 72, 80–2, 85, 92–3, 129, 132, 134, 176
Plato *passim*
  'Attic Moses', 67
  cosmologer, 24
  poet and aesthete, 206
  moral philosopher, 71, 86–7, 246
  political philosophy, 96–8, 204, 236–8, 241, 246–249
  putative sexual depravity of, 77
  and Scepticism, 232–3, 273, 298–307
  style, 6, 87, 92, 306
  supposed Trinitarianism, 24, 56, 69, 75, 134–5
  see also Socrates

Plato's dialogues (*indicates those of doubtful attribution)
*Alcibiades**, 74
Apology, 3–4, 74, 233n, 303
*Axiochus**, 71, 126n
Charmides, 3
Cratylus, 89
Crito, 74
*Erastae**, 247
*Eryxias**, 243
Euthyphro, 122–4, 292
Gorgias, 253, 273
*Hippias Major**, 243
Hippias Minor, 243
Ion, 3, 13, 16, 229, 230, 234, 235, 243, 253
Laches, 3, 233
Laws, 8, 74, 97, 302, 325
Letter VII, 96, 273, 326, 327
Lysis, 243
Meno, 9, 24, 39, 139, 146, 148–9, 212, 219, 221, 253
Menexenus, 70n, 229, 243
Parmenides, 3, 5, 39, 69, 118, 209, 253, 272, 273, 332
Phaedo, 3, 8, 9, 24, 39, 54, 69, 74, 92, 139, 146, 151, 165–6, 176, 182, 217, 219, 221, 229, 233n, 247, 272, 303–5, 320
Phaedrus, 9–11, 13, 14, 16, 62, 76, 140, 142, 149, 173, 210, 212, 219, 221, 243, 246–7, 253, 260, 263, 272, 274, 275, 292, 293–5, 297, 320, 322, 335
Philebus, 3, 253
Protagoras, 233n, 253
Republic, 3–6, 8, 9, 11–14, 16, 43, 17, 69–70, 90, 93–9, 103, 106, 107, 118, 151–2, 172, 182, 212–16, 219, 221, 229, 231, 233–6, 239, 243, 246–9, 251, 253, 255, 258, 259, 263, 272, 275, 291, 292, 301, 302–5, 316, 319, 325–7
Sophist, 3, 6, 7, 15, 59, 287, 332
Statesman, 253
Symposium, 3, 10, 11, 13, 14, 54, 59, 62, 71, 73, 76–82, 89, 109, 117, 119, 127, 218, 229, 230, 231, 235, 238, 247, 254, 260, 272, 275, 292, 322, 335, 337
Theaetetus, 3, 6, 209, 253, 332
*Theages**, 247
Timaeus, 5, 7, 8, 15, 21, 23–6, 28, 38, 41n, 45, 46, 151, 155, 176, 193–4, 213, 215, 272, 277, 281, 332
Platonic and Neoplatonic concepts and themes
anamnesis see Recollection
Art, 13–15, 24, 336
Beauty, 6, 10, 13, 14, 80, 101, 109, 117–22, 136, 241, 263, 272, 282–3, 290, 307, 319
Cave, 11, 43, 90, 93, 106, 110, 117, 212–13, 215, 237, 272, 275, 296, 301, 305–6, 333, 334, 337–40
Charioteer (*Phaedrus*), 9, 322
City *see* State
cosmos, 23, 315, 157, 282, 315
daimon, 59–60, 283
Demiurge, 7, 8, 15, 21, 194
Dualism, 8, 36, 89, 151, 153, 262, 283, 284, 320, 321
Emanation, 53, 59, 132, 151, 155
Er, Myth of, 203
Forms (Ideas), 4, 6, 8, 9, 10, 11, 14, 54, 59, 97, 207, 246, 260, 262, 271, 172, 273, 284, 286–7, 308, 336
The Good, 6, 11, 23, 26, 117, 173, 236, 239–41, 263, 271, 272, 275, 307, 319, 321, 322, 324, 332, 333, 336
henads, 9
hypostases, 7, 8, 22, 24, 79, 127–8, 134, 164, 281, 287, 309, 313–14
Imitation (*mimesis*), 159–62, 290
Innate ideas, 9, 141–2, 143–6, 149–50, 171
Intellect, 80 *see also nous*
Intelligible world, 17, 30, 32, 33, 35, 196–8, 237, 240, 281–4, 287–8
Light, 21, 90, 167, 172–4, 275, 295, 305–6, 310, 313–14
logos, 21–2, 51, 135, 318
Love, 10, 13, 24, 45–50, 100–1, 109, 113, 119, 126, 271, 275, 313, 320, 322–5, 336, 338, 340: *eros*, 10, 18, 23, 59, 61, 260, 273, 283, 313–14, 319, 322–4, 326, 238, 335, 338–9; *eros/Venus pandemos*, 61, 109, 113; Platonic love, 72, 76–85, 109
Mind (*mens*), 7, 9, 11, 24, 32, 79
nous, 7, 24, 50, 54, 127, 135, 136, 164, 176, 277, 281, 308, 311–15, 318
The One, 5, 7–9, 11, 24, 30, 49, 50, 53, 55, 59, 79, 127, 129–133, 136–7, 164, 197, 273, 282
phantasia, 15–16, 287
Poets/poetry, 12–18: poetic inspiration, 13, 18
Recollection (*anamnesis*), 9, 10, 23, 39, 40, 42, 56, 73, 126, 139–50, 164–5, 167, 204, 207, 208, 212–16, 221, 223, 226, 246, 263, 272, 283, 285, 319, 321, 335
Self-knowledge, 209–10, 249
Soul, 6–10, 24, 30, 32, 33, 40, 42, 53–4, 62, 73, 75, 79–80, 96, 98, 127, 135, 137, 139, 145, 146, 157, 163–5, 167, 170, 172–6, 212–14, 219, 246–7, 277, 281,

Platonic and Neoplatonic concepts and themes (*cont.*)
287, 295, 306, 314, 322, 330: Ascent of the soul, 10, 11, 18, 26, 30, 33, 39, 40, 42, 45, 48–9, 62, 78, 138, 164, 236, 241, 272, 294; Immortality of the Soul 10, 53, 69, 73, 86, 163, 170, 247, 330; Innate ideas, 9, 141–4, 171; Pre-existence of the Soul, 40–1, 53, 73, 75, 145, 146, 164–5, 167, 212–13, 217–19, 221, 226; World soul, 7, 8, 74, 127–9, 136, 277, 281
State, 93–8, 246–9, 272, 291–2, 302, 319, 322, 324–6
Two Worlds, 53–6, 236
Women in the *Republic*, 96: andocentricity, 274
Pléiade, 72
Pletho (Plethon), George Gemistus, 68, 70, 309, 315, 316
Plotinus, 4, 5, 7, 8, 11, 12, 14, 22, 23, 24, 28–30, 39, 54, 55, 57, 59, 61, 67, 69, 74, 77, 100, 121, 126, 129, 131, 135, 136, 151, 153, 154, 159–61, 164, 169, 173, 174, 176, 182, 196, 198, 208, 272, 276–7, 279–81, 284, 287–8, 309–15, 318
Plutarch of Chaeronea, 4, 8
Poets, poetry, 12–18, 234–7, 254, 327–9 *see also* Platonic and Neoplatonic concepts and themes
Poole, Thomas, 208
Pope, Alexander, 183
Popper, Karl, 331
Porphyry, 5, 11, 12, 22–4, 28, 29, 36, 57, 132, 182, 189, 192, 272, 285, 287–8, 309, 310
Porson, Richard, 182
Pound, Ezra, 267, 271–2, 274, 276–8, 302, 308–18, 330
Praxiteles, 16
Priestly, Joseph, 194
Primaudaye, Pierre de la, 71
Proclus, 5, 9, 12, 14, 16–17, 22, 23, 41n, 57, 130n, 182, 217, 218, 272
Pythagoras, 195, 258–9, 266, 285, 288, 308, 310

Raphael, 67, 86, 203
Remigius of Auxerre, 47
Renaissance, 10, 33, 65–138, 260, 263, 282, 309, 316
Reynolds Sir Joshua, 185
Richard of St Victor, 309
Robinson, Henry Crabb, 194
Rolle, Richard, 60–3
Romantic movement, 207–41
Ruskin, John, 206, 264
Russell, Bertrand, 275
Rust, George, 167

Salusbury, Sir John, 119–20
Salutati, Coluccio, 68
Santayana, George, 272, 277
Sappho, 291
Sartre, Jean-Paul, 274
Scepticism, 4, 93, 232, 240, 273, 298, 303
Seneca, 25
Serres, Jean de (Serranus), 70, 74, 75, 118, 122
Sewell, William, 202
Shadwell, Thomas, 258
Shaftesbury, Anthony Ashley Cooper, third Earl of, 183
Shakespeare, William, 100, 107–10, 117–124, 343
Shelley, Percy Bysse, 202, 203, 229–41, 272
Sidgwick, Henry, 249
Sidney, Sir Philip, 72, 85, 100, 103–10, 112, 235
Sidney, Sir Robert, 104
Smith, John, 73, 177
Socrates, 3, 10, 11, 13, 35, 54, 76, 77–80, 89, 91, 92, 94–6, 98, 139, 148–50, 171, 195, 205, 208, 210, 221, 233, 245–7, 249–53, 256, 259, 272, 292, 295, 298–9, 300–1, 303, 316, 335, 338
Xenophons's Socrates, 245–6, 250, 253, 255
Socrates as Silenus, 89–91
Sophocles, 303, 311
Spens, Harry, 182
Spencer, Herbert, 206
Spender, Stephen, 303
Spenser, Edmund, 72, 100, 126–38
Speusippus, 4
Spinoza, Benedict de, 73, 308
Statius, 45
Stephen, J.K., 292
Stephen, Thoby, 293–5
Stephanus *see* Estienne
Sterry, Peter, 73
Stil nuovo, 81, 106
Stoicism, 4, 15, 21, 27, 53
Sturge Moore, T., 279–81
Swift, Jonathan, 184
Swinburne, Algernon Charles, 259
Sydenham, Floyer, 182, 201–2
Symonds, John Addington, 260
Synesius, 137n

Tasso, Torquato, 127
Taylor, A.E., 272
Taylor, Jeremy, 177
Taylor, Thomas, 130n, 182, 184, 186, 189, 196, 201, 217, 272
Theobald, Lewis, 182
Thirlwall, Connop, 205
Thucydides, 218
Toland, John, 183
Tomlinson, Charles, 278
Toup, Jonathan, 182
Traherne, Thomas, 74, 163–4, 167–78
Traversari, Ambrogio, 76
Trevet, Nicholas, 39
Trusler, John, 195
Twisse, William, 75

Utopia, ideal city, 73, 93–8, 292, 299, 301, 306, 393 *see also* Platonic and Neoplatonic concepts and themes

Vaughan, Henry, 74, 163–4, 166–7, 258
Vaughan, Thomas, 146, 166
Verlaine, 286
Vespasian, 317
Vespucci, Amerigo, 97
Villon, François, 286, 314
Virgil, 45
Vives, Juan Luis, 70
Vlastos, Gregory, 272–3

Walpole, Robert, 185
Walton, John, 39
Weil, Simone, 333, 335, 336
Westcott, B.F., 205
Weston, Jessie L., 304
Whichcote, Benjamin, 73, 139, 140–3, 145–7
Whitehead, Alfred North, 272, 281
Wilde, Oscar, 259, 266
William of Conches, 24, 39, 45, 48
Winckelmann, Johan Joachim, 196–7, 262–4
Wittgenstein, Ludwig, 274
Women, 96, 291–2
Woolf, Virginia, 267, 275, 290–7, 331
Wordsworth, Christopher, 222
Wordsworth Dorothy, 218, 220
Wordsworth, William, 167, 192, 204, 213, 217–28, 266

Xonocrates, 4
Xenophon, 245–6, 250, 253, 255, 273

Yeats, William Butler, 181, 187, 259, 267, 271–2, 274–6, 279–89, 330

Zeller, Eduard, 258
Zeno, 265
Zoroaster, 70

Milton Keynes UK
Ingram Content Group UK Ltd.
UKHW010609241123
433177UK00001B/14

9 780521 021685